D0886759

# The Utopian Vision
## of Charles Fourier

# THE UTOPIAN VISION OF CHARLES FOURIER

## Selected Texts on Work, Love, and Passionate Attraction

Translated, Edited,
and with an Introduction by

**JONATHAN BEECHER
and RICHARD BIENVENU**

Beacon Press   Boston

Copyright © 1971 by Jonathan Beecher and Richard Bienvenu
Library of Congress catalog card number: 72–136222
International Standard Book Number: 0–8070–1538–5
Beacon Press books are published under the auspices
of the Unitarian Universalist Association
Published simultaneously in Canada by Saunders of Toronto, Ltd.
Printed in the United States of America

# Contents

Contents :: ix

# *Preface*

Editors who select three hundred pages of texts from an author whose published writings now amount to more than twelve volumes owe their readers an account of what they are trying to do. For some time now anyone who wanted to read Charles Fourier in an English translation could turn only to rare nineteenth-century translations or adaptations of his works or to an English translation of Charles Gide's anthology published at the beginning of this century. That anthology, however, has long been out of print and is practically unobtainable. Our first purpose, then, was to make Fourier accessible to an English-reading public.

Beyond that rather modest goal, we hoped to present a somewhat fuller account of Fourier's thought than that offered in many previous anthologies and studies of his doctrine. Fourier, like most social theorists whose ideas have retained any grip at all on man's imagination, has often been pressed into service to suit the purposes of disparate social movements. The Fourier of nineteenth-century Fourierism, for example, was a respectable and upright socialist who drew up eminently practical, if quaint, plans for cooperative communities. For tactical as well as personal reasons, Fourier's early disciples ignored or suppressed their master's boldest speculations. Because they were shocked and embarrassed, these practical Fourierists drew a veil over the Fourier who dreamed of a new realm of sexual freedom and who, in his manuscripts, tirelessly recounted the amorous exploits of the saints and heroes of his new world. The Fourier of an excellent Marxist anthology, on the other hand, was given credit by his editors for a devastating critique of bourgeois sexual fraud and mercantile hypocrisy, but what these editors often seem to have appreciated most was Fourier's contribution to the thought of Marx and Engels. Finally, there is the Fourier commonly encountered in general histories of nineteenth-century thought. This Fourier is, as he himself would have put it, the Fourier *pour rire*. In these antipathetic, amused, or contemptuous accounts Fourier emerges as a genial madman, memorable chiefly for his personal foibles and his predictions concerning the appearance of domesticated anti-lions and seas of lemonade.

Naturally we do not presume to say that the texts in this anthology present the complete Fourier. Like other readers of Fourier, we have our own image of the man and we have arrived at our own conclusions about what is important in his thought. These conclusions are necessarily based in part on our sense of the significance of Fourier for our own times. Indeed, one of our aims was to draw attention to aspects of his thought that would be relevant to contemporary social theory. Thus we have focused in our introduction and in our choice of texts on the problems of work and love. But our intention has not been simply to present a "modernized" Fourier, a precursor of Marx or Freud. We believe that Fourier's ideas are important in their own right and that his claim to our attention does not rest merely on the fact that he said things which were later said more clearly and more succinctly by others.

We should add a few words about the problems of editing and translating Fourier. It is possible, by judicious use of the ellipsis, to turn Fourier into an orderly and sober social critic and theorist. It is possible to spare the reader most, if not all, of Fourier's intellectual vagaries, his petty bourgeois prejudices, his constant self-pity and paranoia, his nonsense. We have felt, however, that it would be no service to Fourier or the reader to present too "civilized" (to borrow his own term of opprobrium) an edition of his writings. For the man and the system were all of one piece, and it would be difficult to extract the nonsense, childishness, and extravagance from his work without simultaneously depriving it of some of its best qualities. Therefore, we have chosen to translate somewhat longer selections than those contained in most of the French anthologies and to be relatively sparing in the use of the ellipsis. We hope that in doing so we have managed to convey some sense not only of Fourier's style and manner of exposition but also of the man himself.

Fourier's works confront the translator with peculiar problems. Not only was Fourier a self-described "stranger to the art of writing," but he also had a penchant for neologisms and typographical experimentation that some have cited as evidence of his "madness." His ideas are generally couched in a strange private language in which "pivots" and "cislogomeni" mingle with "mixed scales" and "bi-compound accords." We have done the best we could with all of this. But since many of his neologisms steadfastly defy translation, we have frequently followed the practice of his nineteenth-century translators in simply grafting a number of new words into the English language. We hope that the brief glossary at the end of this book clarifies the meaning of some of the more elusive terms.

Our major problems as translators were posed by Fourier's manuscript writings. For the works which appeared during his lifetime represent only a portion of his complete *oeuvre*. At his death he left thousands of pages of manuscript notebooks. Many of these manuscripts were published by his disciples either in their periodical *La Phalange* or in four separate volumes which appeared between 1851 and 1858. Some of them remain unpublished, and one very important volume, *Le Nouveau monde amoureux*, appeared in print for the first time only in 1967. These manuscript writings, on which we have drawn heavily, are for the most part hastily written and extraordinarily digressive. Fourier did not take time to revise them, and often he simply omitted words or phrases when the right expression did not come immediately to mind. To render these writings into intelligible and fluent English it has sometimes been necessary for us to add connectives, to break up sentences, and to rearrange his tortured syntax. We think we have managed to do so without betraying his meaning. And, in general, we hope that our translations convey some of the irony and dry wit that were integral to Fourier's critical stance and his utopian vision.

There are several debts of gratitude which we have had the good fortune to incur. The College of Arts and Sciences and the Department of History of Harvard University provided indispensable money for travel to Paris and for microfilms, while a grant from the American Philosophical Society furnished equally indispensable subsistence funds during a recent summer. Several friends and former teachers helped with advice and encouragement. H. Stuart Hughes and the late Crane Brinton sympathetically aided and abetted each of us in the early stages of this undertaking. Readers who are familiar with Frank Manuel's essay on Fourier will recognize what we owe his work, but we are equally grateful to him for his readiness to share his knowledge of Fourier and for his encouragement of our efforts. Among the French scholars to whom we are indebted in various ways, we would like to single out Madame Simone Debout-Oleskiewicz. Without her painstaking editorial work on the *Nouveau monde amoureux*, this anthology might not have appeared in its present form.

Finally, the ultimate stages of our collaboration were rendered not only possible but also gastronomically elegant, in a way that Fourier himself would have commended, by Roberta Bienvenu who contributed culinary expertise and editorial discernment in the best Phalansterian tradition.

*Columbia, Mo.*                    RICHARD BIENVENU
*Cambridge, Mass.*                JONATHAN BEECHER

September 1970

# The Utopian Vision
## of Charles Fourier

# *Introduction*

THE GENESIS OF A UTOPIA

Charles Fourier liked to say that there were four famous apples in history. "Two were famous by the disasters which they caused, that of Adam and that of Paris, and two by services rendered to mankind, Newton's and my own." Fourier encountered his apple in a Paris restaurant. It cost his dining companion fourteen sous. Having just left a region where better apples sold for fourteen sous the hundred, Fourier was so struck by the discrepancy in price that he began to suspect that something had gone wrong with the economic system. "From that moment were born the investigations which, at the end of four years, made me discover the theory of industrial series and groups and subsequently the laws of universal movement missed by Newton."[1] A few years later, in an obscure provincial newspaper, Fourier notified the world of his discovery. Newton had determined the laws of gravitational attraction, but it had been left to Fourier, "a scientific pariah . . . an almost illiterate shop clerk," to advance from the realm of pure curiosity (the equilibrium of the stars) to that of the most urgent utility (the equilibrium of the passions). His law of "passionate attraction" completed Newton's work and was destined to "conduct the human race to opulence, sensual pleasures and global unity."[2]

This celebration of an apple was not the only story told by Fourier to account for the origin of the doctrine with which, for some thirty-five years, he hoped to metamorphosize a corrupt

---

[1] *Publication des manuscrits de Charles Fourier*, Vol. I (Année 1851), p. 17; *Oeuvres complètes de Charles Fourier* (Paris: Editions Anthropos, 1966–1968), X, 17. These works will subsequently be identified by the abbreviations *PM* and *OC*.

[2] *Bulletin de Lyon*, 11 Frimaire, Year XII (December 3, 1803); *PM*, 1; *OC*, x, 52–53. See below pp. 81–82.

civilization. In his first published book, the *Théorie des quatre mouvements*, he singled out "the incapacity which the philosophers had displayed in their great experiment, in the French Revolution," as "the first consideration which made me suspect the existence of a still unknown social science and inspired me to attempt its discovery."[3] Elsewhere Fourier dated his initial speculations from the year 1789 when, as a raw eighteen-year-old provincial, he had made his first visit to Paris. The revolutionary ferment meant little to him at that time, but he had been amazed by the sheer magnificence of the French capital. The sight of its spacious boulevards, its handsome town houses and its Palais Royal had inspired him to devise the "rules" of a new type of "unitary architecture" which was later to become the basis for the blueprints of his ideal city.[4]

While these stories—and there are others—should perhaps be taken with a grain of salt, they do provide some idea of the scope of Fourier's doctrine, his absolute self-confidence, and his capacity for projecting all of his experience into a single utopian vision. This vision first took firm shape in his mind around 1799. From that time until his death in 1837, it was all that mattered to him. Convinced that all previous philosophers had done nothing to solve the problem of human happiness, Fourier ignored them and their 400,000 nonsensical volumes. Relying on his own imaginative powers and a smattering of scientific knowledge, he spent his remaining years elaborating his theory of "passionate attraction" and setting down on paper a minutely detailed account of the fulfilling life that man was destined to lead in the ideal realm which he called Harmony.

Fourier was blessed with a Petrine faith in the truth of his doctrine and in the eventual flowering of his system of Harmony over the face of the entire globe. Nothing in his external biography could have nurtured such a faith. For when his life was not beset by calamity, it was by the world's and his own standards dull, monotonous, and quite devoid of the epicurean delights that he tirelessly devised for his new world. But for all its outward drabness, his biography will help us to reach a sympa-

[3] *OC*, I, 2–3.
[4] *OC*, II, 209.

thetic understanding of his thought. Its full meaning does not appear in the recorded facts, but in the contrast between these facts and his aspirations.

Charles Fourier was born at Besançon, in France's eastern province of Franche-Comté, on April 7, 1772. He was thus a dozen years younger than his fellow "utopian socialist," Henri de Saint-Simon, and a contemporary of both Robert Owen and Napoleon. In his later years he never tired of pointing out that he had been "born and raised in the mercantile shops." For his father was a prosperous cloth merchant and his mother came from one of Besançon's most prominent commercial families. Charles Fourrier *père* (his son was later to drop the extra "r") died in 1781, and the main influence in the boy's early life was his mother. Like many a well-to-do eighteenth century *bourgeoise*, Madame Fourrier was barely literate. She was also apparently stingy, domineering, extremely prudish, and—as Fourier's first biographer tactfully put it—"scrupulous and unenlightened in her piety."[5] Fourier later recalled that he spent his early years getting dragged from one mass to another; and one of his earliest memories was of being so terrified by sermons on the caldrons of Hell that—at the age of seven—he tried to assure himself of remission from all possible sins by confessing to fornication and simony.

As the only son of a successful merchant, Charles was expected to take charge of the family business when he came of age. This was made very clear in his father's will. It specified that Charles was to receive a patrimony of 80,000 livres—provided he had embarked on a career in commerce by the age of twenty.[6] Otherwise a large part of the inheritance would be withheld. Fourier, who later claimed that he had sworn a "Hannibalic oath" against commerce at the age of seven, had other ideas; and, in fact, most of the tastes and talents that he displayed as a child hardly befitted a future cloth merchant. He seems to have been a

---

[5] Charles Pellarin, *Vie de Fourier* (5th ed., Paris, 1871), p. 71. This devout and charming work, by a disciple who knew Fourier, is the principal source for his biography. In our account most of the details and anecdotes concerning Fourier's personal life are drawn from Pellarin.

[6] At the end of the Old Regime the livre (or franc) was very roughly equivalent in buying power to today's dollar.

precocious, impressionable, and somewhat reclusive boy. According to the reminiscences of his sister, he had a "wonderful aptitude" for music, drawing, arithmetic, and geography, and a passion for sweets and flowers. He loved to spend his time shut up in his room, practicing the violin or poring over a collection of atlases which he had bought with his pocket money. But flowers were his greatest passion. He was so fond of them, his sister recalled, that he turned his room into a veritable greenhouse. Pots and flowers were carefully arranged by color, size, and species in symmetrical patterns which he allowed no one to disturb. As he grew older Fourier was to lose none of his fondness for order and symmetry—in floral arrangements and in all things —and the harmonies of music and mathematics were to serve as his models in the elaboration of his vision of social harmony.

Most of the scholars who have attempted to track down the intellectual "sources" of Fourier's utopia have reached negative conclusions.[7] He was endowed with an excellent memory and the wide-ranging curiosity of the true autodidact. But, so far as one can tell, he never acquired the habit of sustained or thorough reading. He was "bored" by long books and treatises on metaphysics and he boasted that he had not gotten beyond the first page of a summary of the views of the "quibbler," Condillac. The formal education which he received from the secular priests who taught at the Collège de Besançon could not have provided much encouragement. For it was a banal and limited classical education stressing rhetoric, Latin, and above all theology. It did awaken Fourier's interest in mathematics and physics to the point where, for a time, he hoped to enter the exclusive school of military engineering at Mezières. But this would have required letters of nobility which the family did not possess. Thus when Fourier graduated from the Collège de Besançon at the age of sixteen his formal schooling was at an end. He had acquired an intimate familiarity with the catechism, a fair command of Latin, and the ability to sprinkle his writings with inaccurate citations from

[7] See especially the "Etude sur les sources de Fourier" in Hubert Bourgin, *Fourier. Contribution à l'étude du socialisme français* (Paris, 1905), pp. 56–136. For a critique of this study see Emile Lehouck, *Fourier aujourd'hui* (Paris, 1966), pp. 168–172.

Horace, Virgil, and a few of the *philosophes*. His real education was to come from his experience and not from books.

The decisive period in Fourier's intellectual life was the decade of the French Revolution. In 1789, at the age of seventeen, he was sent by his family to work in a banking house at Lyon. He reneged at the last moment, and an attempt the following year to place him with a Rouen textile company was hardly more successful. He found the city disgusting and the work hateful and quit after a few months. But despite his Hannibalic oath, Fourier was unable to escape the vocation for which his father had destined him. In 1791 he was apprenticed to one François-Antoine Bousquet, a wholesale cloth merchant at Lyon, and embarked on a career in commerce which was to last for most of his life.

It was at Lyon that Fourier spent most of the revolutionary period. With its huge silk-weaving industry Lyon was the largest and most advanced manufacturing center of Southern France. Its economic life was dominated by a class of master merchants who were in constant and sometimes violent conflict over wage rates with the mass of silk workers or *canuts*. Fourier was a witness to this conflict and, during the general economic and political crisis of the revolutionary years, he saw unemployment, hunger, and mass poverty of a sort he had never known in his sheltered life at Besançon. Lyon was also a city with a strong tradition of mystical speculation and utopian social thought. It is conceivable that some of Fourier's initial utopian reflections were inspired by the pamphlets of local reformers and revolutionaries.[8] But what is certain is that the city itself, with its poverty and its tradition of social unrest, was a revelation to Fourier. It was during his early years at Lyon that he first began to wonder whether the economic institutions of civilized society were not so many calamities "invented by God to punish the human race."[9]

When he turned twenty-one in 1793, Fourier returned to Besançon to collect half his patrimony. Investing a large part of it in colonial goods, he went into business for himself at Lyon

[8] Notably the quasi-socialist pamphleteer, François-Joseph L'Ange.
[9] *OC*, I, 3.

as a merchant and importer. But only a few months later the city rose in arms against the revolutionary government. From August until November Lyon was put to siege by the troops of the Convention. While Fourier was fighting in the ragtag army of the Lyon Federalists, his goods were requisitioned without indemnity; and when the city capitulated in November he narrowly escaped execution. The experience of the Lyon insurrection was crucial for Fourier in two respects: it cost him a large part of his inheritance and it left him with a lasting horror of political revolution and social turmoil.

At the end of 1793, while Lyon was undergoing its own reign of terror, Fourier managed to escape the city. Reduced to living off the land, he made his way back to Besançon only to be arrested and jailed by the authorities there. The intervention of a Jacobin brother-in-law brought his speedy release. But he then became subject to the *levée en masse*, the decree placing all able-bodied French males on permanent requisition for the revolutionary army. He was drafted into the light cavalry in June of 1794 and he spent the next eighteen months on horseback with the Army of the Rhine. After his discharge he resumed his commercial activities, and he spent most of the Directory (1795–1799) employed as a traveling salesman, voyaging across the south of France for business houses at Marseille, Lyon, and Bordeaux.

If the Lyon insurrection disgusted Fourier with revolutionary politics, it was the financial chaos of the Directory that shaped his economic views. The brief Jacobin experiment in a directed economy was followed by a complete relaxation of economic controls; and the Directory was a period of skyrocketing inflation, industrial stagnation, and widespread food shortages. Fortunes were made overnight through speculation in paper money, profiteering in military supplies, and the creation of artificial shortages. As a commercial employee Fourier saw these abuses at first hand and occasionally participated in them.[10] They

---

[10] In his denunciations of the "crimes of commerce," Fourier often cited an example drawn from his own experience. While working as a merchant's clerk at Marseille during the Directory he had been obliged to jettison a shipload of rice, which his employers had allowed to rot while waiting for a rise in price. *OC*, 1, 239. See below pp. 114–115.

strengthened his conviction that there was something wrong with the whole economic system based on free—or as he called it "anarchic"—competition. He began to formulate a general critique of commercial capitalism which emphasized the parasitism of the merchant and the middleman as the chief cause of economic ills. At the same time that Henri de Saint-Simon was developing his first schemes of social reorganization and Robert Owen was making his first practical experiments in industrial reform, Fourier began to ponder the idea that a cure for many of the ills produced by the system of free competition might be obtained through the establishment—within the capitalist system—of small self-sustaining cooperative communities or associations of producers and consumers.

In addition to his projects of economic reform, Fourier's mind was seething with other schemes related to his experiences as a tradesman and a soldier. Not long after his discharge from the army, he began to bombard public authorities and even the ministers of the Directory with a host of proposals and petitions. These included everything from "important observations" concerning peace treaties and troop movements to suggestions on reforms to be undertaken in the system of military supplies, the organization of commerce, and city planning. In 1797 Fourier traveled to Paris in a vain attempt to get a hearing for his ideas. He had not yet made his crucial "discoveries." But in an epistle addressed to the municipality of Bordeaux in 1796 he was already able to claim that in his travels about France he had been so struck by "the monotony and ugliness of our modern cities" that he had conceived "the model of a new type of city" designed in such a way as to "prevent the spread of fires and banish the mephitism which, in cities of all sizes, literally wages war against the human race."[11]

Proposals like these were not uncommon at the time: unknown provincial philosophers had been submitting them to government officials and learned societies throughout the eighteenth century. But Fourier was no common provincial philosopher; and

---

[11] Memoir signed "Fourrier" to the municipality of Bordeaux, Marseille, 20 frimaire, an V (December 10, 1796). AN, 10AS 15 (18).

in 1797 and 1798 his private speculations began to take a bolder turn. He began to see the problems of urban squalor and cut-throat economic competition as symptoms of a deeper social sickness. The frustrations of his own life and the wretchedness and chaos of post-revolutionary society sufficed in his mind to demonstrate the futility of the Revolution and to discredit the philosophical ideas which had inspired its leaders. As he saw it, the French Revolution was simply a spectacular proof of the vanity of the whole tradition of rationalist and "enlightened" philosophy. The philosophers had always attempted to impose rational norms on human behavior, to repress and stifle the passions. The cause of the failure was quite simply that they had refused to accept man as he was. Institutions could be changed, but man could not. The passions were God-given and they were meant to be expressed.

Fourier's first efforts to bring together all his earlier speculations into a comprehensive view of man and society date from 1799. It was at this point that he began to conceive of his model community not merely as an experiment in city planning or economic reform, but rather as part of a larger theory of social organization designed to provide a useful outlet for every human passion. The task which he set himself was to work out a scheme of "natural association" which would make the gratification of individual desires and passions serve the general good. In his sole surviving account of "the indices and methods which led to the discovery,"[12] Fourier passed blithely over "the stages of my research on the problem of natural association." He merely observed that he eventually hit upon a scheme for the organization of a community—to be called the Phalanx—into small "passional" groups and series in which men would be inspired to work at socially useful tasks by "rivalry, self-esteem, and other stimuli compatible with self-interest."[13] This scheme was based on an elaborate theory of human motivation which Fourier described as "the geometrical calculus of passionate attraction" and which, he claimed, was in "complete accord" with the Newtonian principle of gravitational attraction.

[12] See below pp. 93–102.
[13] *OC*, I, 7.

There is much that remains obscure about these initial discoveries.[14] But it is known that Fourier's crucial break-through came in April 1799. He was then employed as a clerk for a business house at Marseille. Quitting work, he traveled to Paris in order to undertake the scientific studies necessary to "complete" and "confirm" his theory. The "Letter to the High Judge"[15] tells us virtually all that we know about this period of Fourier's life. He soon managed to persuade himself that he had hit upon the key to "the riddle of the destinies." He had discovered the means to gratify and harmonize all the human passions. After less than a year of study, however, a number of "misfortunes"— notably the loss of the remainder of his inheritance—compelled Fourier to give up his studies and return, as he put it, to the "jailhouse" of commerce. In June of 1800, shortly after the *coup d'état* which brought Napoleon to power, Fourier went to work once again for François-Antoine Bousquet, the Lyon cloth merchant with whom he had served his commercial apprenticeship.

#### PROVINCIAL SHOP SERGEANT

The close of the eighteenth century brought two decisive changes in Fourier's life. In the first place, his discovery of 1799 marked the culmination of a long process of intellectual development. By the turn of the century Fourier's formative period was over; his system had begun to take shape. For the rest of his life he was to devote himself to the elaboration and perfection of the "Newtonian calculus" which was the core of his system. Sublimely confident of the truth of his theory and of its imminent acceptance, he withdrew into a private world. He no longer had the slightest interest in the ideas and controversies of other writers and philosophers. Henceforth his reading was confined to newspapers and journals which he culled in search of facts and observations to confirm his own speculations. At the same time writing became a regular part of Fourier's daily routine. Every day after work he would spend at least a few hours working out

[14] See J.-J. Hemardinquer, "La 'Découverte du mouvement social': Notes critiques sur le jeune Fourier," *Le Mouvement social*, No. 48 (July–September, 1964), pp. 49–58.

[15] See below pp. 83–92.

his ideas in an ever-growing set of manuscript notebooks which he jealously guarded and carried about with him on his peregrinations.

In terms of Fourier's personal biography the turn of the century also marked an important break. For with the loss in 1800 of the last remains of his inheritance, he was definitively "declassed." Condemned to a career in the lower reaches of commerce, Fourier was too precise in his habits ever to fall into dire poverty. He always managed to earn just enough to permit himself a few indulgences, and he kept up appearances as best he could. But for the next thirty-seven years, while he mapped out the contours of his ideal city and chronicled the glorious adventures and amorous intrigues of its inhabitants, he was to lead a solitary life of dull work and trivial distractions. He never married and apparently never had a sexual relationship of significant duration; he lived alone in boarding houses and rented rooms, kept cats, tended flowers, and observed a strict daily routine.

Embarked on the exploration of a "new social world," Fourier compared himself to Newton and Columbus. He was convinced that the acceptance of his theory would bring an end to the old mercantile civilization, but in the meantime he was obliged to spend his days in "the jailhouse of commerce."

It is worth recalling [he wrote in 1820] that since the year 1799, when I found the germ of the calculus of attraction, I have been constantly absorbed by my mercantile occupations and scarcely able to devote a few moments to passional problems, a single one of which often requires sustained research for several years. After having spent my days participating in the deceitful activities of the merchants and brutalizing myself in the performance of degrading tasks, I could not spend my nights acquiring a knowledge of the true sciences, which would enable me to draw upon them in the elaboration of my passional theory.[16]

Fourier was eventually emancipated from the necessity of making a living in commerce. But his modest style of life never changed,

---

[16] *PM*, 1; *OC*, x, 23.

and he never acquired the resources to complete his formal studies. Until his last years he remained an isolated and unrecognized provincial autodidact, concocting plans for the regeneration of a world that just wasn't interested. He did have acquaintances who belonged to the learned societies and intellectual circles of Lyon; but none of these friends took his ideas very seriously. To the most eminent of them, the philosopher Pierre-Simon Ballanche, Fourier was simply "a modest person" with a "fine knowledge of geography."[17]

Pained as he was by his lack of recognition, Fourier's only recourse was to make a virtue of it—to boast of his obscurity and to flaunt his lack of academic credentials in the face of the intellectual establishment. Thus, in his first major exposition of the theory he chided his contemporaries for having left the discovery of passionate attraction to a "near illiterate," a "scientific pariah." "It is a *shop sergeant*," he wrote, "who is going to confound all the weighty tomes of political and moral wisdom. . . . Eh! This is not the first time that God has made use of a humble agent to bring low the mighty."[18] Until the end of his life Fourier continued to harp on his lack of intellectual sophistication—to lament it, but also to boast of it. What, he asked, was there to learn from Locke, Condillac, and the whole "philosophical cabal"? Their torrents of enlightenment and their elegant prose had done nothing to increase human happiness. Had he tried to understand their controversies, he would have betrayed his natural gifts and deprived the world of his discovery.

The world should be grateful for my ignorance [he wrote] and it should pay thanks to the fate which, in tearing me away from my studies and in exiling and imprisoning me in banks and business houses, obliged me to cultivate my own faculties, to neglect scholastic controversies, to concern myself only with my own ideas, and to make use of the inventive genius with which nature has endowed me.[19]

[17] *OC*, I, 317.
[18] *OC*, I, 102.
[19] *PM*, I; *OC*, X, 12.

Fourier did not lack self-understanding. He knew that his gifts were unique and quite alien to the conventional wisdom and traditional philosophy of his time. He did not, in fact, have anything to learn from Locke and Condillac. There is nonetheless a hollow note not only in the labored exaggeration of his boasts about his own ignorance and illiteracy but also in his tirades against "the philosophers." For he was desperately eager to win their recognition and totally unable to understand his failure to do so. When his works passed unnoticed or received contemptuous reviews, he could only conclude that a plot was afoot. The "philosophical cabal" was menaced by his ideas and therefore bent on suppressing them.

During the fifteen years that followed his discovery—the whole duration of the Napoleonic period—Fourier remained at Lyon and frequented its banks, its business houses, and its bourse. He changed jobs frequently. For brief periods he worked as a petty functionary at the Lyon town hall and as a cloth inspector in one of the city's military warehouses. Occasionally he did business for himself as a *courtier marron* or unlicensed commercial broker. But throughout most of the Empire he was employed as a clerk and traveling salesman by merchants connected with the Lyon silk and textile industries. His "home" in these years was the quartier des Terreaux, a maze of dark, winding streets, shops, and ateliers which was the center of commercial Lyon. He lived in a succession of rented rooms: on the rue Saint-Come "chez Madame Guyonnet, marchande," the rue Clermont, and the Place du Platre "near the umbrella merchants." Punctual at work, frugal in his habits, scrupulously neat in his dress, Fourier dined in the cheap *tables d'hôte* of the quarter and took his glass of white wine each morning at a small cafe on the rue Sainte-Marie-des-Terreaux. His distractions were those of a hundred other modest employees of the Terreaux: a game of dominos or billiards in the evening after work, a solitary stroll at dusk along the quays of the Rhone, a weekly visit to the flower market on the Quay de Villeroi. He had friends with whom he shared some of his ideas and dreams. But at work he hid behind the mask of a conscientious employee. For as he confided later to an admirer: "You are not aware that a man loses all credit, becomes an object of ridicule in a commercial establishment if he gives the impression that he is writing a book."[20]

As a traveling salesman Fourier had the opportunity to travel widely. Almost every year he bought and sold cloth for his employers at the great trade fairs of Beaucaire, Frankfort, and Leipzig. He also made frequent trips to the chief commercial centers of Italy, Spain, Switzerland, and the Low Countries as well as France and Germany. If, as Fourier so often lamented, his jobs and travels were scarcely conducive to study and writing, they did give him an insight into the actual workings of his society that was denied to his academic contemporaries. He knew the condition of the silk workers, the cheats of commerce, and the machinations of the stock exchange from first hand experience. Pension dinner tables and travel by *diligence* brought him into contact with a wide variety of men and gave him an understanding of their needs and desires that he might never have acquired from books. This experience, together with introspection into his own desires and needs, was the raw material out of which he fashioned his utopia.

Fourier's first attempt to draw attention to his theory came at the end of 1803. The unlikely vehicle which he chose for this purpose was the *Bulletin de Lyon*, a journal read mainly by state functionaries and village mayors and primarily devoted to the publication of government dispatches, exchange quotations, and odes to Napoleon. In a short article entitled "Universal Harmony" he described his doctrine as "a mathematical theory concerning the destinies of all the globes and their inhabitants." He announced that the practical application of his "astonishing discovery" was going to rouse mankind from the "frightful dream of civilization" and usher in an era of universal happiness.[21] More

---

[20] Pellarin, *Vie de Fourier* (5th ed.), p. 89. Pellarin's biography has little to say about Fourier's Lyon years and some of the details in our account are drawn from an examination of his correspondence, AN, 10AS 25, and from an article by Auguste Ducoin, "Particularités inconnues sur . . . Charles Fourier," *Le Correspondant*, XXVII (1851), 480–490 and 541–550.

[21] For the texts of Fourier's article on "Universal Harmony" and his subsequent "Letter to the High Judge," see below pp. 81–92.

articles in the same vein earned Fourier a brief moment of notoriety. But not long after he had dispatched a missive to the government offering Napoleon the honor of becoming the "founder of Harmony," the local authorities put an end to his journalistic career. For some time thereafter Fourier meditated publishing a manifesto against "civilized philosophy" to be entitled *L'Egarement de la Raison*. But it was only in 1808 that his first book appeared. It was an anonymous four-hundred-page "prospectus and announcement of the discovery" entitled *Théorie des quatre mouvements et des destinées générales*.

The *Quatre mouvements* was a diffuse and enigmatic work. Its avowed purpose was not to reveal a body of doctrine which was as yet incomplete, but rather to "announce" his discovery and pave the way for the publication of a comprehensive theoretical treatise. But Fourier's notion of a prospectus was more than a little peculiar. For the book was in fact a veritable crazy quilt of "glimpses" into the more arcane aspects of the theory, "tableaux" of the sexual and gastronomic delights of Harmony, and critical "demonstrations" of the "methodical mindlessness" of contemporary philosophy and political economy. It abounded in long and apparently gratuitous notes and digressions on everything from the decline of the French tragic theatre to the imminent dissolution of the Milky Way. The whole was patched together by a bewildering series of preambles and epilogues, and it culminated with an array of "notes" and "omitted chapters" (containing some of the most essential material) as well as a set of instructions on behavior suitable for "the remainder of civilization." Prior to the book's publication Fourier was already referring to it as a "riddle," and in later years he described it as a "parody" or "intentional travesty" designed to foil potential plagiarists, confuse the censors, and sound out the depths of prejudice which a full revelation of the theory would encounter. The reviews were caustic and commercially it was a disaster.

For all his protestations of naivete and ignorance, Fourier was a man of devious ways. It is very likely that there was an element of cunning design in the bizarre organization of the *Quatre mouvements* and its fragmentary presentation of the doctrine.[22] But if the book was a riddle, it is clear that Fourier was not fully prepared for the "litany of jeers" which greeted its publication. In manuscript writings dating from the last years of the Empire he repeatedly inveighed against his critics, concocted theories attributing the rejection of his work to a conspiracy mounted by the philosophers at Paris, and drafted schemes for the protection of the rights of "unlettered inventors" like himself. Consoling himself in fantasies of revenge, he virtually abandoned his studies between 1809 and 1815. He decided—or so he convinced himself—to exact a "tribute" for civilization by withholding his discovery until a million troops had been lost in the Napoleonic wars. Only then would he deign to resume publication.

Fourier did, in fact, wait fourteen years before publishing a second book. Until the fall of the Empire he remained at Lyon eking out a modest living at a variety of commercial tasks. After 1812, when his mother died, an annuity of 900 francs brought some improvement in his financial situation. But it was only three years later that he was at last able to quit his job and devote all his efforts to the composition of the full-scale theoretical treatise heralded by the *Quatre mouvements*. At the end of 1815 he left Lyon to take up residence with relatives who lived near Belley, a small country town to the east of Lyon.

The five years which Fourier spent at Belley marked the most fruitful period of his entire intellectual life. He at last found the time and the energy to set down on paper a comprehensive exposition of his doctrine. Its rudiments had been clear in his mind since 1799. But what Fourier managed to do at Belley was to refine and systematize his earlier speculations and also explore new branches of the doctrine which he had not previously been able to treat in depth. He devoted particular attention to the analysis of the passions and the perfection of the theory of human

[22] A good selection of Fourier's writings on "the riddle of the *Quatre mouvements*" may be found in the Fourierist periodical *La Phalange*, IX (1849), 193–240. For excellent commentary on these texts and on the whole question of Fourier's guile see Frank Manuel, *The Prophets of Paris* (Cambridge, Mass., 1962), pp. 243–248.

motivation which was the foundation of his system. A "discovery" made in March, 1817, enabled him to work out a theory of group dynamics more subtle and complex than that contained in the *Quatre mouvements*. Spurred on by further discoveries, he devoted much of the following year to an investigation of problems of love and sexuality. In four thick notebooks, collectively entitled *Le Nouveau monde amoureux*, he elaborated a theory of sexual harmony which added a wholly new dimension to his utopian vision.[23] By 1819, after three years of sustained intellectual activity, he had virtually completed the manuscript of a *Grand Traité* to be published in eight volumes. Running to several thousand closely written pages, it was a veritable *summa* of the doctrine of passionate attraction.

Fourier never published his *Grand Traité* in anything like its complete form. Partly owing to financial difficulties, partly as a result of new discoveries, and primarily out of fear of alarming his readers by too full a revelation of his ideas, he decided that it would first be advisable to issue an abridged and expurgated treatise in two volumes instead of the intended eight. For two more years he worked on this abridgment, attempting to purge his original manuscript of those portions—including the sections on love—which might offend the public. Then, in the spring of 1821, he returned to his native city of Besançon where, with the help of friends, he found a publisher. His shortened version of the theory appeared the following year in two seven-hundred-page volumes, under the intentionally modest title of *Traité de l'association domestique-agricole*.

### PARISIAN PROPHET

Unlike most traditional utopias, Fourier's vision of social harmony was not conceived as a model for mere contemplation. It was meant to be put into practice. The means by which Fourier proposed to "realize" his theory was the establishment of a trial community. All he needed was a square league of land and a

---

[23] These notebooks were first published only in 1967 in an edition prepared by Simone Debout-Oleskiewicz. It constitutes Volume VII of the new edition of Fourier's *Oeuvres complètes* (Paris: Editions Anthropos, 1966–1968) which is cited throughout this anthology.

wealthy benefactor or *fondateur* who would proceed according to his specifications. During his early provincial years he made numerous attempts to attract the attention of such a benefactor. His "Letter to the High Judge" of 1803 was meant for Napoleon's eyes; in 1808 he sent copies of the *Quatre mouvements* to princes, bankers, and even to Madame de Staël; in 1816 he talked of making overtures to the Russian Tsar, the Duke of Bedford, the United States Congress, and to millionaires at Brussels and Milan. But at that time his main concern was still to perfect his theory down to the last detail. As he wrote to his first disciple, Just Muiron, in 1816: "The impatience you exhibit about the foundation of a canton of Harmony is premature. . . . First of all a complete treatise, a body of doctrine, is required to provide the necessary information."[24]

Only in 1822, with the publication of the *Traité*, did Fourier turn all his attention to the search for the *fondateur*. He was then just fifty years old and still at the height of his powers. But his development as a social theorist was over. For the rest of his life his unique desire was to simplify his doctrine, to present it in a palatable form that would appeal to the public and win him financial backing. Thus, in his subsequent writings he confined himself to the essentials and said little about love and the other "transcendant" branches of the theory. His later books and pamphlets were filled with lists of potential backers, and in his zeal to gain their support he began to adopt the techniques of modern advertising: pithy slogans, bold and varied type faces, money-back guarantees—anything that would "sell" his theory.

When the *Traité* came off the press at Besançon toward the end of 1822, Fourier had the whole edition of a thousand copies shipped to Paris, and he followed it there soon afterwards to stimulate sales and get a hearing for his ideas. His energy was extraordinary. He dispatched copies to members of the government, the opposition, to influential bankers, peers, philanthropists, scientists, men of letters, donors of prizes, academicians, journal-

[24] Charles Pellarin, *Charles Fourier, sa vie et sa théorie*, 2nd ed. (Paris, 1843), p. 247. This second edition of Pellarin's biography includes lengthy extracts from Fourier's correspondence not contained in later editions.

ists, to anyone in a position to finance—or to convince others to finance—a trial of the theory. With each copy he included a letter, often a short treatise in itself, calling attention to the "special advantages" which Harmony would bestow upon the founder. To the American ambassador at Paris he described his theory as an ideal means of pacifying the Indians; to opponents of the slave trade he guaranteed emancipation; and to the *ultra* minister Villèle he promised the "émigrés billion." A year of Herculean efforts yielded three newspaper reviews (of which two were "insidious") and the sale of a few dozen copies of the book. In 1823 Fourier published a brochure answering the critics and summarizing the principal "selling points" of the theory—such as the abolition of commerce and the liquidation of the French national debt. This, too, fell upon deaf ears.

By 1824, after two years of unstinting efforts to publicize his book, Fourier had exhausted his funds. For a brief period he toyed with the idea of setting himself up as a geography teacher. He even went so far as to publish a pamphlet on the memorization of place names (which included some coy propaganda for his system). But nothing came of this venture. A subsequent effort to find work as an unlicensed broker at Paris failed for want of business connections. Thus, in 1825, Fourier was obliged to return to Lyon to take a job as a cashier at a salary of 1200 francs a year. From Lyon Fourier continued to send letters and copies of his treatise to everybody he thought likely to be interested in his ideas. A sympathetic Irish feminist put him on the track of one of Robert Owen's disciples, and an exchange of letters ensued. For a time Fourier believed that he might convince Owen to turn his community at Motherwell into a Phalanx. But the correspondence ended when Fourier discovered that the Owenite was attempting to convert him.

The lure of Paris was too great for Fourier to bury himself in the provinces for any length of time. Thus, at the beginning of 1826, he returned to the capital and found work in the offices of Messrs. Curtis and Lamb, an American firm of textile importers. He held that job for two years, devoting all his free time to the search for the benefactor and the composition of yet another shortened version of his theory. Published in 1829 under the title *Le Nouveau monde industriel et sociétaire*, it contained the clearest and most succinct formulation of the economic aspects of the doctrine that Fourier was ever to write. Once again he attempted to organize a massive publicity campaign. He sent copies to Chateaubriand, Decaze, Lady Byron, and dozens of others. In 1830 he published a pamphlet condensing the book's main arguments into capsule form. But its immediate impact on the public was scarcely greater than that of the 1822 treatise.

During the last decade of his life, Fourier threw himself into an ever more frenzied search for recognition and financial backing. He refused to leave Paris for extended periods because he was convinced that somewhere in that corrupt city he would find his benefactor. He even made a point of returning to his lodgings every day at noon in case his "candidate" should appear. But none came. In June of 1830 his hopes rose briefly when Baron Capelle, the French Minister of Public Works, responded courteously to a request for an audience. A few weeks later, however, the July Revolution brought down the government, and the audience was never held. Most of Fourier's countless other appeals, letters, petitions, and addresses to men of note did not elicit so much as a reply.

If Fourier was unable to win the backing of the rich and the powerful, he did eventually manage to gain the support of a devoted band of disciples. The first was Just Muiron, a minor functionary at the prefecture of Fourier's native city of Besançon. Muiron, who had come accidentally upon a copy of the *Quatre mouvements* in 1814, described his first reading of the work as a revelation comparable to that bestowed upon Saint Paul on the road to Damascus.[25] Two years later, after a difficult search, Muiron succeeded in locating Fourier, and the two struck up a correspondence that was to last until Fourier's death. Although Muiron was a modest and rather sententious individual, he was fiercely loyal to the doctrines of his Master. During the Restoration he managed to interest a number of his friends in Fourier's

[25] Just Muiron, *Les Nouvelles transactions sociales* (Paris, 1832), p. 149.

ideas and to enlist their help in paying for the publication of the
*Traité* and the *Nouveau monde industriel*. In 1830 the Fourierist
group still consisted of hardly more than a dozen or two small
landowners and *rentiers* from the area around Besançon. But the
change in political climate brought about by the July Revolution
served to swell their ranks. The young Victor Considerant, a
Bisontine and a graduate of the prestigious Ecole Polytechnique,
soon emerged as Fourier's most effective proselyte.

What really served to turn the small Fourierist group into
a movement, however, was a schism among the disciples of Saint-
Simon. Under the authoritarian leadership of Prosper Enfantin
the Saint-Simonian movement had become a religious cult, and
when schism broke out in 1832 some of Enfantin's highly talented
followers found a new prophet in Fourier. The Polytechniciens
Jules Lechevalier and Abel Transon were among the first and
most gifted renegades from the Saint-Simonian religion to be
"converted" to Fourierism. Together with Considerant and
Fourier himself, they held public lectures on the doctrine and
founded a journal, *La Réforme industrielle*, intended to gain support for the establishment of a Phalanx.[26]

The first actual attempt to set up a Fourierist community
took place in 1833. With the help of a member of the Chamber of
Deputies, Dr. A. F. Baudet-Dulary, the disciples obtained 500
*hectares* of land at Condé-sur-Vesgre, near the forest of Ram-
bouillet. Forming a joint stock company, they set to work clearing
the land and building provisional living quarters. Fourier himself had doubts almost from the beginning. He was soon chiding
the disciples for taking liberties with the doctrine; and when the
architect built a pigsty with stone walls eighteen inches thick and
no entrance, Fourier became convinced that he was in the pay of
the Saint-Simonians. Lack of capital forced the disciples to
abandon the project in the middle of 1834. But well before that
time the Master was denouncing it, to all who cared to listen, as
a travesty on his ideas. By the end of his life he had decided that

[26] An excellent detailed account of the relations of Fourier and his
disciples with the Saint-Simonians is given by Henri Louvancour, *De
Henri Saint-Simon à Charles Fourier* (Chartres, 1913).

the only way to put his theory into practice would be to set up a trial Phalanx composed exclusively of children, who had not yet been corrupted by civilization.

Although Fourier never completely lost hope, he became an increasingly bitter and irascible old man. In his last years he was plagued by bad health and tormented by the double fear that his ideas might be stolen from him and that he might not live to see their realization. Mistrustful of everyone, he was ready at the slightest pretext to vent torrents of abuse not only upon "the plagiarists" but also the disciples who were "smothering" him with their attentions and even the Paris wine merchants whose poisonous adulterations were, he felt (and perhaps rightly so), speeding him to his grave. He continued to write ceaselessly; but his voluminous output during the thirties added little to his theory. An 1831 pamphlet, *Pièges et charlatanisme des deux sectes Saint-Simon et Owen*, was an embarrassment to his most devoted admirers; and the two-volume *La Fausse industrie* (1835–1836) was a barely coherent "mosaic" of tirades against his detractors and enticements and bribes aimed at the *fondateur*.

Thanks to the efforts of his disciples more than to his own writings, Fourier acquired a certain amount of notoriety in the last three or four years of his life. Relatively favorable discussions of his ideas were published in the popular press by tolerant non-believers such as George Sand, Louis Reybaud, Xavier Marmier, and others. At the same time, less sympathetic journalists began to resurrect Fourier's early speculations on cosmogony to entertain their readers with accounts of anti-lions and planetary love-making. Tales of Fourier's "extravagances" gained such currency that now and then children who encountered him walking in the garden of the Palais Royal would taunt: "Voilà le fou: riez!"

But finally neither the taunts nor the sympathy appeared to make much difference to Fourier. For at the end he retreated into an almost impenetrable shell, and when he appeared in public or dined out he remained silent and impassive, keeping his true feelings to himself. One of his admirers described him at the age of sixty-four as a man of "imposing calmness" whose "cold and meditative attitude" was animated upon occasion by "an air of divine enthusiasm." But the best portrait of the man in his last years is probably the one left by his devoted disciple and biographer, Charles Pellarin:

The thing that first struck everyone who met Fourier, the most simple man in the world in his dress and manners, was his piercing glance. Above this eagle eye . . . rose a broad, high and remarkably beautiful forehead. The frontal parts of his skull, the seat of the intellectual faculties according to the phrenologists, were extraordinarily large compared to the rest of his head which was rather narrow. His aquiline nose had been bent to the left as the result of a fall in his youth; but this did not harm the harmonious quality of the whole face. His thin lips, habitually pressed tight together and drooping at the corners, denoted perseverance, tenacity, and gave to Fourier's physiognomy a certain expression of gravity and bitterness. His blue eyes seemed to dart lightning in moments of animated conversation when, for example, he was doing justice to some sophistical attack on social truth or confounding a civilized quibbler. But at other times his eyes shone with a gentle, melancholy and sad lustre.[27]

Towards the beginning of 1837, Fourier's health began to decline markedly. He was unable to assist his disciples in the launching of a new journal, *La Phalange*, or even to take his accustomed stroll to the Tuileries each morning to witness the changing of the royal guards. By the end of the summer he was complaining of violent stomach pains and had virtually ceased to eat. Although several of the disciples were doctors, he refused to take their medications or even to be examined by them. He was insistent that no one be allowed to take care of him. During his last weeks only an old cleaning lady had free access to his rented room on the rue Saint-Pierre-Montmartre. On the morning of October 10, 1837, she found him dead at his bedside, dressed in his old frock coat.

### AN ENEMY OF CIVILIZATION

Fourier was a self-taught social thinker, fiercely proud and obsessively jealous of his independence and isolation. The most that he was willing to admit was that distant precursors like Descartes

[27] Pellarin, *Vie de Fourier* (5th ed.), p. 123.

had anticipated, however imperfectly, his revolutionary methods of social analysis: "absolute doubt" and "absolute deviation." Absolute doubt, as outrageously and misleadingly naive as most of Fourier's ideas, consisted simply of doubting all opinions absolutely and indiscriminately, including those that were generally received. Above all, absolute doubt required Fourier to doubt civilization itself: "to doubt its necessity, its excellence, and its permanence."[28] The other component of his method, absolute deviation, required him to dismiss the doctrines, teachings, and moral codes of all previous thinkers and philosophers.

Fourier was thus not a critic of his society but an enemy. He always insisted, often with great vehemence, that his attack on civilization was radical, absolute, uncompromising. In his reply to one well-meaning critic who obviously had not grasped the meaning of absolute doubt, Fourier made it clear exactly how far he went in his condemnation. M. de Jouy, Fourier complained, admitted "that I have good reason to complain about our imperfect civilization. IMPERFECT!!! I have proved, on the contrary, that it pushes perfidy, rapine, egoism and all of the vices to the supreme degree."[29] This sort of language is difficult to take seriously, and Fourier usually has not been taken seriously: "absolute doubt" seems at best to be a mere rhetorical flourish, another of this isolated man's charming and meaningless conceits. Yet, if one takes the trouble to read Fourier from his first attacks on commercial dishonesty and inefficiency to his mature speculations on incest, his spirited defense of sexual perversion and his minute specifications for a social system designed to facilitate universal sexual gratification, it gradually becomes clear that Fourier took his method seriously.

Many pages of Fourier's works are devoted to scientific analyses of the evils of civilization. The science usually consisted of what Fourier thought was a revealing mathematical operation—enumeration. Civilization, for example, was characterized by "seven scourges," and his science could discern thirty-six different kinds of bankruptcy or nine degrees and seventy-two species

[28] *OC*, I, 3–5.
[29] *OC*, II, 78.

of cuckoldry. By the time he had completed his audacious attack he had subjected every institution of civilization to scrutiny and rejection. But at the beginning he fastened on civilization's most obvious flaw, poverty. Anyone who troubled to look around himself, Fourier believed, had to conclude that civilization was absurd. "Yes, the absurdity is general so long as you do not know how to remedy the most scandalous of social disorders, POVERTY. So long as poverty subsists," civilization's profound sciences are nothing but "certificates of insanity."[30] In Fourier's analysis, the shameful poverty of civilization originated in the three branches of its economic system: commerce, distribution and consumption, and production. In the critical portion of his system, Fourier first exposed the roots of physical poverty in the commercial system of his day.

His indictment of commerce began with catechetical innocence: "Now, what is Commerce?" His answer, subsequently the theme of infinite development and variation, was as straightforward as the question: "It is falsehood with all of its paraphernalia, bankruptcy, speculation, usury and cheating of every kind."[31] These are the crimes that Fourier singled out as the blackest mercantile sins. Because he knew commerce at first hand his critique was merciless. Standard zoological epithets such as "bloodsuckers," "vultures," and "parasites," were not strong enough to express the horror that this Bisontine salesman felt; he conjured up more grisly images. The cornerers of foodstuffs during times of scarcity, for example, he likened to a "band of executioners" who scurry over "the field of battle to rip and enlarge the wounds" of the soldiers lying there.[32] Even when the commercial classes were not engaged in the crimes of commerce, Fourier felt, they constituted a burden on society. Merchants were like a horde of monks who produced nothing, consumed a great deal, and removed large numbers of men from productive occupations.

This diatribe would seem to give Fourier a place in the anti-

[30] *OC*, I, 185.
[31] *OC*, I, 227.
[32] *OC*, I, 237.

commercial tradition which, following Aristotle and the Fathers of the Church, condemned mercantile activity as ignoble, dishonest, parasitical, and corrupting. This prejudice against the merchant established itself so securely in socialist and radical thought that the very idea of buying and selling was banished from many of the heroic but grimly austere visions of a socialist future. Fourier, however, cannot be fitted into this tradition. While his condemnation of civilization was absolute, he astutely distinguished between that which was intrinsically evil and that which had been perverted by civilization. Recognizing that the act of buying and selling was not in itself corrupting, he condemned neither the merchant's calling nor the desire to make money, increase profit or, earn interest. Because he appreciated the joys of selling and shopping, he made provisions for them in Harmony: in the new societary order, the intelligent and discerning consumption of well-made and honestly priced goods would become a rich source of pleasure and social utility.[33] So long as civilization subsisted, however, commerce would remain vicious, "a simple and brutish impulsion," driving men to deceit and limitless self-aggrandizement.[34] Yet the systematic dishonesty and rapacious egoism of commerce was but part of the reason for the poverty of civilization. For Fourier contended that after the producer had been robbed by the merchant, he cheated himself by failing to end the irrational organization and waste that characterized consumption in civilization.

In Fourier's mind the cause of this immense waste of food was clear: men lived in "isolated, incoherent households." He offered a simple remedy which he named *Association agricole*, or *Association Domestique-Agricole*. The inept, chaotic, and fragmented methods men used to care for and distribute food had to

---

[33] It is interesting to note that Robert L. Heilbroner, a benevolent critic of Marxist economics, gently chides Marxists for their inability to rid themselves of Marx's fear of money and the market. Heilbroner's contention that "trading and bargaining and 'shopping,' when conducted in an atmosphere free of duress, can be a source of pleasure for buyer and seller alike," is, we suggest, in the tradition of Fourier. See "Marxism: For and Against," *New York Review*, XII, No. 11 (June 5, 1969), p. 18.

[34] *OC*, III, 224.

be replaced by scientific, rationalized, and cooperative distribution and consumption. The new system would produce "enormous economies" and "colossal profits."[35] Fourier never tired of describing, cataloging, and calculating what hungry men (or debt-ridden nations[36]) would gain by this simple but revolutionary change. To make his point, Fourier often singled out the haphazard fragmentation and unnecessary duplication of storage facilities, transportation, fuel consumption, and essential industries like wine-making and brewing. These activities were especially good examples of civilization's wasteful methods. Instead of using one vast, well-maintained granary, men built three hundred inferior storage bins in which precautions against fire and spoilage were never effective. Fourier loved, but could seldom afford, his country's best wines. He was appalled by the incompetence and "extreme ignorance" of the thousands of domestic brewers and wine-makers who scandalously wasted these precious staples. The operation of three hundred individual ovens in a single village instead of three large efficient ones, to take another example, meant that fuel in an already deforested nation cost even more. These were but a few of the cases that Fourier cited to prove his point: the needless duplication of facilities for consumption and living was the source of irrational and costly waste.

Cheating and waste—these were the two vices that afflicted distribution and consumption; and it was the shock of encountering these two vices that drove the young Fourier to seek a way out of civilization. He proposed to eradicate these vices by inaugurating a strictly regulated "truthful commerce" within the framework of the Phalanx, a new community for cooperative consumption and production. Fourier freely admitted that the idea of consumers and producers in cooperative communities was not original with him, but his modesty did not go beyond that. For Fourier felt that, among all philosophers and moralists, he alone deserved to be called the "Messiah of Reason." He alone had solved the eternal riddle of social philosophy: the problem

[35] *OC*, III, 11–12.

[36] See, for example, Fourier's "Post-Ambule"; "England's Public debt paid off in six months by means of hens' eggs." *OC* IV, 206–211.

of liberating mankind from the painful and loathsome work to which the God of the Old Testament had condemned him.

### WORK IN CIVILIZATION

The problem of work emerged as one of the central concerns of European social thought by the beginning of the nineteenth century. Economists and moralists, political reformers and uto-pians were all engaged in attempts to reassess, or to assert the social, psychological, and moral importance of productive labor. The most striking aspect of this relatively new concern was the almost universal attempt to establish productive work as the prime activity of a healthy society and the mark of a virtuous man and citizen. The campaign to reevaluate work and rescue it from cen-turies of classical and Christian denigration did not begin, of course, with Fourier's generation. As soon as economic activity became extensive enough to create a self-conscious and literate class of producers, men who worked began to insist that working was as dignified and as honorable as fighting, praying, or ruling. Naturally, the movement to reassess work was led by middle-class theorists who first sought to justify their own lives and, later, to educate the pre-industrial working classes to the joys and benefits of disciplined labor in the factory. Yet the rehabilitation of work was not solely a middle-class enterprise. Early socialist writers who were influenced by the social thought of the *Encyclopedia* and the French Revolution, also preached a gospel of work. Thus, Fourier's arch-rival, Henri de Saint-Simon, announced what was to become a dominant theme in nineteenth century socialism when he proclaimed a new social commandment in 1802: "All men shall work."[37]

Fourier, too, was convinced that work was a central social problem and that labor was the key to human happiness. But he would not join the chorus of classical economists, bourgeois moralists, and socialist theorists who were singing the praises of work. He scornfully rejected any attempt to infuse human labor, as it was practiced in civilization, with fraudulent theological or

[37] Saint-Simon's announcement appeared in his *Lettres d'un habitant de Genève*. See, *Oeuvres de Saint-Simon et d'Enfantin* (Paris, 1865–1878), XV, 55.

social value, and he despised as hypocrites and charlatans the philosophers who tried to deceive the masses into loving work because it was a religious or a social duty. Work was a man's destiny, but so, too, were happiness, comfort, and rich passionate fulfillment. The work which so many of Fourier's contemporaries sought to make men love was, in his mind, a hideous corruption of God's design. The enticements and threats to which civilization subjected her recalcitrant workers were shameful—and ineffective. To despise and denigrate labor was not, Fourier believed, a sign of immorality and egoism but of good sense. He agreed with Saint-Simon that work occupied a low place in European society's scale of values, that there existed a deep "disdain for agriculture and honest work." But he did not think that this attitude was merely the product of a retrograde feudal-aristocratic mentality. If, in their hearts, men had little love for work, it was with good reason.

Fourier insisted that it was futile to condemn workers who showed a preference for idleness or to attempt to inculcate a love for work or a sense of its dignity. Had not Scripture itself always recognized that "work is a punishment for man," and that human-kind's primeval happiness consisted in "having nothing to do"?[38] But for decisive proof that civilized labor was an evil, Fourier turned to nature, that great fount of eighteenth century en-lightened moral theory. The savage, he often pointed out, was "profoundly contemptuous" of the civilized order; the strongest curse that a savage could devise for an enemy was to wish the civilized man's fate on him: "May you be reduced to tilling a field."[39]

Free men justifiably abhorred work, Fourier believed, be-cause civilization forced them to labor under conditions that ruined their health and stifled their spirit. His observations on the physical conditions of work are scattered throughout his writings. Nowhere did he approach the systematic investigations, such as the studies by Villermé and Engels, that began to appear at mid-century. But whatever statistical and methodological shortcom-

[38] *OC*, IV, 554.
[39] *OC*, I, 277; III, 249.

ings Fourier's descriptions reveal, they nevertheless show that he knew well enough what an honest day's work in civilization meant.

It was, in the first place, an atrociously long, monotonous day. "From morning to evening, all year and all of his life," the worker does the same thing.[40] Forced to "spend twelve, often fifteen consecutive hours," at boring tasks, the man who labors in this "veritable industrial hell," finds that his life is a perpetual torture.[41] The worker, moreover, spends these fifteen hours "crouched in an unhealthy workshop."[42] Here again civilization displayed its characteristic perversity. It surrounded "unproductive functions" with enticing luxury, but allowed workshops which produced essential goods to become disgusting, ugly, and filthy. Long hours spent in airless and dingy shops ruined the worker's health: Fourier contended that it was not uncommon to find "one-eighth of the working-class population suffering from hernia," fever, and malnutrition.[43] Work in factories like chemical plants or glass works was, he believed, a form of murder. The "vaunted spinning mills of England" were especially ruinous to the worker's health: there men and even children worked —under the whip—for fifteen hours a day, sacrificing their health and falling susceptible to "fever and epidemics" for which they could not afford medical treatment.[44]

Fourier was not, of course, the only social critic who was moved to condemn the working conditions imposed on the victims of nascent industrialization. Others, like the widely read French romantic liberal Jules Michelet, were also shocked by the degrading existence of the urban factory worker. But the concern that many liberal and conservative romantics, both in England and France, professed for the unfortunate industrial workers did not originate entirely in heartfelt sympathy. They exposed the physical, moral and, above all, the social evils created by factory work in the cities partly so that they could exalt the

[40] *OC*, II, 149.
[41] *OC*, IV, 515; II, 149.
[42] *OC*, IV, 525.
[43] *OC*, VI, 75.
[44] *OC*, IV, 408.

life and work of that quintessential Frenchman—or Englishman—
the peasant. Fourier, a *bourgeois* and a merchant, was not taken
in: he exploded the bucolic myths of well-bred poets with some
of his most rigorous and unrelenting sarcasm.

Life in the open air, he pointed out, is no guarantee of health.
The sturdy peasants praised by *littérateurs* were actually "sad
and dirty."[45] More "*living automatons*" than men, farmers were
remarkable chiefly for their "extreme coarseness," a characteristic
which made them more akin to animals than to humans.[46] No
apologist for civilization could say that the peasant was happier
than the city dweller until he had traveled through France and
seen the wretched food eaten in the country. And what of work
in the fields, that dignified labor that binds a man to his country?
The poets might discern indescribable and ineffable pleasures,
but Fourier confessed that he could find nothing touching or delightful about a band of agricultural workers who suffered from
hunger and thirst and subsisted on black bread and water.[47] Such
a life, he concluded, destroys the body and kills the spirit.

Civilization had not only turned man away from his destiny
by making work repulsive; true to its usual penchant for perfecting vice, it had consistently failed to provide enough of its
repulsive work. Chronic unemployment was the only evidence
Fourier felt he needed to reject civilization and its political doctrines. Poverty and unemployment could not be hidden behind
the mask of irrelevant political theory. Fourier refused to discuss
political concepts. He would not debate, as he put it, on those
"renewed reveries of the Greeks, these Rights of Man that have
become so ridiculous." Political controversies would only engender bloody upheavals like the French Revolution, if civilized
men persisted in neglecting the "first right, the only useful right,"
the right to work. Social disorder would plague mankind, Fourier
warned, until a way was found to provide all men with work.
For politics there was only one problem: "*To find a new Social
Order* that insures the poorest members of the working class sufficient well-being to make them constantly and passionately prefer

[45] *OC,* IV, 494.
[46] *OC,* I, 67.
[47] *OC,* IV, 499–500.

their work to idleness and brigandage to which they now aspire."[48]

Civilization, therefore, corrupted everything. It was an order that fostered social parasitism on a colossal scale and condemned the men who by their toil kept it alive to a miserable existence, to an "industrial hell." Yet Fourier's attack did not rest merely on this exposure of tangible economic injustice and physical pain. In his analysis of the psychological effects of labor, Fourier showed that civilization is, and has always been, "the antipode of wisdom and happiness, the absence of the beautiful and the good."[49]

Fourier attacked the liberal conception of freedom as empty and formalistic. He was not alone when he rejected political liberalism. Others before him, especially during the Revolution, had insisted that political freedom was fraudulent unless it was accompanied by social freedom based on the right to work. Yet Fourier's critique of work in civilization went far beyond the social radicalism of the *sans-culottes* or left-wing Jacobins; his radicalism was above all psychological. He investigated the relationship between liberty and work with a characteristic mixture of idiosyncratic terminology and insight, adding to the concept of freedom a psychological dimension that the conventional libertarian theory of his day failed to encompass.

Philosophers who discussed the problem of liberty, he charged, were unable to see that freedom from slavery and political despotism, or the right to participate in the political process were relatively superficial kinds of liberty. True, or bi-compound, freedom in Fourier's language also involved the quality of a man's relationship to his work, both in an economic and psychological sense. In the first place, Fourier estimated that of all the members of society, only a "very small minority" of rich idlers or men holding lucrative positions enjoyed even a crude sort of freedom: they were free from the economic necessity of working. All the rest—more than seven-eighths of society—were free to do nothing but work. Political freedom was meaningless if a man was reduced to working "under the penalty of dying of hunger." A

[48] *OC*, I, 279.
[49] *OC*, II, 178.

man who enjoyed only one day of mere physical freedom each week, was not free. "For him, the workshop is an agreed-upon, indirect form of slavery."[50] Since all poor men were subjected to this disguised servitude, the politicians' concession of the "rights of sovereignty" to the people was nothing but brutal irony. Indeed, the highest form of freedom consisted not merely of the freedom to work or not, as one pleased, but also of freedom from the psychological compulsion to work. Bi-compound freedom, then, was enjoyed only by savages and animals because even those few fortunate civilized men who could live without working were driven to work by an internal compulsion or the fear of social disapproval. For Fourier, freedom included liberation from the work ethic itself.

Fourier's rejection of the commercial and industrial system of his day and his prescription for a social system based on agricultural—indeed, horticultural—production, have caused him to be labeled as a romantic reactionary who looked backward to an arcadian paradise free from the plagues that had already begun to afflict an industrializing society. There is a certain amount of truth in this interpretation. Compared to some of his contemporaries like Owen, Saint-Simon, or the Saint-Simonians, Fourier does appear to be a prophet whose vision was rather myopic. He was not aware that the dominant social fact of the coming century would be the exploitation of a new industrial working class by capitalists. Nor did he believe, along with Saint-Simon, Owen, and Marx, that the very satanic mills that were devouring the workers would one day be transformed into beneficent engines of social and moral regeneration.

It is not really surprising, however, that a man who so thoroughly exposed the misery and suffering lurking behind all of civilization's facades did not make more of the wretched existence of factory workers. There is nothing in Fourier's writings to equal the book-length chapter on the working day in *Capital*, primarily because Fourier wrote on the conditions of work before factories had become a prominent feature of the French economic

[50] *OC*, III, 155.

landscape. The most advanced form of economic organization that Fourier had constantly before his eyes was the silk industry in Lyon, where silk was still produced by handloom weavers, most of whom worked in their own homes or in small *ateliers* even when they owned neither their tools nor raw material. Mechanization and the factory system had not progressed far enough in France to strike Fourier as the most characteristic aspect of civilized work.

He was, it is true, somewhat aware of the importance of the new, large manufactory, but almost only in a negative sense. Like many another early nineteenth century socialist or conservative observer, he insisted that the immediate effect of vaunted technological progress was chronic unemployment, brutal working conditions, and increased poverty. In general, Fourier's attacks on factories and mechanization were often merely *pro forma*, inspired by his anglophobia and based largely upon his voracious reading of newspapers. Compared to his contemporaries and, above all, to somewhat later writers like Marx and Engels, Fourier often seems hopelessly retrograde, an economic and technological *naïf*. On the other hand, there are more significant reasons for his relative indifference toward the machine and the large factory. Both his conception of nature and his method of "absolute doubt" led him to slight the emerging industrial revolution. Fourier was neither a theoretical luddite nor an apostle of technology. He did not think that machines were in themselves evil and he described himself as "far from endorsing the views of the fools who would like to tear down the factories."[51] But if machines had a role to play in Harmony, that role would be secondary, simply because a good life for all did not depend upon their proliferation. Fourier believed that nature, like most women, was essentially accommodating and generous. If she withheld her favors from civilization, it was because she had been maltreated. The Saint-Simonian vision, as well as the subsequent Marxist dream, of mechanized socialist mankind wresting a bountiful living from a stingy and hostile environment would have seemed a horrible nightmare of rapine to Fourier, for he knew that the natural destiny of the globe

[51] See below, p. 127.

was to become a horticultural paradise, an ever-varying English garden.

Machines, then, were not essential. Nor did Fourier attempt to make them scapegoats for civilization's perversities. *Le doute absolu* required Fourier to give civilization its due in all of its aspects. This is why, it seems to us, he did not emphasize exploitation, especially the exploitation of workers massed together in a factory. It is possible to find here and there in Fourier's works a phrase which evokes that great socialist theme of the nineteenth century—exploitation. It is even possible to detect anticipations of the more subtle and complex idea of alienation. But he never developed the themes of alienation and exploitation in a sustained fashion, not because he failed to perceive these evils clearly, but because his critical vision encompassed a wider universe of social evil.

Even without exploitation, civilization would remain a perverse social order. Life and labor under the execrable moral system of civilization, Fourier insisted, would be but slightly improved by the end of exploitation. Poverty, starvation, and wage-slavery did not exhaust the catalog of civilization's torments. Nor were the working classes civilization's only victims. Fourier's critical attack was fundamental; his social sympathies were not class-bound. Many other critics of emerging industrial society lavished their social pity on the working classes because they felt, often for selfish political motives, that these were the men most in need of sympathy and help. Fourier, on the other hand, condemned all of civilization and pitied all of its victims, even those members of the petty bourgeoisie who toiled away in clerical or service occupations. The "little people" of the lower middle class were not always starving or in rags, but they were prey to anxieties and emotional deprivation that were often worse than merely physical suffering. Fourier's keen sense of the psychological costs of pinched, drab lives, insecurity, class jealousy, and the dread of pauperization or *déclassement*, is not often encountered in social thinkers before the massive social dislocations of our own century.

Some of Fourier's concern with the sufferings of the middle classes can be attributed to his own experience as a self-taught and isolated intellectual forced to eke out a living in the lower reaches of French commercial life. But, it seems to us, the real source of what Edmund Wilson calls Fourier's "almost insane capacity for pity"[52] lies neither in the man's unappeased desires nor in the crochets of a lonely old bachelor, but rather in Fourier's refusal to accept either physical suffering or emotional deprivation as necessary, eternal aspects of the human condition. This refusal led to his angry rejection of a tragic or ascetic view of man's destiny. Moralists and divines had always sought to convince other men that a substantial amount of physical suffering and a narrow range of gratification were natural and inevitable. For Fourier, such doctrines were both hypocritical and pathogenic. His refusal to accept their view of life gives Fourier's analysis of the worker and his working day, whatever its defects, a vibrancy absent from most nineteenth century critiques of commercial or industrial capitalism.

### THE ANATOMY OF THE PASSIONS

Fourier's exposure of the crimes of commerce and his analysis of the inefficiencies of fragmented production, preparation, and consumption of consumer goods were for a long time the most widely admired aspects of his critique of civilization. His psychological radicalism was seized upon by the Surrealists, but most of Fourier's disciples and students were intimidated or scandalized by his psychological speculations. Even Charles Gide, who admired Fourier greatly and did much to rescue his thought from undeserved and condescending neglect, preferred not to follow Fourier into the "labyrinth of his psychology," and dared not contemplate his teachings on the "relations between the sexes" because they originated in a code of morality so lax that it went beyond "free love" itself.[53] More recently, however, there has been a resurgence of interest in Fourier as a psychologist, and the best recent studies have followed the Surrealists in insisting that

[52] *To the Finland Station* (Garden City, N.Y., 1953), p. 87.

[53] Gide makes these remarks in the otherwise sympathetic and useful chapter in the venerable text he wrote with Charles Rist, *Histoire des doctrines économiques*, 2nd ed. (Paris, 1913), pp. 286–298.

Fourier's vision is a whole and cannot be conveniently separated into sensible doctrines and mad speculations.[54]

This has been a change in the right direction because it emphasizes the fact that Fourier was no mere humanitarian critic of emerging industrial capitalism who cried out that men did not get enough to eat. He believed, rather, that he had found a way to liberate all of man's passions, a way to ensure man an emotional life immeasurably richer and freer than a repressive civilization had ever afforded him. Fourier's psychology is at the center of his thought, and to neglect it is to misunderstand him completely. In fact, he himself rested his claim to historical fame greater than that of Newton on the sole basis that he had completed Newton's work by discovering the laws governing men's passions. It was this concern with man's emotional life that convinced Fourier that his indictment of civilization was utterly devastating. He could prove not only that civilization starved and killed millions each year, but also that it subjected all men to a life of emotional deprivation which reduced them to a state below that of the animals, who at least were free to obey their instinctual promptings.

Everything in Fourier's speculations, down to the most minute details of Phalansterian life, labor, love, architecture, and gastronomy, was designed to ensure all men a life rich in gratified desire. The great discovery that was to make such a life possible was the law of passionate attraction. At the outset of *Le Nouveau monde industriel* Fourier defined it in these terms: "Passionate attraction is the drive given us by nature prior to any reflection, and it persists despite the opposition of reason, duty, prejudice, etc."[55] Although few of the eighteenth century psychologists had denied that men were creatures of passion, most of them held that men were also endowed with a rational faculty which would or could enable them not only to organize their sense experience but also impose effective checks and limits on their passions. Breaking decisively with this tradition, Fourier

---

[54] The essays by Frank Manuel and Daniel Bell are good examples of this kind of treatment. See our Bibliographical Note.

[55] *OC*, VI, 47.

maintained that men were moved by instinctual forces over which they had no real control. His primary concern as a psychologist was to specify and analyze these drives. For the passions were the "mistresses of the world"; and only when they had been recognized and allowed free expression could man attain the happiness for which he was destined.

Although Fourier was acutely aware of the diversity of man's instinctual promptings, he believed they could all be subsumed within a basic classification of recurring or "radical" passions which—like the signs of the zodiac, the Greek Gods, and the Christian apostles—were twelve in number.[56] In discussing these twelve radical passions, he generally employed the simile of a tree. From the trunk of the tree, which he called "Unityism," sprang three sets of branches. The first set consisted of five passions corresponding to the five senses. Fourier called these the "luxurious" passions because their gratification was dependent not only on health but also on wealth—on the kind of material luxuries that only a rich man could afford in civilization. Such was the inequity of the civilized state that men with "brilliant" appetites and strong stomachs lived on the brink of starvation and others with magnificent ears lacked the money to buy tickets to the opera. In Harmony, Fourier insisted, a minimum of gratification would be provided for each of the five senses and notably for the two most "active" ones: the sense of taste and the sense of touch.[57]

Fourier's second category included the four affective passions: friendship, love, ambition, and parenthood (or "famillism"). These four passions tended to bring people together in groups. Like the other passions, they expressed themselves with varying degrees of intensity in different individuals. But whereas the sensual drives remained relatively constant throughout the lifetime of a single individual, the strength of the affective passions varied with a person's age. Children were prone to be dominated by friendship, young people by love, mature individuals by ambition, and old people by "famillism." Many of the

[56] See the texts below, pp. 215–219.
[57] *OC*, I, 77; VII, 440–443.

evils of civilization stemmed from the fact that the elderly had succeeded in imposing "their" passion on the rest of society. For love, friendship, and ambition were continually frustrated by the "insidious" alliance of the familial passion with the institution of monogamous marriage. In Harmony the family passion would not disappear; but with the abolition of marriage—and of the lugubrious family meal—it would assume new, unrepressive forms.

The last and loftiest set of branches on Fourier's "passional tree" included the three distributive or "mechanizing" passions—so named because their free expression was essential for the gratification of the other nine. These were the Cabalist or intriguing passion; the Butterfly or the penchant for variety and contrast; and the Composite or the desire for the sort of happiness which could only be found in the mixture of physical and spiritual pleasures. Useless and even harmful in civilization, these three distributive passions were to become the "mainsprings of the social mechanism" in Harmony. Their combined action would keep the other nine passions in a state of perfect equilibrium and permit the formation of the "passionate series" which were to be the basic forms of association within Fourier's ideal community.[58]

Although Fourier's psychology began with the identification and description of the twelve radical passions, it did not end there. For, as he sometimes put it, the passions were only the alphabet of his science; there was also a passional grammar with its own declensions, conjugations, and syntax. A very large part of Fourier's writing was devoted to the delineation of the various links which might be established among the different passions and the permutations which they would undergo when placed in combination with one another. Without delving too deeply into the more subtle refinements, one can say that each of Fourier's passions could be divided into a host of nuances, each had its own "exponential scale" of degrees of intensity, and each was endowed with particular "subversive" tendencies which would become manifest whenever the "harmonic" tendency was denied gratification. Thus when ambition was perverted or repressed it could express itself in destructive competition, and the aural pas-

[58] See below, pp. 217–219 and 228–232.

sion in a love of mere noise. Similarly hatred and jealousy were "subversive" manifestations of the passion of love.

These twelve basic passions were the materials out of which Fourier constructed an elaborate classification of personality types which was to serve as the model for his theory of social organization.[59] He maintained that each of the passions played some role in the psychic life of every human being. But the intensity with which the different passions were felt varied greatly from one individual to another. Everyone was ruled by one or several dominant passions, and these "dominants" in turn expressed themselves in various ways depending on the "tonic" or nuance of the passion. Thus the hero of Molière's *The Miser* was dominated by ambition with avarice as its tonic; similarly an inveterate drinker was dominated by the passion of taste with drink as its tonic. Fourier claimed that most men and women were dominated by some nuance of a single passion; they were the "monogynes" or "solitones" who would be the common soldiers in the ranks of Harmony.

Much rarer, but far more interesting to Fourier, were the "polytones" or "polygynes," complex personalities who were dominated by more than one passion. In discussing these types Fourier generally cited historical examples which were well known to his readers. Louis XIV, for instance, was a bitone dominated by the two passions of ambition and love. Robespierre and Lycurgus were tritones, and Nero was a tetratone with four dominant passions. In running the gamut from the solitone to the pentatone, Fourier asserted, one would find a total of 810 distinct personality types, each of which represented some combination of the twelve basic passions. These 810 types did not exhaust the potential of the human species—there were also the extremely rare hexatones, heptatones, and omnitones—but they did constitute what Fourier called the "general scale" or "keyboard" of personality types. They represented the minimal level of psychic diversity necessary for the maintenance of "passional equilibrium" within Fourier's ideal community.

[59] See the texts below, pp. 220–224, and also Fourier's manuscript "Du Clavier puissanciel des caractères" published in *La Phalange*, V (1847), pp. 5–47, 97–135.

Whether Fourier was writing about the 810 personality types or the twelve basic drives, he insisted on the permanency of the passions. They were God-given and as immutable as the species of the eighteenth century naturalists: they could never be destroyed or permanently altered. They were the source of all human activity, and it was up to man to shape his institutions in accordance with their laws. Civilization had engendered universal and perpetual misery, Fourier maintained, precisely because its philosophers had failed to recognize the supremacy of the passions. Some of them, like the wealthy and comfortable Seneca, had preached hypocritical doctrines of moderation; others had vainly urged that men "smother their passions" and aspire to lives of ascetic virtue. Fourier conceded that the priests of civilization had displayed a certain "political sagacity" in exploiting the credulity and ignorance of the multitude; their celestial paradise and caldrons of Hell were "cunning" inventions which had seemingly reconciled men to lives of poverty and deprivation.[60]

The result of all these repressive doctrines, however, was only to create a state of "internal war" within every man and to set his passions "at odds with accepted wisdom and the law."[61] And this was a war that could never be won, Fourier insisted, for the passions were imperious and they could be denied only at the price of pain and mental disease. Fourier emphasized that there was no distinction to be made between the force of a man's hunger for bread and his hunger for anything else that his passions demanded, whether it was intrigue, change, beautiful flowers, or orgasm. To deny any passional need was to engender psychic aberration.

It is easy to compress the passions by violence [he wrote]. Philosophy suppresses them with a stroke of the pen. Locks and the sword come to the aid of sweet morality. But nature appeals from these judgments; she regains her rights in secret. Passion stifled at one point reappears at another like water held back by a dike; it is driven inward like the humor of an ulcer closed too soon.[62]

[60] *OC*, XII, 611–612, 661.
[61] *OC*, III, 241.
[62] *OC*, VI, 403.

Thus each stifled passion would only reappear and make its demands felt more urgently. If the passion was particularly strong it would reappear in a vicious or "subversive" form.

In one of the most suggestive passages from his notebooks on sexual relations in Harmony, Fourier observed that repression ruined God's handiwork by turning essentially benign and socially useful penchants into painful mental sickness, often into criminal disease. Referring to the case of a woman whose repressed and unconscious lesbian tendencies drove her to sadistic practices, Fourier commented: "Every passion that is suffocated produces a counterpassion, which is as malignant as the natural passion would have been benign."[63] Even if a perverse counterpassion was not produced, Fourier contended, the suffocation of a passion could still cause pain and anxiety. Many men, although fortunate by the world's standards, were nevertheless condemned to the "perpetual anxiety" which resulted from "the pressure of a suffocated dominant, that is, from an imperious passion that they cannot satisfy." The dominant passion of a man unable to appease his desires could become a true "vulture of Tityus," a source of constant torment. "How many civilized men are plunged into this state," wrote Fourier, "by the suffocation of some dominant passion!"[64]

Fourier never tired of insisting that the pain and anxiety caused by repression were unnecessary. For the passions were benign and harmonious if afforded maximal expression. The source of evil was the unnatural set of institutions and moral codes known as civilization. There was "nothing vicious but civilization" which drove "all the passions in a direction contrary to their natural course" and turned them into "unchained tigers, incomprehensible enigmas."[65] Fourier's belief in the inherent goodness of man and his passions was so firm that he refused to find even his arch-fiend, the merchant, personally guilty of the crimes of commerce. In expressing opinions which were "not very flattering for commerce," he reminded his readers that he was criticizing only a perverted profession and not the men who

[63] *OC*, VII, 390. For the complete text see below, pp. 353–354.
[64] *OC*, III, 323.
[65] *OC*, II, 153–154; IV, 33.

practiced it. "One should never blame the passions of individuals," he wrote, "but rather the civilization which forces men to practice vice by offering the passions only vices for their satisfaction."[66]

Mankind would wander in this labyrinth of passional deprivation, anxiety, and disease until it discovered how to construct a social order which would allow the passions to satisfy themselves and, through gratification, create the concord and social unity toward which they always naturally tended unless diverted by unnatural interference. Fourier's system of Harmony was such a social order and it was to be based upon human nature as it naturally was, and not as moralists vainly insisted it must become. Harmony would usefully employ the very passions which civilization called "indestructible vices." It would in fact depend upon them, thrive upon them. So-called vices like gluttony and gallantry would be very much in evidence in the most productive Phalanxes. Indeed, every one of Christianity's seven deadly sins— including sloth!—would have its uses. Take the child, wrote Fourier, whom civilization considers to be "thoroughly rotten" simply "because he is gluttonish, quarrelsome, fanciful, mutinous, insolent, curious and indomitable." In Harmony such a child would become "the most perfect of children . . . the most ardent at work."[67]

If the passions naturally tended to social harmony, then the most peaceful and productive society was the one which best satisfied, developed, and refined the passions. The goal, according to Fourier, was complete gratification: the perfect hedonist was necessarily the perfect Harmonian. Man's destiny was the "flowering of the passions," and the real task of reason was to seek ways in which man's passions could be "continually refined." Instead of wasting itself in dangerous and futile attempts to smother passion, reason should have sought "to widen the circle of our pleasures" and to increase their intensity. "Happiness," wrote Fourier, "consists in having many passions and many means

[66] *OC*, I, 223–224.
[67] *OC*, I, 71–72. For Fourier's amusing account of the uses to which the seven deadly sins would be put in Harmony see his manuscript "De la méthode mixte" published in *La Phalange*, VII (1848), pp. 113–114.

to satisfy them."[68] Fourier called for the complete gratification of every man's desires. But he assured his readers that the quest for pleasure, no matter how selfish it might seem, was identical with the practice of social virtue: in Harmony "the man who devotes himself most ardently to pleasure becomes eminently useful for the happiness of all!"[69]

### WORK IN HARMONY

It was Fourier's emphasis on passional fulfillment that made his utopia so unusual. The great task of social thought, he believed, was to show how work and the apparently incompatible desire for pleasure could be reconciled. Many eighteenth century utopians had been content to remain rather vague about work, falling back on conventional literary images of sturdy independent farmers. But Fourier insisted on a meticulous discussion of the subject. Although he was an optimist who believed that the problem of scarcity was largely man's creation, he nevertheless knew that men must work to produce life's necessities and luxuries. Consequently, the basic social and economic unit of his system—the Phalanx—was much more than a planned community designed to put production and consumption on a rational basis. The elaborately contrived structure of life on the Phalanx would create the natural and proper relationship between the passions and work. This relationship, as Fourier saw it, was absolutely reciprocal: the appeasement of man's desires depended on the products of labor; but work, in turn, could be nothing but "eternal torture" unless it was performed at the urging of the passions. Fourier offered to do no less than to free man from the biblical curse, to liberate him from work that was painful, enslaving, and destructive of his integrity.

Such a metamorphosis was long overdue. Neither economic development nor the progress of the arts and sciences had enabled civilization to solve the problem of human labor. Everyone agreed that workers labored "without ardor, slowly and with loathing" and were driven to their work only "by the fear of

[68] *OC*, I, 92.
[69] *OC*, IV, 419.

famine and punishment." Fourier argued, however, that there existed a "more noble" solution, one worthy of a just God. That solution, devised by God and discovered by Fourier, was "industrial attraction" or "attractive labor."

Fourier laid down a number of conditions that had to be met if work was to be transformed.[70] Some of these conditions are not especially original; they can be found in many radical or proto-socialist programs. Fourier proposed, for example, to abolish work for wages by establishing a system in which all members of the Phalanx would receive dividends proportional to their contributions in work, capital, and talent.[71] He also insisted that Harmony's workshops, fields, and gardens had to be elegant, clean, and alluring. The other conditions, however, are uniquely Fourier's. They constitute the mainsprings of attractive labor. Labor could be made truly attractive, Fourier contended, only if men were able to work at as many tasks as they chose—at least eight during the course of a day—in groups of friends and lovers who were spontaneously drawn together by fondness for the work at hand, for its product, or for each other. Finally, as the key social principle of Phalansterian life and work, Fourier prescribed what he called the "social minimum." Essentially a guaranteed annual income, the social minimum provided economic security and, above all, made psychological liberation possible by freeing men from the necessity to work. Once men no longer felt themselves to be "slaves of work," they would become psychologically capable of looking upon work as a pleasure.

All the elements of Fourier's design for attractive work were organically related in the strictest sense: if any one of them was removed the mechanism would not function. Piecemeal reform of working conditions was hopelessly inadequate; the new relationships among passions, freedom, and work prescribed by Fourier had to be established together, integrally. It would do no good, for example, to establish the social minimum unless working conditions were also changed. Work in civilization was so repulsive

[70] See the text below, pp. 274–275, on "The Seven Conditions and the Social Minimum."

[71] Fourier's scheme of remuneration is outlined in the text below, pp. 249–252, on "Administrative Institutions and Practices."

that if workers were freed from the necessity of working they would prefer to remain idle. Similarly, it would be wasted effort to clean up the workshops and establish humane working conditions unless the social minimum were also established. For without a guaranteed income, work would still be a necessity, the worker still a kind of slave.

The task that Fourier set himself was that of establishing a system in which all men would want to work, a system replete with a baroque assortment of incentives, allurements, and enticements. But his mechanism was no ordinary set of worker-incentives. In fact, Fourier's conception of the psychology of work sets him apart both from subsequent socialist thinkers and from the industrial psychologists and management experts of modern industry. He was not at all concerned, for example, with the problem that haunted so many socialist theorists who believed that they had to discover socialist incentives to work if they were ever to succeed in building a society free of the profit motive. Still enthralled by a work ethic which viewed even creative activity as painful, socialists looked for moral equivalents to capitalism's incentives. Fourier did not make such a search because he believed that most socially necessary work was attractive in itself, unless, of course, it had been perverted and made loathsome by civilization. Men were naturally active beings who, if left perfectly free to remain idle, would not choose to do so, as long as work was attractive. And Fourier believed that very few tasks were utterly distasteful to all men. Many seemed unattractive because civilization condemned men to one kind of work. Collecting garbage, digging ditches, or working in the stables were not in themselves degrading tasks. Nor were they completely devoid of attraction for a larger number of men than one might imagine. Such tasks were made loathsome because civilization seized a man who might have eagerly looked forward to pitching hay or shoveling manure once a week for two hours and forced him to *become* a garbage collector, a farm laborer, or a clerk. Because no one in Harmony would ever be transformed into a function, almost no task would lack empassioned devotees.

Fourier's conception of the relationship between psychological drives and work was rooted in the belief that men did not really need to be enticed, entrapped, or deceived into working. He insisted that in most cases Harmony would not have to resort to contrived work incentives because men would be *impelled* toward work by their own individual needs and desires, by their own configuration of "work instincts."

Since Fourier has sometimes been described as a precursor of "Taylorism" or of the "human relations" school of industrial psychology, it should be emphasized that his work incentives had nothing in common with those engineered by modern industry. Harmony's incentives originated within the worker's psyche. Fourier believed that men were impelled toward certain tasks by their own drives and for their own reasons. He insisted that work could become a means of self-expression in a very fundamental sense only when and if men became free to work out of internal necessity and for no other reason. This autonomy was not the independence of the civilized man who worked and strived because he had been converted to a stern ethic of work for God's or society's sake. The internal necessities of the worker in Harmony sprang from his own personality or, in Fourier's terms, his passional type, not from an internalized sense of duty driven into his psyche by his family, his society, or his religion.

The basic mechanism that would permit work to become the free activity of a free man was what Fourier called the "passionate series" (*série passionnelle*). He defined it as a "league of various groups, graduated in ascending and descending order, passionately joined together because they share a common liking for some task, such as the cultivation of a fruit."[72] Each series was to be divided into a number of groups devoted to special tasks. If a series was dedicated to growing hyacinths or potatoes, for example, each of its groups would work with a different type of hyacinth or potato. Fourier arranged the groups within each series according to a "geometric" scheme of classification, division, and subdivision.

Geometrical refinements aside, the truly significant aspect of Fourier's theory of groups was this: despite the apparently great degree of rigidity and regimentation, membership in a special

[72] *OC*, VI, 52. For texts on the passionate series and their groups see below, pp. 225–232.

work group was absolutely voluntary or, to be more exact, instinctive. The members of a group had to be "passionately engaged" in their work and not driven to it by motives of "need, morality, reason, duty and constraint." A series, moreover, was not a bland gathering of men and women with identical tastes and personalities. In fact, the proper functioning of a series depended upon the creation of a sort of ordered discord and rivalry among its members. For this reason variety and inequality were essential; each series had to be composed of individuals who differed greatly in their "personalities, tastes, instincts, wealth, pretensions and intelligence." Among Fourier's examples of typical series, he seems to have had a special preference for the pear-growers. Since all other series were to be organized in like fashion, this one may serve as the paradigm of the organization of work in Harmony.

## THE PEAR-GROWERS' SERIES[73]

| Divisions | Numerical Progression | Types |
|---|---|---|
| 1. Forward outpost | 2 groups | Quinces and abnormally hard types |
| 2. Ascending wingtip | 4 groups | Hard cooking Pears |
| 3. Ascending wing | 6 groups | Crisp Pears |
| 4. Center of the series | 8 groups | Juicy Pears |
| 5. Descending wing | 6 groups | Compact Pears |
| 6. Descending wingtip | 4 groups | Mealy Pears |
| 7. Rear outpost | 2 groups | Medlars and abnormally soft types |

The series were designed to provide a mechanism that would utilize the three distributive passions—the Butterfly, the Cabalist, and the Composite passions—in work. To satisfy the Butterfly passion's thirst for "periodic" variety, Fourier devised a unique pattern of work that enabled each worker to spend about an hour and a half, but never more than two hours, at each task. In

[73] *OC,* I, 294.

this way a man could work at "seven or eight kinds of attractive work" during the course of a day, and even vary his work from day to day by joining an entirely different set of work groups each day during the week. The Butterfly passion thus impelled Harmonians to "flutter about from pleasure to pleasure," from job to job. Fourier was aware that economists and industrialists would contend that such constant flitting about would waste time and money. His defense was simple: the five to fifteen minutes that Harmonians would require to change jobs would be an insignificant loss, more than offset by the increased productivity of impassioned workers. Moreover, by bowing to the demands of the Butterfly passion, Harmony would escape the hidden human costs that civilization had always neglected to enter on its balance sheets. For, insisted Fourier, a man's physical and psychic health were "necessarily injured" if he labored for twelve hours at any task such as "weaving, needlework, writing or any other job" that did not "successively exercise all the parts of his body and mind."[74] The deformed bodies and stunted minds that civilization routinely wrote off would disappear in Harmony, where even potentially murderous occupations such as work in chemical plants and glass works would be made harmless by limiting workers to "short sessions of two hours" no more frequently than "two or three times a week."

This fundamental need for job variation meant that every Phalanx would have to organize a large number of series. Fourier pointed out that the number of work series would vary according to the terrain and desires of each community. But he insisted that "*at least* forty-five to fifty" series would be necessary in order to permit every worker to do as many jobs as he chose. Eventually every Harmonian would be attracted to forty or more occupations and all would be capable—thanks to Phalansterian education—of laboring skillfully in each of them.

Variety and a kind of freedom in work that civilized economists and industrialists would judge frivolous—these were the two principal attributes of attractive labor. They explain Fourier's untiring insistence that the whole gamut of emotional types

[74] *OC*, vi, 74–75.

be represented on each Phalanx. Fourier's calculations led him to believe that a fairly random sampling of 810 men would yield, for practical purposes, the necessary range of types and tastes. He multiplied this figure by two—there were to be women, of course —and arrived at the optimal figure of 1,620 Harmonians per Phalanx. Once these men and women were assembled and transformed by Harmonic life and education, Fourier explained, their personalities would blossom. The hidden work instincts, repressed sexual and gastronomic preferences, even the apparently perverse manias that civilization tried to smother, would emerge and make it possible to provide the right personality for each necessary task or function.

No Phalanx could hope to succeed unless it provided a personality for every job. If the Brook Farm fiasco proved anything it was that Fourier's transatlantic converts had not read his specifications carefully enough. When Hawthorne complained that "a man's soul may be buried and perish under a dung-heap or in a furrow of the field, just as well as under a pile of money," he had only himself to blame, not Fourier's theory.[75] A proper Phalanx would have provided scores of enthusiasts of manure and the plow. To entice followers and to illustrate how the Butterfly passion operated, Fourier described a typical summer's day in the life of Mondor, a rich Harmonian.[76] In the course of a single day Mondor would eat five meals, attend mass, two public functions, and a concert (or a ball), and spend an hour and a half at the library. In addition, thanks to the system of groups, he would perform eight different tasks. In the morning he would hunt, fish, garden, and tend pheasants, and then in the afternoon he would spend his time at the fish-tanks, the sheep pasture, and in two different greenhouses. Finally, just before supper, he would attend a session of the Exchange to plan his activities for the following day.

Harmonians were never bored and always worked ardently,

[75] Letter of Nathaniel Hawthorne to his wife (June, 1841) in Newton Arvin (ed.), *The Heart of Hawthorne's Journals* (Boston, 1929), p. 74. We are indebted to Manuel, *Prophets of Paris,* p. 229, for this reference.

[76] For a complete schedule of Mondor's day as well as that of Lucas, a poor Harmonian with a rural background, see below pp. 276–277.

but their enthusiasm at work depended on more than gratifying the Butterfly passion. The other distributive passions—the Cabalist and Composite—had to be called into play. Man's penchant for intrigue and rivalry originated in the passion that Fourier named the Cabalist. Its principal role in work was to generate "discord or emulative rivalries" that would inspire each group to perfect its product. Like the Butterfly, it would inspire "extreme ardor at work," but it would also encourage "great intimacy among the members of each group," and intense rivalry between different groups. For all of its intensity, however, rivalry on the Phalanx would never become disruptive, for the Butterfly and Cabalist passions would function within the series mechanism to create "general benevolence" amid truly violent competition. As Fourier explained it, the Butterfly passion would disseminate the workers of one specialized group into a hundred other groups. This aspect of Harmony, known as "meshing" or "linking," would prevent the groups from hardening into exclusive and selfish corporations. Since every group would have "friends in all of the other groups," hostility and enmity would be banished.[77]

The Composite passion completed the serial mechanism. While the Cabalist was essentially a passion of calculation, the Composite was the free, blind enthusiasm that would be engendered when both the spirit and the senses were stimulated. Attractive labor would stimulate the spirit by fostering a sense of fellowship among coworkers. The senses, on the other hand, would be charmed by the excellence of the goods produced by the work groups.

The series and their groups were Fourier's basic solution to the problem of work. The mechanism he invented was designed to employ the fundamental sources of power in the social universe—man's twelve passions. This subordination of every detail of social and industrial organization to man's emotional nature is obvious in all aspects of work in Harmony. The supreme rule was that work could become attractive only when it served the passions. This principle is nowhere clearer than in Fourier's

[77] *OC*, VI, 85.

choice of the kind of work that was to be done on the Phalanx.

The most striking characteristic of work in Harmony was the predominance of agriculture, and within agriculture, of horticulture. Fourier specifically relegated manufacturing to a secondary role and banished the prospect of anything approaching the massive concentration of factories that was to characterize modern industrial society. Harmonians would be primarily growers of fruit, vegetables, and flowers, and breeders of animals useful and ornamental. Fourier admitted that manufacturing was necessary, but he insisted that it could be made attractive only with great difficulty. The discovery of this truth surprised and momentarily perplexed him; but he soon realized that this was God's design. The solution was simple: manufactured goods in Harmony would be extremely well made and durable. Since they would outlast civilization's shoddy products by at least ten years, Harmonians would consume as "little as possible" in clothing and furnishings and "as much as possible" in foodstuffs.[78]

There would, nevertheless, be manufactures and they had to be chosen with extreme care. According to Fourier's basic principle, a specific manufacture would be suitable only if it could be allied with one or more of the Phalanx's agricultural specialties. Fortunately indispensable manufactures such as carpentry and shoemaking fulfilled this condition. Fourier labeled all other industries "speculative" industries and warned that any industry which failed to arouse "interest and passion" among the members of a Phalanx was to be avoided.

Even eminently suitable and necessary manufactures would not excite interest, however, if they were allowed to become as "disgustingly filthy" as the workshops of civilization. Cleanliness and even luxury were necessary to gratify the five sensual passions. Thus Fourier insisted that every effort be made to build factories that were elegant and luxurious enough to attract men by their beauty alone. The furnaces of the confectionery, for example, could be made elegant by the judicious use of marble veneers and frequent repainting. Elegance was in fact an essen-

[78] *OC*, IV, 209–210. For Fourier's discussion of this question, see below, p. 288.

tial aspect of Fourier's solution to the problem of repugnant work, for he believed that many of the occupations which men avoided could be made attractive by uniting efficiency and beauty.

There remained those jobs which were generally considered repugnant and dishonorable, even under the best conditions. These occupations would be officially designated as "Drudgery," and included tasks like mail delivery, night guard duty, and carillon playing. All of these jobs were deficient in direct attraction because they had to be performed in isolation. To provide the necessary attraction, membership in the series of Drudges would bring a supplementary dividend and other favors. But, above all, the Drudges—who served only once or twice a week— would be "individuals whose temperament can adjust to the job," men who would "make a game" of their chores. Fourier realized that these precautions would seem "superfluous" to civilized men who were in the habit of taking "oppression for moral wisdom." Harmonians would know, however, that nothing is more important than infusing "repugnant and disdained work with gaiety."[79]

Fourier's ultimate solution to the problem of thoroughly repugnant work can be found in his description of "The Little Hordes," the bizarre organization, which is perhaps the most widely known of Harmony's institutions.[80] The Little Hordes were designed to put the passions, energy, and inclinations of children to good use. Fourier maintained that fully two-thirds of all sub-adolescent boys between the ages of nine and fifteen were attracted to filth. They loved to wallow in mud and "play with filthy things." Such children were "unruly, peevish, scurrilous and overbearing." Coarse in speech and noisy, they were willing to brave bad weather and danger "simply for the pleasure of wreaking havoc." In Harmony these hitherto insupportable habits would be put to use by enrolling the children in Little Hordes which would perform any kind of work that might degrade a group of workers. Highly honored and given first place

[79] *OC*, IV, 37; VI, 137. See below, pp. 314–315.
[80] On the Little Hordes see *OC*, V, 138–166; VI, 207–214. The later text is translated below, pp. 315–322.

among the Phalanx's corporations, the Little Hordes would be allotted "foul functions" such as maintaining the sewers, caring for the dunghill, and cleaning the slaughterhouses.

Fourier's goal was the perfect integration of man's passional drives and work. The fullest expression of that ideal was his vision of Harmony's "industrial armies." Once life and labor in Harmony had cured humanity of the psychological disorders engendered by civilization, wondrous armies would appear. Fourier foresaw the convocation of "a million industrial athletes" and outlined a magnificent program of bridge-building, reforestation, and land reclamation. Anticipating stupid criticism, Fourier pointed out that the world could well use this new industrial power: civilization had so devastated the earth that it would "take at least a hundred years" merely to reforest the slopes of the Alps and Pyrenees "that our scientists have allowed to be denuded while they were leading us to the perfectibility of metaphysical abstractions."

The armies of Harmony would differ in every possible way from the war machines that civilization maintained at ruinous expense. Recruitment, for example, would be based on attraction. If civilization "enrolled its heroes by putting chains around their necks," Harmony would recruit its heroes and heroines with the prospect of "magnificent feasts"—amorous as well as gastronomic —that civilization conld hardly conceive. For a third of each army would consist of young women who would work alongside the young men. Like everyone else in Harmony, they would be organized into corps according to their capacities and inclinations. The most renowned corps would be that of the Vestals, modest young virgins whose beauty would serve as an inspiration to all. Pursued by numerous suitors, they would choose their first lovers at some point during a season's "campaign." No less important, however, were the experienced and energetic young women known as Bacchantes. These sexual athletes, Fourier promised, would provide sexual satisfaction and solace for the rejected suitors of the Vestals and for any other troops whose feelings might be wounded in the amorous skirmishes and festivities which would occur after the day's work was done.

### THE LIBERATION OF INSTINCT

The Harmonious Armies, with their unique blend of labor and love, of pomp and social utility, afford us a glimpse into the higher stages of Harmony, a promised land of complete instinctual liberation that Fourier kept all but hidden from the public after the appearance of his first book, the *Théorie des quatre mouvements*. In that work he drew the curtain back slightly and revealed a few details of amorous relations in Harmony, but only to titillate *"les voluptueux,"* the sensualists. For the rest of his life he deliberately refrained from publishing any detailed account of the radical transformations that amorous relationships were to undergo. Instead, he recorded these details in the crowded pages of his notebooks, collectively entitled *The New Amorous World*. These manuscripts are confused, digressive, and unfinished, but they provide fascinating evidence that Fourier was the most audacious utopian of his era, a visionary whose speculations took him far beyond the important but preliminary problems of production and consumption.

The men and women of Fourier's new amorous world were Harmonians who belonged to work groups, lived on Phalanxes, and performed attractive labor within the serial mechanism. But they were somehow different from the inhabitants of the first Phalanxes described in Fourier's published works. For one thing, Fourier changed the setting for their adventures. These Harmonians lived not in Europe but under the bright Mediterranean sun of Asia Minor. The existence of a literary tradition certainly played a part in Fourier's decision to move his Harmonians. When he situated a Phalanx on the site of the old Greek city of Cnidos, he was following Montesquieu who had already celebrated the erotic finesse of its inhabitants.[81] But there were other, more compelling reasons for this transposition. It seems obvious that Fourier set his new amorous world in those alluring lands to emphasize the fact that he was describing a different order of men. His Cnidians, Babylonians, and Armenians were all sons and daughters of Harmony, they were children completely un-

[81] In *Le Temple de Gnide* (1725).

tainted by the psychic diseases of civilization. As he explained in his manuscripts, he was not writing about men and women as civilization knew them. He would not "speculate on civilization." Rather, he intended to describe an "order of things in which the least of men will be rich, polished, sincere, pleasant, virtuous and handsome (excepting the very old); an order of things in which marriage and our other customs will have been forgotten, their very absence having inspired a host of amorous innovations which we cannot yet imagine."[82]

In *The New Amorous World* Fourier set out to describe the institutions of what has become known as a non-repressive civilization: a social order which is able to provide the material basis of a decent life—security and comfort—without requiring its members to pay an excessively high price in instinctual self-denial. Fourier believed that his writings on the series, attractive labor, and Phalansterian life had conclusively demonstrated that the material or technological basis for such a society was well within man's capabilities. The ultimate purpose of the Phalanx was not merely to satisfy man's physical needs; Fourier's utopia was designed to permit man to free himself from self-imposed emotional bondage. In *The New Amorous World* this strange prophet of the passions revealed that complete instinctual liberation was the destination toward which he had always been leading the lost children of civilization.

The new liberated man that Fourier described would appear only after a fundamental right had been recognized. Harmony had to grant to every mature man and woman a "sexual minimum."[83] In Harmony all adults would be entitled to a satisfying minimum of sexual pleasure. The sexual minimum would play the same role in the world of amorous relationships that the social minimum played in the world of work. The metamorphosis of labor from self-denial and servitude into self-expression and freedom was based on the principle of the social minimum: just as a guaranteed income freed men from the ne-

[82] *OC*, VII, 51.

[83] Fourier's argument for the sexual minimum (*OC*, VII, 439–445) is translated below, pp. 336–340.

cessity of working, so too would the sexual minimum transform amorous relationships by purging them of any tinge of coercion and necessity. Sexual relations, Fourier insisted, are necessarily corrupted or falsified unless the elemental sexual drive is satisfied. Until the fear—and the fact—of sexual deprivation was banished, men and women would not be free to obey their deepest promptings or to develop their latent potentialities.

Fourier's argument for the sexual minimum was, on its surface, rather utilitarian, especially for a thinker whose amorous imagination was anything but pedestrian. He seems to have approached the subject of erotic satisfaction in an unexpectedly naturalistic fashion. Sexual pleasure, he argued, was primarily a pleasure of the sense of touch. It was, to be sure, a basic need, as imperious as the demands of the sense of taste, but no more important. Despite this apparently narrow view of erotic pleasure, Fourier was not really intent on reducing love to a mere physiological act, the "rubbing of one membrane against another," as Diderot put it.[84] Fourier began his discussion of love with the orgasm, but he did not end it there. He deliberately treated the question in a naturalistic fashion because he felt that it was essential to demystify the sexual act. By guaranteeing orgasm, Fourier sought to liberate men from an unhealthy fixation on coition. If Fourier implied that the act of love is basically a discharge of pent-up energy or the satisfaction of a physiological need, it was because he looked beyond orgasm to a world of more subtle and complicated human relationships which were themselves made possible only if the sexual appetite were appeased. The goal of the sexual minimum, then, was a higher order of erotic pleasure. Fourier's apparent naturalistic reductionism was actually intended to overcome the tyranny of the genitals, not by falsely pretending to transcend sexuality, but by incorporating it in all amorous relationships.

Most amorous disorder originated, Fourier believed, in civilization's refusal to recognize the absolute right of every man and woman to the sexual minimum. Because it permitted sexual

---

[84] In his *Supplement to the Voyage of Bougainville*. See Diderot, *Oeuvres philosophiques* (Paris: Garnier, 1956), p. 510.

gratification only within the narrow confines of monogamous marriage, civilization excluded large numbers of men and women from legitimate sexual pleasure and debased even those unions it claimed to bless. The erotic impulse, according to Fourier, was an extraordinarily complex force. When it was subordinated to the narrow utilitarian purpose of Christian marriage, it was perverted, its natural development arrested, its vast potential for social good destroyed. It was obvious, he wrote, that "both the law and religion admit only one goal in love and that goal is procreation. They permit only one kind of union and that is marriage or enslaved monogamy; they both require that the union be consummated physically; they forbid purely sentimental relationships, for those unions would produce neither Christians nor citizens. . . ."[85] Under the guise of sanctifying a physical union, Christian marriage actually debased love; it tacitly approved even the most brutal sort of sexual unions and encouraged the worst kinds of tyranny. "Here," Fourier argued, "civilized perfectibility reveals itself at its most brilliant. A young girl, harassed by parents and superiors, allows herself to be led to the altar. Her marriage is the most flagrant kind of constraint: she loves someone else and has absolutely no sentimental illusions about her marriage. No matter: her deflowering, a veritable debauch, an obvious case of rape, is no less sacred in the eyes of the law and of religion."[86]

If Christian marriage tended to brutalize sexual relations, civilized morality was guilty of the worst sort of hypocrisy and ineptitude. According to Fourier, love was naturally destined to be a compound passion. It aspired to "spiritual" as well as to physical satisfaction. People had long paid lip-service to this truth. Since antiquity, poets and philosophers had celebrated sentimental love. And they had concurred in describing it as a "higher" form of pleasure than physical love. But all this meant nothing under a moral code which permitted physical satisfaction only when it had been sanctified by marriage vows. It was sheer hypocrisy to vaunt sentimental love in civilization, for "these sentimental

[85] *OC*, VII, 69.
[86] *OC*, VII, 71.

masquerades are a very useful device for so many hypocrites who play the virgin in public and behave like whores in private."[87] Although civilization pretended to subordinate physical sexual pleasure to sentimental love, it was actually obsessed with orgasm. "The physical principle in love" actually reigned in secret; either sentimental love was entirely excluded from erotic relationships or else it was "the humble slave" of sensual pleasure. This pernicious imbalance, Fourier maintained, degraded the erotic life by reducing sex to a simple, brutish impulsion, devoid of sentiment, beauty, and real attachment. Love, the divine source of social unity, was transformed by civilization into an egocentric, selfish, and aggressive activity which drove men and women apart. As a result, all sexual or amorous relations in civilization were poisoned. Civilization's "amorous regime" permitted no one to escape its evil effects. Even the dissidents, the sexual insurgents who practiced free love could not find real gratification: their illicit relationships were essentially unsatisfying and egoistic, devoid of generosity. Consequently, the "bond of marriage, the only one permitted by law," satisfied no one. Husbands, the "privileged class" of civilization's amorous regime, were content only when they were able to practice adultery freely. But most of them would not have been "content if they knew what their wives were secretly doing"; both husband and wife were driven to fraud and deceit, and their lovers were unhappy because morality and the laws forbade them to "effect a union with the object of their love." Was it possible, Fourier asked, to imagine a more ridiculous system of sexual morality? Was there any reason to be astonished that "everyone is involved in a secret conspiracy to violate the civil and religious laws which govern or pretend to govern the amorous world?"[88]

To replace the old amorous system which benefited no one and which no one respected, Fourier proposed a radically different set of laws and institutions. Harmony's laws would govern the amorous world by collaborating with man's sexual instincts, while its network of amorous institutions were specifically designed not

[87] *OC*, VII, 37, 95.
[88] *OC*, VII, 75.

only to permit but also to foster the most diverse kinds of sexual gratification. Harmony would rehabilitate and socialize sensual pleasure in all of its manifestations. For love was not a mere diversion or recreation for the Harmonians; it was an essential part of their communal life. It was one of the principal means for establishing harmonious relations between the rich and the poor. The prime source of social solidarity, love's binding power, would be felt even in Harmony's kitchens and at its dinner tables. As Fourier wrote in one of his manuscript fragments: "Love in the Phalanstery is no longer, as it is with us, a recreation which detracts from work; on the contrary it is the soul and the vehicle, the mainspring of all works and of the whole of universal attraction."[89]

The amorous institutions which Fourier described in his notebooks had much the same basic purpose as the passionate series: they established a concord between instinctual gratification and social welfare. When civilized morality restricted the enjoyment of sexual pleasure to the conjugal bed, Fourier argued, it had tacitly denied the possibility of integrating sexual drives in the fabric of man's productive, civic, and spiritual life. Civilization grudgingly tolerated sexual gratification only because it was an inescapable aspect of the procreative process. On that narrow utilitarian basis alone did civilization deem sexual pleasure socially useful. For the natural tendency of the sexual drives, according to the moralists, was to create a host of private relationships which undermined social solidarity. Sexual passion, civilization concluded, had to be rigidly confined within the framework of monogamous marriage. Fourier, on the other hand, insisted that such a mean view of God's design was blasphemous. In *The New Amorous World*, he set out to show that virtually every kind of sexual gratification could be made to foster social harmony and economic well-being.

In a very curious way, then, Fourier's utopia belongs to the eighteenth century tradition which called for the end of purely private pleasures and egocentric preoccupations. Like Rousseau and Montesquieu, Fourier believed that narrow selfishness was

[89] *La Phalange*, ix (1849), 200.

socially vicious: no measure of freedom and self-realization was possible in a society that had not discovered a means of transcending the pursuit of selfish interests. But civic-mindeness in Rousseau's republic was purchased at the price of self-denying virtue; its citizens cultivated the hard and manly virtues that Rousseau associated with the vigorous military city-states of antiquity. Harmonians, on the other hand, would rise to heights of civic virtue and would enjoy a keen sense of social solidarity by freely gratifying their desires, even when these included "manias" like amorous heel-scratching or hair-plucking.

All of Harmony's amorous institutions were designed to guarantee a basic human right: "No one capable of love," Fourier promised, will ever "be frustrated in his or her desire." The first step, of course, was the abolition of monogamy, for love could not fully express itself (save for short periods of time) in exclusive relationships based on jealousy and the selfish exclusion of others. In Harmony, then, love was to be "free." Fourier did not, however, wish merely to establish universal polygamy. He also proposed to rehabilitate those sexual practices that civilized morality and the church had absolutely forbidden. It was urgently necessary, Fourier believed, to abandon the notion of sexual perversion. The perversity lay not in unusual sexual tastes but rather in a repressive civilization which forced natural and potentially useful "manias" such as sapphism, pederasty, or flagellantism to develop in a vicious and harmful fashion.

The institutions of the new amorous world would promote the universal gratification of sexual desire, even when desire did not have "normal" heterosexual congress as its object. Fourier did not, as many scholars have claimed, look forward to the end of so-called "perverse" sexual practices.[90] Rather, he called for the enfranchisement of the sexually oppressed. The only kind of sexual activity that Fourier condemned as vicious or unnatural —truly perverse—was that in which a person was abused, injured, or used as an object against his will. In his comments on the "Case of Madame Stroganoff," Fourier argued that the sadistic infliction of pain was evil in that instance because Madame

[90] See for example Frank Manuel, *The Prophets of Paris*, p. 234.

Stroganoff's sadism was merely a symptom of her unconscious lesbian desires for the slave who was her victim.[91] When pain was freely given and freely received for sexual purposes, as in the case of active and passive flagellants, it was permissible.

Fourier's solution of the problem of sexual liberation was characteristically institutional. The amorous affairs of every Phalanx were to be run by an elaborate hierarchy of officials—high priests, pontiffs, matrons, confessors, fairies, fakirs, and genies. Each of these dignitaries played a role in the sessions of the Court of Love which were held in the evening after the children and the chaste Vestals had been put to bed.[92] The Court of Love was both a judiciary body and a recreational institution. Its sessions provided opportunities for the formation of amorous ties. Its officers were in charge of organizing the fetes, entertainments, and orgies. The Court was also responsible for the enforcement of a minutely detailed amorous code which regulated the sexual activities of the members of the community.

The amorous code, like the series mechanism, seems oddly out of place in a completely libertarian society; but the code was no more coercive than the work series. Membership in the various corporations was purely voluntary; the code enforced authenticity and sincerity; it did not regiment sexual life. Young men and women who belonged to the Damselate, for example were bound by the rules of their corporation to practice fidelity. If a young woman transgressed the rule often enough, she would be "sentenced" by the Court of Love to quit the ranks of the Damsels and join some other group such as the Bacchantes, whose rules were more consistent with her inclination. But if she wished to remain a Damsel, the court would grant her an "indulgence," provided that she perform some virtuous act, such as placing herself at the disposition of an elderly or needy member of the Phalanx for a day or two. Infidelity was no crime in Harmony, but inauthenticity was. The "penances" inflicted by the Court of Love were designed to discourage deception and make it impos-

91 See below, p. 353.
92 See below, Section VII, for details on Harmony's amorous corporations, dignitaries, and regulations.

sible for anyone to claim to be what he or she was not. Fourier's system of indulgences was thus both a clever parody of the way in which Catholicism dealt with sin and a skillfully designed philanthropic institution. For the virtuous acts required of those who transgressed the rules which they had freely chosen to obey always served to provide sexual gratification for those who needed it. "Indulgences" and "penances" guaranteed that "no one capable of love" was "frustrated in his or her desire."

Variety was to be the essence of Phalansterian life, and many individuals would have amorous needs and penchants which could not be gratified within the compass of a single community. There would consequently be a great deal of movement and travel in the new order. Bands of adventurers, troubadours, and knights-errant would traverse the globe, sometimes in the company of the industrial armies and sometimes by themselves, in search of pleasures and companions unobtainable in their own localities. People subject to extremely rare manias, that is, "perversions," would meet regularly at international convocations which would be pilgrimages as sacred for them "as the journey to Mecca is for Muslims."[93]

In this atmosphere of ceaseless movement, total strangers were constantly encountering one another and forming new relationships. To make these encounters as rewarding as possible, the amorous hierarchy of each Phalanx had to make elaborate preparations to entertain the hordes of visitors. The tasks of these officials included the organization of festivals and various sorts of orgies,[94] but their most important duty was the administration of an elaborate system of erotic personality matching.

The task of matching the visitors with appropriate partners would be facilitated by the compilation of a card file which would identify the passional types and amorous proclivities of each of the members of the Phalanx. Travelers, too, would carry papers indicating their individual needs and penchants. Since there was a little of the Butterfly in everyone, a traveler might have immediate needs and momentary inclinations at variance with

[93] *OC*, VII, 387. See below, p. 348.
[94] For a typical Harmonic orgy, see below, pp. 391–392.

the basic configuration of his passions. Thus everyone would undergo periodic interviews in order to ascertain his libidinal needs of the moment. These interviews would be conducted by a group of wise and elderly psychologists—women, for the most part—known as Confessors. They would be assisted in their work by psychologically acute Harmonians officially designated as matrons, fairies, and fakirs. The important task of psychological analysis, Fourier insisted, could not be performed by young people. Amorous experience and, above all, female intuition were required. Thus Harmony would provide employment, prestige, and a rich sexual life for one of the classes most oppressed by civilization—the elderly. For the confessors, both male and female, would not only be held in great esteem; often they would find it necessary to intervene personally and minister directly to the sexual needs of their younger clients.

Fourier's solicitude for the elderly, the poor, the "perverts," for all of those to whom civilization denied sexual gratification, led him to create a variety of "philanthropic" corporations composed of erotic saints and saintesses, heroes and heroines[95] who would provide erotic gratification for the less appealing members of the community.

Fourier's sexual fantasies were often wild and uncontrolled, perhaps because they were too closely related to his own frustrations. Nevertheless, his excesses—if one can use that term when speaking of a utopian—should not distract us from his fundamental qualities of balance and, oddly enough, moderation. Fourier wished to transform men, but not by transcending human nature. Like Rousseau he sought to give men back to themselves. This could be accomplished, he thought, only if man's passional needs were fully satisfied. Complete satisfaction, however, depended upon more than an economy of plenty; it also required self-knowledge and a society which would permit self-realization. Fourier shared Rousseau's desire to enable men to be "authentic," to accept themselves, and become "transparent." And he also felt that new social, educational, and political institutions had to be

[95] Such as the "Angelic couple." See below, pp. 373–378.

devised to make men whole. But the similarity of these two enemies of civilization goes no farther. The Harmonian of Fourier's vision is neither the saint of Christian utopias nor Rousseau's virtuous and humorless citizen. In the midst of his bacchantes, fairies, and fakirs, Fourier managed to preserve a detached, even wry, view of the new men and women. He predicted that Harmonians would have a sense of humor about themselves, for they would be willing to accept one another, and even strive to satisfy one another, no matter how richly endowed they might be with the bizarre tastes and needs that civilization, in unwitting self-accusation, had castigated as perversions.

### THE PROPHET TODAY

Ridiculed during his lifetime, Charles Fourier has not fared much better at the hands of the sober and judicious historians of nineteenth century socialism and social thought. His name continues to evoke a patronizing smile. His bizarre style, his extravagant cosmogony, and his quaintly precise specifications concerning rose-growing and animal-breeding in Harmony have all helped perpetuate his reputation as a harmless and entertaining crank. Because Fourier elaborated his utopia in such outrageous detail and because he expected all his specifications to be carried out to the letter, he has been hard to take seriously. Sympathetic readers have, to be sure, detected a grain of sense even in some of Fourier's strangest theories. And it has long been recognized that a few of his ideas played a significant role in the shaping of the socialist tradition. For this reason Fourier has always enjoyed a secure position in the diverting company of "utopian socialists," those forerunners whose fantastic schemes often concealed valuable and interesting "anticipations" of mature socialist thought. But Fourier conceived of himself as the "Messiah of Reason" who had come to save mankind. He would have angrily refused to play the role of a clownish John the Baptist amusing the audience while it awaited the appearance of the creators of scientific socialism. And perhaps we owe it to Fourier to keep his own aims and ambitions in mind in judging both his thought and his role as the founder of a social movement.

By Fourier's own standards the achievement of his disciples

was modest indeed. He would surely have rejected as travesties the dozens of under-manned and under-capitalized experimental Phalanxes set up on four continents after his death. It is also most unlikely that he would have approved of the reformist and political turn taken by the Fourierist movement in France during the 1840s. But this is not to say that Fourierism was of no consequence as a social movement. On the contrary, in the decade that followed his death his doctrine gained a following that it had never had in his lifetime. During the 1840s Fourierist groups and movements sprang up in most of the European countries and in America. The French disciples led by Victor Considerant went on to turn Fourierism into a socialist movement for "peaceful democracy" which became an intellectual and even political force of some significance during the last years of the July Monarchy and the early phases of the 1848 revolution. In America, where Fourierism was implanted by the astute journalist Albert Brisbane, some three dozen Fourierist communities were in existence by 1843. Even in Tsarist Russia, where there was no real possibility for the establishment of a "movement" or a viable community, Fourier's ideas cast their spell on the radical Westernizer, Alexander Herzen, and his circle; and the Fourierist study group formed at St. Petersburg around 1845 by M. V. Butashevich-Petrashevsky attracted a remarkably talented group of young intellectuals, including Dostoevsky and the philosopher Danilevsky.

But the heyday of the Fourierist movements was short-lived. The exalted conversations of the Petrashevtsy were brought to an abrupt end in the spring of 1849 by the intervention of the Tsarist police. Of the American communities, Brook Farm had a certain *éclat* while it lasted. But it was never run on strict Fourierist principles, and it had lost most of its members by 1846 when its principal buildings were destroyed by fire. Few of the other American Phalanxes survived for more than two or three years. They were badly financed to start with; and experience showed that, like the Icarian and Owenite ventures, they lacked the cohesiveness of the sectarian religious communities established in America. Many of them were organized by gentle and well-born Whig intellectuals who sought momentary escape from the harsh realities of post-Jacksonian America but soon found the theory too exacting. The Fourierist communities organized in Europe fared no better. There, too, the brief history of practical Fourierism was marred by schism and lack of capital, and most of the communal experiments were short-lived.

In France the Fourierist movement led by Considerant met its downfall, along with all of the other socialist *écoles*, in 1848. After the June insurrection of that year, its program of "peaceful democracy" ceased to have any political meaning. Considerant and his followers were drawn into an alliance with the neo-Jacobin Left, and after their participation in the abortive insurrection of June, 1849, they were obliged to leave France. Subsequently Considerant emigrated to the United States and received some support from Albert Brisbane for the establishment of a Fourierist community near Dallas, Texas. Although this final venture survived for two decades, it was never particularly successful. Long before its failure Considerant returned to Paris. He died there in 1893 at the age of eighty-five, confessing that he had lost his faith in the law of passionate attraction.

If Fourierism was a failure in its communitarian and political phases, there is one aspect of Fourier's legacy which remains to be considered. This concerns the relationship between his ideas and the emergence of the cooperative movement in France. One of the major themes of Fourier's economic critique had been the defense of the consumer against the parasitism and dishonesty of the merchant and middleman. The idea of an association of producers who would work together and market their goods in common was also an integral part of Fourier's utopian vision. Did his writings on these subjects have a significant influence on the development of the cooperative movement in France? Charles Gide, Jean Gaumont, and several other French scholars have answered this question in the affirmative.[96] In support of their

---

[96] See Charles Gide, *Fourier, précurseur de la coopération* (Paris, 1922–1923) and the first volume of Jean Gaumont, *Histoire générale de la coopération en France*, 2 vols. (Paris, 1923). Gide devotes considerable attention to the gradualist schemes devised by Fourier as an alternative to the immediate establishment of a trial Phalanx. Recent research by Henri Desroche and others tends to confirm Gaumont's claim that the main

claims it can be said that a large number of consumers' and producers' cooperatives were actually established by admirers of Fourier. Some of them—such as the cooperative iron-works or *Familistère* founded at Guise in 1859 by J. B. A. Godin—were both long-lived and successful. But most scholars concede that the link between Fourier's writings and cooperative practice is somewhat tenuous. Fourier's doctrines never provided more than provisional recipes for the practical endeavors of the French cooperatists, and the element of "Fourierism" in their schemes rarely amounted to more than plans for profit-sharing or direct marketing. Certainly the cooperative movement owed less to Fourier's ideas than to the theory and practice of Buchez and Louis Blanc in France and the Rochdale Pioneers and the Owenites in England.

It would scarcely be doing justice to Fourier to limit a discussion of his intellectual legacy to the rather forlorn history of the experiments in practical Fourierism undertaken by his nineteenth century disciples. As has often been pointed out, these disciples were for the most part well-meaning but cautious reformers who were only too eager to "improve" a civilization that their master wished to destroy. And while they did much to popularize Fourier's doctrine, the disciples also transformed and emasculated it in the process, practicing what one of them described as a "useful weeding out" of its "extravagant elements." They reprinted Fourier's major works and published some of his manuscripts. But, fearful of compromising their movement, they often bowlderized his texts and they allowed his most audacious writings to languish in obscurity. It was only with the publication of *The New Amorous World* in 1967 that Fourier's utopian vision became known in its entirety.

Despite—or perhaps in part because of—the prudence of the disciples, Fourier's ideas did have an undeniable influence on the generation of European radicals and socialists who reached ma-

---

impetus for the establishment of "Fourierist" cooperatives came from a group of dissident disciples hostile to the politicization of Fourierism by Victor Considerant.

turity in the 1840s. This influence was probably greatest in the sphere of social criticism, where Fourier's writing had a comprehensiveness, a vigor, and a psychological acuity not to be found in the work of any of his contemporaries. Fourier's analysis of the "anarchic" character of early capitalist production and his brilliant depiction of the frauds of the marketplace were assimilated not only by Considerant and his school but also by Proudhon, Louis Blanc, Constantin Pecqueur, and many others. The appeal for the right to work, which Fourier voiced at the very beginning of the nineteenth century, became a battle cry in 1848. But for all its satirical verve, Fourier's critique of *laissez faire* economics was in many ways less penetrating, and ultimately less influential, than that developed by more sophisticated economists such as Sismondi and the British Ricardian socialists. It was as a critic of bourgeois society rather than capitalist economics that Fourier probably made his most original and enduring contribution to radical thought. His indictment of "civilized" morality, his attack on the family system, and his plea for the emancipation of women all made their way into the developing socialist tradition. In a less obvious but equally important way his social criticism helped mold the mentality of the generation which fought on the barricades in 1848. His exposure of pain and suffering that others took for granted and his sympathy for all the outcasts of civilized society did much to give socialist thought the moral and humanitarian dimension which was its hallmark in 1848. Fourier's comprehensive view of civilization as an order founded on the repression of man's instinctual drives may be more readily comprehensible to our post-Freudian generations than it was to his contemporaries. His defense of erotic minorities was not even known—let alone appreciated—in his own time. But what mid-nineteenth century radicals could and did appreciate was the sense of moral outrage which informed even Fourier's driest and most ironic commentary on the fraud and hypocrisy, the waste and needless suffering of civilization.

If Fourier's social criticism was admired and echoed by many mid-nineteenth century radicals, the influence of his positive utopian vision would seem at first glance to have been much slighter. Outside the Fourierist school, the Phalanx was almost always an object of ridicule. It is true that in a general way Fourier and his disciples helped make the organization of work one of the main themes of socialist agitation in the 1840s. It is also true that a number of early socialist writers took an interest in specific aspects of Fourier's theory of association. Proudhon in particular was intrigued by Fourier's speculations concerning industrial series and groups; and a few minor communists such as Theodore Dézamy and Joseph Rey incorporated Phalansterian institutions into their own utopian schemes. But after 1848 the main elements of Fourier's utopian vision were rejected by almost all socialist and radical writers. The failure of the Owenite and Icarian—and Fourierist—communities in the New World marked the end of the communitarian phase in socialist experimentation. With the advance of industrialization, Fourier's pastoral utopia had come to seem increasingly anachronistic. Furthermore, the combined effect of the post-1848 political reaction and the growing self-consciousness of the industrial working class made Fourier's dream of social harmony and class reconciliation appear far less persuasive to most radicals than the Marxian and syndicalist theories of class conflict.

In their sympathetic and perceptive assessments of Fourier's thought, Marx and Engels frequently paid tribute to Fourier's talents as a social satirist and to his "remorseless unbearing of the material and moral misery of bourgeois society." But of his "fantastic blueprint" for future society, the best they could say was that it contained a "vein of true poetry."[97] According to them Fourier's thought was flawed in two related ways. He completely misunderstood the significance of the industrial revolution, and his notion of how his utopia might be brought into existence was hopelessly naive. What Fourier failed to grasp, in their view, was the fact that the growth of the factory system was itself creating

[97] Friedrich Engels, *Socialism: Utopian and Scientific*, in Marx and Engels, *Selected Works*, 2 vols. (Moscow, 1962), II, 123–124; Karl Marx and Friedrich Engels, *The German Ideology* (Moscow, 1964), p. 508. Engels' essay contains the classic Marxist appreciation of Fourier's thought.

the material conditions both of proletarian revolution and of man's ultimate social and moral regeneration.

The "poetry" which Marx and Engels detected in Fourier's utopia was his vision of man's potential—his awareness of what man might become in a humane and rationally ordered society. Although Fourier lacked Saint-Simon's and Owen's appreciation of modern industry, he saw much more clearly than they the necessity of psychic as well as economic liberation, the possibility of the flowering of man's personality as well as the satisfaction of his hunger. And it was this insight that made Fourier's thought so congenial to Marx and Engels. The "great germ" which they observed beneath the "fantastic covering" of Fourier's system was his insistence on the primacy of self-development and self-expression *within* the world of work and society.

The essential element in Fourier's utopian vision was of course his theory of "attractive labor." But this is an idea that neither Marx and Engels nor virtually anyone else has been willing to accept as a serious goal for a socialist society. When Marx and Engels first began their lifelong collaboration they did appear to believe that labor under scientific socialism might indeed resemble the Phalansterian ideal. In *The German Ideology* they predicted that socialist modes of production would make it "possible for me to do one thing today, another tomorrow, to hunt in the morning, fish in the afternoon, rear cattle in the evening, engage in criticism after dinner, just as I please. . . ."[98] This, obviously, is a rather limited version of a summer's day on the Phalanx, not quite as active or colorful and betraying a Germanic penchant for higher intellectual activities, but a day on the Phalanx all the same. Later, however, Marx rejected this ideal as unrealistic and criticized Fourier for adopting a frivolous attitude toward the serious problem of work. The notion of truly "attractive labor," Marx concluded, was chimerical. Fourier was

[98] Marx and Engels even made a slight concession to the Butterfly passion by indicating in the margin of their manuscript an alternate set of activities: "cobbler in the morning, gardener in the afternoon, and actor in the evening." *Die Deutsche Ideologie, Marx-Engels Gesamtausgabe*, Part One (Berlin, 1932), V, 22, 572.

guilty of dealing with a profound problem in the manner of a coquettish shopgirl.[99]

Marx rejected the idea of attractive labor because he made a philosophical distinction between necessity and freedom, while Fourier had been content to make only a psychological one. Man was destined, Marx insisted, to live at least part of his life within the "Kingdom of Necessity." Since man would always have to work to survive, a certain portion of his labor would be unfree, imposed on him from without. Marx did predict that necessary work, or the kind of "labor which is determined by need and external purposes," would one day be made immensely less loathsome and fatiguing.[100] Yet, despite all of the improvements that socialization would bring, work within the kingdom of necessity would still remain painful; it would still bear the marks of Yaweh's curse. From this point of view, Fourier's transformation of repulsive work into attractive work was somewhat fraudulent. He attempted to abolish the kingdom of necessity with a kind of psychological sleight of hand. The social minimum would really give the Harmonians only the illusion of freedom. They would in fact be even less free than the inhabitants of the highly industrialized socialist society envisaged by Marx: Harmonians would spend most of their time at work. This argument has been advanced against attractive labor by successive generations of Marxists, but Fourier probably would have replied that it confirmed rather than refuted the theory of passionate attraction.

The fact that work would always remain objectively necessary mattered little to Fourier because he did not sense an irreconcilable antagonism between man and nature. Despite the decidedly romantic elements in Fourier's vision, his conception of man in nature was rooted in eighteenth century classicism. Harmonians would work arduously, but their productive activities would be as elegant and graceful as taste and intelligence could

[99] *Grundrisse der Kritik des Politischen Oekonomie, Rohentwurf, 1857–1858* (Berlin, 1953), p. 505.

[100] Karl Marx, *Selected Writings in Sociology and Social Philosophy*, T. B. Bottomore and Maximilien Rubel, editors (London, 1956), pp. 254–255.

make them. Nature, Fourier believed, was neither harsh nor hostile and Harmony would have no room for the Promethean dynamism or the sweating bodies and calloused hands celebrated in many nineteenth century socialist visions of the future. Fourier asserted that mankind was naturally endowed with immense creative energies which had been repressed or abused, not only by an inefficient and unjust economic system but also by codes of morality which engendered anxieties and compulsions. The social minimum, according to Fourier, would liberate man's capacity for self-realization and passional enjoyment. Thanks to the intricate series mechanism and to Phalansterian vocational education, even "necessary" or difficult work would always be self-expression and self-realization.

Instinctual self-denial would cease to exist in Harmony because there work itself would appease almost all of every individual's unique needs. Although these needs were often in the realm of illusion and imagination, they were, Fourier insisted, legitimate and worthy objects of scientific speculation. The human mind was not limited to a purely objective interpretation of its predicament. In fact, once man had received what was objectively necessary—the physical security and erotic satisfaction provided by the two Fourierist minima—his passions would then seek to satisfy themselves by freely creating "illusions" and "fantasy." For Fourier, then, the kingdom of freedom was as wide as men wanted to make it. Physically, Harmony was based on the concrete facts of a rational technology, but its emotional life was founded on the deliberate and selfconscious production and refinement of illusion. It was possible, Fourier agreed, to "do without all of the illusions that constitute life's principal charm. A husband and wife can do without sentimental love and nonetheless their purely sensual union will produce offspring. We can do without the spirit of patriotism because wheat will grow as well in a field sown by a slave without a country as it will in one planted by a fervent citizen. But who is wiser: the man who plants flowers along life's way or the man who makes it bristle with thorns?"[101]

Fourier believed that mankind had it in its power to plant

[101] *OC*, VII, 155.

flowers along life's way. He insistently urged his readers to put his theories to the test. No one has ever subjected "passionate attraction" and the institutions of Harmony to a real test on Fourier's terms. The feasibility of Harmony must remain, in that sense, a moot point. It now appears certain, however, that the social order of complete liberation which Fourier described was hardly within the reach of his own generation. Early nineteenth century Europe probably lacked the productive capacity necessary to achieve the high standard of living that Fourier promised for all of his Harmonians. Yet, if Harmony, with its orchards and gardens, its perpetual *fêtes champêtres,* and its universal gastronomic and sexual gratification was fundamentally utopian in the worst sense of the term in Fourier's day, how much farther has it receded from the grasp of a post-industrial society which has increased the comfort of many of its members but also improved on most of the vices Fourier described as already perfect in the early years of the nineteenth century?

Man's destruction of his environment had, Fourier thought, reached catastrophic proportions in his own time; it now seems almost irreversible. That twentieth century cities are and may well remain unlivable is now a banal observation, but the rural exodus which Fourier thought had to be reversed continues apace. Fourier's often sadistic prediction that more civilization inevitably meant more war and carnage has been fulfilled in ways which even that enemy of civilization must not have imagined. Even the very real industrial and technological progress that is civilization's pride has served only to push the prospect of Harmony further and further into the distance. Overpopulation has made it necessary to accelerate rather than curtail massive concentrations of large-scale industry. Although the now quaint horrors of the Victorian factory are disappearing, there is little evidence that the higher technology will ever be willing to subordinate maximum efficiency to passionate gratification. Despite Fourier's hopes, agriculture itself will probably never become the great source of passionate attraction, if only because the pressures of population appear destined to force men to exploit endless and unattractive fields of grain or other, less appealing, basic crops.

The globe of the future will have little room for Harmony's orchards and glades.

The joys and pleasures that characterize life on the Phalanx are almost certainly destined to extinction by the development of technology and the plague of overpopulation. Yet, industrial progress and the extension of affluence have at the same time made certain aspects of Fourier's vision appear less incredible. In some ways we are closer to Fourier's goal of a non-repressive society than his scandalized contemporaries would have thought possible. During the last few years a growing number of philosophers, social critics, or ordinary victims of civilization have begun to repeat the same criticisms and voice the same hopes that earned Fourier more than his share of ridicule. The steady growth of our productive capacity and the liberating potential of automation have encouraged critics of industrial society to question the necessity of a work ethic which still condemns most men to repulsive, meaningless, or boring work. Others assert that the discontents of work and conventional morality—postponed or forbidden gratification—are simply too high a price to pay for the dubious pleasures of life in civilization; they withdraw into cooperative communities and attempt to emancipate themselves from civilization's repressive moral codes as well as its work ethic.

It would be ridiculous to suggest that those who are now trying to establish a philosophical foundation for a non-repressive culture are Fourierists; the new communities are certainly not Phalanxes and the new sexuality, despite its similarity to certain aspects of Harmony's new amorous world, would probably have struck Fourier as rather too self-conscious and potentially tyrannical. Fourier's thought has not directly inspired either the new radical critics of modern society or the new utopians who are seeking an alternative to industrial civilization. Until very recently, in fact, Charles Fourier was familiar only to scholars and those socialists who cherished the memory of one of the early fathers of the socialist tradition.

Only now, with civilization on the threshold of its post-industrial stage, does Fourier seem to have found the audience that he was never able to attract during his lifetime. It could be argued, of course, that Fourier's striking modernity is largely spurious, for in no way did he foresee the technological developments that alone could make Harmony possible. This judgment is accurate but hardly fair to the isolated and ridiculed thinker who had the courage and perspicacity to urge his generation to reject the new chains that were being forged for it in the guise of an ennobling and holy ethic of work. Years before Marx demonstrated that "scientific" social theory was often merely an ideology serving the interests of a dominant class, Fourier had exposed even the most libertarian political and social doctrines of his own day as fraudulent and oppressive. And long before twentieth century man began to suspect that he had built his own prison and sown briars along life's way, Fourier had tried to convince the "civilized" to throw off their self-imposed yoke of psychological and erotic immaturity. For this reason, it seems to us, the *Phalanstérien* has a claim on our attention.

# Note on the Sources

The majority of the texts translated in this anthology have been taken from the most recent and fullest edition of Fourier's writings: *Oeuvres complètes de Charles Fourier*, 12 volumes, Paris: Editions Anthropos, 1966–1968. Each selection from this edition is followed by the abbreviation *OC* and the appropriate volume and page reference. Since every volume but one of this new Anthropos edition is a photographic reproduction of earlier editions, we are providing a full reference to each volume here at the outset.

*OC*, I: *Théorie des quatre mouvements et des destinées générales.* 3rd ed. Paris, 1846.

*OC*, II–V: *Théorie de l'unité universelle.* 4 vols. 2nd ed. Paris, 1841–1843. (This work was originally published under the title *Traité de l'association domestique-agricole.*)

*OC*, VI: *Le Nouveau monde industriel et sociétaire.* 3rd ed. Paris, 1848.

*OC*, VII: *Le Nouveau monde amoureux*, Paris, 1967. (This volume, edited and with an introduction by Simone Debout-Oleskiewicz, consists almost entirely of previously unpublished manuscripts.)

*OC*, VIII–IX: *La Fausse industrie morcelée, répugnante, mensongère.* . . . 2 vols. Paris, 1835–1836.

*OC*, X: *Publication des manuscrits de Charles Fourier. Année 1851. Année 1852.* 2 vols. Paris, 1851–1852. (This volume of the Anthropos edition has two paginations, which are referred to as *PM*, I and *PM*, II.)

*OC*, XI: *Publication des manuscrits de Charles Fourier. Années 1853–1856. Années 1857–1858.* 2 vols. Paris, 1853–1858. (This volume of the Anthropos edition also has two paginations. They are referred to as *PM*, III and *PM*, IV.)

*OC*, XII: This volume includes a number of manuscript writings by Fourier which his disciples originally published in their journal *La Phalange* between 1845 and 1849.

Since the *Oeuvres complètes* are less than complete, we have taken a few texts from other sources. References for these texts are given in full. We have also drawn some material from Fourier's unpublished writings at the Archives Nationales in Paris. Such material is cited by the abbreviation *AN* and its *cote* or classification at the archives. In presenting the texts we have generally chosen our own titles. Those which are inside quotation marks, however, are Fourier's. Footnotes by Fourier are indicated as such; the rest are by the editors.

# I

## First Proclamations

I ALONE shall have confounded twenty centuries of political
imbecility, and it is to me alone that present and future
generations will be indebted for their boundless happiness.
Before me, mankind lost several thousand years in fighting
madly against nature. I am the first who has bowed before
her by studying attraction, the organ of her decrees. She has
deigned to smile upon the only mortal who has brought
incense to her shrine; she has delivered up all her treasures to
me. I come as the possessor of the book of Destiny to banish
political and moral darkness and to erect the theory of
universal harmony upon the ruins of the uncertain sciences.

*—OC,* I, 191

Fourier often claimed that his readers were like men operated on
for cataracts: they had to be exposed gradually to the sunlight.
Thus he began most expositions of his doctrine by stating his
main points in concise summary form. Only after titillating his
readers with a suitable array of *aperçus* and *abregés* did he
proceed to expound the theory in full detail. This custom will be
respected in the present anthology. Before initiating our readers
into the deeper mysteries of passionate attraction, we will begin
with three texts which should provide a general introduction both
to Fourier's theory and to the man himself. The first two of these
texts date from the very outset of his career. Written in 1803, they

are Fourier's first public proclamations of the "discovery" which
he had made four years earlier. The third text is an excerpt from
the "Preliminary Discourse" of the *Théorie des quatre
mouvements* (1808), Fourier's first major work.

While the third text speaks for itself, a few words may be
necessary to help situate the first two. "Universal Harmony"
appeared as an article in the *Bulletin de Lyon* on December 3,
1803. At that time Fourier was thirty-one years old and employed
as a traveling salesman and clerk for a Lyon cloth merchant. Best
known among his friends as a zealous amateur geographer, he had
already published some verse and a few rather trivial articles in
the local journals. But he had also begun to discuss his theory in
public with anyone who cared to listen, and he had even
composed a number of brief poems on passionate attraction for
circulation among friends and "adepts who have conversed with
me." It was at the request of one of these "adepts"—a woman who
is known to history only as "Madame Amélie F."—that he
published "Universal Harmony."

The appearance of this article touched off a lively
controversy in the Lyon press. For a few weeks Fourier became
"the man of the day," celebrated in the pages of the *Bulletin* as "a
deep thinker, a universal genius" and ridiculed in the rival *Journal
de Lyon* as a candidate for the madhouse at Charenton.
Emboldened by his notoriety, he soon published another article
entitled "Continental Triumvirate" in which he prophesied a
cataclysmic war between France and Russia to be followed by an
era of perpetual peace. This brought Fourier to the attention of
Lyon police. For in Napoleonic France an attack on civilization as
a "frightful dream" could be dismissed as a harmless extravagance;
but to discuss the prospects for war was to violate one of the
journalistic canons of the period. Fourier was reprimanded by the
local police commissioner and eventually ordered to cease
publishing. But before doing so, he took his case to higher
authorities.

During the Consulate the *Grand Juge* (to whom Fourier
addressed the second of the texts translated here) exercised
judicial and police functions roughly equivalent to those of an
American attorney general. In writing this dignitary Fourier

explained his difficulties with the Lyon police and also attempted to secure official sanction for the publication of further articles on his doctrine. But his real hope was that the letter would reach Napoleon's eyes. It did not. Instead it remained buried in the Paris police archives with the following comment scrawled on its margin: "Almost every day the journals contain some new piece of madness signed 'Fourrier.' . . . Would it not be advisable to forbid the journals to insert any political article by this individual."

Both "Universal Harmony" and the "Letter to the High Judge" were written hastily and in a tone that can only be described as Fourier's exalted mode. Yet they provide a relatively comprehensive summary of his doctrine at its formative stage. He was subsequently to modify points of detail and to focus on the organization of the ideal community while minimizing the importance of his speculations on cosmogony and metempsychosis. Nevertheless, Fourier first conceived of his theory as a universal science; and he never completely abandoned the hope, so urgently voiced in these texts, of revealing all "the destinies."

### "UNIVERSAL HARMONY"

The calculus of Harmony, for which Madame A. F. seeks publicity, is a discovery that the human race was far from expecting. It is a mathematical theory concerning the destinies of all the globes and their inhabitants, a theory of the sixteen social orders which can be established on the diverse globes throughout eternity.

Of the sixteen possible societies, only three are to be seen on our globe: Savagery, Barbarism and Civilization. Soon they will come to an end, and all the nations of the earth will enter the fifteenth stage which is Simple Harmony.

Great men of all the centuries! Newton and Leibnitz, Voltaire and Rousseau, do you know in what you are great? In blindness. You will soon seem like no more than great madmen for having thought that civilization was the social destiny of the human race. How could you have failed to understand that these three societies, the savage, the barbarian and the civilized, are but rungs to be climbed, that they are reason's age of childhood and imbecility, and that God would be improvident if he had conceived of nothing better adapted to human happiness? These three societies are the most disastrous among the sixteen. Of the sixteen there are seven which will see the establishment of perpetual peace, universal unity, the liberty of women.

I owe this astonishing discovery to the analytic and synthetic calculus of passionate attraction which our savants have deemed unworthy of attention during their two thousand five hundred years of study. They have discovered the laws of material movement; that's all very well, but it doesn't get rid of poverty. It was necessary to discover the laws of social movement. Their invention is going to lead the human race to opulence, to sensual pleasures, to the unity of the globe. I repeat, this theory will be geometrical and applied to the physical sciences. It is not an arbitrary doctrine like the political and moral sciences, which are going to meet a sad fate. There is going to be a great disaster at the libraries.

If ever war was deplorable, it is at this moment. Soon the victors will be on the same level as the vanquished. What point is there in conquests when the entire globe will comprise but a single nation, will be run by a single administration? In spite of this unity, there will be no equality in harmony.

To the chief of France can be reserved the honor of extracting the human race from social chaos, of being the founder of Harmony and the liberator of the globe. The rewards which this honor entails will not be modest, and they will be transmitted in perpetuity to the descendants of the founder.

Some readers will cry out: "dream," "visionary." Patience! In a short time we will wake them from their own frightful dream, the dream of civilization. Blind savants, just look at your cities paved with beggars, your citizens struggling against hunger, your battlefields and all your social infamies. Do you still believe that civilization is the destiny of the human race? Or was J.-J. Rousseau right in saying of the civilized: "These are not men; there is a disorder in things, the cause of which we have not yet fathomed."

–*PM*, 1; *OC*, x, 52–53

## "LETTER TO THE HIGH JUDGE"

Lyon, 4 Nivose, Year XI[1]

Citizen High Judge:

It is with respect to a trivial matter that I am going to bring you great news. Allow me half a page concerning this trifle which is the occasion for the revelation of universal harmony.

I have been informed that a few individuals have sent you their critical comments about my article on the "Triumvirate" of which I am enclosing a copy. It seems to me that the police commissioner handles the matter perfectly well. I have talked with him, and I will follow his instructions.

On a number of occasions I have sent political missives to the Directory or to the Ministry of Foreign Affairs. I have always received complimentary letters in reply. I presume that the article on the "Triumvirate" will likewise be appreciated in its essence, even though it might be deficient in its style since it was written hastily. Although the ideas which it contains run counter to current policies, they are only all the more worthy of attention. The situation is menacing. Upon the outbreak of continental war, one of the two German empires will be divided up, and then the triumvirate will be a reality. From the outset it will actually be no more than a duumvirate; for Germany, unprotected and caught between the two rivals, will become a vassal of one or the other. But the duumvirate will still be only a trap for France; and when I warn my country that it is likely to be defeated in a subsequent conflict, that Russia will have the means to strike some decisive blows, and that France will have very few advantages in its favor, I am asserting nothing that I could not prove in the greatest detail. I dare to believe that this warning will win the approbation of the government rather than its disapproval, and that the printer who published it, out of confidence in me, will be given no trouble.[2]

[1] This letter was written in great haste and inadvertently misdated by Fourier. The correct date should be 4 Nivose, Year XII, according to the revolutionary calendar, or December 26, 1803.

[2] In this paragraph Fourier summarizes the argument of his article "Continental Triumvirate" published in the *Bulletin de Lyon* on 25 Frimaire, Year XII (December 17, 1803).

But this is not the matter which I propose to discuss with you. These disputes of civilization are no more than child's play in the present circumstances. An event of much greater importance is brewing, and I wish to make it known to the government:

*Universal Social Harmony and the Imminent Collapse*
*of the Civilized, Barbarian and Savage Societies.*

I am the inventor of the mathematical calculus of the destinies, a calculus which Newton had within his grasp without realizing it. He determined the laws of material attraction, and I have discovered those of passionate attraction, a theory approached by no one before me.

Passionate attraction is the archetype according to which God has regulated all the modifications of matter, the order of universal movement and the social movement of the human inhabitants of all the worlds.

As long as a globe fails to calculate the laws of attraction by analysis and synthesis, its reason advances from shadow to shadow; it cannot acquire the slightest notion of the laws which govern the universe, of the social destinies, the goal of the passions, etc.

The theory of the destinies can be divided into three principal branches:

First. The theory of the creations, that is to say the determination of the plans adopted by God concerning the modifications of matter, including everything from the cosmogony of the universes and the invisible stars to the most minute alterations of matter in the animal, vegetable and mineral kingdoms. The plans followed by God in the distribution of passions, properties, forms, colors, tastes, etc. to the diverse substances.

Second. The social movement, that is to say the future and past destinies of human societies on the diverse globes, their ordonnance, their revolutions, their characters, etc.

Third. Immortality or the future and past destiny of God and of souls in the diverse worlds which they have traversed and will traverse throughout eternity.

You see, Citizen Minister, that the complete elaboration of this prodigious theory would be much too difficult a task for one man or even for several. Thus I have devoted myself primarily to the most urgent calculation, that of the social movement and the societary destiny of the industrious nations. I have determined the whole mechanism of Harmony in its smallest details, from the methods of its central administration down to the most minute aspects of its domestic relations, which are diametrically opposed to our own.

As for calculations other than that of the social movement, I have limited myself to finding the key, to making trials in each of the fixed sciences[3] and even in the fixed arts like music. I will hand over that key to the savants; it will be a prize which will provide them with ample means of winning fame. I will keep for myself only the honor of having opened the way for them, but I will have all to myself the honor of the discovery of the laws of universal harmony.

It is obvious that if this discovery could not satisfy the passions of great men and sovereigns, it would be useless and ridiculous to announce the imminence of Harmony; if it offered them no more than three times the advantages of their present situation, they would decide to remain in civilization. This is something which I had to anticipate. But their pleasures in the new order will be so prodigious that they will become its most enthusiastic partisans, for their souls and senses are more practiced than those of the vulgar, more apt at appreciating and savoring states of happiness.

The laws of Harmony should have been discovered 2300 years ago; they have remained unknown due to the inadvertence and pride of the three metaphysical, moral and political sciences. These sciences have failed to determine the functions and duties of God. They should have recognized that God owes men a social code. To discover this code they should have opened an inquiry concerning the means of revelation employed by God to make his designs known to us. Attraction, which explains the designs of God with regard to the stars and the animals, is also the organ of God with regard to human beings. Its synthesis forms the code for the reign of social harmony which is going to

[3] The natural sciences.

last approximately sixty thousand years. After that, the cooling of the globe will bring a marked decline in luxury. With the final disappearance of luxury, which is the pivot of Harmony, the human race will fall back into subversion. Mankind will complete its course as it began by traversing the civilized, barbarian and savage societies and others which belong to the subversive order.[4]

Since the announcement of this discovery will help bring about peace in the measure that it wins the confidence of the government, I ought, Citizen High Judge, to explain it to you in a detailed memorandum. But since my right hand is sprained and in bad condition for writing, I cannot devote myself now to the composition of a lengthy essay. The details of Harmony are so extraordinary that a superficial explanation would be quite inadequate. If you wish, I will go into a few details; but given the state of my sprained hand, I can scarcely promise more than two large sheets like this one.

Being the sole possessor of the theory of social movement, I shall not give it away to the public. Instead I shall make known only the superficial aspects of the calculus, taking precautions so that its essence and the solutions to the problems it raises may be safeguarded for the French government. Thus the First Consul cannot be beaten out by any other prince in the establishment of Harmony. He will be assured of no competition for the title of Primate or Emperor of the Globe, a title to be conferred by right upon the founder. There is no impertinence or charlatanism about this, for the calculus is correct, mathematical and invariable.

Do not suppose, Citizen High Judge, that this discovery could become a rallying point for fanatics and intriguers. On the contrary it offers a sure means of foiling the civil and political trouble makers of all countries. For the whole earth is going to enjoy a better lot. Poverty will be completely eliminated; and a graduated metamorphosis will turn the poor class into a middle class, will bring opulence to the bourgeois, splendor to the opulent, and so forth. This perspective, which is well substantiated

---

[4] According to Fourier's elaborate cyclical-stadial theory of history, the 60,000 (later: 70,000) year reign of social harmony was destined to be preceded and followed by a number of "subversive" epochs during which the passions would be in conflict. See below pp. 189–196.

and confirmed by all conceivable proofs, will wither the seeds of civil or political discord and calm the most turbulent individuals.

Permit me a few lines of argument. Poverty is the principal cause of social disorders. Inequality, so much maligned by the philosophers, is not displeasing to men. On the contrary, the bourgeois delights in hierarchy; he loves to see the bigwigs decked out and parading in their best finery. The poor man views them with the same enthusiasm. Only if he lacks what is necessary does he begin to detest his superiors and the customs of society. This is the origin of social disorders, crimes and of the gallows, that sad bastion of the civilized order. It is easy to prove that all social crimes committed out of ambition proceed from the poverty of the people, from their efforts to escape poverty, from the anxiety which is instilled in society by the presence of poverty, from the fear of falling into it, and from disgust for the odious habits which it encourages.

For social science there is thus only one problem to resolve, that of the graduated metamorphosis which I have mentioned. By this I mean the art of raising each of the classes of civilization to the condition of the class above it. Then indigence and discomfort will be eliminated, since the lower class will have become the middle class and will enjoy an honest comfort like our petty bourgeois who are far removed indeed from a spirit of sedition.[5] When the people enjoy constant comfort and a decent minimum, all the sources of discord will be dried up or reduced to very little. Administration will become child's play, and in Harmony the government of the whole planet will be much less complicated than that of a civilized empire.

To eliminate poverty it was necessary to conceive of an industrial system more productive than our own. Such will be universal harmony which will produce at least triple—yes, without exaggeration—at least triple the yield of the civilized system in a

---

[5] Like most social theorists of his time, Fourier was often vague and ambiguous in his discussion of social class. Even in his mature writings he generally divided society simply into the rich, the poor, and the middle class or bourgeoisie. In this text the expression *classe populacière* (here translated as "lower class") is used interchangeably with *classe pauvre* and simply *le peuple*.

well-cultivated empire. Accordingly, while Harmony will greatly increase the wealth of the well-to-do, it will bring about an excessive increase in that of the people, to whom it will guarantee a salary or in old age a decent *minimum* below which they cannot fall. This beneficence will be all the more simple in that humanity will reproduce much less in Harmony than in civilization.

This is far removed from the theories of the philosophers, some of whom, the *Demagogues*, seek to rob the rich to provide for the poor.[6] The others, who are called the *Economists*, do not have the welfare of the people in mind.[7] They think only of enriching empires without worrying themselves about the fate of the individual. Thus the theories of the Economists have greatly enriched England without enriching the English. According to the *Tableau de Londres*[8] you can find 115,000 paupers, prostitutes, thieves, beggars and unemployed in the city of London alone; the workers of Scotland live in a frightful state of misery. This is nonetheless the consequence of the modern systems which claim to alleviate the suffering of the people.

Furthermore, just as Steuart[9] prophesied, none of the philosophical theories has proved adequate to deal with the problem of excessive population. The civilized reproduce too much, produce too little, and waste vast quantities of food, labor, time, energy, etc. Count Rumford[10] and Cadet de Vaux[11] are the only writers I

[6] It is possible that Fourier has the Babouvists in mind. But it is more likely that he is referring here to the more radical Jacobin orators and publicists of the Revolutionary period, such as Marat and Chalier. The latter was the leader of Lyon's Jacobin group and his ideas were doubtless well known to Fourier.

[7] The classical liberal political economists who adhered to the ideas of Adam Smith.

[8] Probably a reference to P. H. Langlois (tr.), *Le Tableau de Londres et de ses environs en 1802* (Paris, 1802).

[9] Sir James Denham Steuart (1712–1780) was a Scottish economist who advocated mercantilist ideas and was best known for his *Inquiry into the Principles of Political Economy* (1767; French translation, 1789).

[10] Benjamin Thompson Count Rumford (1753–1814) was an English scientist, philanthropist, and social reformer. He made significant contributions to the study of heat, but he was interesting to Fourier chiefly as a partisan of soup kitchens and other forms of public aid to the poor.

[11] Cadet de Vaux (1743–1828) was a French chemist and agronomist, an

know who have understood the vice of civilized societies. These societies are going to reduce the common people to the most frightful poverty everywhere except in new areas like the United States where labor is lacking. The source of this widespread indigence is excessive procreation. Nevertheless humanity will be able to multiply for about eighty more years in order to bring the globe to its full size of three billion inhabitants. Once this number is reached, however, the population will remain fixed in Harmony. What would be the point of having swarms of excess population once wars are abolished? Excessive numbers of people will become so useless that France, for its part, will disgorge about five million of its inhabitants who will find homes in Spain, the Ukraine, etc.

Let us summarize the problem which I have just raised: it is to prove that three billion inhabitants in the order of Harmony will be just as productive as nine or ten billion in civilization. Of course this prodigious increase in wealth would be illusory if Harmony failed to eliminate the seeds of human discord, such as war, which neutralize the efforts of men and absorb the fruits of their industry, no matter how great they may be.

Note well that this prospect of future happiness does not rest solely upon an enormous increase in wealth. For even a Lucullus would be most unhappy if his dominant passions were not satisfied. The opulence of Harmony will merely be an agent of happiness, merely a means for the development and gratification of a huge number of brilliant passions which are unknown in civilization and will be revealed in Harmony. For what is it to be happy if not to feel and gratify an immense number of harmless passions? Such will be the lot of men when they are delivered from the civilized, barbarian and savage states. Their passions will be so numerous, so explosive and so varied that the rich man will spend his life in a sort of permanent frenzy and the twenty-four hours of his day will fly by like one.

You can tell from this sketch, Citizen High Judge, that the

---

advocate of experimental farming, and a staunch partisan of the potato. Fourier frequently praised him as an early defender of the idea of agricultural association.

announcement of this discovery will be a source of concord, a balm poured on the wounds of the human race. The certainty of such a brilliant metamorphosis will paralyze the ambitious and throw trouble makers into a state of apathy; it will inspire a profound disdain for the tumult, the torment, the perfidies and the injustices of civilization; the widespread feeling to which it will give rise will be that of Charity. Everyone will understand the necessity of working together to ease the lot of the poor until the establishment of Harmony will free them from want. This charitable impulse will be the more spontaneous in that when the Spherical Hierarchy is constituted, it will reimburse all the alms which have been provisionally voted.

It is necessary, Citizen High Judge, to advise you of a comic incident which will follow the revelation of the theory of social movement. It is going to deal a mortal blow to the political and moral philosophies and, in addition, an incurable wound to metaphysics. These three sciences have engendered and sustained poverty, perfidy and ignorance of the destinies. . . . The disgrace of these three sciences will be a misfortune of very little importance. As soldiers say: "You cannot make an omelette without breaking eggs." Thus, in the encounter of truth and sophistry, some sciences have got to crack. Humanity will lose a great many books, but it will win happiness, affluence and peace for sixty thousand years. That's sufficient consolation! . . .

You may be astonished that I have waited four years before publishing my discovery. Here is the explanation for this delay. At the time of the discovery, I was a merchant's clerk at Marseille. I quit work to go to Paris to study the fixed sciences and apply them all to the calculus of passionate attraction. I studied with ardor, and in three or four years I would have applied all the sciences. But after eight or nine months misfortunes befell me. I had to break off my studies and resume my work as a merchant's clerk at Lyon where I found a job. Driven to despair by this bad turn of events, I wished to safeguard my discovery until I regained the wealth necessary to continue my studies. I was too proud to share the glory with the savants. But since then I have undergone so much disgrace and illness that I renounce my plans for study. I will no longer deprive the physicists and naturalists of

the honor of embellishing the core of my theory with the demon-
strative analogies which their sciences can provide once I give
them the appropriate clues. As a result of this delay, the calculus
will have undergone the trial advised by Horace: *novum pre-
matur in annum*.[12] It was quite unnecessary, for passionate attraction is as invariable as physics. If there are seven colors in the
spectrum, there are seven primitive passions in the soul. If there
are four arcs in a conic section, there are four groups of passionate
attraction, and their properties are just the same as those of conic
sections. Nothing can vary in my theory.

In order that this invention may provide me with a refuge
from the poverty which pursues me, I have decided to open a
subscription. It will be a success if the government grants me just
one favor: I simply need permission to publicize the invention in
the Paris journals. . . . Without your authorization, Citizen
High Judge, my subscription will fail, the journals will not want
to concern themselves with this discovery. I dare hope for the
protection of the government, since it can be certain that I will
not divulge any solutions and that the curious would vainly split
their heads trying to solve the problems which I will leave un-
answered. If they don't know the secret, their efforts will be in
vain. In any case there are not two people on the globe who have
a ·flair for the problems of passionate attraction; they are too
overwhelming in their immensity and in their frightful simplicity.

In unveiling before you the prospect of the welfare of all
humanity, perpetual peace, the imminent cessation of poverty
and crime, and the elevation of the First Consul to a position of
world supremacy, I am sure, Citizen High Judge, to provoke not
your doubts but your hopes concerning the veracity of the calculus. If it had not been revealed earlier and if the First Consul
were now acquainted with the laws of social movement, he would
be able to fool England completely by signing a peace treaty
based on the expectation of the coming revolution. This humilia-

---

[12] Horace, *The Art of Poetry* 388: "Yet if you ever do write anything,
let it enter the ears of some critical Maecius, and your father's, and my
own; then put your parchment in the closet and keep it back till the ninth
year."

tion of a trouble-making cabinet would be a brilliant jest with which to bring an end to civilization.

Among the social benefits which I have unveiled before you, I should not forget to announce that two years after the establishment of Harmony we will see the end of all accidental ills, venereal epidemics, smallpox, yellow fever, etc. As soon as the Spherical Hierarchy is constituted, it will impose a quarantine on syphilitic diseases. At the same time the Primate of the globe will recruit about twenty million pioneers to cleanse foul regions. Thus the extinction of accidental maladies will take place within two or three years.

Any brilliant discovery subjects its author to the attacks of the envious. If Columbus, Galileo and other great men could be excommunicated for being ahead of their time, people may also try to blacken my reputation. But we are no longer living in an age of superstition. The conqueror of destiny fears nothing under the reign of the conqueror of success.

I summarize, Citizen High Judge, the two requests which I have to make of you:

1st: the authorization to have separate articles inserted in the Paris journals, leaving them the latitude to make all necessary corrections, according to the intentions of the censorship which I shall try to anticipate.

2nd: the communication of my letter or a copy to the First Consul. I do not know how to get it directly to him, and I am counting on your help in this matter. He cannot fail to be moved at the idea of rescuing the human race from social chaos, of banishing poverty and crime forever from the face of the earth, and of becoming the terrestrial arm of God, of directing mankind to its destiny. He will not mistrust the man who offers him such a future. Extremes touch; if I am unknown and destitute, I expect to inspire the confidence of the first of men by the very excess of my obscurity.

I have the honor to offer you my respectful salutations,

Fourrier
Chez Madame Guyonnet, marchande
rue Saint-Côme, à Lyon

—Charles Pellarin (ed.), *Lettre de Fourier au Grand Juge*

(Paris, 1874), pp. 14–28. Also published as an appendix to J.-J. Hemardinquer, "Notes critiques sur le jeune Fourier," *Le Mouvement social*, No. 48 (July–September, 1964), pp. 59–69.

"INDICES AND METHODS WHICH LED TO THE DISCOVERY"

I was thinking of nothing less than of research concerning the Destinies; I shared the widespread view which considers them to be impenetrable and which relegates any calculation about the destinies to a place among the visions of the astrologers and the magicians. The studies which led me up to the discovery centered simply around the industrial and political problems that I am now going to discuss.

After the philosophers had demonstrated their incapacity in their experimental venture, in the French Revolution, everyone agreed in regarding their science as an aberration of the human mind; their floods of political and moral enlightenment seemed to be nothing more than floods of illusions. Well! what else can be found in the writings of these savants who, after having perfected their theories for twenty-five centuries, after having accumulated all the wisdom of the ancients and moderns, begin by engendering calamities as numerous as the benefits which they promised, and help push civilized society back toward the state of barbarism? Such was the consequence of the first five years during which the philosophical theories were inflicted on France.

After the catastrophe of 1793, illusions were dissipated, the political and moral sciences were irretrievably blighted and discredited. From that point on people should have understood that there was no happiness to be found in acquired learning, that social welfare had to be sought in some new science, and that new paths had to be opened to political genius. It was evident that neither the philosophers nor their rivals possessed a remedy for the social distresses, and that their dogmas only served to perpetuate the most disgraceful calamities, among others poverty.

Such was the first consideration which led me to suspect the existence of a still-unknown Social Science and which provoked me to try to discover it. Far from taking fright at my lack of knowledge, I thought only about the honor of laying hold of what the savants had been unable to discover for twenty-five centuries.

I was encouraged by numerous symptoms of the aberration of reason and particularly by the spectacle of the calamities afflicting social industry: poverty, unemployment, the success of rascality, acts of maritime piracy, commercial monopoly, the abduction of slaves, finally other misfortunes too numerous to mention and which give one cause to ask whether civilized industry is not a calamity invented by God in order to punish the human race.

All this led me to suppose that some reversal of the natural order had taken place within industry; that it was perhaps functioning in a manner contrary to the designs of God; that the tenacity of so many scourges could be attributed to the absence of some arrangement willed by God and unknown to our savants. Finally I thought that if the human societies are suffering, as Montesquieu put it, "from a lingering disease, an inner vice, a secret and hidden venom," one might find the remedy by avoiding the paths followed for so many centuries and with such bad luck by our uncertain sciences.[13] Thus I adopted as my rules of research the principles of ABSOLUTE DOUBT and ABSOLUTE DEVIATION. These two methods must be defined, since before me no one had ever made use of them.

1st. ABSOLUTE DOUBT. Descartes had an inkling; but while praising and recommending doubt, he used it in a limited and inappropriate way. He raised ridiculous doubts; he doubted his own existence and spent more time distilling the sophisms of the ancients than looking for useful truths.

Descartes' successors made even less use of doubt than he. They applied the method only to things which displeased them; for instance, they raised questions about the necessity of religions because they were the antagonists of the priests. But they were very careful not to raise questions about the necessity of the political and moral sciences which were their means of subsis-

[13] By contrast to the natural or "fixed" sciences, Fourier referred to metaphysics, politics, political economy, and morality as the four "uncertain" sciences. The citation from Montesquieu, which was one of Fourier's favorite *devises*, comes from the *Lettres persanes*, Letter CXII.

tence, and which are today recognized as very useless under strong governments and as very dangerous under weak governments.

Since I had no relations with any scientific party, I resolved to apply the method of doubt to the opinions of all the parties without prejudice, and to suspect even those dispositions which had won universal assent. Such is civilization, which is the idol of all the philosophical parties and to which they attribute the ultimate of perfection. However, what is more imperfect than this civilization which drags all calamities in its wake? What is more questionable than its necessity and its future permanence? Isn't it probable that it is only a stage in the life of society? If it has been preceded by three other societies, Savagery, Patriarchate and Barbarism, does it follow that it will be the last because it is the fourth? Could not others still be born, and won't we see a fifth, a sixth, a seventh social order which will perhaps be less disastrous than civilization, and which have remained unknown because we have never attempted to discover them? Thus the method of Doubt must be applied to civilization; we must doubt its necessity, its excellence and its permanence. These are problems which the philosophers don't dare to face, because in suspecting civilization, they would call attention to the nullity of their own theories, which are all linked to civilization, and which will all collapse with it as soon as a better social order is found to replace it.

Thus the philosophers have limited themselves to a *Partial Doubt* because they have books and corporate prejudices to uphold; and fearing to compromise the books and the coterie, they have always equivocated on the important questions. But I who had no party to defend could adopt the method of Absolute Doubt and apply it first of all to civilization and to its most deeply rooted prejudices.

2nd. ABSOLUTE DEVIATION. I had presumed that the surest means of making useful discoveries was to deviate in every way from the paths followed by the uncertain sciences, which had never made the slightest discovery useful to society, and which, in spite of the immense progress of industry, had not even succeeded in warding off poverty. Thus I made it my business to remain in constant opposition to these sciences. Taking into consideration the multitude of their writers, I presumed that any subject which they had treated ought to be completely exhausted, and I resolved to apply myself only to problems which none of them had treated.

Accordingly, I avoided any inquiry into matters concerning the interests of the throne and altar, about which the philosophers have busied themselves ceaselessly ever since the origin of their science. They have always sought social welfare in administrative or religious innovations. I applied myself, on the contrary, to seeking the good only in operations which would have nothing to do either with administration or with the priesthood, which would rely only on industrial or domestic measures, and which would be compatible with all governments without requiring their intervention.

In following these two guides, *Absolute Doubt* concerning all prejudices, and *Absolute Deviation* from all known theories, I was sure to discover some new field of speculation, if any remained; but I scarcely expected to grasp the calculus of the Destinies. Far from aiming so high, I devoted myself at first only to very ordinary problems such as *Agricultural Association*. . . . When I began to speculate on this matter, I would myself never have presumed that such a modest calculation could lead to the theory of the Destinies. But since it has become the key to the theory, it is indispensable for me to speak about it at some length. . . .

More than once people have supposed that incalculable savings and ameliorations would result if one could bring together the inhabitants of a village in an industrial society, if one could associate two or three hundred families of unequal wealth according to their capital and their work. At first the idea seems completely impractical because of the obstacle that would be presented by the human passions. The obstacle seems particularly great because the passions cannot be overcome by gradual degrees. It is scarcely possible to create an agricultural association of twenty, thirty, forty or fifty individuals. But at least eight hundred are necessary to establish a NATURAL or ATTRACTIVE association. I mean by these words a society whose members would be inspired to work by rivalry, self-esteem and other stimuli compatible with self-interest. In the order to which I refer we will become passionately enthusiastic about agricultural work which is so irksome today that we only do it out of necessity and the fear of dying of hunger.

I will not discuss the stages of my research concerning the problem of natural association. It is a system so foreign to our ways that I am in no hurry to describe it in detail. It would seem ridiculous if I did not first provide the reader with a glimpse of the immense advantages which it will yield.

An agricultural association of roughly a thousand people offers such immense advantages that it is difficult to explain the fact that our modern philosophers have shown no interest in the idea. There is a group of savants, the economists, who are supposed to be particularly interested in industrial ameliorations. Their failure to search for a method of association is all the more inconceivable in that they have themselves indicated several of the advantages which will result from association. For instance, they have recognized, as anyone else could have done, that three hundred families of associated villagers could have just a single well-kept granary instead of three hundred run-down granaries, a single wine-vat instead of three hundred poorly maintained vats. In many cases, and especially in summer, these villagers could have just three or four large ovens instead of three hundred. They could send a single dairymaid to town with a wagon bearing a cask of milk and thus save a hundred other dairymaids the time and trouble it takes to carry their pitchers into town. These are just a few of the savings that diverse observers have recognized; and yet they have not indicated one-twentieth of the advantages which will result from agricultural association. . . .

Disputatious people are sure to raise objections. "How can you form an association out of families when one may have 100,000 livres and another may be penniless? How can you reconcile so many conflicting interests and desires? How can you absorb all their jealousies in such a way as to serve everyone's interest?" My reply to all this is: by the enticement of wealth and pleasure. The strongest passion of both peasants and city people is the love of profit. When they see that a societary community yields a profit THREE TIMES that of a community of incoherent families and provides all its members with the most varied pleasures, they will forget all their rivalries and hasten to form an association. The system will be adopted everywhere without the application of any form of constraint, for people everywhere are passionately devoted to wealth and pleasure.

To summarize, this theory of agricultural association, which is going to change the condition of the human race, appeals to the passions which are common to all men; it seduces them with the enticements of profit and sensual pleasure. That is why it is sure to succeed among the savages and barbarians as well as the civilized, for the passions are the same everywhere.

There is no urgency about making known this new system to which I will give the name PROGRESSIVE SERIES, or SERIES OF GROUPS, PASSIONATE SERIES.[14] By these words I mean to designate an assemblage of several associated groups whose members are devoted to different branches of a single industry or a single passion. . . . The theory of PASSIONATE SERIES or PROGRESSIVE SERIES has not been conceived arbitrarily like our social theories. The ordonnance of these series is entirely analogous to that of a geometrical series. Both have the same properties such as the balance of rivalry between the extreme groups and the intermediate groups of the series. . . .

People have regarded the passions as enemies of concord and have written thousands of volumes against them. These volumes are going to fall into nothingness. For the passions tend only to concord, to that social unity which we have thought was so alien to them. But the passions can only be harmonized if they are allowed to develop in an orderly fashion within the PROGRESSIVE SERIES or SERIES OF GROUPS. Outside of this mechanism the passions are only unchained tigers, incomprehensible enigmas. For this reason the philosophers have claimed that they must be repressed. Their opinion is doubly absurd since the passions cannot be repressed and since, if they could, civilization would rapidly disappear and man would rapidly fall back into a nomadic state in which the passions would be even more harmful than they are

[14] On the passionate series and the whole theory of passionate attraction see the texts below in Section IV.

now. I have no more faith in the virtues of the shepherds than in those of their apologists.

The societary order which is going to replace the incoherence of civilization has no place for moderation or equality or any of the other philosophical notions. It requires ardent and refined passions. As soon as an association is formed, the passions will harmonize with greater ease if they are more intense and more numerous.

This is not to say that the new order will change the passions. Neither God nor man is capable of changing them; but it is possible to change their direction without changing their nature. . . . Thus if I maintain that in the societary order men will acquire tastes which are different from those which they have at present, that they will prefer to live in the country rather than the city, one should not believe that in acquiring new tastes they will acquire new passions. They will still be guided by the love of wealth and pleasure.

I insist on this point to meet an objection which has been raised by certain obtuse individuals. When they hear me talk about the new tastes and customs which will emerge in the societary order, they immediately exclaim: "so YOU WANT TO CHANGE THE PASSIONS!" Certainly not. But what I do want to do is to provide them with new means of expression, to assure them three or four times the development which they have in the incoherent order in which we live. This is why we will see civilized people acquire an aversion for habits which please them today, such as family life. In the family system children spend all their time crying, quarreling, breaking things and refusing to work. But when these same children have joined the PROGRESSIVE SERIES or SERIES OF GROUPS, they will become industrious; they will try to emulate each other's accomplishments without any outside encouragement; they will enthusiastically try to inform themselves about agriculture, manufacturing, science and art; they will perform useful tasks while they think they are amusing themselves. When fathers witness this new order of things, they will find their children adorable in the series and detestable in the incoherent household. Then they will observe that in the residence of a PHALANX (this is the name I give to the association which farms a rural area) people are served marvelous food. . . . Finally they will discover that in the activities and relations of the series there is never any cheating, and that people who are so dishonest and crude in civilization will become paragons of honesty and refinement in the series. When they have seen all this they will acquire an aversion for the household, the cities and the civilization of which they are now so fond. They will want to associate themselves in the series of a Phalanx and live in its edifice. Will they have changed their passions in becoming disdainful of the customs and tastes which please them today? No, their passions will have changed their means of expression without having changed their nature or their ultimate goal.

Thus one should beware of supposing that the system of the progressive series, which will be entirely different from that of civilization, will bring about the slightest change in the passions. The passions have been and will remain immutable. They will produce conflict and poverty outside of the progressive series and harmony and opulence in the societary state which is our destiny. The establishment of the societary order in a single community will be spontaneously imitated everywhere thanks to the immense profits and innumerable pleasures which that order will assure to all individuals, however poor or wealthy they may be.

I shall turn now to the results of this discovery from a scientific standpoint. . . . As to the new sciences which it has revealed, I shall confine myself to indicating the two most important ones. Since these matters will not interest most of my readers, I shall try to be as brief as possible.

The first science which I discovered was the theory of passionate attraction. When I recognized that the progressive series assure full development to the passions of both men and women, of the young and the old, and of people in every social class, when I discovered that in this new order a great number of passions will be a guarantee of strength and wealth, I surmised that if God had given so much influence to passionate attraction and so little to its enemy, reason, His purpose was to guide us to the system of progressive series which is completely consistent with attraction. Then I supposed that attraction, which is so much maligned by the philosophers, must be the interpreter of the designs of God concerning the social order. By this means I arrived at the ANALYTIC AND SYNTHETIC CALCULUS OF PASSIONATE ATTRACTIONS AND REPULSIONS. This calculus cannot fail to culminate in agricultural association. Thus if anyone had attempted to study attraction analytically and synthetically, he would have discovered the laws of association without seeking them. This is something that no one has ever dreamed of. Even in the eighteenth century, when analytical methods were so popular, no one ever tried to apply them to attraction.

The theory of passionate attractions and repulsions is an exact science and wholly applicable to geometrical theorems. It has great ramifications and can become the sustenance of the philosophers who are, I believe, very much in need of some luminous and useful problem on which to exercise their metaphysical talents.

I continue my discussion of the filiation of the new sciences. I soon recognized that the laws of passionate attraction were in complete accord with the laws of material attraction, as explained by Newton and Leibnitz, and that there was a UNIFIED SYSTEM OF MOVEMENT GOVERNING THE MATERIAL WORLD AND THE SPIRITUAL WORLD.

I suspected that this analogy might apply to particular laws as well as to general ones, and that the attractions and properties of the animals, vegetables and minerals were perhaps coordinated with the same scheme as those of man and the stars. After making the necessary investigations, I became convinced of this. Thus a new exact science was discovered: *the analogy of the material, organic, animal and social movements*, or *the analogy of the modifications of matter with the mathematical theory of the passions of man and the animals*.[15]

The discovery of these two exact sciences revealed others to me. It would be useless to list them all here. But they include everything up to literature and the arts, and they will permit the establishment of exact methods in all the domains of human knowledge.

[15] On the theory of universal analogy and some of the other "new sciences" discovered by Fourier see the texts included in Section VIII of this anthology.

Once I had discovered the two theories of attraction and the unity of the four movements, I began to make sense of the book of nature. One by one, I found the answers to its mysteries. I had lifted the veil that was supposed to be impenetrable. I advanced into a new scientific world. It was thus that I arrived by gradual degrees at the calculus of the Universal Destinies, or the determination of the fundamental system governing all the laws of movement, present, past and future.

*—OC*, I, 2–12

# *II*

# *Commerce, Industry, and Work in Civilization*

I am a child of the profession, born and raised in the mercantile shops. I have seen the infamies of commerce with my own eyes, and I will not describe them from hearsay as do our moralists.

—*OC*, VI, 398–399

The philosophers tell us that civilization is the culmination of the social destinies; in fact it is merely the *fifth* of thirty-two possible societies, and one of the most wretched.

—*OC*, I, 35

Civilization was a pejorative term in Fourier's vocabulary, a synonym for perfidy and constraint. The attack which Fourier leveled against the institutions, ideologies, customs, manners, and vices of civilization was both penetrating and extraordinarily comprehensive. In its scope, its intransigence, and its psychological insight it repeatedly brings to mind Rousseau's earlier challenge to civilized society and culture. But whereas Rousseau was very much concerned with the problem of how man should live in a depraved society, Fourier's sole aim was to bring an end to civilization. His rules of method—Absolute Doubt and Absolute Deviation—implied a total rejection of civilization as a way of life. "We must apply doubt to civilization," he wrote, "we must doubt its necessity, its excellence and its permanence."

There was no doubt a good deal of nonsense, pettiness, and prejudice in Fourier's indictment. His writing on civilization was punctuated by outbursts of rage against the Jews, the English, the Parisians, and the "philosophical cabal" which, he believed, was deliberately suppressing his ideas. His personal hatred of commerce was such that he often described the merchant as a villain whose machinations were the unique source of poverty and hunger. But even at its pettiest and most myopic, Fourier's attack on civilization had qualities not to be found in the writing of any other social critic of his time. His lack of education, his *déclassement*, and his sense of total alienation from the intellectual establishment were sources of insight as well as resentment. They heightened his contempt for conventional wisdom and sharpened his awareness of ills which other more successful and worldly men simply took for granted. For all of its intellectual naïveté and personal rancor, Fourier's social criticism was that of a man who absolutely refused to be taken in by the lofty abstractions which others used to rationalize or hide the physical suffering and emotional deprivation that were the lot of most men in civilization.

Fourier never tried to conceal the fact that his hatred of civilized society was born of his own experience. The psychological roots were probably buried deeper than he knew. But the autobiographical text which opens this section is interesting as his own account of his discovery that civilized ideals were not consistent with civilized practice. Like the young Rousseau Fourier was shocked to discover, at the age of six, that society punished honesty and betrayed innocence. He later claimed that this painful but enlightening experience caused him to seek a new social and economic order which would reward honesty. He first directed his anger against the commercial world because he was forced to make his living in it and to cooperate in its crimes. But eventually he broadened his investigation to include the whole of civilized society; and everywhere he looked he found the same fraud and deception, the same contradiction between the ideals men professed and the way they actually lived.

Although the texts in this section are but a small sampling from Fourier's writings on commerce, industry, and work, they should convey some idea of his main preoccupations and his various critical techniques. If Fourier's favorite analytical genre —the enumeration—is amply represented here, it should be pointed out that his brief list of the "vices of commerce" is by no means complete. By the end of his life Fourier could boast of having compiled a list of seventy-two distinct commercial vices, each of which included a host of varieties, types, and species. Fourier's amusing account of a "sentimental bankruptcy" shows just what he meant by the analysis of a species and it reveals him as a social satirist comparable to Balzac (who admired Fourier's typologies and tried his own hand at a classification of bankruptcies in *César Birotteau*).

Some of the limitations of Fourier's economic critique are illustrated by the text on "Industrial Anarchy." As this text shows, when Fourier attacked the factory system of his day, he aimed most of his criticism at hated England and was content to rely on the flimsy and incomplete evidence he could glean from newspapers. Often his "sources" were French translations of English articles or reports published years before he used them. The reasons for Fourier's rather superficial treatment of the factory system—and for his preoccupation with the misdeeds of the merchant—have been suggested in our Introduction. It was only during Fourier's last years that large industrial enterprises began to assume a prominent role in French economic life. Throughout his long years at Lyon the most advanced industry which he had before his eyes—the Lyon silk industry—was dominated by a small nucleus of master merchants and run on the "putting out" system.

Although Fourier never neglected an opportunity to expose the miserable working conditions that civilization imposed on urban and rural workers, the texts on "Work, Anxiety, and Freedom" show that he was particularly concerned with the psychological costs of work. In "The Worker's Misfortunes," for example, intangible but real psychological deprivations figure more prominently than do physical torments. Because he insisted that freedom included freedom from anxiety and compulsion, Fourier was able to show that all but the wealthiest men were subject to a kind of servitude in work. At the very time when most left-wing critics of capitalist exploitation were making common cause with middle class entrepreneurs to praise labor, Fourier, with rare insight, condemned the work ethic as a form of servitude.

# 1

# CRITIQUE OF COMMERCE

### FOURIER AND COMMERCE

To unveil the intrigues of the stock exchange and the brokers is to undertake a Herculean task. I doubt that the demi-god felt as much disgust in cleaning the Augean stables as I feel in probing the sink of moral filth which is called the bordel of exchange and brokerage. This is a subject that science has not even touched upon. To discuss it you need a practitioner grown grey in the service and raised in the mercantile pen, as I have been since the age of six. At that age I began to notice the contrast which exists between commerce and truth. I was taught at catechism and at school that one must never lie; then they took me to the store to accustom me to the noble trade of deceit or the art of selling. Shocked by the cheating and deception which I witnessed, I began to take the merchants aside and tell them what was being done to them. One of them, in his complaint, made the mistake of betraying me, and this earned me a hard spanking. My parents, who saw that I was addicted to the truth, exclaimed reproachfully: "This child will never do well in commerce." In fact, I conceived a secret aversion for commerce; and at the age of seven I swore an oath like that which Hannibal swore against Rome at the age of nine: I swore myself to an eternal hatred of commerce.

They got me into commerce against my will. I was lured to Lyon by the prospect of a trip; but at the very door of Scherer's banking house where they were taking me, I deserted, announcing that I would never be a merchant. It was like backing out of a marriage on the altar steps. They took me to Rouen where I quit a second time. In the end I bent to the yoke, and I lost the best years of my life in the workshops of deceit. Everywhere I went I heard echoes of the sinister prophecy: "What a fine, honest lad! He will never do well in commerce." In fact, I have been duped and robbed in all my undertakings. But if I have no talent for the practice of commerce, I am quite able to unmask it.

—"Analyse du mécanisme d'agiotage," *La Phalange*, VII (1848), pp. 9–10.

THE RISE OF COMMERCE AND THE BIRTH OF POLITICAL ECONOMY

Well! Why have nations taken so long to realize that the commercial order is a temporary monstrosity, an utterly senseless system that places the three productive classes—proprietors, farmers and manufacturers—at the mercy of a parasitical class which has no national loyalty and which can do whatever it wishes with the fruits of industry over which it exercises arbitrary control? So faulty a system is obviously the result of a failure in social science. Commerce could have seemed tolerable in the childhood of human societies, although even then it was scorned. But it is unworthy of the modern age which aspires to enlightenment and perfectibility, and which boasts of seeking the truth—of which commerce is the mortal enemy. Let us then investigate why the invention of a better system has been put off until our own time and why no effort has been made to discover some means of liberating society from the influence of commerce and deceit.[1]

I have already said that the wise men of antiquity never made commerce an object of study; they simply treated it with the scorn which it deserves. The masters of the world, the Alexanders and the Caesars, would have smiled with pity if someone had advised them to subordinate their policies, in today's fashion, to the interests of dealers in oil and soap. The privileges that commerce had enjoyed at Carthage[2] were alone sufficient to debase it in the eyes of Rome; thus the Roman writers relegated it to a place among the filthy professions.

As for the small republics of Tyr, Carthage and Athens, which were devoted to traffic, they never influenced opinion in the great empires. They vaunted their trade for the same reason

[1] This text is from the preamble of a manuscript written in 1810 and entitled "On the Federal Warehouse or the Abolition of Commerce." The "better system" to which Fourier refers is a credit scheme designed to facilitate the gradual transition from civilization to Harmony by freeing agriculture and industry from "the speculative extortions of commerce."

[2] Fourier often referred to the Carthaginians as a people who had been corrupted by the mercantile spirit. They were the forebears of the English ("modern Carthaginians") and of the Jews (a people "addicted to traffic, to usury and to mercantile depravity"). On Fourier's anti-semitism see below p. 199.

that brigandage was vaunted by the Tatars and piracy by the Algerians. They fleeced their neighbors as often as possible, and they were regarded as birds of prey whose voracity is abhorred but who are tolerated because they are not entirely useless. . . .

The role of commerce in antiquity amounted to very little. Just what was the vaunted trade of Tyr, Carthage and Athens? I would say that the activity of these three ports was barely equal to that of three of our small ports, like Nice, Bayonne and Dieppe, in peacetime. At that time there was little to exchange among the states on the shores of the Mediterranean. Since the goods which they produced were just about the same, farming and industry provided few occasions for trade. The backwardness of navigation prevented them from finding markets for their goods in the torrid and cold zones. . . . It is clear that the commerce of antiquity must have been quite insubstantial when we consider that its most important branch, the grain trade, was frequently controlled by rulers. We read that Hiero, the King of Syracuse, made shipments of wheat to the Roman Senate. Thus in the nations of antiquity commerce was only a shadow—no more than a tenth—of what it is today. For this reason it is not surprising that the statesmen of that time paid little attention to their merchants and scorned their wiles without trying to reform them, just as the gross customs of the lower classes are disdained but tolerated today. Antiquity neither could nor would devote itself to the search for another mode of exchange; it simply tolerated commerce as a vulgar vice.

Circumstances are very different today. Various unforeseen events have produced a colossal growth in commerce. Progress in the art of navigation, the discovery of the East and West Indies with all their resources, the extension of farming to northern latitudes, the establishment of communications between the three zones, the rapid development of manufacturing, and the competition for trade among a multitude of nations—all these factors have led to a prodigious increase in the volume of commerce. It can be said to have increased ten-fold since Antiquity. Trade has now become one of the principal branches of the social mechanism; it has finally drawn the attention of the philosophers; they have ceased to ridicule it. Among them one group of men, who are called the Economists, has devoted itself to the study of industrial policy. . . .

When political economy emerged as a science, commerce was already powerful and revered. The Dutch had already accumulated their hoards of gold; they had discovered the means to bribe and corrupt kings and their courts long before anyone had heard of the Economists. At the outset, then, commerce was a giant and political economy was only a dwarf. When political economy entered the lists against commerce, the ports were already swarming with wealthy ship-fitters and the great cities were full of those dandified bankers who are intimate with ministers and give orders to diplomats. It was no longer possible, as in antiquity, to treat commerce as a laughing stock; for there is no greater title to respect in civilization than a bulging safe. The first efforts of political economy were all the more modest in that its authors possessed neither wealth nor an established body of doctrine. Since the legacy of antiquity amounted to no more than a few jeers about commerce, they had to create everything for themselves. Deprived of the wisdom of antiquity and thrown back on their own resources, the poor Economists were obliged to adopt modest and timid dogmas. This was only becoming in a few unknown savants who had to enter the scientific world by doing combat with the Croesus of the age.

There could be no doubt about the outcome of such a combat. Political economy made only a faint gesture of resistance. Praise for that gesture is due to Quesnay, the leader of the French sect.[3] Trying to make the truth known, he propagated

---

[3] François Quesnay (1694–1774) was court doctor under Louis XV and leader of the group of Physiocrats. The first true school of French economists, the Physiocrats held that land is the only source of wealth. They are best known for their advocacy of a single tax to be levied on land. Although they regarded commerce as necessary to assure the circulation of wealth throughout society, they held that in itself commerce was a sterile and unproductive activity. It was this—and not their endorsement of the doctrine of *laissez faire*—that made Fourier sympathetic to them. See *PM*, III; *OC*, XI, 158: "A reasonable sect had emerged in France, the sect of Quesnay who wished to subordinate the whole industrial mechanism to the needs of agriculture. Quesnay had too little esteem for manufactur-

dogmas which tended to subordinate commerce to the interests of agriculture. But the English cabal, which had sold out to commerce, triumphed with the help of a few religious intrigues. Philosophy, which had opened hostilities against the priesthood, was in need of reinforcements; it prudently decided to ally itself with the money-bags and to flatter commerce, which was beginning to acquire a great influence. Thus the Economists hitched themselves to the wagon of commerce. They proclaimed it infallible like the ancient popes. They declared that a merchant's dealings could never fail to promote the public interest and that the merchant ought therefore to enjoy an absolute liberty. All the dogmas were adapted to this paradox.

Soon merchants were being showered with adulation. Raynal, Voltaire, and all the most eminent philosophers could be seen kneeling before the golden calf. But they secretly scorned it; for when Voltaire dedicated his play *Zaïre* to a London merchant, whom he overwhelmed with banal compliments, he was no more sincere than when he dedicated his *Mahomet* to Pope Benedict. Voltaire was himself a consummate practitioner of mercantile trickery; he excelled at duping book-sellers. Thus he knew the true worth of the fine art of trade; he knew that merchants detest learning, that they scorn the sciences and the arts, that they are bored even by the flattery of writers when it does not serve to line their pockets. But the philosophical party was in need of new recruits, and so they praised the merchants to the skies. . . .

It must be said in defence of the philosophers that during the eighteenth century commerce was not as perverse as it is today. There were relatively few merchants then and they made their profits easily. Thus they did not need to resort to the innumerable subtleties and audacious tricks that degrade their profession today. This is so true that elderly merchants are constantly voicing their stupefaction at today's wiles; they are agreed in describing modern commerce as a snare, a Black Forest, by comparison

---

ing which must be distinguished from commerce. . . . Quesnay ignored this distinction and, like all systematic thinkers, he adopted extreme views. Nonetheless he was heading in the right direction since he wished to subordinate commerce to agriculture."

with the friendly spirit in which trade was carried on before the Revolution. We should add that at that time the English monopoly was not yet dominant; France was still standing up to England and, along with its allies, it had a very substantial monopoly of its own. That is why the French philosophers were not alarmed by an abuse from which their own nation benefited. Everything conspired to make this mismatch seem attractive to philosophy. In associating itself with commerce philosophy behaved just like a young noblewoman who marries a commoner whom she supposes to be an honest man. And, in fact, it was impossible at that time to predict the immensity of vices and scourges that commerce was going to inflict upon the nineteenth century.

But now the mercantile spirit has shown its profound malevolence. The mask has fallen; monopoly and deceit are now revealed. Philosophy can no longer deceive itself about the infamies of the serpent with which it has been associated. It is time for philosophy to break with commerce and return to the path of Truth, which is wholly alien to the mercantile spirit. A discovery is about to banish commerce from the womb of civilization. If it was pardonable to encourage commerce when there was some doubt about its perversity, it would be odious to do so today, now that Truth has unmasked it and cast it into disgrace.

—*PM*, iii; *OC*, xi, 78–86

Within the last half-century the capriciousness of fashion has given commerce a major influence on civilized politics. The politicians would have been a good deal wiser if they had given their support to the manufacturing industries and not to commerce, brokerage and speculation, which are the natural enemies of manufacturing and of all productive industries.

I will demonstrate later that commerce, which is mistakenly classified among the productive forms of work, ought to be ranked first among the parasitical professions like those of monk, soldier, lawyer, etc. The reduction of all these professions should be the constant aim of any sound political system.

By its growth and influence the merchant class has done much more harm to industry than have the monks and lawyers.

For the monks merely deprive the farms and workshops of their labor. The lawyers' fault is somewhat graver, since they distract others from labor and rob them without producing anything themselves. But commerce is guilty of both these vices and it adds a third: it diverts and turns against industry capital which, under a better system, should be devoted uniquely to the improvement of farming and manufacturing.

The commercial systems are, for the moment, Europe's most fashionable chimera. Authors who wish immediate renown, write a brochure on credit, exchange, duties and paper money. Tell us in your learned investigations why cottons have "weakened" and sugars are "wavering." Say why one empire has exported more ells of cloth than its neighbor. If you explain these great mysteries to us in pounds, sous and deniers, the temple of fame is open to you. Don't forget to dedicate your work to one of the saints of the day, one of those bankers whose name makes all knees bend, even at the court. Don't go after the protection of official dignitaries; senators and generals are and should be only in the second rank since they know nothing about commerce or banking. Even kings will soon be proud to bear the title of "merchants" as they once boasted of being "Fathers of the people"; and to maintain their popularity they will have to appear in public with a bale of cotton for a throne, a measuring rod for a sceptre, and with a coat of arms consisting of a few rolls of tobacco emblazoned against a background of bars of soap. Ah! don't the monarchs owe thanksgiving to commerce? It was a trade rivalry between France and England that toppled their thrones; it was a competition for sugar and coffee that sent Louis, his family, and the elite of France to the scaffold. Has politics ever had such a bad effect on industry as it has in recent times? Was there ever so much bad faith among tradesmen, so much encouragement to speculation and bankruptcy, as there has been since the court and the academies were infected by the mercantile spirit?

—*PM*, III; *OC*, XI, 6–7 (Written in 1803)

## CRITIQUE OF ECONOMIC LIBERALISM

Despite all its vices, commerce is regarded as a perfect method of exchange because the contracting parties are free to come to terms or to decline to do so. This freedom is only a negative benefit. It has no value except by comparison with the methods of the barbarians, with requisitions, maximums, tariffs, etc. It is far from sufficient in itself to secure equity, fidelity, confidence or economy in exchanges. These and other benefits have no place in the commercial order, which establishes all the opposite vices. Commerce allows deceit and plunder to triumph; it creates a climate of mistrust which impedes the development of economic relations and necessitates expensive precautions. Finally it hinders and complicates the whole process of exchange.

*—PM*, I; *OC*, x, 248

Commerce, which is vaguely defined as free exchange, is merely one method of free exchange, and not the best. To define it more precisely, commerce is a mode of exchange in which the seller has the right to defraud with impunity and to determine by himself without arbitration the profit which he ought to receive. The result is that the seller is the judge of his own case while the buyer is deprived of protection against the rapacity and cheating of the seller. It makes no sense to say: "Good faith ought to reign in commerce." One should say: "Good faith ought to reign in order to destroy commerce."

*—PM*, III; *OC*, xi, 16–17

The fundamental principle of the commercial systems is: "Let the merchants have complete freedom." This principle concedes to them absolute ownership of the commodities in which they deal. They have the right to take their goods out of circulation, to hide them, and even to burn them as was done more than once by the Dutch East India Company which publicly burned supplies of cinnamon in order to raise its price. What it did with cinnamon it would have done with wheat, had it not feared the anger of the common people; it would have burned a part of its wheat, or allowed it to rot, in order to sell the rest at four times its value. Well! Every day on the docks can you not see people throwing into the sea supplies of grain that a merchant has allowed to rot while waiting for a rise in prices. I have myself presided as a clerk over these foul operations, and one day I jettisoned twenty thousand quintals of rice which could have been sold before it rotted for a fair profit, had the owner been less greedy for gain. It is society as a whole which suffers by such waste, which you can see taking place every day under the cover of the philosophical principle: *Laissez faire les marchands*.[4]

Let us suppose that in a famine year like 1709 a rich company of merchants observes this principle by cornering all the grain in a small state such as Ireland. Let us further suppose that the general scarcity and the restrictions on exports in neighboring states have made it impossible to find grain abroad. Having cornered all the available grain, the company refuses to sell it until the price has tripled or quadrupled, saying: "This grain is our property; it pleases us to sell it at four times its cost. If these terms don't suit you, find your grain somewhere else. While we are waiting for the price to rise a quarter of the population may die of starvation, but that doesn't bother us. We are sticking to our speculation, in keeping with the principles of commercial liberty, as consecrated by modern philosophy."

I ask in what respect the actions of this company differ from those of a band of thieves, for its monopoly compels the whole nation to pay a ransom equal to three times the value of the grain —or else die of starvation.

According to the rules of commercial liberty the company has the right to refuse to sell at any price, to allow the wheat to rot in its granaries while the people are starving. Can you believe that the starving nation is in conscience bound to die of hunger for the honor of the fine philosophical principle: *Laissez faire les marchands?* Of course not. Then admit that the right of commercial liberty should be subject to restrictions consistent with the needs of society as a whole. Admit that a person who possesses a superabundance of a commodity which he has not produced and which he will not consume, ought to be regarded as a CONDITIONAL TRUSTEE of that commodity and not as its absolute owner. Admit that the dealings of merchants and middlemen should be subordinated to the welfare of the mass of society, and that these individuals should not be free to impede economic rela-

---

[4] "Let the merchants do as they please."

tions by all those disastrous maneuvers which your economists admire.

Are merchants alone exempt from the social obligations imposed on all the other classes of society? When a general, a judge or a doctor is given a free hand, he is not authorized to betray the army, despoil the innocent or assassinate his patient. Such people are punished when they betray their trust; the perfidious general is beheaded; the judge must answer to the Minister of Justice. The merchants alone are inviolable and sure of impunity! Political economy wishes no one to have the right of controlling their machinations. If they starve a whole region, if they disturb its industry with their speculation, hoarding and bankruptcies, everything is justified by the simple title of *merchant*. This is like the quack doctor in the play who, having killed everyone with his pills, is justified because he can say in Latin: *medicus sum*. In our century of regeneration people are trying to convince us that the plots hatched by one of the least enlightened classes of society can never do harm to the welfare of the state. Once upon a time people talked about the infallibility of the pope; today it is that of the merchant which they wish to establish.

—*OC*, I, 239–241

### THE VICES OF COMMERCE

What are the vices inherent in the commercial mechanism? Others have defined it in flattering terms; I am going to adopt a very different tone and show commerce to be the source of all sorts of crimes and misdeeds. I will refer to just seven.

The first disorder is *Bankruptcy* which scoffs at the efforts of legislators and triumphs in spite of all their legal codes.[5] Just recently French legislation was put to shame when it purported to repress bankruptcy with a new code of commerce. Bankruptcy has only become bolder and more confident in changing its form, and the new code is merely a weapon with which the bankrupt threaten the creditors whom they wish to rob.

[5] Fourier refers to the fraudulent or profitable declaration of insolvency which enables "any merchant to steal from the public a sum equivalent to his wealth or credit." The following text provides an example.

The second vice is *Smuggling* by which commerce rebels openly against authority and forms industrial Vendées against which the state must maintain parasitical armies of customs officers. Certain cities like Basel and other such centers of contraband exploit neighboring empires in the same way that the Algerian pirates exploit seafarers. The ones are sea-robbers and the others are land-robbers. I shall prove in one of the chapters of this work that, by means of its contraband, the city of Basel alone exacts an annual tribute of several million from France. You can draw your own conclusions about the extent of the smuggling carried on each year over the whole territory of France, Germany, Spain and Italy.

What shall I say of the *Usurers* who, under the name of bankers, are waging war against property owners? Take for example the hordes of Jews and vagabonds who have practically overrun the four departments on the right bank of the Rhine. They would soon have gobbled up most of the French property there if the government had not restrained them by decrees and by means of an economic struggle that involved the Bank of France, which is an agent of resistance against usury.

*Speculation* is the fourth of the plagues to which I am calling attention; it is another one of the weapons used by commerce against governments. Speculation abuses public confidence and makes sport of the ascendency of the noblest heroes. Witness the campaign of Austerlitz during which a horde of Parisian speculators ravaged French industry, discredited the Bank of France and the government bonds, and created all the symptoms of a panic at the very moment when the Empire was echoing with cries of admiration and blind confidence in its illustrious chief.

*Hoarding* is not the least of the mercantile feats. It creates famine in the midst of abundance; by means of contrived panics it can double the price of goods and exploit society in the interest of the commercial vampires.

*Parasitism* is a less obvious but not less harmful disorder. Hosts of merchants encumber the cities, and the streets are cluttered with solicitors who swarm without limit or purpose. There was competition enough when their number was only a quarter of what it is today, and then agriculture profited from the capital and labor of the crowd of parasites with which commerce is now inundating the cities.

Of all the commercial vices *Cheating* is the one which is making the most rapid progress. Today it has reached such a point that merchants of the old type are thought to be incompetent because they don't know the tricks to which abusive competition has given rise.

—*PM*, III; *OC*, XI, 73–75

### A SENTIMENTAL BANKRUPTCY

Each of the generic features of commerce, such as speculation, bankruptcy, etc., includes a vast array of species and varieties which should have been analyzed and classified. . . . In discussing the hierarchy of bankruptcy I have made up a list comprising 3 orders, 9 generic types and 36 species of bankruptcy.[6] This list could easily be tripled or quadrupled. For bankruptcy has become such an art that every day someone invents a new species, especially in the realm of governmental bankruptcies where France has just made an innovation: the *doubledupe* or *amphidupe*, which has provided the nation with a new means of despoiling itself.

Our century obliges people to adopt a facetious tone in criticizing vice: *castigat ridendo*.[7] We are supposed to avoid the grim tone of the moralists of the last century. This would have been easy for me since in my hierarchy of bankruptcy I have described each of the 9 types and 36 species in amusing terms. Take for example the fifth type, the tactical bankruptcy. This includes 5 species: 17) the bankruptcy by squadrons; 18) the firing line bankruptcy; 19) the close column bankruptcy; 20) the wide formation bankruptcy; 21) the sharp-shooter's bankruptcy. These five species comprise one of the types in the center of the series. They correspond exactly to military maneuvers. Thus I have called this type the "tactical" and the one that precedes it the "maneuvering" bankruptcy.

It would be very easy, then, to satisfy the oratorical insistence on amusing criticism—*castigat ridendo*—while providing a frank

[6] Fourier's complete "hierarchy" of the varieties of fraudulent bankruptcy may be found in *OC*, IV, 124.
[7] "Criticize in laughing."

and truthful analysis of the vice. I could, according to the method of the journalists, present a list of the species of bankruptcy to make the reader desire a chapter on each one of them. Everyone would be interested to see how I define such species as these.

Sentimental, infantile, well-to-do, cosmopolitan;
Gallant, sanctimonious, unprincipled, amicable;
Stylish, preferential, wide-netted, miniature;
Break-neck, stealthy, Attila-like, invalid's;
Swindler's, jail-bird's, ninny's, visionary;
Posthumous, familial, re-decked, push-pin.

An analysis of all these species of bankruptcy would produce many amusing chapters, particularly since I am a child of the profession, born and raised in the mercantile shops. I have seen the infamies of commerce with my own eyes, and I will not describe them from hear-say as do our moralists who know nothing more about commerce than what they hear in the salons of the speculators and who know only the respectable side of bankruptcy proceedings. According to them any bankruptcy (especially that of a broker or banker) becomes a sentimental incident in which the creditors themselves are beholden to the bankrupt party for having palmed off his noble speculations on them. The notary brings them the news as if it were an accident of fate, an unforeseen catastrophe caused by the misfortunes of the times, critical circumstances, a deplorable turn of events, etc. This is the way one usually begins a letter announcing a bankruptcy.

According to the notary and his accomplices, *who secretly derive ample remuneration from the loss*, these bankrupt individuals are so honorable, so worthy of esteem!!! A tender mother who is sacrificing herself for her children; a virtuous father who is teaching them to love their constitution;[8] a tearful family which is worthy of a better fate and inspired by the most sincere love for every one of its creditors! Truly it would be a crime not to aid this family to recover; it is the duty of every honest man to help them.

[8] *La Charte*, or the constitutional charter of the restored Bourbon monarchy.

At this point a few moral shysters appear on the scene, their palms well greased, to talk of lofty sentiments and the pity which misfortune must inspire. They are helped out by pretty female petitioners who are very useful in calming down the more recalcitrant creditors. Shaken by all these intrigues, three-quarters of the creditors arrive at the judgment session unsettled and disoriented. In advising the creditors to take a loss of 70%, the notary depicts the 30% rebate as the effort of a virtuous family which is impoverishing itself and making every sacrifice to satisfy the sacred duties imposed by a sense of honor. The creditors are told that in all conscience they ought to accept a loss of 80% in order to pay homage to the noble qualities of a family so worthy of esteem and so zealous in defense of the interests of its creditors.

A few barbarians may wish to object to such terms. But the accomplices who are spread about the room whisper that these recalcitrant individuals are IMMORAL people: that one of them does not go to church regularly; that another keeps a mistress; that another is known to be a Harpagon, a usurer; that still another has already gone bankrupt himself and is a hard-hearted man with no indulgence for his fellows. Finally most of the creditors give up and sign the contract, whereupon the notary declares that it is "a highly advantageous settlement for the creditors" in that it has saved them the expense of legal fees and provided them with the opportunity to do a good turn to a virtuous family. Everyone (or at least all of the fools who comprise the majority) leaves filled with admiration for the virtue and the lofty sentiments of which this worthy family is the model.

Thus concludes a *sentimental* bankruptcy in which the creditors are looted for at least two-thirds of their money. For a bankruptcy would only be *honest* and not sentimental if the settlement was fixed at 50%. Indeed, 50% is so normal a rate that the bankrupt party has no need of utilizing artistic refinements if he is willing to settle at this modest rate. Unless he is an imbecile he is sure to make at least a 50% profit on his bankruptcy.

If someone had published a work describing a hundred

species of bankruptcy, with more details than I have given here on the *sentimental* bankruptcy, this book would have made known one of the pretty traits of commerce, one of its true features. Other works dealing with other features, such as speculation and hoarding, would have opened people's eyes and raised doubts about the commercial mechanism known as *free competition*, which is the most anarchic and perverse mode of exchange that can exist.

—*OC*, vi, 396–400

# 2

# WORK AND INDUSTRY IN CIVILIZATION

### "INDUSTRIAL ANARCHY"

To dispel the illusions of happiness which are founded on industry I will first examine the plight of England, the country whose industrial development is most advanced. It is the country which the Economists hold up to us as a model. Let us analyze the well-being of its people.

In prosperous times the poor of London number about 230,000. 115,000 of them are in the care of the parishes; 115,000 are beggars, thieves, vagabonds and vagrants. The latter category includes 30,000 prostitutes. There are in London some 3000 receivers of stolen goods, one of whom is worth twenty million, and 3000 Jews who distribute bad money and encourage domestic servants to steal from their masters and children to steal from their fathers. These extracts from the *Tableau de Londres* would suffice by themselves to convey an idea of the happiness provided by civilized industry.[1]

Let us move from the capital to the provinces. Let us listen to what trustworthy individuals have to say about provincial poverty. Let us first of all listen to the assembly of the principal artisans of Birmingham (March 21, 1827) attesting that "the industriousness and frugality of the worker cannot keep him safe from poverty; that the majority of workers employed in agriculture and industry are destitute; that the people are literally dying of hunger in a country where the supply of food is plentiful."

This is the fruit of the systems of industrialism which serve to enrich finance, big business and the great property owners, and leave the people nothing but hunger and nakedness as the wages of slave labor which is often performed in workshops where men are locked up for eighteen hours a day.

Here is a curious testimonial on the subject. In the House

---

[1] Although this text dates from 1828, Fourier appears to be citing the same *Tableau de Londres* which he drew upon in 1803 when writing his "Letter to the High Judge." See above p. 88.

of Commons on February 28, 1826 M. Huskisson, the Minister of Trade, says: "Our silk manufactures employ thousands of children who are kept at work from three o'clock in the morning until ten at night. How much are they paid a week? A shilling and a half or 37 French sous, which means about five and a half sous a day for nineteen hours of work."

Since living costs are greater in England than in France, their salary of five and a half sous a day is the equivalent of four French sous.

M. Huskisson neglects to point out that these children are watched over by foremen provided with whips to strike any child who stops an instant, and that they are not even permitted to leave to go to the bathroom: they have a toilet in the workshop itself. They are subjected to a hundred other vexations.

Thus, thanks to the bragging perfectibilities of industrialism and productionalism, slavery had been reestablished in fact, and it is more onerous for them even than for the Negroes who are at least given time to rest. The English people, with their liberties and their sovereignty, are tortured by their mercantile chiefs just as the Negroes are tortured by the savage planters of the Antilles.

English soldiers fare no better. Sir R. Fergusson has presented to Parliament a list of the numbers of whippings, beatings and other tortures inflicted on the artillery, which is everywhere the most disciplined of all forces. I regret having lost this list which puts English soldiers on a level with Negroes as to punishments.

Well, what is the result of these tortures perpetrated on the lower classes? Colossal wealth for three hundred aristocratic families and a few merchants; but altogether England is so poor that out of fourteen million inhabitants (England and Scotland) there are six million whose annual wage is no more than one hundred francs in a country where everything costs more than in France. These people are naked and dying of hunger, as the Birmingham assembly attests. In Ireland, an agricultural country, the poverty is just as frightful if not worse.

The existence of the vicious circle is amply demonstrated: England with its system of large estates and Ireland with its small holdings have both succumbed to the same peril, that of extreme poverty. Such are the fruits of civilized industry. . . . Its principal fault is the parceling out of land; but in countries of large-scale agriculture there are a hundred other vices which produce the same result, the poverty of the multitude.

And in France, the so-called *belle France*, is the worker less wretched than in England? You must see first hand the food, dress and lodging of the inhabitants of such industrious provinces as Auvergne, Limousin, Cévennes, Brittany, the Alps, the Jura, and even in the great manufacturing centers like Lyon and Paris. Just take a look at the condition of the workers in the glass-works in the Faubourg Saint-Antoine.

Switzerland, so widely praised for its liberty and its morality, exhibits the same degree of poverty even in its most laborious cantons. No one is as poor as the workers of Saint Gall and the other Swiss manufacturing centers. Incidentally Switzerland sells men to all sovereigns. If the Swiss peasant were happy in his homeland, he would not sell himself in order to get out.

In the barbarian or mixed countries the working class is equally wretched. The Chinese and the Hindus, justly renowned for their agriculture and their manufactures, are so poor that the people eat just one meal a day, a small ration of rice cooked in water without salt. Then, to satisfy their hunger, these people eat the vermin which cover them. This is the frightful result of parceled out industry, organized according to the family system or the swarm of small households.

This mode of industry is evidently a mockery of nature against the civilized and barbarian peoples. It is clear that an excess of work brings them to the same poverty as does excessive idleness. The apathetic Spaniard has at least one advantage: he is assured of finding work when he wants it. There is no such guarantee for the wage-workers in France and England and in the industrious provinces of Spain like Catalonia.

What good are industrial prowess and economic theory if the results they yield are always contrary to their promises and if they leave the people worse off than the savages who, even when poor, have a triple advantage over our wage-earners:

liberty, freedom from worry, and the hope of abundance after a good hunt. In our countries, on the contrary, the members of the productive class spend the best years of their lives trying to earn enough so as not to die of starvation in old age. There are very few workers who attain that goal, and even those who do are wretched, for they acquire the means to live comfortably only at an age when life has lost its savor.

Recent events such as the plethoric industrial crisis of 1826 have so thoroughly dissipated illusions that the economists are beginning to denounce their own science.

A dispute broke out not long ago between two of the chieftans of Economism, Messrs. Say and Sismondi.[2] When the latter returned from a visit to the perfectibilities across the channel, he declared that England and Ireland, despite their colossal industrial development, are no more than great dens of paupers and that the promises of industrialism still belong to the realm of chïmeras.

His colleague, J.-B. Say, attempted to defend his science. But to speak frankly that poor science was confounded by the plethoric catastrophe of 1826. The crisis has shown the commercial system to be incompetent and evil. . . .[3]

Another economist, M. Charles Dupin,[4] has very recently claimed that the poverty of civilization could be ended if the working people were better trained and educated. He proposed the provinces of the north of France as a model for the south.

---

[2] Both Jean-Baptiste Say (1767–1832) and Simonde de Sismondi (1773–1842) began their careers as orthodox liberal political economists. Say remained faithful to the doctrines of Adam Smith and Ricardo. But, as Fourier's comments suggest, Sismondi became increasingly disturbed by the human consequences of industrial crisis and eventually elaborated a strong, if rather despairing, critique of some of the main tenets of economic liberalism.

[3] Although Fourier attributed most of the economic ills of his time to the machinations of the merchant, he recognized that the main cause of the international economic crisis of 1826 was overproduction. Much admired by Marx, his analysis of this "plethoric crisis" may be found in *OC*, VI, 392–396.

[4] Charles Dupin (1784–1873) was a French liberal economist and mathematician.

His work includes a map on which the illustrious Touraine, the garden of France, is colored black for its unenlightened attitudes and its refusal to clear its land.

By way of reply, let us examine the happiness of the provinces of northern France. Amiens, Cambray and Saint-Quentin are celebrated industrial centers. Right between these three cities, however, in the area around Péronne, you can see the peasant of Picardy living in such poverty in his earthen hut that he does not even have a bed. In winter-time he sleeps on a pile of leaves which rapidly turns into a worm-infested compost heap. When his family wakes up, they have to pull the worms out of their flesh. The food served in these huts is just as elegant as the furniture.

This is the condition of the people who manufacture the muslins and kashmir shawls which protect our fine ladies. The workers in the hills around Saint Etienne who make famous ribbon finery have been reduced to the same state of poverty. A master manufacturer there would refuse work to a family which wished to eat anything besides turnips or potatoes.

Such is the result of excessive competition: the more active the mercantile rivalry, the more the worker is starved and victimized by the greedy manufacturer. Striving to cut wages so as to increase his own wealth, the manufacturer obliges his competitors to follow his example. The worker, who has no other choices but starvation or the gallows, is forced to accept even the most thankless work. It is by means of this increasing pauperization of the worker that such renowned manufacturing centers as Saint-Gall, Roubaix and Nîmes manage to meet the competition of England, a country which, with its mummeries of liberty, has surpassed all other nations in the art of torturing the productive class and which is little by little imposing its way on its competitors. The result of our frenzy of industrialism is thus to reduce the peoples of Europe to a state of poverty equal to that of the Chinese and the Hindustanis.

Do the masses of a nation derive any profit from this frenzy of industrialism, from this pauperization of the working classes? No. The only people who profit from this odious system are a few manufacturers and a few parasitical speculators and mercantile cossacks. The proprietor and those who work the land gain nothing.

Occasionally the economists acknowledge some of the vices of industrialism. Both M. Malthus and Steuart have recognized the part played by the unlimited increase in population in the vicious circle of civilized industry. M. de Sismondi has likewise denounced the phenomenon of inverse consumption which, catering to the whims and refinements of the idle, denies the original producer a share in the goods he has created.

What is the point of acknowledging two symptoms of evil when there are a hundred others? Our system of agricultural fragmentation and commercial trickery is a vicious circle which consists of more than a hundred ills. They must all be denounced; half-hearted criticism only serves to worsen the evil.

A comprehensive analysis of all the ills of the present economic system would show that any one of them is bound to prove fatal to modern industry and that, instead of illusory and limited reforms, the whole system must be attacked. Such an analysis would show the necessity of devising an order based on different foundations than those of the present system. It would show the necessity of establishing a societary and truthful order in the place of the system of fragmentation and deceit which is called perfectible civilization. . . .

In criticizing civilized industry, I am far from endorsing the views of the fools who would like to tear down the factories. I merely wish to prepare men's minds for an examination of the societary mechanism, or the system of industrial attraction and guaranteed truth, which will bring a four-fold increase in economic productivity . . . and establish a system of distribution which will assure the lower classes of a proportional share in the increased wealth and a *minimum* sufficient for a decent life. . . .

The mechanism of civilized industry is distorted in its four bases:

In *production* by the parceling out of agricultural and domestic functions and the subdivision into families. For the family is the smallest, the most inefficient and most wasteful of groups: the family system often requires one hundred workers to do a job which might be done by a single individual under societary management.

In *consumption* where the affluence of the idle takes precedence over the well-being of the producers, peasants and workers who are so poor that they have no share in the wealth that they have produced. The French peasant sells his wheat in order to eat cheap barley-bread; he sells his good wine and keeps only the worst for himself.

In *distribution* by a competition in poverty which tends to reduce wages and to turn starved workers into serfs. Civilized industry brings increased prosperity only to the wealthy classes.

In *circulation* or exchange by the independence accorded to the intermediaries known as merchants, who become the owners of the goods they handle when they should only be subordinate agents. They excel at falsehood; they adulterate foodstuffs and raw materials; and they do harm to every branch of industry with their schemes in hoarding, speculation, bankruptcy, and usury. All of their maneuvers serve only to despoil agriculture and property and to concentrate all wealth in the hands of the great merchants.

It is thus evident that civilized industry is at the antipodes of reason; it is a world gone wrong, a faulty mechanism resting on four faulty bases.

The first economists, the Smiths and Quesnays, could not have failed to perceive this disorder; they should have denounced it, condemned the whole system of civilized industry, and attempted to devise another system which would rest on four bases contrary to those which I have just analyzed.

—*De l'anarchie industrielle et scientifique*
(Paris, 1847), pp. 18–25 (written in 1828).

## CIVILIZED WORK IS UNPRODUCTIVE

Even though civilized writers have composed innumerable treatises on political economy, nothing is more ridiculous than the confusion that characterizes work in civilization. In our societies the healthiest men may often be seen performing tasks fit for four-year-old girls. In the streets of our large cities you can see strong men busy shelling peas, peeling vegetables, and cutting paper to make candy wrappers. These trifling tasks should be performed by the groups of little children who help out in the kitchens and workshops. . . .

Is it not also common in all our cities to see strong young men of twenty who spend their days armed with napkins and carrying about cups of coffee and glasses of lemonade? If men of twenty or thirty had to perform such trifling functions in the combined order, then four-year-old children would have to do the plowing!

This strange division of labor is characteristic of all work in the incoherent order. Should a young man of twenty spend his time crouched in an office and scrivening? If the young men of Harmony performed such sedentary functions, then the old men would have to go out and work the pumps to water the gardens!

In Harmony all scissors and needle work will be performed by a few women who are too young or too old to assume more arduous tasks. All the bookkeeping will be done by aged men or women, who, possessing cool heads and lacking the strength necessary for active work, will enjoy keeping the accounts of the Phalanx. They will be sorry to leave the groups devoted to outdoor work; but in their declining years they will be delighted to participate in this way in the activities of the groups to which they formerly belonged.

The source of the industrial confusion which prevails in our societies is that an individual has just one profession which is itself divided into some thirty branches. In the combined order the individual practices just one branch in thirty different professions. For example, if a group which works with fruit trees gathers to rid the trees of caterpillars, two-thirds of its members may be absent. The absentees would include all those who have an aversion for this part of the job. The next day the caterpillars will have vanished, and the absentees will congratulate their colleagues all the more heartily in that they took no part in the task despite their great concern for the success of the fruit trees. The diverse members of a group will thus be continually congratulating each other; each will encourage the others in their work because each member will perform only the task that pleases him. Each will soon excel at the specific task which he has chosen. But if men are forced, as they are in civilization, to perform all the branches of a job, they will soon succumb to the disgust and imperfection which are associated with all work in civilization.

One of the principal savings of the combined order will result from the gathering together of all minor domestic jobs or household tasks. Let's take for example the handling of liquids like milk and wine.

In a civilized village there may be a hundred women who waste a whole morning going to town to sell a jug of milk. Instead of these hundred women, a Phalanx will send a carriage bearing a barrel of milk and accompanied by just one man to take care of the horse and the carriage. We might add that to pick up and purchase the milk brought to the city by a hundred village women, civilization sends out three hundred servant-girls who work in three hundred incoherent kitchens. So it takes one hundred village women and three hundred servants to perform a task which can be done by one man and a horse; for when a barrel of milk arrives in a Phalanx, it will go straight to a warehouse divided into three or four categories, as I shall explain further on.

Such prodigious savings of labor will mark all aspects of life in the combined order, and they will make our most economical forms of work seem ridiculous. A wine-making community which now has two or three hundred poorly tended vats will have five or six vats to divide the wine according to its quality. Sometimes a given field will be jointly owned by several Phalanxes; then the whole yield may be fermented in the same vat and the wine divided proportionately among the Phalanxes. Thus it may be said without exaggeration that most of the work in the combined order will involve only a twentieth or a thirtieth of the number of workers who perform the same tasks in the incoherent order.

*—PM*, 1; *OC*, x, 141–143

### "UNPRODUCTIVE CLASSES IN CIVILIZATION"

What is the number of *active* and *positive* workers today? It amounts to no more than one-third of the population. . . . If one compares work done in civilization and in Harmony, it will be evident that TWO-THIRDS of our population consist of *worthless* or *negative* workers. Here is the list:

## TABLE OF UNPRODUCTIVE CLASSES IN CIVILIZATION

| Domestic Parasites | Social Parasites | Accessory Parasites |
|---|---|---|
| 1. Women | 4. Armies | 9. Unemployed |
| 2. Children | 5. Fiscal Agents | 10. Sophists |
| 3. Servants | 6. Manufactures | 11. Idlers |
| | 7. Commerce | 12. Drop-Outs |
| | 8. Transportation | |

Y  Agents of Positive Destruction
X  Agents of Negative Creation

Domestic Parasites. 1. Three-fourths of the WOMEN who live in cities and half of those who live in the country. They are unproductive because they are absorbed in household work which entails the wasteful duplication of functions. This is why the political economists consider a woman's working day to have only one-fifth the value of a man's.

2. Three-fourths of all CHILDREN. City children are utterly useless and those who live in the country are only slightly useful, given their ineptitude and mischievousness.[5]

3. Three-fourths of all household SERVANTS. Most of the work that they do, not counting gardening, is unnecessary. This is especially true of kitchen work. Half of all grooms, manservants and workers in luxury trades will be superfluous in association because they owe their jobs to the civilized system of piecemeal labor.

[5] One day I watched five children tending four cows. (More herders than cows.) How well were they doing their job? They were letting their cows get into green, unripened wheat. I advised the first child to take the cow nearest him out of the wheat. He replied: "It's not my cow." I said the same thing to the next child and got the same answer. From what they said, it seemed that none of the four cows belonged to any of the five cowherds. I went on my way, shrugging my shoulders at our economic perfectibilities. . . . (Fourier's note.)

These three classes of household members form a separate category in the series of parasites. They will play no role whatsoever in the societary state. In that order men and women will be asked to perform only those domestic tasks for which they are suited. This will reduce to one-fourth or one-fifth the number of people required by the current system of isolated households and incoherent families.

Social Parasites. 4. ARMIES and NAVIES divert strong young men from useful work and consume most of the state's revenue from taxes. They encourage idleness and depravity by forcing young men to waste the best years of their lives, and by depriving them of the chance to learn useful occupations. The apparatus of men and machines which is called an army spends its time producing nothing and waiting to be used for destructive purposes. . . .

5. FISCAL and ADMINISTRATIVE AGENTS. In France the customs service alone absorbs 24,000 men. Add to that the government tax collectors and the other armies of clerks, watchmen, gamekeepers, spies, etc. All the members of overlapping or useless administrative bodies belong in this category. Fiscal agents, to cite only one example, will be superfluous in an order in which each Phalanx will pay its taxes at a stated time upon the simple notice of the minister.

6. Clearly half of all reputedly useful MANUFACTURES are *relatively* unproductive owing to the poor quality of the goods they produce. If all manufactured goods were of a uniformly high quality, losses due to depreciation could be cut in half and production costs would decline accordingly. Costs might be reduced by three-fourths in work undertaken for the government which everyone conspires to defraud.

7. Nine-tenths of all MERCHANTS and commercial agents are social parasites. Under the societary method of truthful commerce the exchange and distribution of goods will require only one-tenth of the personnel employed by the present system. . . .

8. Two-thirds of the agents employed in land and sea TRANSPORT are unproductive, although in a different sense from the members of the commercial class. They transport goods by unnecessarily circuitous routes and engage in risky ventures, notably

on the seas where their incompetence and imprudence multiplies shipwrecks. Let us put *smuggling* in this category. It often requires ten times the travel and men that direct transportation would entail. In order to get from Dover to Calais, drygoods have been known to pass through Hamburg, Frankfort, Basel and Paris. That makes five hundred leagues for seven, all for the equilibrium of commerce and perfectibility.

Accessory Parasites. 9. Those who are legally, accidentally or secretly UNEMPLOYED are accessory parasites. This category includes people who are idle either because they are out of work or because they are relaxing. If labor were made attractive, they would refuse to be inactive. But now, on the contrary, they double the idleness legally permitted by lazing through *Holy Monday*, which is the most ruinous of all the holy days since it is observed 52 times a year in factory towns.

Let us add guild holidays, revolutionary holidays, carnival days, patron saints' days, marriage celebrations, and many other similar festivities. People will no longer want to observe these holidays in a society whose work sessions will be more enjoyable than civilization's festivals and dances.

In a discussion of unemployment accidental stoppages should also be taken into account. If the master is out of sight, his workers will stop at the slightest pretext. Let a man or a cat go by and there they are, all in a flutter, foreman and workmen, leaning on their shovels and gaping in order to pass the time. Forty times, fifty times a day, they lose five minutes in this manner. Their week hardly amounts to four whole days. There is so much idleness without industrial attraction!

10. The SOPHISTS and all those who thrive on controversy are accessory parasites. This category includes those who read their writings and are inspired by them to get involved in party intrigues and unproductive cabals. Controversy muddles every subject; it produces political disturbances and distracts people from their work.

The list of controversialists and sophists would be much longer than one might think, even if it were limited to jurisprudence which seems to be an excusable sophism. Let us suppose that in the societary order there will be only one-twentieth as

many lawsuits as there are now, and that the means of settling
these few disputes will be as simple as today's are cumbersome.
The conclusion is that nineteen-twentieths of the members of the
bar are parasites, as are the litigants and their witnesses. Of course
there are a great many other sophistical parasites, beginning with
the economists who rant against parasitism while they practice it.

11. The IDLE, the men of good breeding who spend their
lives doing nothing, are accessory parasites. And let us not forget
their valets and all those who serve them. The man who serves an
unproductive person is himself unproductive. Such is the case of
the solicitors, of whom there are as many as 60,000 in the city
of Paris alone. All qualified voters likewise belong in this category.

Prisoners constitute a class whose idleness is involuntary. The
same may be said of the sick. Among native Harmonians there
will not be a tenth as many sick people as one finds in civilization. For, while sickness is unavoidable, it can be greatly reduced.
Out of ten sick people today, nine are suffering from the effects
of civilized food and eating habits. With all due respect to our
doctors, these nine men would be healthy in the societary state.

12. The DROP-OUTS, people in open rebellion against work,
laws, customs and established practices. This category includes
those who run lotteries and gambling-houses (true social poisons),
adventurers, prostitutes, vagrants, beggars, pick-pockets, brigands
and other drop-outs. Their number is increasing and, to control
them, we are obliged to maintain a police force which is just as
unproductive as they are.

Pivotal Classes. Y. Agents of POSITIVE DESTRUCTION: those
who organize famine and plague, or bring about war. The civilized order does all it can to protect the agents of famine and
plague. It dotes on speculators and swindlers. It encourages any
kind of invention capable of increasing the ravages of war: Con-
greve rockets, Lamberti cannons, etc.

X. Agents of NEGATIVE CREATION. I have already proven that
they are excessively numerous and that most of their projects,
such as the building of walls and fences, are unproductive in a
relative sense. Some of their accomplishments are illusory due to
their ignorance and incompetence. Take, for instance, buildings

that collapse, bridges that must be relocated and roads in constant need of mending. Others are indirectly destructive: a hundred workers appear to be doing useful work clearing a forest, but in fact they are in the process of ravaging the countryside. Their work does more harm to the land than the ravages of war, which may be repaired. Others have harmful consequences like the repercussive scourges of which political economy is so proud. Such is the invention of a new fashion in dress which may reduce twenty thousand workers to a state of poverty and eventual unrest.

*—OC*, IV, 173–179

### THE BUCOLIC MYTH

These tableaux [describing farming operations in Harmony] would be charming merely in a simplistic way if their *dramatis personae* were today's starving wretches whose fate we should pity. They would present a picture of the beautiful isolated from the good and would be in accordance with the method of civilization which is able to create the *beautiful* only at the expense of the *good*. Thus, everything that civilization offers as beautiful in gardening and architecture is unproductive. And, on the other hand, those places where the good can be found—such as factories and cultivated fields—are a distressing spectacle for a sensitive man. In these places one can see starving farmers and workers, three-fourths of whom do not eat enough to satisfy their hunger. On the hottest summer days they have neither a glass of wine to ward off sun-stroke nor a mobile tent to shade them while they harvest. Meanwhile, in the neighboring town, loafers and gapers gather together under gaudy flounced tents and gorge themselves on ices, fine liqueurs and cool drinks. . . .

One forgets the meanness and poverty of civilized agriculture as one listens to the poets describing rustic pleasures. Delille,[6] freely using the freedom poets have been granted to lie, assures us that the fields are places of ineffable delight and that we cannot SAVOR them. That is how he puts it.

---

[6] Jacques Delille (1738–1813) was a classical nature-poet much admired in his time.

But few can enjoy their touching delights,
We need more than our senses to savor them properly.

What does he find so touching about the sensual delights of
a band of workers who, exposed to the hot summer sun, suffer
from hunger and thirst? What are the delights of men who at
noon dolefully eat a crust of black bread with a glass of water,
and sit by themselves because the man who has a piece of rancid
bacon does not want to share it with his companions? What is
there to SAVOR in the privations of these poor people? To fob off
such pastoral buffoonery Delille needs all of his prestige. In matters of morality, Delille is another CHAPELAIN, "Who, with his
heavy hammer, pulverizes common sense."

At the beginning of his poem Delille calls for a "practiced
eye and delicate senses," to taste the pleasures of the countryside.
A few pages later he would exclude the senses from the game and
have us "savor" the touching delights which, as he himself recognizes, are not very pleasing for the senses.

The soul does not find these delights any more tasty. In fact,
300 families living in a fairly large town cultivating 300 fields of
cabbage would derive from their work nothing that could stimulate friendship, love, ambition or the 10th, 11th, or 12th passions,
the distributive passions.[7]

12th. There would be no COMPOSITE intrigue. In their miserable fenced-in gardens there is nothing to charm either body or
soul. The worker is driven only by the dismal motives of escaping
from starvation and providing himself with a few bad heads of
cabbage to support his starving wife and children. (Not to mention the motive of watching out for his neighbors who try to
steal his cabbages at night.) All of these calculations are hardly
the enthusiasm required by the 12th passion.

10th. There would be no CABALISTIC intrigue. When he
grows his bad cabbages "the peasant" is not inspired by rivalry.
It does not occur to him to work with a single type of cabbage
nor to form a club with fellow growers. His only goal is to fill
his poor philosophical pot with the most detestable cabbages
while saying: "May God always grant us these."

[7] On the distributive passions see below pp. 218–220 and 275–283.

11th. There would be no intrigue for the BUTTERFLY. While eating his wretched soup made with cabbages hardened for want of irrigation he cannot use different varieties nor "savor" during the course of the year a hundred kinds of cabbages from his own district as well as those near-by. These varieties would constitute a new enticement for the farmer.

—*OC*, IV, 498–501

### THE RIGHT TO WORK DENIED

Our social compacts are utterly unable to provide the poor man with a decent level of subsistence consistent with his education. They cannot guarantee him the first of the natural rights, the RIGHT TO WORK![8] By these words "natural rights," I do not mean the chimeras known as "liberty" and "equality." The poor man does not aim so high; he does not wish to be the equal of the rich; he would be quite content to eat at the table of their valets. The common people are even more reasonable than you wish them to be. They will consent to submission, to inequality and to servitudes, provided you can find a way to aid them when political vicissitudes have deprived them of their work, reduced them to famine, to opprobrium and despair. It is just at this point that they are abandoned by political philosophy. What has it done to assure them in bad times not of help but merely of the chance to do the customary work on which their subsistence depends. Among the lower and even the educated classes there are hosts of wretched individuals who vainly seek employment while their fellow creatures live contentedly in idleness and abundance. Why does philosophy jest with these poor creatures by offering them the rights of sovereignty when they demand only the rights of servitude, the right to work for the pleasure of the idle?

Will you tell the pauper that there is a place for him in the

[8] Although the right to work was recognized by Turgot and in the French Constitution of 1793, Fourier has frequently been described as the first writer in the socialist tradition to formulate the right to work. See for example Engels' letter to Bernstein, May 23, 1884, in Karl Marx and Friedrich Engels, *Selected Correspondence* (Moscow, n.d.), p. 447, and Charles Gide and Charles Rist, *Histoire des doctrines économiques*, 6th ed. (Paris, 1944), p. 332. The present text, which is an excerpt from one of Fourier's earliest manuscripts, dates from no later than 1806.

army or on the farm? Are these satisfactory expedients for a father burdened with children or for women who are even more likely than men to lack work and to earn so little that they can provide for themselves only through prostitution? Is a man who has spent his youth studying the liberal arts fit to bivouac on the snow or to drive a plow? To offer him the plow, the rucksack and the workhouse is to present him with the cup of hemlock. These things are more repulsive to an educated man than death itself. To be forced, after having lived among the educated class, to mingle with the gross populace is to sink living into the tomb. Is it through such remedies that your social compacts are to surpass the bounty of nature? To equal nature's bounty you must give us at least what it gives to the savages and the wild animals, a job which pleases them and to which they have become accustomed during the course of their lives, a job with creatures whose society suits them. Similarly, give the civilized man a job which is his own inalienable property and which he can practice as he likes, when he likes, without taking orders from an unjust superior, without mixing with people whose manners and customs are loathsome to him. Give the civilized man the same privileges as those of the savage who cannot be deprived of the right to the same sort of work as the chiefs of his horde, the right to hunt and fish and to keep his catch for himself and not for a master.[9] Finally, with all your learning, do as much for the pauper as nature does for the savages and the wild animals without the aid of your sciences.

—*OC*, XII, 624–625

[9] Fourier maintained that man in the savage state possessed seven natural rights: the right to hunt, to fish, to gather food, to pasture animals, to steal from strangers, to form alliances with his fellows, to be free from worry. Civilized man had been deprived of all these rights and compensated with an illusory political liberty and other "reveries and gasconades." In the present text Fourier is not arguing that the rights of the savage should simply be restored but rather that they should be reformulated in such a way as to provide modern, industrial man with a freedom "equivalent" to that enjoyed by the savages. See *OC*, III, 163–187 and the first of the texts translated below under the heading "Work and Compulsion."

# 3

# WORK, ANXIETY, AND FREEDOM

After health and wealth nothing is more precious than freedom. But there are two sorts of freedom: physical freedom and social freedom. The second variety is not the one that the sophists wish to procure for us.

The sophists are used to considering nature in a simplistic manner, and they have allowed their mania for simplification to confuse the debate about freedom. They have not been able to distinguish between the simple, compound and bi-compound varieties of freedom. For more than a thousand years they neglected the first of the freedoms, material or bodily freedom. It was the Christian religion which finally intervened powerfully to emancipate the slaves. But before Christianity the philanthropists of antiquity were used to turning human beings into beasts of burden and to obliging slaves to kill each other in mass combats for the amusement of the virtuous citizens of Rome. When the Romans did not wish to see twenty thousand slaves slaughtered en masse, they had two hundred massacred one by one in gladiatorial combats. These performances repeated with more civic pomp by the virtuous republicans of Sparta. To reduce their slave population the Spartans would gather two thousand of their most faithful slaves, crown them with flowers, parade them around the city, and then slaughter them. The Spartans dispatched their most faithful slaves in this way because they did not want to see them die of slow torture in the galleys. Such were, for a thousand years, the noble ideas of Philosophy about physical freedom. Every good republican applauded these massacres; and if Christianity had not intervened, things might still be at the same point.

If someone had consulted the oracles of wisdom, the Platos and the Aristotles about the emancipation of the slaves, they would have replied with the fine word "impossibility" which France has inherited. The enlightened Aristotle was so sure that slaves were beasts of burden, creatures outside the human race, that he laid down the principle that "There is no virtue proper to a slave." He wished to reduce them to the status of brute beasts, devoid of the rational faculty and of virtue itself. . . .

Under the last Caesars the philosophers saw the granting of bodily freedom, which they had so long regarded as impossible, was in fact quite feasible. They should then have recognized the error of their science with its assumptions about impossibility and its conviction that "nature is limited to known means." But they learned nothing from this lesson, and their secret indifference with regard to freedom is proven by the fact that they made no effort to analyze and spread word of the means by which emancipation had been brought about.

The ideas that people now have about emancipation are superficial and highly impractical. Thus in recent times the attempt to grant bodily freedom to the Negroes was a failure. It was in 1789 that Philosophy undertook the task. Instead of seeking appropriate methods and adopting a policy of judicious philanthropy, Philosophy relied solely on the spirit of partisan politics. It succeeded only in turning Santo Domingo into a bloody battle-ground under the banal pretext of liberty.[1]

Philosophy thus stands convicted of complete incompetence in matters related to bodily or physical freedom and the process of emancipation, whether sudden or gradual. . . . Has Philosophy shown any more skill in the matter of social freedom? This question prompts us to distinguish three kinds of freedom. . . .

1. *Simple or Physical Freedom* without social freedom. This is the condition of a poor man who has a very small fixed income, only enough to provide the barest necessities, a military ration. He enjoys an *active physical* freedom because he is not forced to work like the laborer who has no independent income. Yet his passions are completely unsatisfied. Phebon is quite free to go to the opera. But it costs a crown to get in and Phebon has only enough money to feed himself poorly and to dress himself shabbily. He is free to aspire to the rank of Deputy, but this requires a far greater income than he has. He may take pride in

---

[1] Fourier refers to the decade of fighting which followed the Negro rebellion led by Toussaint L'Ouverture at Haiti during the French Revolution.

the fine title of Free Man, but his social freedom is a sham. The doors of the inn and the opera are closed to him, and he has no place among the electorate.[2] He is only a passive member of society. His passions cannot express themselves in an active way, and his opinions are held in contempt.

Such a man is, nonetheless, considerably more free than the laborer who is obliged to work lest he die of starvation and who has just one day a week of *active* physical freedom—Sunday. For the other six days of the week the laborer is in a state of passive physical freedom. He has consented to the form of slavery represented by the workshop. But compared to the idleness and well-being which he enjoys on Sunday, this indirect form of slavery is not any less physically constraining than real slavery.

A distinction can also be made between active and passive social freedom. For the time being let us simply point out that the two classes of men just cited do not enjoy social freedom. They only possess simple or physical freedom: it is active for the man with a small fixed income and passive for the laborer. But the laborer is himself much better off than the slave who is denied physical freedom in both its active and its passive forms.

2. *Divergent Compound Freedom.* This includes *active physical* freedom and *active social* freedom, and it permits the complete satisfaction of the passions. Such is the condition of the savages, for they enjoy both these freedoms. A savage deliberates on questions of peace and war just like a cabinet member in civilization. He enjoys, insofar as it is possible in his horde, the complete satisfaction of his soul's passions. Above all, he enjoys freedom from worry, a good almost unknown to civilized men. It is true that he must hunt and fish for his subsistence, but this work is *attractive* to him and no threat to his active physical freedom. Work which is pleasing is not a form of servitude. While the savage would feel enslaved behind a plow, his hunting is an amusement just as selling is the merchant's amusement. Do

[2] According to the French electoral laws which prevailed in 1822, when this text was published, the right to vote was contingent upon the payment of at least 300 francs a year in direct taxes. To run for elective office a man had to pay at least 1000 francs in taxes. In all of France only 110,000 "electors" and 16,000 eligible office holders met these qualifications.

you think that a merchant has experienced physical discomfort when he spends his morning setting out a hundred bolts of cloth, lying to his clients and selling many pairs of breeches? The fatigue he may feel is a pleasure, for his work is attractive and he possesses physical freedom. This is proved by the fact that our merchant who is quite content today will be glum and surly tomorrow if the customers don't come and he is unable to lie and to sell.

We have seen that the freedom of the savage is a compound freedom because it is both physically and socially active. But these two *activities* are *divergent* from man's destiny which is attractive labor. If the savage is to enjoy *active, convergent* freedom, he must be offered attractive *productive* work which is carried out in passionate series. Then he will advance to the third type of freedom.

3. *Convergent Compound* or *Bi-compound Freedom.* This consists of two independent elements, *active physical* freedom and *active social* freedom in alliance with *attractive productive work.* It presupposes unified adherence, the individual consent of every worker—man, woman and child—and their impassioned collaboration in the performance of work and in the maintenance of the established order. This third sort of liberty is the destiny of man.

—*OC*, III, 152–156

### WORK AND COMPULSION

Freedom from worry is a form of happiness experienced by the animals. But it is also a human right, although it can only be enjoyed in Civilization by the very rich. Far from being careless of the morrow, nine-tenths of civilized men are worried about the present day because they are obliged to devote themselves to loathsome work that is forced upon them. And so on Sunday they go to cafes and places of amusement to enjoy a few moments of the sort of carefreeness that is vainly sought by so many rich men who are themselves pursued by anxiety. *"Post equitem sedet atra cura."*[3]

---

[3] "Black care rides behind the horseman." Horace, *Odes* bk. III, i, 40.

Quibblers will say that freedom from worry is a state of mind and not a right. But it becomes a right insofar as it is proscribed in the state of civilization where any sign of carelessness is held in dishonor and resolutely condemned. Let the father of a poor family try to devote himself to his own pleasures without worrying about his workshop and without saving up money for taxes, rent and future needs. Then public opinion through its criticism and the tax collector through his agents will let him know that he does not have the right to be carefree, to enjoy life like the savages and animals. They will tell him that he must master his carefree inclinations. Civilized education, moreover, intervenes systematically to fight against our desire to be carefree, a desire that will be unfettered in Harmony.

As for the Savage, it is obvious that he enjoys his carefree life and does not want to concern himself with the future. Otherwise he would worry that his children and his horde might suffer from hunger. He would then accept the agricultural implements and farming equipment that civilized governments try to offer him. But he doesn't want to give up any of his seven rights. In this he is correct because if he gave up his right to freedom from worry he would lose all his other rights one after the other. Doubtless he does this without calculating, but nature has done his thinking for him. Attraction leads him along the right path. . . .

The only plausible objection that can be raised against the happiness of the Savages is that women do not share it. Although women constitute one-half of the human race, their condition among the Savages is quite servile and very unfortunate. . . .

I have already established that the savage is more advanced than we are in his enjoyment of freedom because he has achieved *compound divergent* freedom. That is, savage males enjoy the seven natural rights. They are thus quite superior to us because we deprive the vast majority of either sex of the advantage. . . .

To indemnify a civilized man for the loss of his seven rights our publicists fob him off with a few promises and tall stories. They offer him the dignity of possessing the fine title of a free man and the happiness of living under the Charter of 1815. These silly promises don't even deserve to be called illusions. They are incapable of satisfying a wage earner who wants above all to eat to fill, to live happily and free from worry, to hunt, fish, intrigue and steal like the Savage. . . .

When it deprives man of his seven natural rights, Civilization never gives him agreed-upon equivalents. Take an unfortunate worker who has neither work nor bread and is pursued by creditors and tax collector. Ask him if he would not prefer to enjoy the rights of hunting and fishing and to have trees and flocks like the Savage? He will not fail to prefer the life of the Savage. What is he given as an equivalent? The happiness of living under the Charter. But an indigent man cannot satisfy himself by reading the Charter instead of eating dinner. To offer him that sort of compensation is to insult his poverty. He would consider himself happy if he could enjoy the seven natural rights and freedom as does the Savage. But he will not find these in the civilized order.

—*OC*, III, 167–170

The exercise of the industrial faculty which is a delight for the free animals—the beavers, bees, wasps and ants—is a torment for man, who escapes it as soon as he acquires his freedom. Civilized man aspires only to inertia, and the supreme curse which the savage shouts at his enemy is this: "May you be reduced to plowing a field!"

Since we are evidently destined by God for agricultural and manufacturing labor, how has it happened that we have thus far received from him neither a social code regulating our industrial relations nor a natural enticement to work? Why is work, which is said to be our destiny, only a torment for civilized and barbarian wage earners and slaves, who are in constant rebellion against the obligation to work and who would quit working altogether if they were no longer constrained by the fear of punishment?

Work is nonetheless a delight for many creatures such as the beavers, bees, wasps, and ants, who are perfectly free to lapse into a state of inertia. God has provided them with a social mechanism which attracts them to work and makes it a source of happiness for them. Why should he have failed to grant us a benefit which he bestows upon the animals? There is a huge difference between their work and ours! The Russians and the Algerians work out of fear of the whip or the cudgel; the English and the French work from fear of the hunger which besets their poor households. The liberty of the Greeks and Romans is much vaunted, but they had slaves who worked out of fear of being executed just like the Negroes in our colonies today. Such is the happiness of man in the absence of the *attractive industrial code;* such is the result of human laws and of the philosophical constitutions: they make humanity envy the lot of the industrious animals, for whom Attraction turns wearisome tasks into sources of pleasure.

Our happiness would be great indeed if God had treated us like these animals, if he endowed us with *passionate attraction* for the work which we are destined to perform! Our life would be but a succession of delights, and these delights would be a source of great wealth to us. In the absence of the system of attractive labor, however, we are no more than a society of slave-laborers in which a few people manage to avoid the necessity of working and form coalitions in order to remain in a state of idleness. These people are hated by the masses who share their desire to free themselves from work. This is the source of revolutionary ferment. Agitators promise to make the people happy, rich and idle; but once they have gained power, they oppress the multitude and reduce it to a more complete state of servitude in order to consolidate their own position as idlers or as managers of those who work. The latter are no different from the idlers.

In this miserable condition we are reduced to envying the lot of the animals and insects, and bemoaning a providence which appears to have regarded these creatures with a solicitude which it has not had for us. For, if one is to believe the philosophical prejudices, God has not prepared a social code for us, nor a sure industrial mechanism, nor industrial attraction to make our work enjoyable, nor even the guarantee of the work we need for our subsistence. . . .

Our philosophers would be vain in claiming that their vague wisdom and their oppressive laws could ever provide us with an attractive *industrial code*. They are vain in promising in their innumerable constitutions to make life enchanting for our wage-earners. All their theories only serve to make work more loathsome and to add to the horror of the seven lymbic calamities.

—*OC*, III, 249–251

### THE WORKER'S MISFORTUNES

The common people have not even reached the level of simple pleasure on the scale of happiness. They do not have enough for subsistence or to satisfy their sense of taste. This is the most imperious of all the senses and its satisfaction is the *sine qua non* of happiness. Rather, the common people are overwhelmed by a host of privations which transform their lives into a permanent hell. These privations constitute all of the degrees of unhappiness: simple, compound, super-compound, bi-compound, and quintessentially subversive or omni-compound, unhappiness.

As many as 16 causes of despair can be enumerated. They assail the common people of civilization in varying degrees at every moment according to the following scheme.

### MISFORTUNES OF WORKING PEOPLE

PRESSING EVIL. 1. The burden of taxes: pursuits of fiscal agents who come to extract the few pennies that a man has painfully amassed to support his unfortunate family.

2. The necessity of endangering his health in excessive and unhealthy work in order to provide for his own subsistence and that of his children.

DIRECT EVIL. 3. Repercussion of poverty, shared suffering, or the faculty of feeling the misfortunes of his family whose privations add to his own pain.

4. New misfortunes that redouble his suffering just when he thinks he has endured the worst that fate had in store for him.

5. Unjust stigma of shame: the opprobrium and defamation which plague the poor man because of his destitution and expose him to a disdain which merely increases with his penury.

INDIRECT EVIL. 6. The sight of fortune's favorites to whom chance, intrigue or crime brings affluence. This can only increase the despair of the honest worker who is led by his own probity deeper and deeper into the abyss of indigence.

7. Relative regression caused by the progress of luxury which increases the sufferings of the multitude in the same proportion that it creates new means of pleasure for the rich. Deprived of life's necessities, the civilized worker is tormented by a display of increased affluence which the savage does not see.

8. Frustration in seeking legal redress through lawsuits and other claims. He lacks the money and the credit to pay lawyers' fees.

ACCESSORY EVIL. 9. Social snare, or the constant danger of being cheated by his fellow citizens, of meeting nothing but a swarm of cheats or disguised enemies in the social world.

10. Poverty anticipated in the present, or the fear of unemployment, which never troubles the savages and the animals.

11. Scientific mockery, or the illusory help of literary charlatans who, while promising the people that they will soften their misfortunes, overwhelm them with new calamities.

12. The trap of morality, or the persecution he attracts when he practices virtue, because virtue shames perverse rivals, excites them to calumny which is always well-received in civilization.

PIVOTS. Y. Loathing for work, and deprivation of the prerogatives enjoyed by animals such as beavers, bees, etc., who are attracted to work and find their happiness in that work which is the civilized man's torture.

YY. Betrayal of nature, or the martyrdom of attraction. The goad of numerous desires which the civilized man cannot satisfy and which lead him to ruin; whereas nature endows animals with only those passions which are suited to guide them and which they have the right to satisfy.

TRANSITIONS. KK. Wearisome reflections on the past, the memory of numerous miseries already endured and yet to be feared.

K. Suffering anticipated in the future, or the awareness that in his old age, in the distant future, he will meet with increased misfortunes and be unable to escape them.

Such is the lot of the common people whom the sophists describe as making great strides toward perfectibility. In fact their condition is worse than that of the wild animals. The lion, for example, is well clothed, well armed, and takes its subsistence where it finds it; it is a hundred times more fortunate than the common people of civilization who are dragged off to the gallows if they ask for any one of their natural rights or for the primordial social right to a *minimum* of subsistence.

Is someone going to object that the common people are so brutish that they are incapable of feeling the enormity of their misfortunes? In that case just what is the significance of the pretension of our sages to spread enlightenment, to give us delicate senses and to refine our minds' perceptions of sensations? Here one might be inclined to praise the obscurantists who want to brutalize the common people. Since all of civilization turns in a vicious circle, the obscurantists may well be right in more than one case.

—*OC*, IV, 191–193

### LOATHSOME WORK: GOD'S CURSE

"We must love work," say our sages. Well! How can we? What is lovable about work in civilization? For nine-tenths of all men work procures nothing but profitless boredom. Rich men, consequently, find work loathsome and do only the easiest and most lucrative kinds of work such as managing companies. How can you make a poor man love work when you are not even able to make work agreeable for the rich? This would require elegant workshops, division of tasks and courteous, loyal, and polished fellow-workers. All of these conditions are impractical in civilization. They can exist only when work is organized in passionate series.

In addition to all the obvious drawbacks of civilized work such as the filthiness of certain workshops, the coarseness of the peasants, theft, complications, isolation, boredom, the risk of loss, etc., there is a still greater drawback. That is the necessity of watching over all phases of a particular kind of work and often of performing all of them oneself. A certain rich man, for example, would very much like to grow flowers and fruits. But he hasn't the courage to order seeds and plants because he is afraid of being cheated by the merchants. (He most certainly will be cheated.) He is discouraged at the prospect that a negligent son or son-in-law may allow his plantings to perish after him. He is surrounded by maladroit, careless, thieving, and hateful workers; by mocking and ignorant neighbors who ridicule his work; by children who come and spitefully lay waste to his flower beds; and by women who devastate his gardens even more stupidly. For women know nothing about flowers and think that they are doing the flower-grower a great honor by cutting and chopping up his flower beds, when they are not able to recognize the different species nor praise the grower intelligently. How can we make work agreeable for the poor man when all kinds of obstacles conspire to disgust even the rich?

*—OC,* IV, 520–521

Work, say the Scriptures, is a punishment for man: Adam and his children were condemned to earn their bread by the sweat of their brows. Before the infliction of this punishment, man's primeval happiness consisted in having nothing to do, as in the case now for our populace on Sunday. It is thus well recognized, even by religion, that civilized work is a state of unhappiness for man. Religion admits that man is closer to nature when he indulges in enchanting illusion rather than when he listens to philosophy's promises about the charms of life in a thatched hut. Yet when Scripture told us the truth concerning the unhappiness attached to work today, it did not say that this punishment would not end one day, nor did it claim that man would never be able to return to the happy state he first enjoyed.

*—OC,* IV, 554–555

# III

## *Philosophy, Morality, and Sex in Civilization*

I once saw some philosophers making fun of the 200,000 volumes of theology which are assembled in the main gallery of the Bibliothèque de Paris. They were expressing amazement at the folly of the human mind which had spent eighteen centuries spawning visions that were reduced to nothing by a glimmer of good sense. This was in 1800, a time when theology was completely useless. I told these philosophers who were so amused by the disaster of the 200,000 theological volumes that the 400,000 volumes lining the walls of the philosophical gallery would soon meet the same fate.

*—PM*, 1; *OC*, x, 21

Fourier was seldom able to conceal the personal rancor which motivated his sweeping condemnation of philosophy and philosophers. Condemned to obscurity and genteel poverty, his works either ignored or reviewed contemptuously, Fourier hated the successful philosophers and publicists of his time with all of the energy of a genius whose opponents refuse even to argue with him. He probably found some comfort in scribbling devastating ripostes on scraps of paper. Was not "every new discovery attacked at first: vaccine, steam, Columbus"? Were not his enemies cowards? "They call it nonsense because they want to avoid combat."[1] Although he was usually able to control his rage in his published writings, Fourier's bitter frustration was never far from the surface.

The first group of texts in this section provides an introduction to Fourier's anti-philosophical polemic. The jealousy which often inspired his *ad personam* attacks should not be allowed to obscure the value of his observations. Perhaps we should not take him too seriously when he charges that the *philosophes* assembled behind the "banners of deceit, that is, of Commerce," for motives of personal gain. On the other hand, his assault on the philosophers was often effective and revealing precisely because Fourier refused to argue philosophically: he would not discuss political ideas in the abstract. His fundamental accusation was that civilized philosophy was not authentic. Its doctrines had no real relationship to the way men lived in the world, and most of the "philosophical cabal" were great hypocrites, like the wealthy Seneca, who intended their fine doctrines of moderation, self-denial, or docility for the edification of men less fortunate than they. But the ills of society were too obvious to be ignored. When abstract philosophical concepts like "equality of rights," or "fraternity" were judged in the light of social reality, they were exposed as chimeras, mere words without meaning. As Fourier argued in typical fashion, it was impossible for the sentiment of sweet fraternity to exist between the refined sybarite and the coarse peasant who was covered with vermin, afflicted by mange, and infected with typhus.

Fourier's critique of civilization was all of one piece, and the texts on "Marriage and the Family System" show that he regarded civilized sexual mores as marked by the same spirit of fraud, duplicity, and anarchic individualism that prevailed in the economic sphere. Just as the principle of laissez faire had provided merchants with a philosophical sanction for dishonest business dealings, so, maintained Fourier, had the repressive institution of marriage fostered universal deception and sexual

---

[1] AN, 10AS 21.

dishonesty. The lofty abstractions of political economy cloaked monopoly, exploitation, and social irresponsibility; but civilization's celebration of life in the "happy family" barely concealed what everyone knew. Marriage was a state of "domestic warfare" in which the "virtuous wife" and the "faithful husband" were no less determined to deceive one another than the two parties to a business transaction. Since neither partner gained by the family system, it could only be described as "the work of a third sex which seeks to torment the other two."

The "Hierarchy of Cuckoldom" is probably the best known of Fourier's satirical attacks on civilized sexual behavior. But it is more than a brilliant dissection of adultery, and it should be read along with his uncondescending rehabilitation of the rights of women. For the "Hierarchy," like all of Fourier's discussions of love in civilization, has a sociological dimension and a revolutionary purpose. As an easy mark for the satirist's ridicule, the horned spouse had long been a stock figure in literature and popular entertainments. But Fourier, even while ridiculing the cuckold, transformed him into a sociological datum. He did not draw up his taxonomy of marital infidelity merely to prove that men were faithless, women fickle, and moral pretensions always fraudulent. His social satire, in other words, was not just a cynical exposure of human frailty, but rather an attempt to prove that civilized institutions were ridiculous and evil because they thwarted basic human inclinations.

The taste for variety in sexual partners was perfectly natural, Fourier insisted. Like many other so-called perversions, this penchant was a source of social disruption only because a false morality had warped its development and forced men and women to practice deceit. As these texts show, Fourier believed that a consideration of sexual practices in antiquity as well as a comparative study of non-European cultures would prove that in other eras and other societies men had ordered their amorous relationships in ways that were imperfect but more in harmony with natural penchants than the sexual system imposed by Christian Europe. The new social order which he proposed to establish would be based on the liberation and utilization of erotic energies that had long been ignored, misused, or misdirected.

Fourier's critique of civilized commerce, work, love, and philosophy forms a coherent whole which won the admiration of many nineteenth century radicals who had little sympathy for the constructive aspects of his vision. In his own presentation of the doctrine, however, Fourier rarely allowed his social criticism to stand by itself. Generally he placed his accounts of the vices and suffering of civilization in close juxtaposition with his descriptions of the delights of Harmony. On other occasions (notably in his early writings) he attempted to subsume the critique of civilization within a panoramic vision of the whole course of human history. The final group of texts in this section illustrates some of the facets—and ambiguities—of Fourier's historical vision.

By and large Fourier's elaborate cyclical-stadial view of history played a decorative rather than an essential role in his doctrine. He never explored its pessimistic implications and he used it primarily as a means of dramatizing the ills of his own age. It is true that several generations of Marxist historians have followed Engels in maintaining that Fourier's "masterly" use of historical dialectics represented a great contribution to socialist thought. But their case often seems to rest on little more than a few verbal parallels between Fourier's writings and those of Marx. Fourier did describe civilization as caught in a "vicious circle" of "contradictions"; he maintained that societies give rise to the forces that destroy them; and he often talked of a "class war." His concept of class, however, was at best rudimentary, while the "struggle" which he discerned was simply the war between rich and poor, or between the merchant and his victims. Some of the texts in the final group also suggest that, at least in his initial writings, Fourier was groping toward a theory of social change in which sexual rather than economic relations played the decisive role. But Fourier could permit himself to be inconsistent on this matter. Speculations on historical development were secondary to a man who expected the collapse of civilization to come about through the intervention of a single wealthy capitalist.

# 1

# CIVILIZED PHILOSOPHY

Celebrated philosophers have long recognized the existence of a great unfathomed mystery; they have understood that man had failed in the study of nature and missed the paths which would have led to individual and collective happiness. In ages less vain than ours savants have deplored this failure and looked forward to a time when the human race would arrive at a happier destiny than that of civilization. We find such prognostications in the writings of the most renowned authors from Socrates, who prophesied that "some day the light would descend," to Voltaire who, impatient to see it descend, exclaimed: "How dark a night still veils all nature's face."[1]

Plato and the Greek sophists expressed the same misgivings in other terms. Their utopias were an indirect accusation of the social thought of their age which could not conceive of anything beyond the systems of civilization and barbarism. These writers are regarded as oracles of wisdom, and yet from Socrates to Montaigne we find the most eminent of them deploring the insufficiency of their ideas and asking: "What do I know?" Today people talk in a different tone, and Voltaire was right to complain that the cry of the modern sophists is: "What don't I know!"

All the honorable philosophers, those who have not engaged in idle controversy, have recognized the falseness of our social theories. Montesquieu thinks that "the social world is suffering from a chronic sickness, an inner vice, a secret and hidden venom." J.-J. Rousseau, in speaking of the people of civilization, says: "These are not men; there is a disorder in things, the cause of which we have not yet fathomed."

There are nonetheless people who vaunt the progress of our political sciences and the perfection of reason. This is an in-

[1] Fourier's writings abound in such citations, gathered more or less by chance from the writings of the philosophers. This quotation, one of his favorites, comes from Voltaire's *Discours sur l'Homme*, VI, 11.

decent boast and it has been cruelly refuted by the general misfortune, by the disastrous consequences of the so-called enlightened theories which gave birth to the storms of revolution. Was there ever a time like the present to stigmatize the regenerating sciences en masse! They have already been condemned by their own authors. Before the Revolution the compiler Barthélemy said (in his *Voyage d'Anacharsis*): "These libraries, the so-called treasure-houses of sublime knowledge, are no more than a humiliating repository of contradictions and errors; their abundance of ideas is in fact a penury." What would he have said a few years later if he had seen the philosophical dogmas put to the test? No doubt like Raynal he would have made a public confession of ignorance and said with Bacon: "We must revise our whole understanding of things, and forget all that we have learned."

A scholar could gather pages of such citations in which modern philosophy denounces its own wisdom. I am merely citing a few imposing authorities who have preceded me in drawing attention to the spurious quality of our present enlightenment. I wish only to make it clear that the greatest geniuses have prophesied and called for the discovery of a social theory other than the Philosophy which they blame for having misled human reason.

What is the error committed by the philosophers? What branch of learning have they failed to investigate? There are several, and notably the branch with which they claim to have been particularly concerned: I mean *the study of Man*. Although they claim to have exhausted the subject, they know absolutely nothing about it. They have concerned themselves with superficial problems, like that of Ideology,[2] which are meaningless so long as we remain ignorant of the fundamental science which deals with man's basic impulses. It is impossible to understand

[2] Fourier uses the term "ideology" here in its original sense to refer to the doctrine of Destutt de Tracy (1754–1836) and the other *idéologues*. For them *idéologie* was an attempt to establish a science of psychology which would explain human behavior in purely biological terms. It was only later that the term acquired the broader associations which it now has.

the nature of these impulses and their goal without a knowledge of the analytic and synthetic calculus of passionate attraction. . . .

So long as the human mind has not discovered the calculus of the social destinies, interpreted by the synthesis of attraction, we must remain in a state of political cretinism. Our progress in a few of the natural sciences—in mathematics, physics, chemistry, etc.—is useless, for it has not provided us with a remedy for any of man's ills. The accomplishments of these sciences only serve to emphasize the confusion of social thought which has done nothing to promote human happiness and which, after thirty centuries of correctives and reforms, has left all social evils as deeply rooted as ever. . . .

What have we learned about man and his social destinies? There are four sciences which claim to solve the riddle. One of them, called *Ideology*, is only concerned with the surface of the question. It has lost itself in quibbles and subtleties concerning the analysis of ideas and failed to study the real question, which is that of the functions and uses of the passions and the laws of passionate attraction. . . .

Three other sciences—politics, moral philosophy and political economy—also claim to explain the problem of our destinies. Let us analyze these sciences.

Politics and political economy advocate theories which run counter to human destiny. They encourage us to submit passively to civilization, with its system of incoherent and loathsome work, when we should be trying to attain our true destiny which is societary work.

A fourth philosophical science, moral philosophy, which also boasts of making man its study, does just the opposite. The only art that the moralists know is that of perverting human nature and repressing the soul's impulses or *passionate attractions* on the grounds that they are not suited to the civilized and barbarian order. The real problem on the contrary is to discover the means of escaping the civilized and barbarian order. This order is in conflict with man's passions and inclinations, all of which tend to unity, to domestic and agricultural association.

These four uncertain sciences vaunt the system of incoherent and piece-meal work in order to dispense themselves of the task of inventing the societary system. Having failed to perform their appointed task and having misled us for three thousand years, they will come to the same end as all the anarchists who delude men with their promises of happiness and finally destroy one another.

Such is the status of the philosophical sciences today: like the revolutionary parties, they are destroying one another before our very eyes. One of the most reputable of these sciences, *Moral Philosophy*, has recently been overwhelmed by a party of new savants called the *Economists*. The Economists have won favor by encouraging the love of wealth whereas morality advised men to throw their wealth "into the womb of the avid seas." By hoisting the banner of wealth and luxury, and thus yielding to the first dictate of attraction, the Economists were sure of crushing the moralists. For the moralists wish us to scorn wealth only because they lack the means to obtain it for us; like the fox in the fable they call the grapes too green because they are unable to reach them.

What has civilization gained by changing its banner, by forsaking the moralists in order to follow the Economists? It is true that the economists permit us to love wealth, but they don't make us wealthy. On the contrary, the influence of their dogmas has only served to double the weight of taxes and the size of armies, to promote poverty, deceit and all the scourges. Its material consequence has been the devastation of forests; in the political sphere its fruit has been monopoly, both naval and corporate. Is there any vice which has not been aggravated by the intrusion of these dangerous doctors? . . .

If we consider that the present state of generalized deprivation is the fruit of a hundred thousand social systems, can we believe in the good faith of those who have amassed this clutter of dogmas? Should we not divide the authors of these systems into two categories, one composed of charlatans and the other of dupes? For we must consider as dupes those who have believed that civilization was man's destiny and have sought to perfect it instead of looking for a way out of it.

Let us then distinguish those who, in agreement with the

Montesquieus, the Rousseaus and the Voltaires, have been suspicious of philosophy and civilization. We will give the name of *Expectant* Sophists to all those writers who, since Socrates, have sought the enlightenment which they admitted was not to be found in their own learning; and under the term *Obscurantist* Sophists we will designate all those quacks who vaunt their nostrums of perfectibility, although well aware of their worthlessness.

We can recognize a category of very pardonable Obscurantists. This would include the men who take fright before a new discovery is tested, fearing that it might become a dangerous weapon in the hands of agitators. Such doubts are praiseworthy prior to verification. But under the term Philosophical Obscurantists I mean to include only those haughty men whose motto is *nil sub sole novum*,[3] and who pretend that there is nothing more to be discovered, that their science "has perfectibilized all perfectible perfectibilities."

This distinction of the philosophers into *Expectants* and *Obscurantists* allows everyone the chance to justify himself. A philosopher is exonerated in placing himself in the category of the Expectants who are waiting for enlightenment, and in condemning the four sciences that are indulgently described as uncertain when they might better be called deceiving. What other name can be given:

To modern Metaphysics which has spawned the sects of Materialism and Atheism and cast the intellect into a scientific dead-end by bogging it down in the useless controversy over ideology. Had the metaphysicians devoted themselves to their assigned task, the study of attraction, this would have led in a few years to the discovery of the laws of passional harmony.

To Politics which vaunts the rights of man but fails to guarantee the first right and the only useful one, which is the right to work. The acknowledgement of this right would have sufficed to cast suspicion on civilization which can neither recognize it nor grant it.

To Economism which promises wealth to nations but only

[3] "There is nothing new under the sun."

teaches the art of enriching financiers and leeches, the art of doubling taxes, of devouring the future through fiscal loans, and of neglecting all research on domestic association, the basis of the economy.

To Moralism which, after two thousand years of advocating the scorn of wealth and the love of truth, has just recently begun to extol the civilized commercial system with its bankruptcy, usury, speculation and freedom of deception.

Such are the four sciences which direct the social world, or rather which have been misdirecting it for twenty-five centuries. These sciences are already suspect in the eyes of the revolutionaries whom they have begotten. Bonaparte eliminated them all from the Institute, and this was perhaps the most sensible act of his reign.[4]

*OC,* iii, 109–123

### CRITIQUE OF THE REVOLUTIONARY IDEALS

Philosophy was right to vaunt *liberty;* it is the foremost desire of all creatures. But philosophy forgot that in civilized societies liberty is illusory if the common people lack wealth. When the wage-earning classes are poor, their independence is as fragile as a house without foundations. The free man who lacks wealth immediately sinks back under the yoke of the rich. The newly freed slave takes fright at the need of providing for his own subsistence and hastens to sell himself back into slavery in order to escape this new anxiety that hangs over him like Damocles' sword. In thoughtlessly giving him liberty without wealth, you merely replace his physical torment with a mental torment. He finds life burdensome in his new state. . . . Thus when you give liberty to the people, it must be bolstered by two supports which are *the guarantee of comfort* and *industrial attraction.* . . .

*Equality of rights* is another chimera, praiseworthy when considered in the abstract and ridiculous from the standpoint of the means employed to introduce it in civilization. The first

[4] Allusion to Napoleon's suppression in January 1803 of the section of the French *Institut* which was concerned with the study of the moral and political sciences.

right of men is the right to work and the right to a *minimum*. This is precisely what has gone unrecognized in all the constitutions. Their primary concern is with favored individuals who are not in need of work. They begin with pompous lists of the elect from privileged families to whom the law guarantees an income of fifty or one hundred thousand francs for the simple task of governing the people or sitting in an upholstered seat and voting with the majority in a senate. If the first page of the constitutions serves to provide administrators with guarantees of affluence and idleness, it would be well for the second page to pay some attention to the lot of the lower classes, to the *proportional minimum* and the right to work, which are omitted in all constitutions, and to the right to pleasure, which is guaranteed only by the mechanism of the industrial series. . . .

Let's turn to *fraternity*. Our discussion here will be amusing, at once loathsome and learned. It is amusing in view of the imbecility of the theories which have purported to establish fraternity. It is loathsome when one recalls the horrors that the ideal of fraternity has masked. But it is a problem which deserves particular attention from science; for societies will attain their goal, and man his dignity, only when universal fraternity has become an established fact. By universal fraternity we mean a degree of general intimacy which can only be realized if four conditions are satisfied:

Comfort for the people and the assurance of a splendid minimum;

The education and instruction of the lower classes;

General truthfulness in work relations;

The rendering of reciprocal services by unequal classes.

Once these four conditions are met, the rich Mondor will have truly fraternal relations with Irus who, despite his poverty, will have no need of a protector and no motive to deceive anyone, and whose fine education will enable him to associate with princes. . . . As for the present, how could there by any fraternity between sybarites steeped in refinements and our coarse, hungry peasants who are covered with rags and often with vermin and who carry contagious diseases like typhus, mange, plica and other such fruits of civilized poverty? What sort of fraternity could ever be established between such heterogeneous classes of men?

—"De la méthode mixte," *La Phalange*,
VII (1848), pp. 117–119.

### POLITICS AND POVERTY

By dint of compiling the reveries of classical antiquity, modern philosophers have come to espouse the prejudices of their fore-fathers, and notably the most ridiculous prejudice, the conviction that the good can be established by governmental action. Neither the ancient nor the modern civilizations have ever conceived of a measure which did not rely on government. Are they unaware that any civilized administration, however organized, prefers its own good to that of the people? What has been the result of the theories designed to curb the powers of government? What has been the use of ministerial responsibility, the balance of powers, and other notions equally devoid of sense? Experiments with these scientific visions have only served to convince us that the nature of the civilized mechanism imposes the prompt reestab-lishment of the abuses that we try to banish. Civilization is a social plague on the planet, and vices are just as necessary to it as is a virus to disease. The reforms that you seek to impose by governmental action only serve to confirm existing abuses. After much effort you bow under their yoke, and all you gain for your efforts is the conviction of an inexorable bondage.

What fatal circumstance has caused the modern sciences to attain gigantic stature in physics and the arts and to remain dwarfs in the subalternate science of politics? Civilized genius, even in its most brilliant periods, has never created anything for the happiness of the common people. At Athens as at Paris, the beggar standing at the palace gate has always served to demon-strate the nullity of your political wisdom and the reprobation of nature against your social theories. You have not even man-aged to accomplish half of the reforms which were possible in civilization. Although you could not have rooted out the vices which degrade civilization, you could have mitigated them. You could have given civilization a polish of splendor and unity which would have made its present situation seem like a state of ruin. All you can do is to look backwards in politics; you praise yourself for the avoidance of evil before attaining the good. Like the child who thinks himself a mighty man at the age of four because he has beaten up a three year old, you think yourself wise for having banished from your societies a few of the horrors which reduce the barbarian to an even lower condition than your own. But just how much progress have you made toward the good when mendacity and thievery, venality and bribery, reign perpetually in your disgusting civilization?

*—PM*, 1; *OC*, x, 220–221

MORALITY AS PREACHED; COUNTER-MORALITY AS PRACTICED

Ten thousand systems of morality teach us to repress our passions; twenty or thirty thousand systems encourage us to satisfy them. The theater and the novel provide us with a barely camouflaged COUNTER-MORALITY which indulges the passions, engenders them, stimulates them, and shows us the tricks necessary to satisfy them. . . .

Any play that was truly moral and devoid of amorous intrigue would never find an audience. In fact plays and novels are constantly inciting people to yield to love and to ignore the obstacles and objections raised by fathers, moralists and priests. Those who love one another despite the powers that be are presented as heroes. The love affair gets legitimized by a marriage at the end of the book or in the last act; but during the first nine-tenths of the play, or for four-and-three-quarters acts, the young have been taught to disobey the commands of their superiors and to have their fun on the sly. At the end their misdeeds are discovered as a result of some blunder. But every intriguer tells himself: "I would not have been so stupid." Thus everyone leaves the theater sympathetic to vice and inclined to practice it in affairs of interest as well as in love. . . .

Counter-morality has gone practically unstudied. It is a subject on which one could write a most interesting book and a very irritating one for the moralists whose systems it would confound. It can be divided into nine branches which have not yet been distinguished. These are: 1. theaters; 2. novels; 3. the genteel world; 4. occupational ethics; 5. submissive women; 6. rebellious children; 7. social outcasts; P. high society; T. necessary usages. Each of these nine varieties includes many sub-species. I am only indicating the principal ones.

Let's take a look at this gallery of counter-moralists in which the lessons taught in *plays* and *novels* are so well practiced by the *genteel world*. What does it care about the 10,000 systems of sweet and pure morality which forbid a girl to have a lover, much less two or three? Just try advising a girl to leave her lovers and to go taste the charms of moral virtue. She will tell you that virtue consists in having just one true lover plus a prosperous protector. Similarly every portion of the genteel world has its own well-established counter-morality with principles and doctrines which are observed to the letter. The dogmas of morality, on the other hand, are never put into practice; they are the masks worn by hypocrisy.

Let's turn to *occupational ethics*. Can you convince a tenant farmer that he is immoral when he pilfers from the landowner? As for tradesmen who cheat their customers, will they listen to moral remonstrances such as Fénélon's claim that it is better to die than to tell a lie? Try to preach this morality to a salesman.

Every trade has its counter-morality and its principles. Take the servant for example. He says: "A man who eats and drinks well does his master no harm." By virtue of this principle he makes off with the most costly foods and the best wines.

Big business is in a class by itself in counter-morality; it sees virtue in great crimes. To starve a country and to paralyze industry through the hoarding of commodities is the way to win the respect of the merchants and even of the moralists, who praise all successful crimes. By means of its monopolistic connivings commerce can sometimes topple an empire (Napoleon). That is counter-morality on a grandiose scale.

*Women* of good character play a disguised role in counter-morality; they are all in agreement to elude the sacred laws of conjugal fidelity (while avoiding publicity). Their refrain is:

"If there is no scandal and if things are carried on discretely, there is no harm done." In return for this they have the right to carp about the misdeeds of the genteel world to which they do not belong—*so they say.*

*Children* are nature's echoes against morality; they are all in league to escape its rules. Their only source of happiness lies in activities forbidden by their moralistic teachers—in breaking, destroying, quarreling and insulting. They honor a person who excels in these respects, and they tease and abuse those who are inclined to obey the authorities.

Next come the *social outcasts,* and first of all the passive ones or slaves. Aristotle did not know of any virtue proper to a slave. Why then does your perfectible civilization persist in creating whole classes of men who are lacking both in virtue and in good character? A master rapes or seduces the wife or child of his slave, and morality obliges the slave to endure everything, even the whippings that he will receive if he complains about the rape of his wife.

Then there are the active *social outcasts* such as swindlers, prostitutes, agitators, and among the lesser breeds: pickpockets, highwaymen, ex-convicts steeped in the counter-morality of the jail-house and the prison, calculating beggars with their chiefs and their own special rules. This whole category of men who have broken with society forms another powerful cohort in the ranks of counter-morality.

P. Finally *high society* and courtiers: these people do not think themselves obliged to practice morality; they regard it as a means of restraining the common people and the bourgeoisie. In their eyes morality is an intellectual police force which protects their own security. They control morality and do not obey it; the only thing they follow is their own anti-moral whims.

T. *Subjugated people,* the victims of circumstance: Soldiers whose profession prevents them from thinking of marriage, unless there is a large dowry, are obliged to seek out illicit relationships, adulterous affairs, fornications. The same applies to travelers, celibate priests, poor young people and unwedded girls; this whole class has been won over to counter-morality. . . .

Deducting this litany of classes addicted to counter-morality, what classes remain for morality? Those who preach it by profession. Does it follow that they practice it?

*OC*, IX, 765–771

### THE VARIETIES OF CIVILIZED EDUCATION

For all their insistence on unity of action, our politicians have not observed that in any system of civilized education a child is subject to indoctrination by four incongruous agents. All four of them compete to subject the child to contradictory pressures which are absorbed during puberty by a pivotal pressure which is *the worldly spirit* or *prettied-up immorality*. Let us analyze this bizarre mechanism.

Prior to adolescence a child from a well-to-do family ordinarily receives four types of education: 1. The Dogmatic; 2. The Grasping; 3. The Insurgent; 4. The Evasive; P. The Worldly or Absorbing.

1. DOGMATIC EDUCATION is ostensibly provided by tutors and professors who are full of nonsensical advice about the merits of scorning perfidious wealth and imitating the virtues of the two Brutuses, one of whom immolated his sons and the other his father. Or else they vaunt the virtues of the young republicans of Sparta who hunted helots and stole their supplies and practiced collective pederasty as a prelude to the patriotic virtues of maturity.

In truth a few excellent precepts are mixed in with this liberal nonsense, but they are not emphasized. The result is that the child takes what is most dangerous from a mixed-bag of twaddle and rejects the little that is good. The cause for his confusion lies in the conflict of the other pressures which we are going to describe.

2. GRASPING or unsocial education is secretly provided by fathers who teach their children that money is the sinews of war and that above all else one has to make money *per fas et nefas*.[5] Fathers don't dare to be too explicit about this odious principle, but it underlies everything they say. They prevail upon the

---

[5] "By fair means and foul."

child to be very accommodating about any possibility of making money and to learn how to adapt morality to the dictates of self-interest. . . .

3. INSURGENT EDUCATION is provided cabalistically by a child's comrades. In their turbulent league against teachers and fathers their rule is always to do the opposite of what they are told; to jeer at morality and the moralists; to break things, quarrel and plunder when they have an instant's liberty; to avenge their necessary subjection to authority by means of secret rebellion and studied dissimulation; to make a point of honor out of the spirit of revolt by being contemptuous and cruel to those who cooperate with the authorities.[6]

4. EVASIVE EDUCATION is provided furtively by servants who help the child to escape the parental yoke, who toady to him and treat him secretly to stolen goodies in order to be praised to the father. They give help to the child and advise him in all his efforts to free himself from the fetters of morality. Thus the rich child looks upon servants as his secret allies; and the servants are not wrong to play this role, for fathers and mothers are unreasonable enough to dismiss a servant merely because he is not liked by their child or by one spoiled child.

These are the systems of education which contend for a child until he reaches the age of fifteen. At that point a fifth and stronger combatant appears on the scene and takes control. . . . This victor is:

P. WORLDLY or absorbing education: it must be placed in the pivotal position, for it caps the four other varieties and eliminates or modifies everything about them which is not to its liking.

At the age of sixteen when a child enters the world, he receives a wholly new education. He is taught to make fun of the dogmas which intimidate and bridle schoolboys, to conform to the customs of sophisticated society and to laugh, as it does, at the moral doctrines which put a crimp on pleasure. Shortly thereafter, when he turns from love affairs to affairs of ambition, he is taught to make fun of visions of probity, to entangle him-

[6] In his own theory of education Fourier attached great importance to the discipline provided by a child's peers. See below pp. 261–262.

self in huge expenditures and usurious loans, and finally to spread his depravity among all the women with whom he consorts.

In this quadrille of different types of education the four varieties are in competition until the child reaches adolescence; at that point the pivotal type proceeds to overshadow and absorb all the others. Prior to adolescence the first type of education, that provided by the savants, only has an apparent influence; it is only the three others that really matter. They usurp the heart, the mind and the senses of the pupil; and when he reaches the age of fifteen, all that remains of his dogmatic education is a small stock of moral precepts, most of which are dangerous if followed literally and which only carry weight insofar as they can be reconciled with the worldly pressures.

This intricate complex of rival teachers is certainly the very opposite of unity. The moralists pretend to ignore this quadruple conflict; it suits them to hide it so as to make their own services seem valuable. Would they not fall into great disfavor if people recognized that the whole institutional scaffolding of civilization is simply a conflict of incompatible elements, a monstrous assemblage of all the duplicities of action?

—*OC*, v, 201–205

# 2

## MARRIAGE AND THE FAMILY SYSTEM

### "AMOROUS ANARCHY"

Of all our social relations there is none more false than that of love. Dissimulation has become so much a part of love that it is no longer possible for us to read the works of an earlier day in which the subject was treated frankly; we are shocked even by Plutarch, Virgil and others who were models of decency in their time. During antiquity homosexual love was tolerated. But if the great men and women of Greece returned today they would all be burned alive. Solon, Lycurgus, Agesilaus, Epaminondas, Sappho, Julius Caesar and Severus would be put to the stake for pederasty or lesbianism. These very people, the great of antiquity, had nothing but scorn for commerce and deceit, which are now honored; and they criticized bankruptcy and speculation, which have become practices as innocent as homosexual love was once thought to be. There is something for the ancients and the moderns to quarrel about! People vaunt the chaste morals of the Roman ladies who piously participated in the worship of the phallus. Which of the two ages comes closer to following the dictates of nature? This is a new question and it is not yet time to treat it. Let us confine ourselves to pointing out that in love as in commerce the progress of civilization is merely progress in social falsehood. To find tangible proof of this increase in falsehood, one need only compare one century with another. Today people find it hard to endure the comedies of Molière because they deal frankly with cuckolds and cuckoldry. The academies would like to have the word which designates the deceived husband expunged from the French language. Is this a proof that people detest adultery and that there are now fewer cuckolds than there were in Molière's time? The number of adulterers has not diminished and it is certain that amorous license has increased. There are three reasons for this increase:

1. *The growth of the fiscal and mercantile system* which, by concentrating wealth in the great cities, has served to increase their venality and corruption. The corruption spreads subse-

quently into rural villages which become accustomed to the ways of the city thanks to the spread of commerce and other factors. In the most insignificant hamlets today there are cafés such as existed only in the large cities a century ago. Has amorous license made less progress in these hamlets than greed and gluttony? It has made more. The secret orgies of the rural areas are even worse than those of the town.

2. *The weakening of various restraints* such as the decline in the prestige of religion and the reduction of the threat of venereal disease. Better understood and better treated, venereal disease no longer inspires the terror that it once did. As for religious restraints, they were destroyed by the Revolution, and it would take another century to make the peasants believe in Hell again. Women are even less intimidated by Hell in matters concerning love, which they call God's secret. Young women are so convinced that love has divine sanction that armies of priests could not make them change their minds or discuss their love affairs in the confessional.

3. *Revolutionary customs.* A counter-revolution can change rulers and laws but it cannot change secret customs. It could not keep the invading armies from spreading their spirit of lust about the countryside, nor could it prevent retired French soldiers from practicing their debaucheries in the most isolated rural areas.[1] I have witnessed in a hamlet of forty households where I had gone to work on this book; I have witnessed, I say, secret orgies as well organized as in a big city; young women twenty years old more experienced, more jaded than Laïs and Phryne at forty; peasant women who were used to seeing their daughters deflowered at the age of ten; fathers and mothers who knew all about the whole business and who played along as dispassionately as the mothers of Tahiti collaborated in the prostitution of their daughters. All of this debauchery was nicely covered up, nicely powdered with prudery, communion and sacrilege.

That's what you can see everywhere just as I saw it in a

[1] This text dates from 1818. Fourier alludes to the foreign troops who occupied France in 1814 and after, and to the *demi-soldes*, the members of the Napoleonic armies who were retired on half pay after the fall of Napoleon.

hamlet. At the time I had recently left a large city in which cuckoldry was not exactly outmoded; for while I was there I had drawn up a list of 72 distinct varieties of cuckolds, each one of whom had a well-known living model.

In this state of affairs when you hear the philosophers boasting about social perfection and the progress of reason, you might well think that they have identified the perfection of reason with that of deceit. For the other branches of the civilized system—commerce, legal chicanery, etc.—have, like love, made colossal advances in deceit. Our savants who claim that they are looking for the august truth had better look to something else than civilization.

Let us briefly unravel these contradictions. Civilized lawmakers and moralists are incapable of inventing anything. The result is that they accept prevailing practices as natural and as the ultimate destiny of man. Having found society dominated by exclusive marriage and arbitrary commerce, they extolled these customs and they continue to extol them. They are incapable of conceiving of anything else.

Nonetheless, each of the seven societies prior to Harmony has its own method of conjugal union between the sexes and its own method for the social exchange of commodities. Complete liberty in love and complete truth in commerce will reign only in Harmony, the eighth period. Thus there are seven other methods which might be studied by the law-makers. If they had any knowledge of the workings of society, they would make a list of the seven methods of conjugal union and the seven methods of social exchange which precede the reign of complete truth. Then, after examining the fourteen methods, they would choose two. . . .[2]

[2] Fourier goes on to comment that patriarchal societies are dominated by "mixed monogamy with simple concubinage"; barbarian societies by "forced polygamy or the harem"; and civilization by "exclusive and permanent monogamy." He concludes by noting that the sixth and seventh historical stages of Guaranteeism and Serisophie will be characterized by "modes of conjugal relations . . . highly preferable to our own, although complete liberty and complete truth will only be attained in the eighth period."

Marriage has suffered the same fate as all other civilized customs: it has led to results contrary to those intended. It has produced widespread secret debauchery and it has given legal protection to those who are most audacious in violating its sanctity. People mock justice in saying that it hangs only the petty thieves while letting the big ones slip by. In this fashion the laws protect debauchery when it is practiced by genteel ladies who do not ask for money or talk of marriage. Such women are protected by all of society: by fathers and mothers who are quite content to see their sons satisfied by women who cost nothing and who needn't be married; by the young men themselves who are delighted to get their share of the spoils; and finally by other women, by young ladies who have a taste for pleasure and find it at the houses of these genteel ladies for whom innocence is just a mask.

The philosophers should take account of these observations; they should watch how people actually behave and try to make some use of conduct which they are unable to prevent. What, for example, is the mode of sexual relationship most prevalent in a country like France or Italy? Are legitimate relationships more common than illicit ones? No, it is surely the latter which predominate. Without exaggerating one can estimate the number of forbidden love affairs as seven times that of sanctioned conjugal relationships. Since such infractions are only increasing and since the law is powerless to prevent them, would it not be wise to widen the scope of legitimate amorous relationships? . . .

Too many restraints have been imposed on the passion of love. This is proved by the fact that no man wishes to obey the legal injunction to practice continence outside of marriage. The infractions of men have inspired those of women, and love in civilized society is nothing but universal anarchy and secret insurrection.

*PM*, IV; *OC*, XI, 219–226

THE DEGRADATION OF WOMEN IN CIVILIZATION

Don't the philosophers realize that perpetual fidelity in love is contrary to human nature; and that if you can make a few simpletons stick to a single spouse, the mass of men and women will never be reduced to monogamy? Don't they understand that any form of legislation which requires behavior so incompatible with the passions can only produce contradictions in theory and chaos in practice, since all of society will be tacitly in league to authorize infractions of the law? Isn't this the result of the amorous system which has prevailed for the past 2500 years? This system is simply a continuation of the oppressive customs that reigned in the dark ages, customs which are becoming ridiculous in an age when people brag about their reason and their respect for the designs of nature.

It is not astonishing that the ancient philosophers of Greece and Rome disdained the interests of women. For these rhetoricians were all wild partisans of pederasty, which was highly esteemed in noble antiquity. They cast ridicule on those who consorted with women, and they considered the love of women to be a dishonorable passion for a man. The code of Lycurgus encouraged young men to practice sodomy, which the Spartans described as "the path of virtue." This sort of love was also promoted in the less austere republics. The Thebans, for example, formed a battalion of young pederasts. These practices won the unanimous approval of the philosophers who, from the virtuous Socrates to the fastidious Anacreon, flaunted sodomy and contempt for women who were relegated to their rooms, shut up as in a harem and banished from the company of men.

Since these bizarre tastes have not won favor among our contemporaries, there is cause to wonder at the fact that our philosophers have inherited the hatred that the savants of antiquity bore toward women. It is also strange that they continue to disparage the fair sex on account of a few wiles to which women are driven by the oppression that weighs upon them; for any word or thought consistent with the dictates of nature is imputed to women as a crime.

Steeped in this tyrannical spirit, the philosophers prattle to us about a few shrews of Antiquity who replied coarsely to polite words. They vaunt the customs of the Germans who put their wives to the rack for a single act of infidelity. They debase the fair sex even in the flattery they pay it; for what is more inconsistent than the opinion of Diderot who claims that to write to women "you must dip your pen in the rainbow and sprinkle your writing with the dust of butterfly wings"? Women can reply to the philosophers: Your Civilization persecutes us when we obey Nature; it obliges us to assume an artificial personality, to behave in ways that are contrary to our desires. In order to make this doctrine palatable to us, you find it necessary to utilize illusions and deceitful language as you do with the soldier whom you lull with laurels and talk of immortality so as to make him forget his pitiful state. If he were really happy, he could be talked to in the simple and truthful terms which you refrain from using. Women are just the same; if they were free and happy, they would be less eager for illusions and coaxing, and it would no longer be necessary to write to them with the help of "rainbows and butterflies." If soldiers and women, and even the common people as a whole, need to be continually deceived, it is an indictment against philosophy which has failed to organize anything in this world but pain and servitude. And when philosophy jests about the vices of women, it is criticizing itself. It is philosophy which produces these vices through a social system which, repressing the development of women's faculties in childhood and throughout the whole course of their lives, forces them to resort to deceit in order to obey their natural impulses.

To attempt to judge women by the defective character that they display in Civilization is like trying to judge the nature of man by the character of the Russian peasant who has no conception whatsoever of honor or of liberty. It is like judging beavers by the sluggishness that they show in captivity whereas in a state of liberty and coordinated labor they become the most intelligent of all the quadrupeds. The same contrast will reign between the enslaved women of Civilization and the free women of the Combined Order. They will surpass men in dedication to their work, in loyalty and in nobility; but outside the free and combined state woman becomes, like the tame beaver or the Russian peasant, a creature so inferior to its destiny and its powers that it is easy to scorn it when one judges it superficially and on the basis of appearances. Thus it is not surprising that Mohammed, the Council of Mâcon and the philosophers have questioned the existence of a soul in women and have tried to forge their chains instead of breaking them.

Women appear to be more in need of masters than of liberty; thus among their lovers they often give preference to those whose conduct merits it the least. But how could a woman avoid having servile and perfidious penchants since her whole education has accustomed her to smothering her natural character and adapting herself to the first comer whom chance, intrigue or avarice may bring her as a husband? . . .

And you, oppressing sex, would you not outdo women in shortcomings if a servile education had molded you to think of yourselves as automatons meant to submit to prejudice and to cringe before a master whom chance has imposed on you? Have we not seen your claims to superiority confounded by Catherine who trampled upon the masculine sex? In dealing with her favorites she dragged man in the mud and proved that, for all his liberty, man can debase himself below woman whose degradation is imposed on her and thus excusable. To confound the tyranny of men there should exist for a century a third sex, both male and female and stronger than men. This new sex would prove with the lash that men as well as women are made for its pleasure; and then you would hear men protesting against the tyranny of the hermaphroditic sex and admitting that strength should not be the sole rule of right. Just why do they refuse to grant women the privileges and the independence which they would demand from the third sex?

I do not mean to criticize civilized education here nor to suggest that a spirit of liberty should be inculcated in women. Certainly, in each social period youth must be made to venerate the dominant absurdities. In the barbarian order it is necessary to brutalize women, to convince them that they have no souls, so as to dispose them to allow themselves to be sold on the market and shut up in a harem. Similarly in the civilized order it is necessary to stupefy women from their childhood, so as to make them fit the philosophical dogmas, the servitude of marriage and the debasement of falling into the power of a husband whose character will perhaps be the opposite of their own. Just as I would condemn a barbarian who raised his daughters according to the ways of a civilization in which they would never live, I would also find fault with a civilized man who raised his daughters in a spirit of liberty and reason suitable to the sixth and seventh periods which we have not yet attained.

If I attack contemporary education and the servile spirit which it inculcates in women, I am speaking comparatively with regard to other societies in which it will no longer be necessary to warp the female character with prejudices.[3] I am showing them the eminent role that they can play by following the example of women who have overcome the influence of education and resisted the oppressive system necessitated by the bond of marriage. In drawing attention to the women who have managed to realize their potential, from viragos like Maria Theresa to milder types like the Ninons and the Sévignés,[4] I am justified in saying that woman in a state of liberty will surpass man in all the mental and bodily functions which are not related to physical strength.

Man already seems to have a premonition of the future; he becomes indignant and alarmed when women belie the prejudice which accuses them of inferiority. Masculine jealousy has burst out especially against women writers; philosophy has refused them academic honors and has consigned them ignominiously to the tasks of housekeeping.

Was not this affront deserved by educated women! The slave who tries to ape his master merits nothing more from him than a disdainful glance. Why should women have bothered about the banal glory of writing books, of adding a few volumes

[3] Fourier's acute awareness of the relativity of sexual attitudes and relations is manifest in a number of other passages included in this anthology. See above p. 171 and below pp. 333 and 335.

[4] Ninon de Lenclos (1620–1705) and Madame de Sévigné (1626–1696) were women celebrated for their wit and intelligence during the reign of Louis XIV.

to the millions of useless ones already in existence? What women should have produced was not writers but liberators, a political Spartacus, a genius who would devise means of raising their sex from degradation.

It is women who suffer most from civilization; it was up to them to attack it. What sort of life do they lead today? Theirs is a continual state of privation, even in industry, where man has taken over everything down to the meticulous tasks of sewing and scrivening, while women may be seen plugging away at laborious farm work. Is it not scandalous to see strong men of thirty bent over their desks or transporting cups of coffee with their shaggy arms, as if there was a shortage of women and children to attend to the trifling functions of the office and the household?

Just what are the means of subsistence of impoverished women? The bedpost or else their charms, when they have any. Yes, prostitution more or less prettied up is their sole means of support, and philosophy begrudges them even that. This is the abject condition to which they have been reduced by civilization with its conjugal slavery. They have not even thought of attacking it; and their failure to do so has been unpardonable ever since the discovery of Tahiti; its manners and customs were an admonition of Nature and should have suggested the idea of a social order which could unite large-scale industry with amorous liberty. This was the sole problem worthy of occupying women writers; and their indolence with regard to it is one of the causes which have made men scornful of them. A slave is never more contemptible than when his blind submission convinces the oppressor that his victim is born for slavery.

—*OC*, I, 145–150

Is not a young woman a piece of merchandise put up for sale to the highest bidder? Is she not tyrannized by prejudice from childhood and obliged to consent to any marriage that may be arranged for her? People try to persuade her that she is only bound by chains of flowers. But can she really doubt her degradation? Even in nations that are bloated with philosophy, such as England, a man has the right to take his woman to the market, with a rope around her neck, and sell her like a beast of burden, to anyone who can pay his asking price. On this point we have hardly made any progress since that crude era when the Council of Macon, a true council of vandals, debated whether or not women had a soul and decided in the affirmative by a majority of just three votes. English legislation, which is so highly praised by the moralists, grants men a number of rights which are no less dishonoring for the fair sex. The English husband, for example, has the right to demand a monetary indemnification from the recognized lover of his wife. The French style is a little less gross, but the same sort of slavery exists in France. Here as everywhere you can see young women languishing, falling ill and dying for want of a union which is imperiously dictated by nature but stigmatized by prejudice until the girl has been legally sold. Although such cases are rare, they are still common enough to testify to the slavery of the weaker sex, the prevailing scorn for the will of nature, and the absence of all justice with regard to women.

—*OC*, 1, 130–131

### THE PERILS OF MARRIED LIFE

Morality considers love to be no more than a secondary matter. It places man's true happiness in the pleasures of family life and the practice of the rustic virtues. Before adopting its opinions, we should take a closer look at familial relations. Let us distinguish between the PLEASURES OF MARRIAGE and the PLEASURES OF PATERNITY.[5]

The list which I am about to present refers only to the vast majority of people, whose wealth is scarcely greater than their needs. The wealthy class constitutes an exception which should not be taken into account in a general analysis and which only serves to confirm the rule.

---

[5] The text translated here is followed by a similar "Scale of the Seeds of Discord between Civilized Fathers and Children."

## SCALE OF MISFORTUNES IN MARRIED LIFE

### K Widowerhood

1. Chance of unhappiness.
2. Disparity of tastes.
3. Complications.
4. Expense.
5. Vigilance.
6. Monotony.

### Y Sterility

### KK Compound Orphanhood

7. Discord in education.
8. Jobs and dowries.
9. Departure of children.
10. Disappointing in-laws.
11. Incorrect information.
12. Adultery or cuckoldry.

### YY False Paternity

1. *Chance of unhappiness* and anxiety by anticipation. Is there any game of chance more frightful than an exclusive and indissoluble tie on which you stake a lifetime's happiness or unhappiness? Men and women have been known to start worrying about marriage several years ahead of time; and rightfully so. What a mistake in social conduct to make one's whole future depend on a very bad bet!

2. *Disparity of tastes and personalities.* It often emerges on the very morrow of the wedding, if only in disputes over food which cannot be of two kinds in small households. Then there are disagreements about clothing and company: the tender wife wants to entertain and spend her time with certain friends and relatives whom she calls the most proper people, true friends of commerce and the Charter; the husband has no sympathy for their ideas. In short, a newly married couple can hardly go two weeks without discovering incompatible tastes and habits on both sides. Their hopes of marital happiness are quickly disappointed; their illusions are dissipated from the very beginning.

3. *Complications.* It is rare for a marriage to last six months without something happening which changes everything. I once knew a young husband whose father-in-law went bankrupt after two months and paid the dowry with a statement of insolvency. The worst of it was that the son-in-law had given receipts for the unpaid bills and was so compromised that he was forced to pay back the dowry that he had never received: 80,000 francs.

This is a case involving a passion in the major mode, ambition; others concern passions in the minor mode like love. For instance, after a month of marriage a husband may recognize that his wife is a Messalina and that if he wants to end her intrigues it may be necessary to go to court.

You could fill a hundred pages with tales of similar incidents which quickly dispel the charm of married life and show the husband or the wife the trap into which he or she has fallen. Sometimes the husband's disillusionment begins on the very first night when he fails to find everything he had expected. Women are not less subject to disappointments and tricks.

4. *Expense*. In general, everything conspires to involve young husbands in heavy expenditures. You can hear many of them complaining about it and urging their wives to be more economical. In reply the wives accuse their husbands of stinginess. Housekeeping is so costly that people always exceed their budgets; then they have to cut back. When married people argue about such matters, love vanishes. The illusion vanishes; the chain remains.

5. *Vigilance*. The obligation to oversee the running of a household in which it is imprudent to rely blindly on the wife. If she has everything her way, her clothing will be considerably more elegant than the meals she serves. How many other dangers require the husband to exercise a vigilance which was quite unnecessary when he was a free man!

6. *Monotony*. It must be great in the household since, despite the distractions provided by their work, husbands are always running off to public places, clubs, cafes, theaters, etc. to divert themselves from the boredom they find, as the proverb puts it, "in always eating from the same plate." The monotony is much worse for women if they wish to be faithful to their duties.

7. *Discord in education:* a source of misunderstanding when the father, wiser than his wife, will not allow her to spoil the children. A father gets sick of their crying, complains and finally leaves. The wife seeks consolation with another man and discord arises from the very children whom morality offers us as a pledge of ineffable harmony.

8. *Finding jobs for sons and dowries for daughters*. These

tasks are enough to make any man sick of the delights of marriage. But his daughters will remain on his hands until he can find them a dowry. How will he do it if his income is limited? Then there is the problem of finding jobs for his sons and paying for their education. People describe the marital state as a flowery path, but how many thorns do the flowers conceal!

9. *Departure of children.* If there are only daughters, they will follow their husbands wherever they may go. Usually parents are deprived by marriage of their favorite daughters. They remain melancholy and abandoned. Sons, too, will leave to seek their fortunes elsewhere. Most parents are eventually deprived of the company of all their children. If some children stay nearby, they are usually the ones the parents like the least, and in any case they live in separate households where fathers are not wanted.

10. *Disappointing in-laws:* the annoyances caused by one's new relatives. In their subsequent conduct these relatives-by-marriage rarely live up to one's hopes and expectations, and they often prove to be deceitful. Their misconduct results in quarreling and discord instead of the sweet familial pleasures promised by morality.

11. *Incorrect or misleading information* about events transpiring before or during marriage, about one's wife or her parents. How many husbands who think they have married an angel of virtue have cause to exclaim after the marriage: "If I had known that, I would never have married the girl!" How many fathers say the same thing about their daughters' husbands! Marital inquiries are so unreliable that three-fourths of all husbands and fathers have such complaints to make.

12. *Adultery* which is called by the name of cuckoldry on the French stage. It must be an unfortunate accident since men exhaust themselves in taking precautions against it. Nonetheless, every husband can be certain, before his marriage, of suffering the common fate that he has inflicted on so many others. The analysis of this twelfth misfortune alone would require an article as long as the present section.[6]

[6] For a representative sampling of Fourier's gallery of cuckolds see the next selection in this anthology.

Y. STERILITY. It threatens to frustrate the best laid plans of happiness. The fear of sterility is in itself sufficient to terrify any man who takes a wife in the hope of having children. The poor man always has hordes of children: "to the beggar goes the heavy load." Children come in torrents to people who are unable to feed them, but rich families seem particularly subject to sterility. It foils the designs of husbands and grandfathers and obliges them to leave their patrimony to collateral relatives whose greed and ingratitude drive the donors to despair. It makes spouses hate their sterile partners and the conjugal bond which has deceived all their hopes. Sterility is a true social snare, a disaster in itself and also on the following count.

YY. FALSE PATERNITY. This is the most odious of perfidies engendered by the conjugal system. Nonetheless it is the object of public witticisms in France, even on the stage where people joke about it in verse and prose. This sort of humor is worthy of a social order where everything is false and where nothing succeeds like deception. Both the law and public opinion are united in forbidding the husband from making any complaint about the matter or in nullifying any charges he may bring. The law tells him: "It is not proven.". . . Public opinion tells him: "If people don't know about it, it's nothing at all; if they do know, it's a trivial matter." So the husband gets stuck with someone else's children and people ridicule him for having complained about the matter. Compound injustice, the essence of civilization which never does evil on a small scale.

K. WIDOWERHOOD. It reduces the father of a family to a life of forced labor; it is a much greater misfortune than the mild vexations of celibacy. Unless he is extremely wealthy, a man left with several children must lead the life of a galley-slave if he wishes to bring them up properly. And if the widower takes ill and dies before his children reach maturity, his last moments will be embittered by worries about the fate of his children, the disasters likely to befall his young family.

KK. COMPOUND ORPHANHOOD. The greatest pleasure of the father and mother is to know that their children will be happy. But the conjugal system offers no guarantees if the children are orphaned. The best chosen guardians and trustees may despoil the orphan or be powerless to prevent others from doing so. . . .

I would like to know how many husbands can be sure of escaping these sixteen misfortunes, any one of which would suffice to ruin one's life? Out of one hundred individuals who have been married for ten years could you not find ninety-nine who have suffered not just one but two or three of these misfortunes? Unless a person is extremely wealthy the happiness promised by marriage is nothing but a delusion! The institution of marriage is a proof of the fact that our political and moral philosophers are utterly lacking in inventive genius. For if the barbarian harem made women suffer, marriage is a plague on both sexes. How true it is that civilization reproduces in the compound mode all the vices that one finds in the simple mode among the barbarians!

—*OC*, IV, 69–76

#### ADULTERY DISSECTED: THE HIERARCHY OF CUCKOLDOM

In their studies of adultery, as in their studies of bankruptcy, writers have only skimmed the surface. They have only shown the amusing sides. . . . If the word "cuckoldry" has fallen into disfavor, this only serves to prove the progress of the vice and the weakness of the writers who bow down before it. If they had more courage they would hold up a mirror to its face in the form of a methodical and integral table of the orders, types, species and varieties of adultery. One day a Parisian journal attempted to provide a methodical analysis of adultery. But it only mentioned three species and did not even dare to call them by their names. Is that any way to define a vice whose varieties are innumerable? A complete table is needed, a full series representing all the ramifications and degrees. I could present this hierarchy of cuckoldom as a parallel to my analysis of the types of bankruptcy. . . .

### HIERARCHY OF CUCKOLDOM
arranged progressively by category, type and species.
*Short-horned or Pardonable*

*FORWARD OUTPOST*
1. The Cuckold in the Bud.

AVANT-GARDE

2. The Presumptive Cuckold.
3. The Imaginary Cuckold.

RIGHT FLANK

4. The Warlike or Swaggering Cuckold.
5. The Artful or Crafty Cuckold.
6. The Bantering Cuckold.

RIGHT WINGLET

7. The Pure and Simple Cuckold.
8. The Fatalistic or Resigned Cuckold.
9. The Condemned or Predesignated Cuckold.
10. The Irreproachable or Victimized Cuckold.

RIGHT WING TIP

11. The Prescriptive Cuckold.
12. The Absorbed or Preoccupied Cuckold.
13. The Cuckold for His Health.
14. The Regenerating or Conservative Cuckold.
15. The Propagandistic Cuckold.

## Horned or Amusing

RIGHT WING

16. The Endearing Cuckold.
17. The Tolerant or Compliant Cuckold.
18. The Reciprocating Cuckold.
19. The Auxiliary or Helpful Cuckold.
20. The Hastening or Onrushing Cuckold.
21. The Manageable or Benign Cuckold.

CENTER OF THE SECT

22. The Optimistic or High Living Cuckold.
23. The Converted or Reconciled Cuckold.
24. The Federal or Coalesced Cuckold.
25. The Transcendent or Sublime Cuckold.
26. The Neuter or Impassive Cuckold.
27. The Deserting or Seceding Cuckold.
28. The Supportive or Straw-man Cuckold.

LEFT WING

29. The Babied or Compensated Cuckold.
30. The Bewitched or Blinded Cuckold.
31. The Gleaning or Banal Cuckold.

32. The Subservient Cuckold.
33. The Ceremonious or Mannerly Cuckold.
34. The Mystical or Sanctimonious Cuckold.

*Long-horned or Ridiculous*

LEFT WING TIP

35. The Orthodox or Indoctrinated Cuckold.
36. The Turncoat or Renegade Cuckold.
37. The Subdued or Perplexed Cuckold.
38. The Sordid Cuckold.
39. The Vulgar or Grubby Cuckold.

LEFT WINGLET

40. The Disabused or Dumbfounded Cuckold.
41. The Recalcitrant Cuckold.
42. The Fulminating Cuckold.
43. The Trumpeter Cuckold.

LEFT FLANK

44. The Disgraced Cuckold.
45. The Kept Cuckold.
46. The Dandinesque or Desperate Cuckold.

REAR GUARD

47. The Flag-Bearing Cuckold.
48. The Distaff-Bearing Cuckold.

REAR OUTPOST

49. The Posthumous Cuckold or the Cuckold in Two Worlds.


No. 4. *The Warlike or Swaggering Cuckold* is a man who terrorizes potential seducers in order to foil their designs. Although he congratulates himself on the success of his tactic, he still sports the horns of a cuckold. Usually he is deceived by one of the very people who applaud his blustering and assure him that he is the only man alive capable of preserving the sanctity of his household.

No. 6. *The Bantering Cuckold* is a man who jokes about his colleagues and describes them as imbeciles who deserve their fate. His audience listens bemusedly and tacitly applies to him the words of the Gospel: "You see the mote in your brother's eye, but not the beam in your own."

No. 19. *The Auxiliary or Helpful Cuckold* is a man who

spends little time in his own household and appears only to spread good will and to reproach his wife's bashful lovers for not drinking and making merry. Unwittingly he encourages them to forget their quarrels and to live like good republicans among whom everything is common property. This species aids human intercourse; the cuckold's horns weigh lightly on his head.

No. 20. *The Hastening or Onrushing Cuckold* is a man who strives to precipitate events. He eagerly shows off his wife in society, encourages her to go to the theater, to be affectionate with friends, to move in fast circles. This species is comparable to a package sent by fast mail: it arrives speedily at its destination.

No. 24. *The Federal or Coalesced Cuckold* is a man who accepts the inevitable and concedes his wife a lover—but makes the choice himself. Then, like Pitt and Coburg, the cuckold and the lover form a coalition to isolate the wife and to foil her other suitors.

No. 31. *The Gleaning or Banal Cuckold* is a man who humbly seeks his own small share in the harvest and eagerly plays up to his better half in order to obtain from her what she grants to so many others whose leavings he modestly gleans.

No. 33. *The Ceremonious or Mannerly Cuckold* is a quiet, simple man who never violates the rules of civility and seeks his vengeance only by means of calm discussion. When he finds a man of quality sleeping with his wife, he says: "This is most unseemly, sir. I would not have expected such behavior from a man like you." Sitting in an armchair, he recites a few arguments of the same light weight. The lover, who is bored by this little sermon, gets up in his nightshirt and says: "Sir, pardon me for disturbing you, but you are sitting on my trousers." The husband gets up and says politely: "Oh sir, I didn't see them. Take your trousers, etc." Then he goes on with his calm remonstrances.

No. 35. *The Orthodox or Indoctrinated Cuckold* is the best catechized member of the brotherhood. He is a man of faith who believes in principles and right conduct and thinks, as right-minded people do, that most libertines are merely talkers, that there are more faithful wives than one might think, and that rumors shouldn't be listened to. He does have a few suspicions. But, having been well-trained and catechized, he persists in his faith in the true principles of the brotherhood and places all his trust in the natural goodness of his wife and the influence of morality.

No. 36. *The Turncoat or Renegade Cuckold* is a man who was once a model of reason. But after having recognized the dangers of marriage and having warned others against the conjugal snare, he finally walks right into the trap and makes all the mistakes that he had earlier pointed out and denounced. He has apostatized common sense and been won over by folly. This was Molière's fate. After having done so much to enlighten and disabuse the brotherhood, he finished by sheepishly joining its ranks and reproducing in his own life all the absurdities he had mocked.

No. 39. *The Vulgar or Grubby Cuckold* is a clodhopper who antagonizes the public by the contrast between his own deplorable behavior and the good breeding of his wife. Everyone takes the lady's part and says: "It would be a real pity if she were faithful to a beast like him."

No. 43. *The Trumpeter Cuckold* is a man who takes the public into his confidence, wailing tearfully: "But I caught them in the act, sir." The reply he gets is that this was perhaps only a passing encounter and that he shouldn't be in a hurry to believe the worst. Nevertheless he continues to recoup his losses by telling everyone he meets about the outrage, and he would willingly blow a trumpet to assemble more people and arouse the public against his wife's unfair behavior.

No. 48. *The Distaff-Bearing Cuckold* is a man who takes care of the household while his wife is out on the town. He takes charge of all the womanly chores, is polite to the cavaliers who come to fetch Madame, and during her absence he arranges everything to make the household pleasant for her return. Does he go out for a walk? Madame precedes him with her lover, and he brings up the rear escorting ridicule on one arm and Milady's dog on the other. But his arms are less encumbered than is his forehead.

No. 49. *The Posthumous Cuckold* is a man whose wife bears

children ten or twelve months after his death. The law treats them as his, although he could not have been their father. He is thus a cuckold in two worlds or a cuckold in this life and the next, since after having worn the cuckold's horns in this life, another pair is planted on his coffin. This species may be contrasted with the Cuckold in the Bud, the one being cuckolded before and the other after marriage. They have every right to take their respective positions at the head and the rear of the procession.

*—PM*, III; *OC*, XI, 253–264

# 3

# CIVILIZATION IN HISTORICAL PERSPECTIVE

### THE FIRST AGE OF HUMANITY

Humanity, in its social life-span, is destined to traverse thirty-six periods. I am providing here a list of the initial periods, which will suffice for the material contained in this volume:

## SCALE OF THE FIRST AGE OF THE SOCIAL WORLD[1]

### Periods preceding the development of industry:

K. Bastard, without man.
1. Primitive, known as Eden.
2. Savage state or inertia.

### Fragmented, deceitful and repugnant industry:

3. Patriarchate, light industry.
4. Barbarism, medium industry.
5. Civilization, large-scale industry.

### Societary, truthful and attractive industry:

6. Guaranteeism, semi-association.
7. Sociantism, simple association.
8. Harmonism, compound association.

I am not making mention of the ninth period and those that follow it, since at the present time we are only capable of ascending as high as the eighth period. Nonetheless it will be a period of infinite happiness by comparison with the four existing societies.[2] It will spread suddenly and spontaneously to the

---

[1] In this text Fourier's periods are characterized in economic terms. Other writings suggest that each period also had its distinctive forms of religion, morality, and sexual relations. In his early writings and notably the *Quatre mouvements* Fourier was inclined to regard "amorous customs" (the prevailing mode of relations between the sexes) as the "pivotal" or defining attribute of a given period. See below pp. 194–196.

[2] As this reference suggests, Fourier's historical schema allowed for the coexistence of several periods at once. The "four existing societies" are the Savage state, Patriarchate, Barbarism, and Civilization. Fourier's complete vision of human history encompassed 36 (or 32) stages. After the

whole human race thanks to the influence of profit, pleasure and, above all, industrial attraction, a mechanism of which our statesmen and moralists have absolutely no knowledge. . . .

To create attraction the system of the passionate series had to be discovered. Attraction will be established gradually during the course of the sixth, seventh and eighth periods. The sixth period will be marked by the creation of a semi-attraction which will not be sufficient to interest the savages. The seventh period will begin to win them over, and the conversion of the idle rich will take place in the eighth period. The sixth and seventh periods can be skipped thanks to the invention of the passionate series, which is the mechanism governing the eighth period.[3]

—*OC*, vi, xi–xii

### THE PHASES OF CIVILIZATION

Like the human body, societies have their own four ages, each of which can be distinguished by its own particular attributes. It is impossible to detect progress or decadence until a clear distinction has been made among the attributes which characterize a given society. Our naturalists are very scrupulous about classifying useless vegetables and distinguishing between their varieties. Why don't the politicians follow the same method in

---

onset of "Harmonism" progress would continue until the "apogee of happiness" had been reached. Thereupon the human race would begin its inevitable descent back into "chaos." After precisely 80,000 years the last vestiges of life would disappear from the face of the earth and the planet itself would cease to rotate on its axis. See *OC*, i, 33–37.

[3] Fourier repeatedly insisted that the sixth and seventh periods were "optional": there was no necessity for mankind to pass laboriously through the stages of Guaranteeism and Sociantism on its way to Harmony. Nevertheless, all his major works include detailed specifications concerning a wide variety of schemes (small-sized Phalanxes, producers' associations, credit institutions, etc.) appropriate to the transitional periods. Historians in the cooperatist tradition, such as Charles Gide, have attached considerable importance to these schemes. Unquestionably they did serve as models for many of the attempts made by Fourier's nineteenth century disciples to put his doctrines into practice. But in our view they add little to Fourier's stature as a social theorist; they are important primarily for the role that they played in the history of practical Fourierism.

ascribing to their beloved civilization attributes appropriate to each of its four phases? This is the sole means of telling whether it is progressing or declining.

## THE SUCCESSIVE ATTRIBUTES OF CIVILIZATION
### Ascending Vibration

**CHILDHOOD, OR FIRST PHASE**

| | |
|---|---|
| Simple Germ . . . . . . . | Exclusive marriage or monogamy. |
| Compound Germ . . . . . | Patriarchal or nobiliary feudalism. |
| PIVOT . . . . . . . . . | *Civil rights of the wife.* |
| Counterpoise . . . . . . | Alliance of great vassals. |
| Tone . . . . . . . . . | Chivalrous illusions. |

**ADOLESCENCE, OR SECOND PHASE**

| | |
|---|---|
| Simple Germ . . . . . . . | Communal privileges. |
| Compound Germ . . . . . | Cultivation of the sciences and arts. |
| PIVOT . . . . . . . . . | *Emancipation of those who work.* |
| Counterpoise . . . . . . | Representative system. |
| Tone . . . . . . . . . | Libertarian illusions. |

**APOGEE, OR PLENITUDE**

| | |
|---|---|
| Germs . . . . . . . . . | Navigation, experimental chemistry. |
| Attributes . . . . . . . | Deforestation, fiscal loans. |

### Descending Vibration

**VIRILITY, OR THIRD PHASE**

| | |
|---|---|
| Simple Germ . . . . . . . | Mercantile and fiscal spirit. |
| Compound Germ . . . . . | Shareholding companies. |
| PIVOT . . . . . . . . . | *Maritime monopoly.* |
| Counterpoise . . . . . . | Anarchic commerce. |
| Tone . . . . . . . . . | Economic illusions. |

**DECREPITUDE, OR FOURTH PHASE**

| | |
|---|---|
| Simple Germ . . . . . . . | Urban pawn-shops. |
| Compound Germ . . . . . | Fixed number of masterships. |
| PIVOT . . . . . . . . . | *Industrial feudalism.* |
| Counterpoise . . . . . . | Farmers-out of feudal monopolies. |
| Tone . . . . . . . . . | Illusions about association. |

(*Nota.*) We do not mention here the permanent attributes which characterize all four phases of civilization, but only those which constitute a given phase and the mixed attributes which link two successive phases. For example, the civilization of Athens was an incomplete and tainted example of the second phase in that it lacked the pivotal attribute, the liberty of the working people. It was a bastard and falsified second phase, having as its pivot an attribute of barbarism. When one understands the obscurities of the social attributes, of which I am going to describe eight orders, then it will be simple to dispel all illusions about social progress.

The present civilization of France and England is in the declining portion of the third phase. The attributes of the third phase made their appearance long ago; this civilization is now straining toward the fourth phase for which it has the two germs; but it is ignorant of what it must do with these germs in order to enter the fourth phase. Such an advance would represent very little progress; it would be the least amount of progress possible. But the present state is one of painful stagnation in which man's genius is imprisoned, worn out by its sterility, vainly bestirring itself to produce a new idea. Society is being worn out by its excessively long pause in the third phase.

In the absence of inventive genius, the fiscal instinct will soon discover the means of organizing the fourth phase, which represents an advance, but not an advance toward the good. We will only begin to move toward the good when we organize an ambiguous phase between civilization and guaranteeism. That is the means of attacking liberalism, a stationary mentality which is unable to advance and which is passionately devoted to an attribute of the second phase, to the *representative system*—a tid-bit good in a small republic like Sparta or Athens but wholly illusory in a vast and wealthy empire such as France.

I have pointed out that the anti-liberals, a class no less deluded than the liberals, are making a shocking blunder in trying to fight against the liberal chimeras by calling for a return to the first phase. This tactic is particularly inappropriate in view of the fact that the increase in public debts is sweeping us irresistibly toward the fourth phase or decrepitude.

A detailed examination of the table of the permanent attributes of civilization designated in this chapter would be enough to dispel our illusions about the sublime flight of social progress. It would prove that our flight across the phases of society resembles the backward crawl of the crayfish. To aspire to the fourth phase of civilization, to the decrepitude of a fundamentally rotten period, is to progress if you like, but to progress into decadence. This sort of progress is comparable to that of a woman whose hair turns white when she reaches sixty. She might say that her tresses are improving, that their whiteness is going to rival that of alabaster. She might exclaim: "How sublime is the flight of my tresses towards perfectibilizing perfectibility!" Each of us could only smile pityingly: the body does not become more perfect as it ages.

Such is the illusion of progress in which our old civilization glories as it hastens toward decrepitude. Societies like individuals go to their ruin when they fall into debt and sell themselves to the usurer. This is the fact of our time; we are moving from one loan to another.

"The vase is empty, the fabric has been creased." The crease of fiscal loans is an enduring one; each new ministry will fall more deeply into debt; because, as the proverb says, "You've got to eat when you're in the manger." Whatever party may dominate, finance, which holds the reigns of the chariot, will not turn back toward the way of economy. What will be the result of this fiscal ulcer, of this canker of debts and loans which is growing and swelling in all empires? The denouement will be explained in the chapter which deals with the fourth phase of civilization, a phase in which we are led, by the force of circumstances, toward an abyss which our guides, the economists, cannot even recognize.

They may be compared to the inept horseman of whom it is said: "It is not he who leads his horse; it is his horse who is leading him." Such are our political geniuses: they are not leading civilized government; it is leading them. But it would have been so easy for them to guide us in the direction of real progress, if only they had wished to "get out of the rut," to be done with the prejudices of agricultural fragmentation and commercial anarchy, or individual competition in deceitfulness.

—*OC*, vi, 386–389

### SEXUAL RELATIONS AND SOCIAL CHANGE

Each historical period has an attribute which forms the PIVOT OF THE MECHANISM and whose absence or presence determines a change of period. This attribute is always drawn from love. In the fourth period it is the *absolute servitude of woman;* in the fifth period it is *exclusive marriage and the civil liberties of the wife;* in the sixth period it is the *amorous corporation* which assures women the privilege of which I have already spoken. If the barbarians took up the practice of *exclusive marriage*, this innovation alone would soon make them civilized; if we adopted the *confinement and sale of women*, we would soon become barbarians by virtue of this single innovation; and if we adopted the system of *amorous guarantees* which will be adopted in the sixth period, this measure alone would provide us with a means to escape civilization and to enter the sixth period.

As a general proposition, the Pivotal Attribute which is always drawn from amorous customs gives rise to all the others; but the secondary attributes do not give rise to the pivotal and lead only very slowly to a change in period. Barbarians could adopt as many as twelve of the sixteen civilized attributes, but they would remain in a state of barbarism if they did not adopt the pivotal attribute, the *civil liberty of the wife.*

If God gave amorous custom such influence on the social mechanism and on the metamorphoses which it can undergo, it was because of his horror of oppression and violence. He wished the happiness or unhappiness of human societies to be proportionate to the constraint or liberty which they tolerate. But the only sort of liberty recognized by God is that which is extended to both sexes and not just to one. Thus he decided that all the periods which spawn social horror, like Savagery, Barbarism and Civilization, should have no other Pivot than the servitude of women, and that all other periods which produce social welfare, like the sixth, seventh and eighth, should have no other Pivot, no other guide than the progressive liberation of the weaker sex.

—*OC*, I, 89–90

Among the signs which indicate the good results to come from the extension of women's privileges, we must refer to the experience of all countries. It is known that the best nations have always been those which concede the greatest amount of liberty to women. This is true of the Barbarians and the Savages as well as the Civilized. The Japanese, who are the most industrious, the bravest and the most honorable of the Barbarians, are also the least jealous and the most indulgent towards women. This is so true that Chinamen travel to Japan to yield to the love that is forbidden by their own hypocritical customs.

For the same reason the Tahitians were the best of all the Savages; given their relative lack of natural resources, they made greater advances in industry than any other band of Savages. Among civilized populations the French are the least inclined to persecute their women; they are also the best in the sense that they are the most adaptable of nations, the one from which a skillful ruler can get the best results in any sort of task. Despite a few defects such as frivolity, individual presumptuousness, and lack of cleanliness, the French are the foremost civilized nation owing to this adaptability which is the trait most alien to the Barbarian character.

It can likewise be observed that the most corrupt nations have always been those in which women were most completely subjugated. Witness the Chinese who are the dregs of the planet, the most deceitful, cowardly and greedy of all the industrious peoples, as well as the most jealous and intolerant about love. Among modern, civilized nations the Spanish have been the least indulgent towards the fair sex; thus they have remained behind the other Europeans and have lacked distinction in the sciences and the arts. As for the savage hordes, an examination of their case would prove that the most corrupt are also those which show the least consideration for the weaker sex and in which the status of women is the worst.

As a general proposition: *Social progress and changes of period are brought about by virtue of the progress of women towards liberty, and social retrogression occurs as a result of a diminution in the liberty of women.*

Other events influence these political changes; but there is no cause which produces social progress or decline as rapidly as a change in the condition of women. I have already said that the simple adoption of closed harems would speedily turn us into Barbarians, and the mere opening of the harems would enable the Barbarians to advance to Civilization. In summary, *the extension of the privileges of women is the fundamental cause of all social progress.*[4]

—*OC*, I, 131–133

There was very little that prevented the vandalism of 1793 from suddenly producing a second revolution as marvellous as the first was horrible. The whole human race was approaching its release; the civilized, barbarian and savage order would have disappeared forever if the Convention, which trampled down all prejudices, had not bowed before the only one that had to be destroyed, the institution of marriage. In destroying it, we would have entered the seventh period, skipping the sixth. This is the final blow that the French Convention failed to deliver due to its timidity. How could an assembly which was so strongly hostile to half-measures have limited itself to a half-measure like divorce? How could men who made sport of trampling underfoot the Deity itself have been so weak in dealing with the custom of marriage? This was the last entrenchment of Civilization; it survived to regain the offensive and to win back all the ground it had lost; but what kept it from disappearing?

—*OC*, XII, 622

### "SIXTEEN RECENT DEGENERATIONS"

There has been much bragging about civilized perfectibility, the progress of reason, its sublime flight, the creation of new sciences, etc. A good answer to all this is a list of the ills which philosophy has actually caused in the course of a single genera-

[4] This statement became one of the battle cries of radical feminism in the 1840s. It was to serve Flora Tristan, who knew Fourier during his old age, as the epigraph for her *L'Emancipation de la femme* (Paris, 1845). See also Marx and Engels, *The Holy Family* (Moscow, 1956), p. 259, and Engels, *Anti-Dühring* (3rd ed. Moscow, 1962), p. 355.

tion. Everything in the litany that you are about to read dates from the past forty years.[5]

1. *Progress of fiscal trickery*, systems of extortion, indirect bankruptcy, speculation on anticipated revenue, art of devouring the future. In 1788 NECKER did not know where to raise 50 million to cover the annual deficit. But since the creation of THE SCIENCE WHICH DID NOT EXIST UNDER NECKER, a way has been found to increase annual taxes not by 50 but by 500 million. In 1788 they did not amount to half a billion.

2. *Progress of the mercantile spirit:* encouragement given to commercial plundering and rascality. Speculation given the power to scoff at law, to steal all the fruits of industry, to share in the authority of governments, and to spread everywhere the frenzy of gambling in the public funds.

3. *Urban concentration.* The great cities transformed into bottomless pits which absorb all resources, attract all people of wealth, and increase the disdain for agriculture.

4. *Maritime monopoly.* It was contested and held in check in 1788. Now it is exclusive master, with no chance for the Europeans to reestablish rival navies.

5. *Hereditary evil*, or the custom of adopting established vices. Let the Directory initiate a scandalous practice like the farming out of public gambling; its successors will declaim against it, but maintain the vice. The same pattern is followed in small things and in great, in everything from gambling monopolies to military conscription. The progress of civilization is real enough, but it is progress in the art of legalizing and multiplying every conceivable disorder.

6. *Attacks upon property*, degenerating into a habit under pretexts of revolution, pretexts which become rules for succeeding parties.

7. *Collapse of intermediary bodies*, provincial Estates, parliaments, guilds and corporations, which used to impose limits on

[5] Written in 1823. In the *Nouveau monde industriel* (1829) Fourier published an up-dated and expanded list of the symptoms of civilized degeneration. See *OC*, VI, 418–423.

the central power. Their collapse has enabled the government to increase its annual tax revenue by 500 millions in a country from which Necker was unable to squeeze 50.

8. *Plundering of communes:* among other political evils, it has produced that of town duties, a fine means of alienating city-dwellers and rendering them docile followers of agitators.

9. *Instability of institutions*, condemned to impotence even when wisely conceived, and thwarted by the secret persistence of revolutionary habits among people worn out by excessive taxation.

10. *Deep-rooted discords;* local hatreds and ferments of dis-sension improperly stifled by simplistic methods which suppress the evil instead of absorbing it.

11. *Destructive or accelerating tactics* which quadruple the ravages of war, revive barbarous customs, *Vendées*, guerilla-actions, mass troop levies, and which drag everyone including women and children into war.

12. *Political immorality*, the union of Christianity with the Ottomans against a Christian nation which wishes to avoid being massacred.[6] PASSIVE collaboration for the maintenance of piracy and the slave trade, which could be halted at once if measures were taken against the well-known guilty parties. The shameless-ness of commerce which builds the vessels the Algerians will use to fill their prisons with Christian slaves.

—DIRECT DEPRAVITY OF THE SCIENCES: obstinate refusal to ex-plore neglected areas of study; scorn for experience which shows the sophists that their systems have constantly served to perpetuate the nine scourges;[7] fraudulent pretence that every-thing has been discovered and that men with something new to say should be scoffed at; mercantile spirit of the learned world which reduces the sciences and the arts to a nest of commercial

[6] Greece.

[7] In contrast to the "accidental" symptoms of degeneration enumerated here, Fourier maintained that civilization could be characterized by nine essential and permanent features. These "nine scourges" were: "1. Poverty, 2. Rascality, 3. Oppression, 4. Carnage, 5. Climatic excesses, 6. Contagious diseases, 7. Vicious circle, 8. Universal egoism, 9. Deceit." *OC*, II (*Som-maires*), 13.

intrigue, silencing those who have not won favor with the philosophical cliques.

—INDIRECT DEPRAVITY OF THE SCIENCES. Progress in the science of chemistry, to cite just one example, only serves to plague the poor by providing commerce with the means to debase all commodities: bread made out of potatoes, wine squeezed from logwood, sham vinegar, sham oil, sham coffee, sham sugar, sham indigo. All of our foodstuffs and manufactured goods are adulterated, and it is the poor man who suffers by this chemical cheapening: he alone is the victim of all these mercantile inventions. They could be put to good use under a system of truthful relations, but they will become increasingly harmful until the close of civilization.

—LIBERAL RETROGRESSION, or the accumulation of liberal prejudices which lead to shocking actions such as the granting of the rights of citizenship to the Jews; an act doubly impolitic in that it grafts the third period (patriarchate) onto the fifth (civilization) and opens the door to parasites and unproductive people, all of whom are devoted to trade and not to agriculture. An enlightened policy would have excluded these people as a social contagion. This is a new thesis and one on which I should like to write at greater length.[8] ASKER KHAN, the Persian ambassador at Paris, was not allowed to have his slaves beheaded; Bonaparte told him that barbarian customs would not be tolerated in a civilized country. Why then should civilization put up with patriarchal vices which are equally odious although not sanguinary?

—ILLIBERAL RETROGRESSION or spirit of immobility which is dominant among courtiers and men of eminence. They were very liberal in 1788, but now they are frightened by the alleged advance of civilization and the obvious evils to which it has given rise. They are suspicious of the spirit of social progress when they might better wonder about the false paths it has fol-

[8] There was of course nothing new about Fourier's conviction that the Jews were "a nation of usurers." (*OC*, vi, 421.) But he was one of the earliest if not most strident anti-semites in the socialist tradition. See E. Silberner, "Charles Fourier on the Jewish Question," *Jewish Social Studies*, VIII, 4 (October, 1946), 245–266.

lowed and decide to seek true progress through other means than those adopted by the philosophers.

—*OC*, II, 167–170

### THE IMMINENT SOCIAL METAMORPHOSIS

Our efforts at social reform lead to nothing but discord and disaster. The progress of our societies is like the crawl of the sloth which groans with every step it takes. Like the sloth, civilization moves forward with an inconceivable sluggishness through political storms and revolutions. The new social theories put forward by each generation only serve, like brambles, to draw blood from the people who seize upon them.

At last we have reached the end of our social calamities, the end of the political childhood of the globe. We are on the verge of a great metamorphosis which has begun to manifest itself in a state of universal unrest. Today one can truly say that the present is ripe with the future and that an excess of suffering must hasten the moment of salvation. The prolongation of our political conflicts suggests that nature is making an effort to throw off an oppressive burden. Wars and revolutions are ceaselessly inflaming the globe. As soon as the fires are quelled, they rise up again from the ashes. Partisan conflicts are festering without hope of reconciliation. Civilized society has become mistrustful, spiteful, steeped in vices; it is capable of anything, even of joining forces with the barbarians to persecute Christians. The public funds have become the prey of the vampires of speculation. Industry, with its monopolies and its excesses, has become a form of punishment inflicted on the common people who are undergoing the torments of Tantalus as they starve in the midst of plenty. Colonial ambition has opened a new volcano: the implacable fury of the Negroes may soon turn America into a vast sepulchre, and the destruction of the Negro races will be avenged by the slaughter of the conquerors. Imitating the cannibals, commerce has refined the atrocities of the slave trade and mocked the salutary decrees of a congress of sovereigns.[9] The mercantile spirit has widened the sphere of its

[9] The Congress of Vienna nominally abolished the slave trade in 1815.

crimes; every new war carries devastation into both hemispheres. Our vessels are circling the globe simply to spread our vices and our violence to the barbarians and the savages. The earth is now no more than a dreadful chaos of immorality. Civilization is becoming more odious as it nears its end.

Now that civilization has reached the very bottom of the abyss, a fortunate invention is about to provide it with the *social compass* or the *calculus of attraction*. . . .

At last fortune has begun to smile on us; the fates are appeased, and the invention of the societary theory has opened the doors of the social prison known as civilization. . . .

If this age decides wisely to put the theory to the test, the whole globe will be transformed; humanity will rise from the depths of suffering to the heights of happiness. Everything will transpire in an instant, like a theatrical change of scenes in which Hell is replaced by Olympus.[10] We are going to witness a spectacle which can be seen only once on each globe: the sudden transformation from industrial incoherence to societary unity. This is the most spectacular historical change which can take place in all the universes. Its expectation should console the present generation for all its misfortunes. During this metamorphosis each year will be worth centuries of existence. But the events which are going to transpire will be so remarkable that it would be wrong to disclose them without proper preparation.

Beset by long-standing misfortunes and bound by the chains of habit, the people of civilization have imagined that God destined them to a life of privations or at most to a very limited degree of happiness. It will take some time for them to become accustomed to the idea of the happiness that awaits them. They would react skeptically to an unvarnished account of the delights which they are going to enjoy in the very near future. Yet

[10] Here Fourier is envisaging the possibility that a rich capitalist would appear and establish a trial community in exact accordance with Fourier's specifications. In that case there would be no need for humanity to pass through the "transitional" historical stages of Guaranteeism and Sociantism. Instead the success of the community would be so spectacular as to inspire instant imitation and within "no more than six years" the reign of universal harmony would begin.

the new order is near at hand, for it will take barely two years to organize each of the societary communities and no more than six years at the longest to complete the organization of the globe.

The long delay in the establishment of the societary order will only serve to increase its magnificence. Already in the time of Solon and Pericles the Greeks had sufficient means at their disposal to found a trial community. They had satisfied the principal requirement which is the development of large-scale industry. During the earliest times, when industrial development was limited, the societary order could not have been established and God was thus obliged to leave man in ignorance of his magnificent destiny.[11]

Today our resources in art, industry, material elegance and refinement are at least twice those possessed by the Athenians. Thus the beginnings of the societary order will be twice as splendid. Now at last we are going to benefit from the progress of our physical sciences. Until the present time these sciences have only served to multiply the luxuries of the few and hence to increase the relative deprivation of the impoverished multitude. Until now scientific progress has benefited the idle, but it has tormented the working people. In this odious situation men had but two alternatives: to blame God or to blame civilization. Reasonable men would have opted for the latter alternative.

[11] By "large-scale industry" Fourier of course means something more modest than what the term implies today. Nonetheless he repeatedly insisted that his new social order could not be established until mankind had attained a relatively advanced stage of technological (and cultural) development. In this light he maintained that, for all its evils, "civilization has an important historical role to play. For it creates the means necessary for mankind to advance to association; it creates large-scale industry, the abstract sciences and the fine arts. These means must be put to use if man is to rise on the social scale." (*OC*, VI, 9.)

This point, which Fourier constantly reiterated, is important because it shows that his utopia was not simply the product of rural nostalgia. He believed that man's basic instinctual drives could not be adequately gratified in a thoroughly rural and "backward" setting. Far from sharing Rousseau's hostility to luxury, material elegance and refinement, he maintained that the desire for *luxe* was an innate human disposition. See below pp. 216 and 258.

Instead of posing the problem in this way, the philosophers have attempted to elude it. . . . To avoid making a choice, they adhered during the last century to a bastard conception, that of atheism. Presupposing the lack of a God, atheism exempts the savants from seeking out and determining his designs and it authorizes them to pass off their own capricious and contradictory theories as the rules of social welfare. Atheism is very accommodating to political ignorance, and those who have been described as *strong-minded men* for professing to be atheists have shown themselves to be very weak in inspiration. Afraid of failing in the search for the social plans of God, they have preferred to deny God's existence and to praise the perfection of the civilized order which they secretly abhor. In fact, it is the chaos of civilization which has caused them to doubt God's providence.

The sophists are not the only ones at fault on this point. For if it is absurd not to believe in God, it is equally absurd to believe in him half-heartedly—to think that his providence is incomplete and that he has neglected to provide for our most urgent need, the need of a social order which will assure our happiness. When one beholds the marvels of our industry, such as great clipper ships and other wondrous inventions which are premature in view of our political immaturity, can one reasonably suppose that the God who has lavished such blessings upon us would want to deny us knowledge of the social art which will enable us to put our inventions to the best use. Would not God have been malicious and inconsistent in providing us with so many admirable sciences if those sciences were meant to produce nothing more than barbarism and civilization? At last humanity is going to be delivered from these disgusting and criminal societies, and their imminent downfall will be greeted by universal joy!

—*OC*, ii, *Avant propos*, 69–76

# *IV*

# *The Theory of Passionate Attraction*

My theory is limited to *utilizing the passions just as nature gives them and without changing anything*. That is the whole mystery, the whole secret of the calculus of passionate attraction. The theory does not ask whether God was right or wrong to endow human beings with particular passions; the societary order utilizes them without changing anything and just as God has given them.

—*OC*, v, 157

Both Fourier's critique of civilized society and his utopian plans hinged on a psychological vision which he rightly regarded as the core of his whole system. Men were not fundamentally rational or calculating creatures, he maintained; their behavior was determined by fundamental instinctual drives which could not be permanently altered or suppressed. Only when the primacy and the immutability of these drives was recognized, when philosophers and moralists ceased trying to impose curbs and checks on the passions, would it be possible to construct a society in which men could be free, happy, and productive.

We have already pointed out in the Introduction that Fourier's recognition of the strength of the passions as determinants of human behavior was by no means unusual for its time. Many of the philosophes had regarded the passions as the basic springs of human action. Diderot, Helvétius, and others had exalted them as the principle source of great art and great deeds. But even the most ardent apologists of the passions believed that some restraints were necessary if a good and relatively free society was to be built on earth. To be sure, the image of an idyllic primitive society where men were free to obey their instinctual promptings was present in the minds of most of the eighteenth century philosophers. But few believed that this idyllic state could be recaptured. The greatest of the philosophes —Montesquieu, Diderot, Rousseau—believed that social life necessarily involved constraint; and to them freedom meant the conscious acceptance of constraint, the agreement to abide by law. The essential psychological complement of freedom, as they understood it, was stoic moderation and ascetic self-discipline on the Spartan or Roman Republican model.

Fourier was familiar with this venerable tradition of political theory, and he had nothing but contempt for it. In his writings he repeatedly mocked the republican virtue and Spartan simplicity vaunted by "the philosophers." What was good, he asked, about a society in which men were compelled to live on "republican cabbage," "Spartan gruel," and self-restraint? To his mind self-imposed constraints were no better than constraints imposed from without. There was nothing virtuous or dignified about continence and rational self-discipline. Furthermore, they wouldn't work. The passions clamored for gratification and no matter how "rational" repression might be, its consequences would always be harmful to the individual and ultimately destructive to society. Fourier believed that the only happy and harmonious society would be one which would liberate and utilize the passions.

Fourier's conviction that the passions were meant to be the agents of human happiness and social harmony rested on a set of metaphysical assumptions which are presented in the texts that open this section. Although Fourier was capable of developing his metaphysics at great length, it was at bottom extraordinarily simple. Like many of the eighteenth century deists he believed that the perfectly harmonious Newtonian universe was itself a proof of the existence of an infinitely wise Creator. But Fourier's speculations on the properties of the Deity took him far beyond the wildest dreams of the deists. He maintained that a God possessing such attributes as infinite wisdom and universal providence was bound by His very nature to have devised a "social code" for the terrestrial happiness of mankind. What Fourier had done, quite simply, was to discover this code.

Most of the texts in this section are devoted to the analysis of the passions themselves, those God-given instinctual drives which Fourier regarded as the basic forces in the social universe. Fourier's analysis of the twelve radical passions and his classification of personality types have been amply discussed in the Introduction. But there is one point which deserves further emphasis. For all of his optimism about the uses of the passions, Fourier was far from denying the reality of hatred, anger, jealousy, and aggression. He did maintain that many of these harmful or destructive human impulses were "subversive" or "deviated" manifestations of ungratified desire. Many of them were "counter-passions" produced by the repression of benign instincts. When Society had been organized in accordance with God's plan, much of the hostility and destructiveness which plagued civilized society would simply disappear. But Fourier did not claim that all aggressive and perverse impulses would be banished from his utopia. For many such impulses (including each of Christianity's seven deadly sins!) were in fact natural. They would not be repressed but rather absorbed into the system as a whole and channeled into salutary directions by being appropriately combined with other passions. Fourier's utopia thrived on conflict, competition, and discord. As the texts on *The New Amorous World* will show, there was also a place in Harmony for most of the bizarre needs and fancies that civilization wrongly stigmatized as perversions.

# 1

# METAPHYSICS AND THEODICY

## GOD AND HIS PROPERTIES

The multitude has perennially been deceived into thinking that the designs of God are impenetrable, that men should not even seek to know God. Common sense suggests the contrary; it obliges us to begin our studies with the simplest of all our problems, the problem of God.

In antiquity the Creator was travestied by fables which confounded him with a horde of 35,000 false gods, each more ridiculous than the others. At that time it was assuredly difficult to study the designs of God, to make some sense out of the celestial masquerade. Thus Socrates and Cicero confined themselves to gaining detachment from the follies of their age, and to adoring the UNKNOWN GOD without making further investigations which would have been thwarted by the spirit of the time. Socrates was nonetheless the victim of his age.

Now that these superstitions have been dissipated and Christianity has brought us back to sound ideas, to the belief in a single God, we have a sure guide in undertaking the study of nature.[1] Starting with the principle that all enlightenment must come from God, and that reason can only foster enlightenment insofar as it conforms to the dispositions of the Creator, it remains for us to determine the essential properties of God, his attributes, his designs, and his methods of achieving the harmony of the Universe. On this score, certain rules which are already known can lead us to the discovery of those which remain unknown.

In dealing with this question one must proceed by degrees

---

[1] Although Fourier was a theist, he did not always refer to Christianity in such sympathetic terms. His early writings in particular abound in diatribes against Christian asceticism and the "priestly caste." In his later years, however, he sometimes tried to present his doctrine as compatible with orthodox Christianity. The *Nouveau monde industriel* (1829), from which this selection is taken, includes a lengthy "Confirmation drawn from the Holy Gospel."

and begin by analyzing a very small number of the properties of God, focusing on the most evident, such as the following:

1. The INTEGRAL direction of movement.
2. Economy in the choice of means.
3. Distributive justice.
4. The Universality of Providence.
5. UNITY OF SYSTEM.

1. *The integral direction of movement.* If God plays the most important role in the direction of movement, if he alone is master of the universe, the sole creator and dispenser, it is up to Him to direct all aspects of the universe, among others the most noble aspect, that of social relations. It follows that the laws governing human societies must be the work of God and not of men. If we are to guide our societies toward the good, we must seek the social code that God was bound to compose for us. . . .

2. *Economy in the choice of means.* If the mechanism of societies is controlled by God, it should be distinguished by the economy in the choice of means that we attribute to him in naming him the SUPREME ECONOMIST. But the principle of economy requires him to work with very large social groups, and not with the smallest which we name "the family, the conjugal household." Above all the principle of economy requires God to choose passionate attraction as the driving force in human affairs. . . .

3. *Distributive justice.* There is not a trace of it in civilized legislation which increases the poverty of men in proportion to their industriousness. The first sign of justice should be to guarantee the people a *minimum* which would increase in proportion to social progress. . . . Is there any justice in a state of affairs where the progress of industry does not even guarantee the poor a chance to obtain work?

4. *The Universality of Providence.* Divine providence should be extended to all nations, to the savages just as to the civilized. The savages are truly free men, and any industrial system which they reject is contrary to the designs of God. The form of industry which we offer them, agricultural fragmentation and domestic isolation, is not a part of the providential plan, for this system fails to satisfy the impulses given by Providence

to those who are closest to nature. The same can be said of any order based on violence. Any class that is constrained directly, as are slaves, or indirectly, as are wage-earners, is deprived of the support of Providence which has no other agent on this planet than that of attraction. Therefore the civilized and barbarous order, which is based uniquely on violence, is contrary to the designs of God; and there must be another system applicable to all castes and to all peoples, if it is true that Providence is universal.

5. *Unity of system.* This implies the use of attraction, which is the known agent of God, the mainspring of the social harmonies of the universe, from those of the stars to those of the insects. It is thus by the study of attraction that we must seek the divine social code.

—*OC*, VI, 351–355

### THE DIVINE SOCIAL CODE

Destiny! The word sounds ridiculous. Anyone would fear to be taken for a visionary if he did not scoff at the idea of a pre-established destiny, of a divine and mathematical theory concerning the relations of societies and the mechanism of the passions. Nevertheless, how can one suppose that an eminently wise being could have created our passions without having previously determined their uses? Could God, who has spent an eternity creating and structuring worlds, have been unaware that the first *collective* need of their inhabitants is for a code regulating the social relations of men and their passions?

Under the guidance of our self-proclaimed sages, the passions merely engender calamities which make one wonder whether they are the work of Hell or the deity. Try out successively the laws established by the most revered of men, by Solon and Draco, by Lycurgus and Minos, and the result will always be the nine calamities which constitute the subversive mechanism of the passions. Should not God have foreseen the shameful results of man-made laws? He could have observed their effects on the billion globes created prior to our own. He should have known, before creating us and endowing us with passions, that human reason would be insufficient to harmonize the passions and that humanity would need a legislator more enlightened than itself.

Unless one wishes to regard God's providence as insufficient, limited and indifferent to our happiness, it follows that God must have devised for us a passional code, a system for the domestic and social organization of all humanity, which is everywhere endowed with the same passions. . . .

How can we suppose God to be more imprudent than the least experienced among us! When a man gathers building materials, does he not always make a plan for the use of these materials? What would we think of someone who bought stone and timber and supplies for the construction of a large edifice without any idea of the kind of building he wished to construct? What would we think if such a man admitted he had gathered his materials with no idea of the use to which he would put them? We would take him for a madman. Yet this is the degree of ineptitude that our sophists attribute to God in supposing that He could have created the passions, attractions, character traits, instincts and the other materials of the social edifice without having made any plans as to their use. . . .

God must have composed a passional code regulating our domestic, industrial and social relations. How then can we suppose that he wished to hide this code from man, the only creature who needs to know it? He has not concealed from us a much less important branch of the laws of movement, that of material gravitation and the celestial harmonies. Since Newton's time He has initiated us into the mysteries of the equilibrium of the universe, which had previously been regarded as unfathomable. Why should we suppose that He wishes to deny us knowledge of the system which He must have composed concerning the mechanism of the passions and of societies? For what reason would He refuse us the science which is most directly concerned with our needs, with our industrial relations?

*—OC*, III, 111–115

## THE LAW OF ATTRACTION

We already know that God relies solely upon the force of attraction in guiding the movements of the planets and the suns, which are creatures immensely greater than ourselves, and in guiding the insects, creatures far inferior to us.[2] Could man alone be deprived of the fortune of being guided toward social good by attraction? Why should there be a break in the chain of the system of the universe? Attraction is the divine guide of the stars and the animals and it suffices to place them in harmony. Why should it not be equally sufficient for man, whose place in the universe is midway between the planets and the animals? Where is the unity of the divine system if the mainspring of the general harmony, attraction, is not just as applicable to human societies as it is to the stars and the animals, if attraction cannot be applied to the agricultural and manufacturing industries which are the pivot of the social mechanism?

*OC*, III, 248

Philosophical wisdom and civilization come from men and attraction comes from God; for it acts prior to reason, it even wins over the reasoner who has decided not to obey it. Thus it comes from a power superior to reason and human wisdom. This power can only be God; and if attraction, which comes from God, gives rise to evil in the civilized, barbarian and savage societies created by man, is this not an indication that these societies are incompatible with the designs of God, and that attraction, God's agent, could give rise to good in another society organized in conformity with the designs of God?

Nature shows us, through the example of the animals, that if passionate attraction leads to harmony, it does so *conditionally*, provided the prerequisites of harmony are available. Thus the bees can build a hive with the help of attraction only when they find flowers which are the chief element of their social mechanism. Similarly the beavers could not establish their industrious society in a country like Scotland which lacks wood. Thus for these two species wood and flowers are the essential

---

[2] Fourier's reference to the planets and suns as "creatures" is not fortuitous. He regarded most of the heavenly bodies as living bisexual organisms endowed with their own passions and capable of, among other things, procreation. See below pp. 402–403.

principle of harmony without which attraction could not attain its objective.

Human beings are in a similar position. Their attraction can attain its goal, universe harmony, only when the two prerequisites of harmony are available. These are luxury and the theory. You have already created luxury which is the more important of the two agents.[3] It remained for you to discover the theory. Without both these means at your disposal, you are fettered like beavers who find wood without water or water without wood and are unable to organize their marvelous society. Observe sadly, therefore, that despite the increase in luxury and the development of the arts, you have not yet escaped the poverty which besets nine-tenths of society. You possess luxury without the means to make use of it. This means is the theory of social harmony which must bring a greater or lesser degree of luxury to all the inhabitants of the globe. Reflect upon the truth that the birth of social happiness is dependent on the discovery of two means: 1. luxury, without which harmony cannot be organized; 2. the theory of harmony, without which you cannot make use of luxury. If God had not intended all of you to live in a state of well-being, why would he have endowed all civilized peoples with an insatiable desire for wealth. The cupidity that you take for a vice is, on the contrary, a God-given drive which stimulates you to seek social states other than civilization, in which you recognize happiness without being able to enjoy it. It is now available to you, since the theory of Attraction opens before you the way to harmony.

Since Attraction is ineradicable, it works ceaselessly on men and animals. It is the source of their happiness in harmony and of their misfortune when the conditions that give rise to harmony are absent.

In the latter case Attraction becomes a cause of disorder. Put some bees in an area which lacks flowers, and these heroes of harmony will remain in a state of inertia and discord even though their Attraction is neither changed nor reduced. Attrac-

[3] On the importance of luxury and economic or technological development as prerequisites for the establishment of Fourier's utopia see above p. 202*n*.

tion brings good results only when the prerequisites are available; when they are absent it causes evil. Thus in the civilized, barbarian and savage states, where the preparations for harmony are lacking, it serves only to invert our penchants and to make them sources of disorder. The blame should not be imputed to Attraction, but to circumstances. Have you not observed that man is the only creature which Attraction constantly directs toward evil, while it directs all the other creatures toward the habits and societies for which they are best suited? How are we to explain this strange fact if not by assuming that an accidental subversion has occurred in the mechanism of man's passionate attractions. This state of subversion is the order of the three current societies which constantly thwart the designs of Attraction.

Since you are unable to repress the passions, you study the means of accommodating them to established practices, laws and circumstances. You would do better to study the means of changing circumstances so as to adopt them to the designs of Attraction.

*—PM*, III; *OC*, XI, 328–331

# 2

# THE ANATOMY OF THE PASSIONS

If one compares the immensity of our desires with our limited means of satisfying them, it seems that God has acted unwisely in endowing us with passions so eager for pleasure, passions that seem created to torment us by exciting a thousand desires, nine-tenths of which we cannot satisfy so long as the civilized order lasts.

It is for reasons like this that the moralists aspire to correct the work of God, to moderate and repress the passions which they are unable to satisfy and which they do not even understand. For of the twelve passions which are the soul's principal motivating forces, they are only aware of the existence of nine; and their ideas about the four most important of these passions are most imperfect.

These nine known passions are *the five sensual appetites* which exercise a greater or lesser degree of control over each individual, and *the four simple appetites of the soul*, namely:

6th. The group of Friendship.
7th. The group of Love.
8th. The group of Paternity or Family.
9th. The group of Ambition.

The moralists wish to give to these nine passions an action contrary to the designs of nature. Have they not been declaiming for the past two thousand years about the need to moderate and change the five sensual appetites? Have they not been trying to persuade us that the diamond is a worthless stone, that gold is a base metal, that sugar and spice are abject and contemptible products, that thatched huts and plain, unvarnished nature are preferable to the palaces of kings? So it is that the moralists wish to extinguish the sensual passions, and they are no more sympathetic toward the passions of the soul. How often they have vociferated against ambition. According to them one should only desire mediocre and unremunerative positions; if a job provides an income of a hundred thousand livres, you should only accept ten thousand to satisfy morality. The moralists are even more ridiculous in their opinions about love; they wish love to be ruled by constancy and fidelity, which are so incompatible with the designs of nature and so wearisome to both sexes that no creature remains constant when he enjoys complete liberty.

All these philosophical whims, which are called *duties*, have no relationship with nature. Duty comes from men; attraction comes from God; and to understand the designs of God it is necessary to study attraction, nature by itself without any reference to duty. Duties vary in different centuries and different regions, but the nature of the passions has been and will remain invariable among all people.

—*OC*, I, 72–73

### PASSIONATE ATTRACTION

Passionate attraction is the drive given us by nature prior to any reflection; it is persistent despite the opposition of reason, duty, prejudice, etc.

At all times and in all places passionate attraction has tended and will tend toward three goals:

1. Toward luxury[1] or the gratification of the five senses.

2. Toward the formation of groups and series of groups, the establishment of affective ties.

3. Toward the coordination of the passions, character traits, instincts, and consequently toward universal unity.

First Aim: LUXURY. This includes all the pleasures of the senses. In desiring sensual pleasures, we implicitly seek health and wealth which are the means to satisfy our senses. We desire both *internal luxury* or bodily vigor, the refinement and activity of the senses, and *external luxury* or pecuniary wealth. One must possess these two means in order to attain the first goal of pas-

---

[1] Fourier's French term, *le luxe*, is difficult to translate, for it has a much broader range of connotations than its English cognate. It refers both to things and feelings about things; it suggests elegance, splendor, abundance, profusion, and the feelings of affluence and satisfaction. It could be translated by a different word in each context. But since it is an important part of Fourier's technical vocabulary, we have decided to translate it consistently by the single most obvious English equivalent.

sionate attraction, which is the gratification of the five senses: *taste, touch, sight, hearing, smell.* . . .

Second Aim: GROUPS AND SERIES. Attraction tends to form four types of groups.

| | Type | Symbol |
|---|---|---|
| MAJOR | Group of friendship | Circle |
| | Group of ambition, corporative tie | Hyperbole |
| MINOR | Group of love | Ellipse |
| | Group of paternity or family | Parabola |

All groups formed passionately and freely belong to one of these four varieties. . . .

Third Aim: THE COORDINATION OF THE PASSIONS or of the series of groups; the tendency to harmonize the five sensual passions—1. taste, 2. touch, 3. sight, 4. hearing, 5. smell—with the four affective passions—6. friendship, 7. ambition, 8. love, 9. paternity. This harmony takes place through the medium of three little-known and abused passions which I shall call 10. the *Cabalist*, 11. the *Butterfly*, 12. the *Composite*. Their function is to establish the harmony of the passions in their internal and their external action.

*Internal action:* Everyone would like to keep his passions in a state of equilibrium such that the expression of a single passion would facilitate the expression of all the others. Under such conditions ambition and love would lead only to the formation of fruitful relationships and never to disappointments; gluttony would promote good health instead of ruining it; and in general people would acquire wealth and health in abandoning themselves blindly to their passions. This sort of equilibrium, which comes from an unthinking surrender to nature, is granted to the animals and denied to the civilized man, the barbarian and the savage. Passion benefits the animal, but it leads man to his ruin.

Thus man is at present in a state of war with himself. His

passions thwart each other; ambition counteracts love, paternity counteracts friendship, and so on for each of the twelve. This is the origin of the science called MORALITY which attempts to repress the passions. But to repress is not to coordinate, to harmonize. The aim is to achieve the spontaneous coordination of the passions without repressing any of them. . . .

*External action:* The external regulation of the passions requires that an individual's pursuit of his own interests serve the interests of the mass. At present the contrary occurs: the civilized mechanism is a war of each individual against the mass, a system in which it is to everyone's advantage to deceive the public. This is the external discord of the passions. The third goal of attraction is to put them in internal and external harmony with each other. . . .

In the establishment of this harmony the principal role should be played by the three passions numbered 10, 11 and 12, which are called the DISTRIBUTIVE or MECHANIZING PASSIONS. I am giving each of them three different names, so as to provide punctilious readers with a choice.

10th. The Cabalist, the intriguing or dissident passion.

11th. The Butterfly, the alternating or contrasting passion.

12th. The Composite, the exalting or meshing passion.

Later I will define these three much-misunderstood passions. They are the ones which govern the activity of the passionate series; a series will cease to function when the three mechanizing passions do not have free play.

In civilization these three mechanizing passions are called vices. The philosophers claim that the tenth, the cabalistic spirit, is an evil and that everyone should be like-minded and brotherly. They likewise condemn the eleventh, the Butterfly, the need to vary one's pleasures, to flutter from pleasure to pleasure; and they also condemn the twelfth, the Composite, the need for the simultaneous enjoyment of two pleasures, whose mixture turns enthusiasm into exaltation.

Although everyone adores these three reputedly harmful passions, they are in fact sources of vice in civilization, where they are only able to function within families and corporate bodies. God created them to function within series of contrasted

groups. They tend to form such series, and they can only produce evil when they are employed in a different context.

Among the twelve radical passions the three mechanizing
passions play the principal role; they have control over the nine
others. It is their combined intervention which gives rise to true
wisdom, or the equilibrium of the passions through the counter-
balancing of pleasures.

—*OC*, VI, 47–51

### THE THREE DISTRIBUTIVE PASSIONS

The three *distributive* passions are entirely unrecognized, and
are regarded as vices although they are infinitely precious. These
three passions have the particular function of forming and directing the series of groups which are the mainspring of societary
harmony. Since these series cannot be formed in the civilized
order, the three distributive passions have no use in civilization;
they are very harmful and only serve to cause disorder. Let us
define them:

The CABALIST or partisan spirit is a calculating enthusiasm; it
is the passion for intrigue which is particularly strong among
courtiers, ambitious people, tradesmen, and in elegant circles.
The cabalistic spirit always mixes calculation with passion.
Everything is calculated by the intriguer—even the slightest wink
or gesture; he does everything quickly but reflectively. This
form of ardor is therefore a deliberate enthusiasm.

The COMPOSITE or blind enthusiasm is the contrary of the
cabalist. It is an enthusiasm which excludes reason; it is the seduction of the senses and the soul, a state of drunkenness, of moral
blindness; a sort of happiness which arises from the mixture of
two pleasures, one for the senses and one for the soul. Its particular domain is love; but it also operates upon the other passions, though with less intensity.

The ALTERNATING or BUTTERFLY is the need of periodic
change, contrasting situations, changes of scene, piquant incidents, novelties apt to create illusions, to stimulate both the
senses and the soul. This need is felt with moderation every hour,
and it is acutely felt every two hours. If it is not satisfied, a man
falls into indifference and boredom. It is the passion which in the

social mechanism holds the highest rank among the twelve; it is the universal agent of transition. The complete expression of this passion gives rise to a form of happiness attributed to the Parisian sybarites: "the art of living so well and so fast," the variety and linking of pleasures, RAPIDITY OF MOVEMENT.

These three passions have a single aim: to form series of groups, to graduate them, to contrast them, to set them in competition, to enmesh them.

—*OC*, II, 145–146

### THE CLASSIFICATION OF PERSONALITY TYPES

I am going to provide a survey of the scale or general keyboard of personality types. It is composed of 810 full types and 405 mixed types. I will indicate the number and kind of dominant passions that characterize each type. Everyone has all twelve passions, but a personality type is characterized by the passions which are dominant.

## THE 810 PERSONALITY TYPES IN DOMESTIC HARMONY

| | | | |
|---|---|---|---|
| DO | Solitones | 576 | Any 1 dominant passion. |
| s | f, mixed | 80 | 1 spiritual passion, 1 sensual passion. |
| RE | Bitones | 96 | 2 spiritual passions. |
| s | f, bimixed | 16 | 1 spiritual passion, 2 sensual passions. |
| MI | Tritones | 24 | 3 spiritual passions. |
| FA | Tetratones | 8 | 4 spiritual passions. |
| s | f, trimixed | 8 | 2 spiritual passions, 3 sensual passions. |
| SOL | Pentatones | 2 | 5 spiritual passions. |

The letters *s* and *f* signify sharps and flats, the intermediary keys in the musical and passional scale.

The 405 ambiguous personality types should be added to this list. But let us confine ourselves to defining the full types. First of all there are the 576 solitones: these are people who have a single dominant passion. There is not an equal number of solitones for each of the twelve passions, which would make 48 representatives for each passion. Instead, their number varies. There are many more solitones who are dominated by ambition, love or gourmandise than by the passion for aural pleasures, the pleasures of hearing. Nonetheless there are *auralists* or people who are fanatically fond of music, who live for music, who raise their children to music, and who would not allow their daughter to marry a man who was not a musician.

In brief, the solitones have a dominant passion to which they refer everything. Their tastes are almost unchanging and they have a special aptitude for tasks that take a long time. Their place in the scale of personality types is that of common soldiers in a regiment. On the contrary, the two pentatones, a man and a woman, are the equivalent of colonels. Between the two of them they will play an active role in all the series of a Phalanx; if there are 400 series, each of the pentatones must participate in about 200 series. Thus the pentatones must be unusually energetic people, subtle and very broad-minded, like Voltaire, Leibnitz, Fox, etc. Caesar represents an even higher degree: he was a heptatone with seven dominant passions. Bonaparte and Frederic the Great were hexatones with six dominant passions.

A Phalanx has no special need of hexatones, heptatones, or omnitones. It is enough for it to include two pentatones. By natural right and by common consent, the more sophisticated personality types take charge of the administration of three or four Phalanxes, of a dozen, of forty, and so on, depending on the type they represent. Although each of them lives in a single Phalanx, they are the agents of external harmony.

To continue our list, we have the following external types:

| | | |
|---|---|---|
| s | f, tetramixed | 2 spiritual passions, 4 sensual passions. |
| LA | Hexatones | 6 spiritual passions. |
| s | f, pentamixed | 2 spiritual passions, 5 sensual passions. |
| TI | Heptatones | 6 spiritual passions, 1 sensual passion. |
| DO | Omnitones | 7 spiritual passions. |

This second scale of personality types could be much more fully elaborated. Although these types perform their most significant functions in activities which concern more than one Phalanx, they are also extremely useful in their individual Phalanxes.

I have not discussed the 405 ambiguous types which should

be added to the first list. Nor have I discussed the different degrees of variation to which each of the passions is subject. These are immensely complicated matters. For the present I merely wish to make a few superficial remarks about those personality types which are the most contrary to our prejudices.

Let us begin by pointing out that in the eyes of morality all the most distinguished personality types, the truly sophisticated ones, are dangerous. Morality tolerates such people when they are kings or men of great power. But among the masses it appreciates only the solitones, people who are limited to a single dominant passion. Of course nature does not endow all important individuals with transcendent combinations of passions. It scatters the passions at random; and the omnitone, who holds the highest rank on the two scales, may be a mere shepherd. In civilization those who are endowed with a multitude of dominant passions are frustrated by their education; they rebel against established practices and are thought to be unruly people, enemies of morality. . . .

If the dominant passions are repressed, they become warped and their development is perverse. Civilized education, which gives them a superficial gloss of morality, makes them harmful when they might have been noble. Seneca and Burrhus did not change the character of Nero; they merely perverted it. Nero was a tetratone with four distinct dominant passions: the Cabalist, the Composite, ambition and love.[2] Like Nero, Henri IV was a tetratone; but his character was not twisted by a moral education.

A given personality type will come to no good in civilization when it is dominated by a greater number of mechanizing passions than dominant passions. For example, a woman tritone who is dominated by love, the Cabalist and the Butterfly is likely to be highly dangerous.

The theory of personality types is ideally suited to confound those great intellects who believe that chance has presided over the creation of the passions and that God needs the help of

[2] For a more detailed examination of the case of Nero see below pp. 303–307.

the moralists in harmonizing the passions. In communal interaction the passions are like an orchestra composed of 1620 instruments; and the philosophers who seek to guide them may be compared to a group of intruding children who only succeed in making a terrible racket when they try to play the instruments. Should one conclude that music is harmful to man and that the violins must be restrained, the basses stopped, and the flutes silenced? No, instead the little brats must be dismissed and the instruments given to expert musicians. The passions are no more harmful to man than are musical instruments. Man's only enemies are the philosophers who wish to guide the passions without having the least idea of the mechanism assigned to them by nature. When this mechanism is put to the test, it will become clear that even the most ridiculed personalities, men like Molière's Harpagon, have an eminently useful social role to play.

—*OC*, VI, 340–344

Let us add a minor and comical example to our list of monogynes.[3] Here is a character whom I found remarkable. He was a drinker, a monogyne dominated by the passion of taste with drink as his tonic passion. I encountered him in a public carriage. He was not a simple drunkard, but a man endowed with a marvelous ability to relate all of life's happenings to wine. Like the mystics who see everything in terms of God, he saw everything in terms of wine. For example, instead of telling the time by hours and half-hours, he calculated by bottles consumed. If you asked him, "How far is it to such and such a place?" he would answer, "Why, just enough time to drink four bottles." Once when the horses had stopped, I asked him, "Will we be waiting long here?" He answered: "Why, long enough to drink a quick one." I knew that, according to his arithmetic, "a quick one" meant five minutes and "a bottle" meant ten minutes. Once when another carriage, drawn by tired horses, passed us going downhill, he shouted at it: "Bah! Bah! We'll be drinking before you

---

[3] The present text is just one of numerous "case studies" which Fourier interspersed among his rather dry discussions of the general clavier of personality types. Sometimes, as in this text, he substitutes the terms "monogyne," "bigyne," etc., for solitone, bitone, etc.

will!" What he meant was: "We'll get there before you." For why should one go anywhere if not to drink? . . .

I pricked up my ears when he was in private conversation with one of his comrades. He talked of nothing but rows of bottles and open casks and taking the first drink, etc. In short for this man wine was the focal point of all nature. He judged food by the wines that could be drunk with it; for him a horse was not worth money but rather a certain number of casks of Mâcon wine. No matter what subject he discussed, he managed to relate it to wine with an extraordinary finesse and subtlety. Nonetheless he was no drunkard, but simply a strongly pronounced monogyne with drink as his tonic passion.

—"Du Clavier puissanciel des caractères,"
*La Phalange*, VI (1847), pp. 23–24.

# 3

# GROUP PSYCHOLOGY

### THE STUDY OF GROUPS

The term "group" is conventionally applied to any sort of gathering, even to a band of idlers who come together out of boredom with no passion or purpose—even to an assemblage of emptyminded individuals who are busy killing time and waiting for something to happen. In the theory of the passions the term group refers to a number of individuals who are united by a shared taste for the exercise of a particular function. Three men have dinner together: they are served a soup which pleases two of them and displeases the third; on this occasion they do not make up a group because they are in discord about the function that occupies them. They do not share a common passionate inclination for the soup.

The two individuals who like the soup form a FALSE group. To be properly organized and susceptible to passionate equilibrium a group must include at least three members. It must be arranged like a set of scales which consists of three forces of which the middle one keeps the two extremities in balance. In short no group can be composed of less than three people sharing a common inclination for the performance of a particular function.

One might object: "Although these three men are in discord about the trifling matter of the soup, they are in agreement about the main purpose of the get-together which is friendship. They are close friends." In this case I would answer that the group is defective because it is *simple;* the only tie that binds it is a spiritual one. To make it into a *compound* group, a sensual bond would have to be added, a soup liked by all three members of the group.

"Bah! If the three are not in agreement about the soup, they will have shared preferences for other kinds of food. In any case the group actually does have two bonds; for besides the bond of friendship, these three men are united by the bond of ambition; they are in cabalistic league. They have gotten together for dinner in order to hatch an electoral intrigue. So there's the double link, the compound bond that you require."

This would only be a BASTARD compound relationship, formed by two spiritual bonds. The PURE compound demands a mixture of the pleasures of the soul and those of the senses without any sort of dissidence. In this case the meal begins with a disagreement about the soup and the group is falsified despite the double bond. . . .

Since passionate series are composed only of groups, it is necessary first of all to learn how to form groups.

"Ha! Ha! Groups! What a silly subject that is! It must be very amusing to talk about groups!"

This is the way our wits reason when one talks about groups. At the start you are always subjected to a salvo of stale jokes. But whether the subject is comical or not, it is certain that people know nothing about groups, and that they don't even know how to form a proper group of three people, much less one of thirty.

We have numerous treatises on the study of man. But what can they tell us about the subject if they neglect the essential portion, the analysis of groups. In all our relationships we persistently tend to form groups, and they have never been an object of study.

Civilized people, having an instinct for the false, are constantly inclined to prefer the false to the true. As the pivot of their social system they have chosen a group which is essentially false: the conjugal couple. This group is false because it only includes two members; it is false in its lack of liberty; it is false in the conflicts or differing inclinations which break out from the very start of married life over expenses, food, friends, and a hundred other little details like the degree of heat in an apartment. If people do not know how to harmonize basic groups of two or three people, they must be even less able to harmonize the whole.

I have been speaking only about *sub-groups* whose minimum size is three people. A *full group* in the societary system must include at least SEVEN members, for it must include three sub-divisions or sub-groups. The central sub-group must be stronger than either of the two extremities which it keeps in balance. A group of seven may be divided into three sub-divisions consisting of two, three and two members. Each of these sub-groups devotes itself to one aspect of a given activity. Groups consisting of two members are false when they act in isolation, but here they are admissible since their activity is linked to that of others.

The central sub-group (which consists of three people) is in a state of balance with the two extreme sub-groups (consisting of two members each). The reason for this is that in any activity the central sub-group always performs the most attractive functions; the greater attraction of its functions compensates for its numerical weakness. Thus its influence within the group is equal to that of the four other members who perform two different functions. . . .

A group is sufficiently large if it includes seven members, but it is more perfect with nine members. Then its three sub-groups can be supplemented by a pivot or leader and an ambiguous or transitional member. For example:

| Transition | 1 | ambiguous member |
|------------|---|------------------|
| Higher wing | 2 | intermediate members |
| Center | 3 | initiates |
| Lower wing | 2 | beginners |
| Pivot | 1 | leader |

This division emerges naturally in any gathering for work or pleasure if the passions and instincts are allowed to express themselves freely. Man has an instinctual aversion to equality and a penchant for hierarchical patterns. Thus when free expression is permitted, this nuanced, hierarchical scale will emerge in a series of nine groups just as it will in a group composed of nine individuals.

There must be at least seven members in a full group and at least twenty-four in a full series. But to replace individuals who are sick or absent it is better for each group to consist of twelve and each series of forty members. In this way each group and series will be assured of having its full complement of leaders and ambiguous members.

—*OC*, VI, 55–59

### THE PASSIONATE SERIES

The series of groups is the method adopted by God in the organization of the kingdoms of nature and of all created things. The naturalists, in their theories and classifications, have unanimously accepted this system of organization; they could not have departed from it without coming into conflict with nature and falling into confusion.[1]

If human passions and personalities were not subject, like the material realms, to organization by series of groups, man would be out of unity with the universe; there would be duplicity of system and incoherence between the material and passional worlds. If man aspires to social unity, he should seek it by adhering to the serial order to which God has subjected all of nature.

A passionate series is a league or affiliation of several small groups, each animated by some nuance or *variety* of a passion. The passion in question is the *generic* passion for the whole series. Thus if twenty groups cultivate twenty different types of roses, the generic passion of their series is rose-growing; the groups cultivating the white rose, the yellow rose, the moss-rose, etc., represent its varieties.

To take another example: twelve groups are engaged in the cultivation of twelve different flowers. The tulip is cultivated by one group, the jonquil by another, etc. These twelve groups together constitute a series of flower-growers whose generic function is the cultivation of flowers. The flowers are distributed according to a scale of tastes, each group cultivating the variety of flower for which it has a special fondness.

Passions limited to a single individual are not admissible in the serial mechanism. Three individuals—A, B, C—like their bread salted in different ways: A likes his almost unsalted; B likes his moderately salted; C prefers heavily salted bread. These three

---

[1] For Fourier the series and the group were not merely the ideal forms for the organization of human activity. They were also part of the natural order of things—structural principles governing the organization of the entire universe. The spectrum of colors and the musical scale were but two of the other models to which he referred in his abstract discussions of the properties of the series.

people are in a state of graduated dissonance which does not lend itself to the creation of serial accords. For such accords to take place there must be a number of groups linked in ascending and descending order.

A proper group should have from seven to nine members at the minimum in order to permit the development of balanced or equilibrated rivalries among its members. In the passionate series, then, we cannot base our calculations upon isolated individuals. The intrigues of a series could not be maintained by twelve individuals with a passion for the cultivation of twelve different flowers. This will be proved in the body of the treatise. For the time being it should be kept in mind that the term passionate series always refers to an affiliation of groups and never of individuals.

Thus the three individuals mentioned above—A, B, C—could not form a series of *breadists* or bread-lovers. But if instead of three people we suppose thirty—namely, eight of taste A, ten of taste B, twelve of taste C—they would form a passionate series, that is, an affiliation of groups with graduated and contrasted tastes. Their joint activity and their cabalistic discords would create the intrigues necessary to bake excellent bread and grow fine wheat.[2]

The passionate series always strive toward some useful end such as the increase of wealth or the perfection of work even when they are engaged in leisure activities like music.

A series cannot be organized with less than three groups, for it needs a middle element to keep the two contrasting extremes in balance. A balance may also be established among four groups, provided their properties and relations correspond to those of a geometrical proportion.

When there are more than four groups in a series, they should be divided into three bodies, forming a center and two wings, or into four bodies, forming a quadrille. In each body of

[2] This example suggests a point often stressed by Fourier: the series were not composed merely of consumers (or producers) of a given commodity. One of the main functions of the series in Fourier's scheme of attractive labor was to ally production and consumption.

groups the varieties which are closely allied and homogeneous are united.

The societary order must thus employ and develop all varieties of taste and character in a scale of nuanced gradations. It forms a group to represent each variety without making any judgment concerning the merit of a particular taste. All tastes and penchants are good and they all have their uses, provided they can be made to form a series with ascending and descending wings and transitional groups at either extreme to represent uncommon and peculiar tastes. When a series is arranged in this manner, according to the methods which will be explained in the body of the treatise, each of its groups will cooperate *harmonically* with all the others, be they a hundred in number. The groups will resemble the cogs in a wheel which are all useful provided they mesh properly.

The calculus of the passionate series is going to establish a principle flattering to the whole human race: it will demonstrate that all tastes which are not harmful or annoying to others have a valuable function in the societary state. They will become useful as soon as they are developed in series—that is, according to a graduated scale in which each nuance of taste is represented by a group.

Thus the theory of association is nothing more than the art of forming and activating passionate series. As soon as this science has been discovered on a globe, it can at once establish social unity and attain individual and collective happiness. Thus it is a matter of urgent necessity for the human race to acquire a knowledge of this theory.

The passionate series must be *contrasted*, *interlocked*, and kept in a state of *rivalry* and *exaltation*. A series failing to fulfill these conditions could not perform its functions in the mechanism of Harmony.

A series must be contrasted—that is, its groups must be arranged in ascending and descending order. Thus to form a series of a hundred individuals classed according to age the following division should be adopted:

*Ascending Wing:* Groups of infants and children.

*Center of the Series:* Groups of adolescents and adults.

*Descending Wing:* Groups of aged persons.
The same method should be followed in classifying series of passions and character traits.

This method serves to bring out contrasts and hence to produce enthusiasm in the various groups. Each group becomes passionately addicted to its own dominant penchant or special taste. At the same time it develops contrasting tastes and penchants, and it becomes critical of the penchants and occupations of the contiguous groups in the series, with which it is in rivalry.

This system of progressive or graduated classification creates sympathies and alliances between the contrasted groups, and antipathies or dissidences between contiguous groups with similar tastes.

The series needs discords as much as it needs harmonies. It must be stimulated by a host of rival pretensions which will give rise to cabalistic alliances and become a spur to emulation. Without contrasts it would be impossible to form leagues between the groups and create enthusiasm; the series would lack ardor for its labors, and its work would be inferior in quality and quantity.

The second necessary condition is to establish intrigues and active rivalries within a series. Since this should result from the regularity of contrasts and the graduated distribution of nuances or varieties, it may be said that this second condition is fulfilled once the first is satisfied. Of course there is more to say about the means by which intrigues are created, but that will come later.

The third condition to be fulfilled is that of the meshing or linkage of the different series. This can take place only if the groups change their work at frequent intervals, say every hour or at most every two hours. For example, a man may be employed:

At 5:00 A.M. in a group of shepherds.
At 7:00 A.M. in a group of field-workers.
At 9:00 A.M. in a group of gardeners.

A session of two hours' duration is the longest admissible in Harmony; enthusiasm cannot last any longer than that. If the work is unattractive in itself, the session should be reduced to one hour.

In the example just given the three series of shepherds, field-workers and gardeners will become meshed by the process of reciprocal interchange of members. It is not necessary for this interchange to be complete—for each of the twenty men engaged in tending flocks to go off and work in the fields at 7:00. All that is necessary is for each series to provide the others with several members taken from its different groups. The exchange of a few members will suffice to establish a linkage or meshing between the different series.

A passionate series acting in isolation would be useless and could perform no functions of a harmonic character. Nothing would be easier than to organize one or more industrial series in a large city like Paris. They might be engaged in the growing of flowers or fruit or anything else, but they would be completely useless. At least fifty series are necessary to fulfill the third condition, that of meshing. It is for this reason that the theory of association cannot be tried out on a small number of people, say twenty families or one hundred individuals. At least four hundred people—men, women and children—would be necessary to form and mesh the fifty series required to activate the mechanism of simple association. To organize a compound association at least four hundred series, requiring fifteen or sixteen hundred people, would be needed.

—*OC*, iii, 19–25

# V

## *The Ideal Community*

Instead of studying the problem, our modern philosophers
have drawn back in bewilderment. They have all exclaimed:
"That would be too good; men are not meant to attain such
perfection." Thus association has been for our minds the same
thing that the sun is for our eyes: it is so brilliant that we
cannot fix our gaze on it. Eh! Just because the sun tires our
weak eyes, does that mean it does not exist? This is the sort
of argument put forth by those who claim that association is
impossible because it promises to yield results too immense
for their limited imaginations.

—*OC*, IV, 32–33

"Utopian" socialism, according to Engels, differed from mature
"scientific" socialism in many ways; but one of the most
characteristic aspects of the utopians was their propensity for
drawing up "fantastic blueprints" of future society. By this
standard Fourier must be judged the complete utopian. He
produced thousands of pages of detailed blueprints which
provided, among other things, typical work schedules,
specifications for Phalansterian architecture, color schemes for
work uniforms and festive costumes, designs for nursery
furniture, as well as statistical projections of the rate of profit
growth, egg production and the number of great playwrights
that Harmony would probably produce.

The texts which we have selected for this chapter offer a small but representative sampling of these blueprints. Most of them require no editorial commentary and should be allowed to speak for themselves. We would, however, offer a general observation about Harmony's place in the utopian tradition. As Frank Manuel has shown, pre-nineteenth century utopias were "utopias of calm felicity."[1] They defined happiness in terms of moderation, balance and stability. Their institutions and laws would make man happy by diminishing his needs and desires. It is obvious that Fourier broke decisively with this tradition. Harmony was felicitous but hardly calm. The passionate gratification that the earlier utopias sought to curtail was Harmony's mainspring. In other respects, however, Fourier's relationship to the eighteenth century is somewhat more complicated. Most pre-revolutionary utopias were set in an idealized countryside and were peopled by self-abnegating citizens of stoical or saintly mien. Fourier shared none of the eighteenth century utopian infatuation with the virtuous republics of antiquity and he was never tempted to idealize primitive societies. On the other hand, his aesthetic ideal is clearly based on standards of taste established by the eighteenth century aristocracy.

The geographical context of life in Harmony is rural, but the pleasures of the Phalanx are not simple, frugal, coarse or rustic. It seems clear that the vigorous coarseness of a Brueghel peasant scene was not what Fourier had in mind for his Harmonians and he had no affection for Rousseau's mythic yeoman-citizens or for Montesquieu's less Spartan but rather insipid Troglodytes. In his taste for refinement, elegance, fine music, and elaborately orchestrated sexual and gastronomic experiences, Fourier remained an unregenerated son of the aristocratic eighteenth century. He would have looked with disdain upon the enforced simplicity, the drab middle-class manners, customs, and dress that made their way into most nineteenth century utopian visions.

---

[1] "Toward a Psychological History of Utopias," in Frank Manuel (ed.), *Utopias and Utopian Thought* (Boston, 1967), pp. 72–79.

# NEW MATERIAL CONDITIONS

### THE ESTABLISHMENT OF A TRIAL PHALANX

We will suppose that the trial is made by a monarch, or by a wealthy individual like one of the Devonshires, Northumberlands, Bedforts, the Sheremetevs, Labanovs, Czartoryskis, the Esterhazys, Belmontes, Medina-Celis, the Barings, Lafittes, Hopes, etc., or finally by a powerful company which desires to avoid all tentative measures and proceed directly to the organization of Full Harmony, the eighth period in its plenitude. I am going to indicate the procedure to follow in this case.

An association of 1500 or 1600 people requires a site comprising at least one square league of land, that is to say a surface area of six million square *toises*.[1] (Let us not forget that one-third as much would suffice for the simple mode.)

A good stream of water should be available; the land should be hilly and suitable for a variety of crops; there should be a forest nearby; and the site should be fairly near a large city but far enough away to avoid unwelcome visitors.

The trial Phalanx will stand alone and it will get no help from neighboring Phalanxes. As a result of this isolation, there will be so many gaps in attraction, so many passional calms to fear in its maneuvers, that it will be particularly important to provide it with the help of a good site fit for a variety of functions. Flat country, like that surrounding Anvers, Leipzig or Orleans would be quite inappropriate and would cause the breakdown of many series, owing to the uniformity of the land surface. It will therefore be necessary to select a diversified region, like that near Lausanne, or at the very least a fine valley provided with a stream and a forest, like the valley from Brussels to Halle. A fine location near Paris would be the stretch of land between Poissy and Conflans, Poissy and Meulan.

The 1500 or 1600 people brought together will be in a state of graduated inequality as to wealth, age, personality, and

---

[1] The *toise* was equal to about two yards.

theoretical and practical knowledge. The group should be as varied as possible; for the greater the variety in the passions and faculties of the members, the easier it will be to harmonize them in a limited amount of time.

All possible types of agricultural work should be represented in this trial community, including that involving hot-houses and conservatories. There should also be at least three types of manufacturing work for winter and for rainy days, as well as diverse types of work in the applied sciences and arts, apart from what is taught in the schools. A passional series will be assigned to each type of work, and it will divide up its members into subdivisions and groups according to the instructions given earlier.

At the very outset an evaluation should be made of the capital deposited as shares in the enterprise: land, material, flocks, tools, etc. This matter is one of the first to be dealt with; and I shall discuss it in detail further on. Let us now confine ourselves to saying that all these deposits of material will be represented by transferable shares in the association.[2] Let us leave these minute reckonings and turn our attention to the workings of attraction.

A great difficulty to be overcome in the trial Phalanx will be the formation of transcendent ties or collective bonds among the series before the end of the warm season. Before winter comes a passionate union must be established between the members; they must be made to feel a sense of collective and individual devotion to the Phalanx; and above all a perfect harmony must be established concerning the division of profits among the three elements: *Capital, Labor* and *Talent*.

The difficulty will be greater in northern countries than in those of the south, given the fact that the growing season lasts eight months in the south and just five months in the north.

Since a trial Phalanx must begin with agricultural labor, it will not be in full operation until the month of May (in a cli-

---

[2] Fourier frequently described the trial Phalanx in terms which evoke a joint-stock company, and many of the communities set up by his disciples were actually chartered as such. However, according to his scheme of retribution, labor and talent as well as capital were to be represented by shares in the association. See below pp. 249–250.

mate of 50 degrees latitude, like the region around London or Paris); and since the general bonds, the harmonic ties of the series, must be established before the end of the farming season in October, there will scarcely be five months of full activity in regions of fifty degrees latitude. Everything will have to be done in that short time.

Thus it would be much easier to make the trial in a region where the climate is temperate, for instance near Florence, Naples, Valencia or Lisbon where the growing season lasts eight or nine months. In such an area it would be particularly easy to consolidate the bonds of union since there would only be three or four months of passional calm between the end of the first season and the beginning of the second. By the second spring, with the renewal of its agricultural labors, the Phalanx would form its ties and cabals anew with much greater zeal and with more intensity than in the first year. The Phalanx would thenceforth be in a state of complete consolidation, and strong enough to avoid passional calms during the second winter.

If, instead of being surrounded by civilized populations, the trial Phalanx had neighbors who had been brought up in the seventh period, or merely in the sixth, it could count on moral support which would lend strength to its intrigues and help it in getting organized. But in fact it will be surrounded only by those social vipers who are called civilized—*Progenies viperarum*, as the Gospel puts it—people whose deceitful proximity will be a spiritual menace to the first Phalanx just as a horde of plague-bearers would be a material menace to a healthy city. This city would be obliged to drive them away and to level its cannons against those who approached its walls.

The experimental Phalanx will be obliged to take similar actions, *in a moral sense*, against the contagion of civilized customs. It will be forced to withdraw itself from all passional or spiritual relations with its perfidious neighbors. (It should be recalled that the two terms "passional" and "spiritual" are synonymous by contrast to "material.")

The civilized are so accustomed to falsity that they practice it even in those circumstances when they would like to practice truthfulness. Propriety and morality make liars out of civilized men. With such habits, the civilized would destroy the mechanism of Harmony if they were permitted to interfere.

This mistrust will not prevent the first Harmonians from admitting a few civilized people as spectators consigned to a "moral quarantine," and this conditional admission will be the object of a highly lucrative speculation which will yield a profit of some twenty millions to the trial Phalanx if it handles the matter skillfully. (The figures will be given farther on.)

Let us discuss the composition of the trial Phalanx. At least seven-eighths of its members should be people involved in farming or industry. The remainder will consist of capitalists, savants and artists. . . . The Phalanx would be poorly graduated and difficult to balance if, among its capitalists, there were several worth 100,000 francs and several worth 50,000 francs without any of intermediate wealth. In such circumstances, one should try to find men with fortunes of 60, 70, 80, and 90,000 francs. The most precisely graduated Phalanx yields the highest degree of social harmony and the greatest profits.

In readying the gardens and workshops of the trial Phalanx one should try to predict and estimate the approximate quantity of attraction which each branch of industry is likely to excite. For example, we know that the plum-tree has less attraction than the pear-tree; and so we will plant fewer plum-trees than pear-trees. The quantity of attraction will be the sole rule to follow in each branch of agricultural and manufacturing work.

Economists would follow a different line of reasoning. They would insist that it is necessary to cultivate whatever produces the greatest yield and to produce a large quantity of the most productive objects. The trial Phalanx should avoid this error; its methods should be different from those of the Phalanxes that will follow it. When all regions have embraced Harmony and when they are all organized in combination with each other, then it will no doubt be necessary to adapt farming to the dictates of interest and attraction. But the goal of the experimental community is quite different: it is to get a group of 1500 or 1600 people working out of pure attraction. If one could predict that they would be more actively attracted to work by thistles and thorns than by orchards and flowers, then it would be necessary to give up orchards and flowers and replace them with thistles and thorns in the experimental community.

In point of fact, as soon as it has attained its two goals, industrial attraction and passional equilibrium, the trial Phalanx will have the means to widen the scope of its labors so as to include any useful tasks which may have been neglected at the outset. Moreover, its strength will be doubled when neighboring communities organize their own Phalanxes and when the whole region is able to intervene in the mechanism of attraction. Thus in the initial experiment it is necessary to concentrate on the creation of industrial attraction without being particular about the type of work involved.

I have had to insist on this point because the critics may wonder at the fact that I require for the first community a great many flowers, orchards and small animals but very little in the way of large-scale agriculture. The reason for this is that some of the stimuli which make large-scale farming attractive will only emerge after the establishment of a network of Phalanxes capable of aiding each other. The first community, which will be deprived of such resources, should adopt appropriate tactics and resolve the problem of industrial attraction by the means at its disposal.

The most appealing species of animals and vegetables are fairly well known, and it will be easy to estimate the proportions to be respected in the industrial preparations for the experimental Phalanx. Of course there will necessarily be some errors at the outset, and it will take several years before a Phalanx can make an exact reckoning of the proportions to be established among all types of work.

Yet since the capital invested in the establishment of the trial Phalanx will be reimbursed at a rate of twelve to one, the shareholders will scarcely be inclined to worry about the fact that a few errors in the distribution of labor will reduce profits during the first years. The main point will be to attain the goal of industrial attraction and passional equilibrium. This will be the sign of victory; and the shareholders or founders should keep in mind that when they have obtained this victory, when they have provided a practical demonstration of the equilibrium of the passions and shown the way to a happy future, their fellow men will find all the world's treasures inadequate to reward them for having provided an escape from the labyrinth of civilization, barbarism, and savagery.

—*OC*, IV, 426–433

### THE PHALANSTERY

The edifice occupied by the Phalanx bears no resemblance to our urban or rural buildings; and in the establishment of a full Harmony of 1600 people none of our buildings could be put to use, not even a great palace like Versailles nor a great monastery like Escorial. If an experiment is made in minimal Harmony, with two or three hundred members, or on a limited scale with four hundred members, it would be possible, although difficult, to use a monastery or palace (like Meudon) for the central edifice.

The lodgings, gardens and stables of a society run by series of groups must be vastly different from those of our villages and towns, which are perversely organized and meant for families having no societary relations. Instead of the chaos of little houses which rival each other in filth and ugliness in our towns, a Phalanx constructs for itself a building as perfect as the terrain permits. Here is a brief account of the measures to be taken on a favorable site. . . .

The center of the palace or Phalanstery should be a place for quiet activity; it should include the dining rooms, the exchange, meeting rooms, library, studies, etc. This central section includes the temple, the tower, the telegraph, the coops for carrier pigeons, the ceremonial chimes, the observatory, and a winter courtyard adorned with resinous plants. The parade grounds are located just behind the central section.

One of the wings of the Phalanstery should include all the noisy workshops like the carpenter shop and the forge and the other workshops where hammering is done. It should also be the place for all the industrial gatherings involving children, who are generally very noisy at work and even at music. The grouping of these activities will avoid an annoying drawback of our civilized cities where every street has its own hammerer or iron merchant or beginning clarinet player to shatter the ear drums of fifty families in the vicinity.

The other wing should contain the caravansary with its ballrooms and its halls for meetings with outsiders, who should not be allowed to encumber the center of the palace and to disturb the domestic relations of the Phalanx. This precaution of isolating outsiders and concentrating their meetings in one of the wings will be most important in the trial Phalanx. For the Phalanx will attract thousands of curiosity-seekers whose entry fees will provide a profit that I cannot estimate at less than twenty million. . . .

The PHALANSTERY or manor-house of the Phalanx should contain, in addition to the private apartments, a large number of halls for social relations. These halls will be called *Seristeries* or places for the meeting and interaction of the passional series.

These halls have nothing in common with our public rooms where ungraduated social relations prevail. A series cannot tolerate this confusion: it always has its three, four or five divisions which occupy three, four or five adjacent locations. This means that analogous arrangements are necessary for the officers and members of each division. Thus each Seristery ordinarily consists of three principal halls, one for the center and two for the wings of the series.

In addition, the three halls of the Seristery should have adjoining rooms for the groups and committees of the series. In the banquet Seristery or dining room, for example, six halls of unequal size are necessary:

1 first class hall in the Ascending Wing, about   150 people.
2 second class halls in the Center . . . . . . . 400.
3 third class halls in the Descending Wing . . 900.

Near these six halls of unequal size there should be a number of smaller rooms for the diverse groups which wish to isolate themselves from the common dining rooms of their class. It happens every day that some groups wish to eat separately; they should have rooms near the Seristery where meals are served to the members of their class.

In all social relations it is necessary to have small rooms adjoining the Seristery in order to encourage small group meetings. Accordingly, a Seristery, or the meeting place of a series, is arranged in a compound manner with halls for large collective gatherings and for smaller cabalistic meetings. This system is very different from that employed in our large assemblies where, even in the palaces of kings, everyone is thrown together pell-mell according to the holy philosophical principle of equality. This principle is completely intolerable in Harmony.

The stables, granaries and warehouses should be located, if possible, opposite the main edifice. The space between the palace and the stables will serve as a main courtyard or parade-ground and it should be very large. To give some idea of the proper dimensions I estimate that the front of the Phalanstery should have a length of about 600 *toises de Paris*. The center and the parade grounds will run to about 300 *toises* and each of the two wings to about 150. . . . The gardens should be placed, insofar as possible, behind the palace and not behind the stables, since large-scale farming should be done in the area near the stables. These plans will of course vary according to local circumstances; we are only talking here about an ideal location. . . .

All the children, both rich and poor, are lodged together on the mezzanine of the Phalanstery. For they should be kept separate from the adolescents, and in general from all those who are capable of making love, at most times and particularly during the late evening and the early morning hours. The reasons for this will be explained later. For the time being let us assume that those who are capable of forming amorous relations will be concentrated on the second floor, while the very young and the very old (the first and sixteenth choirs, the Tots and the Patriarchs) should have meeting-halls on the ground floor and the mezzanine. They should also be isolated from the *street-gallery*, which is the most important feature of a Phalanstery and which cannot be conceived of in civilization. For this reason it should be briefly described in a separate chapter.

—*OC*, IV, 455–462

AN ARCHITECTURAL INNOVATION: THE STREET-GALLERY

The street-galleries are a mode of internal communication which would alone be sufficient to inspire disdain for the palaces and

great cities of civilization. Once a man has seen the street-galleries of a Phalanx, he will look upon the most elegant civilized
palace as a place of exile, a residence worthy of fools who, after
three thousand years of architectural studies, have not yet
learned how to build themselves healthy and comfortable lodgings. In civilization we can only conceive of luxury in the simple
mode; we have no conception of the compound or collective
forms of luxury. . . .

The poorest wretch in Harmony, a man who doesn't have a
penny to his name, has a well-heated and enclosed portico at his
disposal when he gets into a carriage; he goes from the Palace to
the stables by means of paved and graveled underground passage-ways; he gets from his lodgings to the public halls and
workshops by means of street-galleries which are heated in
winter and ventilated in summer. In Harmony one can pass
through the workshops, stables, shops, ball-rooms, banquet and
assembly halls, etc., in January without knowing whether it is
rainy or windy, hot or cold. The detailed treatment which I
shall give to this subject entitles me to say that if, after three
thousand years of study, the civilized have not yet learned how
to house themselves, it is no wonder that they have not yet
learned how to direct and harmonize their passions. When one
fails in the most minute material calculations, one is likely to fail
in the great calculations concerning the passions.

Let us describe the street-galleries which are one of the
most charming and precious features of a Palace of Harmony.
A Phalanx which may consist of up to 1600 or 1800 people, is
actually a small town in itself; the more so in that it has a large
number of adjacent rural buildings of the sort that our proprietors and city-dwellers relegate to their country residences.

The Phalanx has no outside streets or open road-ways exposed to the elements. All the portions of the central edifice
can be traversed by means of a wide gallery which runs along
the second floor of the whole building. At each extremity of
this spacious corridor there are elevated passages, supported by
columns, and also attractive underground passages which connect
all the parts of the Phalanx and the adjoining buildings. Thus
everything is linked by a series of passage-ways which are shel-

tered, elegant, and comfortable in winter thanks to the help of heaters and ventilators.

These sheltered passage-ways are particularly necessary in view of the fact that there is a great deal of movement in Harmony. In conformity with the laws of the eleventh and twelfth passions (the Butterfly and the Composite), the sessions of the various work and recreation groups never last more than one or two hours. If the Harmonians were obliged to go out of doors in moving from one hall to another, from a stable to a workshop, it would take just one week of wintry, damp weather to leave even the most robust of them beset by colds, inflammations and pleurisy. A state of things which requires so much moving about makes sheltered means of communication an absolute necessity.

The street-gallery or *continuous peristyle* extends along the second story. It could not be placed on the ground floor since the lower part of the building will be traversed by carriage entrances. Those who have seen the gallery of the Louvre may take it as a model for the street-gallery in Harmony. It will be taller than the Louvre, however, and the windows will be differently placed.

The street-galleries of a Phalanx wind along just one side of the central edifice and stretch to the end of each of its wings. All of these wings contain a double row of rooms. Thus one row of rooms looks out upon the fields and gardens and the other looks out upon the street-gallery. The street-gallery, then, will be three stories high with windows on one side. The entrance to all the apartments of the second, third and fourth stories is located in the street-gallery. Flights of stairs are placed at intervals to ascend to the upper stories. . . .

After thirty years, when permanent buildings are constructed, the street-gallery will have a width of six *toises* in the central portion of the Palace and four *toises* in the wings. But at the outset, since the present poverty of the globe requires modest structures . . . the street-gallery will be only four *toises* wide in the center and three in the wings. . . .

The main body of the building will have a width of about eight *toises*, not including the street-gallery. This will allow room to put alcoves and toilets in all of the apartments. . . . The minimum lodging for a member of the poorest class will thus include a room, an alcove and a private toilet. . . .

The kitchens and some of the public halls will be located on the ground floor. There will also be trap-doors in the floors of the dining rooms on the second story. Thus the tables may be set in the kitchens below and simply raised through the trap-doors when it is time to eat. These trap-doors will be particularly useful during festivities, such as the visits of traveling caravans and legions, when there will be too many people to eat in the ordinary dining rooms. Then double rows of tables will be set in the street-galleries, and the food will be passed up from the kitchen.

The principal public halls should not be situated on the ground floor. There are two reasons for this. The first is that the patriarchs and children, who have difficulty climbing stairs, should be lodged in the lower parts of the building. The second is that the children should be kept in isolation from the non-industrial activities of the adults. . . .

To spend a winter's day in a Phalanstery, to visit all parts of it without exposure to the elements, to go to the theater and the opera in light clothes and colored shoes without worrying about the mud and the cold, would be a charm so novel that it alone would suffice to make our cities and castles seem detestable. If the Phalanstery were put to civilized uses, the mere convenience of its sheltered, heated and ventilated passage-ways would make it enormously valuable.

*—OC*, IV, 462–468

# 2

# THE ORGANIZATION OF COMMUNAL LIFE

### THE PHALANX AT DAWN

Every meal has a character of its own, a tone which is the same in all three classes. I will limit myself to describing the character of the *anthem*[1] or first meal which is served in the very early morning before anyone has left the palace. The anthem is not a very orderly meal; it is marked by a pleasing confusion. Since people get up at different times, it is divided into three stages: there is the first anthem for a few groups who go out to work very early; then there is the big central anthem for the majority of the groups, which set off an hour later; finally there is the post-anthem for late-risers. . . .

The central anthem, which takes place around five o'clock in the morning is gay and attractive in all respects. It provides an occasion for the presentation of distinguished travelers who have spent the night at the Phalanx. As people arrive for this meal, they are able to read reports and news dispatches which have arrived during the night; they learn about the plays to be performed in neighboring Phalanxes, about the movements of caravans and industrial armies, the voyages of the various paladins of the globe. In addition they find the various newspapers which have arrived during the night either from the Congress of Unity, which is located on the Bosphorus, or from the secondary congresses of the Amazon, the Chesapeake, etc.

The anthem also serves as a second Exchange; it is an occasion at which the negotiations of the previous day may be modified if necessary. The news which has arrived during the night may necessitate some changes in the arrangements made earlier, and it is at the anthem that such matters are settled. This

---

[1] Fourier maintained that the active life of Harmony would increase people's appetites so much as to require the serving of five meals a day. He elsewhere refers to this first meal, the "anthem" (*antienne*), by other terms such as *le délité* and *la matine*.

task is confided to special acolytes who serve as peripatetic negotiators during the course of the meal.

All of these distractions make the anthem a very chaotic meal, a most satisfying imbroglio including many other surprises of which I will refrain from speaking since they do not coincide with our customs. I might add that all by itself the anthem would suffice to get the most sluggish individual out of bed by five in the morning, were he not already excited by the desire to participate in the sessions of his groups. Thus by the end of the central anthem, it would be unusual to find one-eighth of the Phalanx still in bed.

In warm weather the central anthem concludes with the little morning parade which I will now describe. I will assume that it is held at five o'clock in the morning.

Shortly before five the peals of a carillon announce the little parade and the hymn to the dawn. Those who are finishing their meal make ready; the musicians get their instruments, the priests and parade officers adjust their decorations, etc. The clocks strike five. The Athlete Conradin, who is fourteen years old and ranks as a Major on the parade staff, gives the command to form groups. I have already said that the officers for the little parade come from the choir of Athletes. Thus Conradin's adjutants are also thirteen or fourteen years old; they are Anténor and Amphion for the groups of boys, and Clorinde and Galatea for the groups of girls. Amphion and Galatea set about bringing together the members of the orchestras, while Anténor and Clorinde start to place people in proper marching order. Ranks are formed in the following manner:

I will suppose that the procession consists of 400 people—men, women and children—and that they make up twenty groups which are all ready to set out into the country. The twenty standard-bearers form a line facing the colonnade. The whole throng is divided like an orchestra into separate vocal and instrumental sections, each of which is headed by its own priest or priestess. Before the priests there are basins of burning incense tended by the Tots. A hierophant or high priest stands between the lines of men and women; the drummers and trumpeters are next to the colonnade; and the animals and wagons are drawn up in the rear. At the center of the entire gathering stands the young Major Conradin. His adjutants are at his side, and he is preceded by four children from the choir of the neophytes. These children carry signal torches which they wave when there are orders to be transmitted to the watch tower. The tower in turn relays the orders to the domes of adjacent castles, to neighboring communities, and to those groups which have already gone out into the countryside.

When all is ready, the drums roll, the crowd falls silent, and the Major orders everyone to bow to God. Then the drums and trumpets sound a mighty fanfare and the carillons peal in unison. Incense rises, flags wave, and the colors are hoisted on the spires of the Phalanstery. The groups which are already in the fields pause to join in this ceremony as do passing travelers and the members of visiting caravans.

When a minute has passed, the hierophant calls for the hymn by striking its first three bars on the tuning fork. The ritornelle is chanted by the priests and priestesses directing each of the vocal and instrumental sections. Then the hymn is sung by all the groups together.

When the hymn is over, the Little Khan sounds the call to the colors. Everyone puts away his instrument and takes his place under the banner of his work group. Each group then marches freely, and not in perfect ranks, toward its animals and wagons. (Since the work groups are made up of people of all ages, they would be ill-advised to march in strict parade order.) Pushing its wagons, each group then parades before the great colonnade where the dignitaries are standing. If the parade is just a small one, one of the king's paladins may be there, but on the days of big parades a paladin of the Emperor of Unity will attend. As each group passes the reviewing stand, it receives a salute equal to its rank. The groups of plowmen and masons, who come first, are given a fine fanfare, and then they proceed to their work.

The salute to God circles the earth along with the sun. At the equinox, a big parade is held at sunrise in every Phalanx. Thus the dawn is greeted by a moving ribbon of Phalanxes which stretches for thousands of leagues, and as the day advances, the hymn to the dawn is sung over the length and breadth of the earth. On the two solstices the hymn is sung simultaneously by the whole human race at the moment which corresponds to noon at Constantinople.

*—OC*, XII, 481–484

### ADMINISTRATIVE INSTITUTIONS AND PRACTICES

The internal administration of the Phalanx will be directed *at the outset* by a regency or council to be composed of those shareholders who have made the greatest contribution in terms of capital and industrial or scientific knowledge. If there are women capable of exercising administrative functions, they should be included on the council along with the men; for in Harmony women are on a par with men in all affairs of interest, provided they have the necessary education.

Harmony cannot tolerate any general community of goods,[2] and there can be no collective recompenses to familial or conjugal groups. Harmony is obliged to deal with everyone individually, even with children who are at least four and a half years old, and dividends must be shared according to each individual's contribution in terms of labor, capital and talent.

It is allowable for relatives, couples and friends to share what they possess, as is sometimes done in civilization. But in the dealings of the Phalanx with its members, even with five-year-old children, individual accounts are kept. A child's earnings are not given to his father; and once he reaches the age of four and a half, a child becomes the owner of the fruits of his own labor, as well as of the legacies, inheritances and interests which he may have acquired. These are kept from him by the Phalanx until he comes of age—that is until he is nineteen or twenty and able to

---

[2] Fourier repeatedly dissociated himself from the egalitarian communism which was characteristic of much eighteenth and early nineteenth century utopian thinking. Although by almost any reckoning he does belong in the socialist tradition, the texts in this section also show that he left a place in his ideal community for a number of distinctly capitalistic economic institutions: the payment of interest on invested capital, inheritance rights, some forms of private property, etc.

advance from the sixth tribe, the *lads* and *lasses*, to the seventh, the *adolescents*.[3]

After having evaluated the land, machines, materials, furniture, supplies and liquid capital contributed by each member, the regency issues 1728 exchangeable shares. These shares are backed by the property of the Phalanx, its land, buildings, flocks, workshops, etc. The regency issues these shares, or portions thereof, to each member in accordance with his contribution to the Phalanx. It is possible to be a member without being a shareholder; it is also possible to be an outside shareholder without being an active member. In the second case a person has no right to the two portions of the revenue of the Phalanx which are assigned to labor and to talent.

The annual profits are divided into three unequal portions and distributed in the following manner:

$5/12$ to manual labor,
$4/12$ to invested capital,
$3/12$ to theoretical and practical knowledge.

According to his abilities, each member can belong to any or all of these three categories.[4]

In connection with its administrative responsibilities, the regency gives each poor member an advance of one year's cloth-

[3] The whole Phalanx was divided into a vast network of overlapping tribes, choirs, hordes, bands and other corporate bodies. For a listing of the sixteen tribes or age groups see below p. 256.

[4] Fourier regarded his principle of remuneration, which is stated here only in its most elementary form, as one of his greatest discoveries. Among all the refinements which he added to it, one point should be emphasized. He did not think of the categories of labor, capital, and "knowledge" or talent as mutually exclusive. He conceded that in the first trial Phalanx much of the capital might have to come from a few individuals, and that most of the labor would be done by people with relatively little capital to invest in the enterprise. However, the whole point of his scheme was to make capitalists out of laborers and laborers out of capitalists and to provide both with sufficient education to make a contribution in talent. Once his new order was well-established, every man would receive some retribution for his contributions in all three domains. Furthermore, those (presumably the poorest members of the community) who held a limited number of shares would receive a far higher return on their capital than the rich.

ing, food and lodging.[5] This advance entails no risk, because it is certain that the work which the poor man will perform under the stimulus of *attraction and pleasure* will produce a yield in excess of the advances made to him. After the annual inventory the Phalanx will find itself in debt to all the poor members to whom it has advanced the minimum. This minimum includes: 1) Board of five meals a day in the third class dining room; 2) Decent clothing including work- and dress-uniforms, as well as all the tools and implements needed for farming and industrial work; 3) Lodging consisting of a private room with toilet, and also access to the public halls and festivities of the third class and to the stalls reserved for the third class at the theater.

At the outset, before the Phalanx makes its first harvests, the regency is responsible for the purchase of provisions; but their use and management is to be entrusted to the gastronomic series.

If the Phalanx is composed of 1500 members, they will be roughly divided into the following gastronomic categories:

> 900 members of the third class,
> 300 members of the second class,
> 100 members of the first class,
> 50 members eating food prepared to order.[6]

In all there will be five series devoted to the preparation of food; in addition to the four categories mentioned above, there will also be separate cooking for the animals who will be plentiful and well-treated in Harmony.

Each of the categories noted above will be divided into subdivisions corresponding to the three sexes.[7] There will be separate types of cooking for men, women and children. . . . Each of the three sexes will have its own tables and dining rooms. They will sometimes eat together in groups of various sizes at lunch or supper. But ordinarily there will be no sexual mixing at

---

[5] On the social minimum, the *sine qua non* of Fourier's theory of association, see also pp. 274–275.

[6] Presumably some of the Phalansterians were away on visits when Fourier made these estimates.

[7] Fourier frequently referred to children as a separate or neuter sex.

dinner, which is a meal during which each of the sexes will engage in its own gastrosophic cabals. . . .

Children will not dine at the same table with their fathers. This civilized custom would put a crimp on the studies of the fathers and the pleasures of the children. It will be enough for them to eat together at the two small meals, the *délité*[8] and the afternoon snack. But the two middle-sized meals, breakfast and supper, as well as the pivotal meal or dinner, will be arranged more methodically and according to the wishes of attraction. These arrangements will be perfectly free; they will be in strict conformity with the wishes of the passions. We are unable to recognize these wishes in the present order which distorts the play of the passions. In reading this sketch a father may say: "But I enjoy dining with my wife and my children, and I will continue to do so, come what may." Such an attitude is quite mistaken. Today, for want of anything better, a father may enjoy eating with his wife and his children. But when he has spent two days in Harmony and taken the bait of the intrigues and cabals of the series, the father will wish to dine with his own cabalistic groups. He will send off his wife and his children who, for their part, will ask nothing better than to be done with the lugubrious family dinner.

Since no coercive measures are tolerated in Harmony, the work to be done is indicated but not ordered by the Areopagus, which is the supreme industrial council. It is composed of the high-ranking officers of each series, and it serves as an advisory body with regard to passional affairs. Its opinions and decisions are subordinated to the wishes of attraction, and each series remains free to make decisions concerning its own industrial interests. Thus the Areopagus cannot order that the mowing or harvesting be done; it can only declare that a certain time is propitious according to the available meteorological or agronomic data; thereupon each series acts according to its wishes. But its wishes can scarcely differ from those of the Areopagus whose opinion is held in high esteem.

—*OC*, IV, 444–447

[8] Breakfast.

### THE EXCHANGE

No series has more members than that of the Exchange. Insofar as possible everyone in the Phalanx gathers at its sessions which are held every day to plan the activities of the following days. They take place at nightfall, at the time when everyone is returning to the Phalanstery and when there is little or no activity in the kitchens and gardens.

There is much more animation and intrigue at the Exchange of a Phalanx than there is at the stock exchanges of London or Amsterdam. For every individual must go to the Exchange to arrange his work and pleasure sessions for the following days. It is there that he makes plans concerning his gastronomic and amorous meetings and, especially, for his work sessions in the shops and fields. Everyone has at least twenty sessions to arrange, since he makes definite plans for the following day and tentative ones for the day after.

Assuming that 1200 individuals are present, and that each one has twenty sessions to arrange, this means that in the meeting as a whole there are 24,000 transactions to be concluded. Each of these transactions can involve 20, 40 or 100 individuals who must be consulted and intrigued with or against. It would be impossible to unravel so many intrigues and conclude so many transactions if one proceeded according to the confused methods employed by our commercial exchanges; operating at their rate it would take at least a whole day to organize half the meetings that the Harmonians must plan in half an hour. I will now describe their expeditious methods.

In the center of the hall there is a raised platform on which the director, the directrice and their secretaries are seated. Scattered around the hall are the desks of 24 negotiators, 12 men and 12 women. Each of them handles the affairs of a given number of series and serves as the representative of several neighboring Phalanxes. Each of the four secretaries corresponds with six of the 24 negotiators by means of iron wires whose movements indicate requests and decisions.

Negotiations are carried on quietly by means of signals. Each negotiator holds up the escutcheons of the groups or Phalanxes which he represents, and by certain prearranged signs he indicates the approximate number of members which he has recruited. Everyone else walks around the hall. In one or two circuits a given individual may take part in 20 transactions, since all he has to do is to accept or refuse. Dorimon suggests that a meeting of the bee-keepers be held the next day at ten o'clock. The leaders of this group have taken the initiative according to the customary procedures. Their job is to find out whether or not a majority of the members of the bee-keeping group wish to hold a session. In this case the decision is affirmative. Each of the members takes his peg from the bee-keepers' board which is placed in front of Dorimon's desk. . . .

At the other side of the hall Araminte calls for a meeting of the rose-growers to be held at the same time. Since many of Araminte's rose-growers are also members of the bee-keeping group, they raise an objection and notify Dorimon. He conveys their message to the directorate which tells Araminte to halt his negotiations. The rose-growers are obliged to choose another hour, since bee-keeping is a more necessary form of work than rose-growing.

Negotiations frequently become so complicated that three, four or five groups, and even complete series, find themselves in competition. Everything is settled by the signals of the negotiators. Their acolytes confer with the leaders of the various conspiring groups by calling them over to one of the desks. Every time someone tries to initiate an intrigue, either to organize a session or prevent one from being held, a conference takes place at some point outside the main promenade area so as not to disturb those who are still walking around the hall, watching the progress of negotiations and making up their minds. . . .

When a session of the Exchange is over everyone writes down a list of the meetings which he has agreed to attend, and the negotiators and directors draw up a summary of all the transactions. This summary is immediately sent to the press and then it is distributed to neighboring communities by a dog who carries it around his neck.

Conflicts and changes of time frequently cause the postponement of sessions. News of such postponements is regularly announced in the main hall of the Phalanstery, where there are always intermediaries or brokers to initiate new activities and plan meetings which could not be arranged at the evening's Exchange due to conflicts and cabales. In all the public halls there are special bureaus to deal with such problems.

All of these transactions will be carried on by methods totally unlike those of our stock exchanges where people try to conceal their thoughts and use crafty tactics. In the Exchanges of Harmony everyone desires to manifest his intentions and to make them known to all.

*—PM*, i; *OC*, x, 191–193

### THE PHALANX ON PARADE: ITS SIXTEEN TRIBES

When a Phalanx gathers for ceremonial occasions such as receptions and important festivities, it forms a vast series consisting of thirty-two choirs (sixteen male and sixteen female) each of which parades with its own special costumes and ornaments. This series, which can be called the basic series, is one of those which has the same distinguishing features throughout the globe. In all countries it adopts the thirty-two colors specified for each of its thirty-two choirs; these colors are required only on its pennants, plumes and distinctive ornaments.

Each of the thirty-two choirs has three uniforms for the three seasons—hot, cold and moderate. Each has its banners, its officers and its own special form of corporate enthusiasm, all of which serve as powerful stimuli in work and other activities. Since I will often be referring to this series, it should be described in great detail. In the outline that follows I designate under the name of tribes the double choirs of men and women and boys and girls who belong to the same age group.

*OC*, xii, 373

## FULL-SCALE PHALANX[9]

### DIVIDED INTO 16 TRIBES AND 32 CHOIRS

| Orders | | Names | Ages | Numbers |
|---|---|---|---|---|
| Ascending | | Nurselings | 0–1 | 72 |
| Complement | | Babies | 1–2 | 60 |
| | | Imps | 2–3 | 48 |
| Ascending Transition | 1. | Tots | 3–4½ | 60 |
| Ascending Wingtip | 2. | Cherubs | 4–6½ | 57 |
| | 3. | Seraphs | 6½–9 | 66 |
| Ascending Wing | 4. | Pupils | 9–12 | 75 |
| | 5. | Students | 12–15½ | 84 |
| | 6. | Striplings | 15½–20 | 93 |
| | 7. | Adolescents | 19–24 | 102 |
| | 8. | Grown | 24–30 | 111 |
| Center | X | Regency | | 81 |
| | 9. | Athletic | 30–37 | 105 |
| | 10. | Viril | 37–45 | 96 |
| Descending Wing | 11. | Refined | 45–54 | 87 |
| | 12. | Temperate | 54–64 | 78 |
| | 13. | Prudent | 64–75 | 69 |
| Descending Wingtip | 14. | Reverend | 75–87 | 60 |
| | 15. | Venerable | 87–100 | 51 |
| Descending Transition | 16. | Patriarchs | 100 and over | 45 |
| Descending Complement | | Sick | | 30 |
| | | Crippled | | 40 |
| | | Absent | | 50 |
| | | | TOTAL | 1620 |

—*OC*, VI, 110–111

[9] For compelling typographical reasons this outline has been slightly simplified by the editors.

# 3

# EDUCATION AND CULTURAL LIFE IN HARMONY

## EDUCATION, REFINEMENT, AND SOCIAL HARMONY

There is no problem about which people have had more foolish things to say than that of education and its methods.[1] Nature has perennially taken a malign pleasure in confounding all our educational theories and their spokesmen. The disgrace of Seneca, who was Nero's teacher, has been matched in more recent times by the failures of Condillac, who trained a political dunce, and Rousseau, who did not even dare to try out his theories on his own children. At least Rousseau showed some wisdom; for had he put his theories into practice, he would doubtless have succeeded like Cicero who had the help of the whole learned crew of Athens and Rome in turning his son into a complete nonentity, an idiot, whose only claims to fame were his name, his inheritance, and his ability to drink a whole jug of wine at a single gulp. . . . One must admit that civilized educational methods only serve to discourage the hopes of fathers for their sons. To escape the chaos of the civilized systems, let us first set down our guidelines. Let us determine the aims of education; then we will consider the means to be employed.

In all the activities of Harmony there is no other aim than unity. To realize that objective, education must be COMPOUND and INTEGRAL.

*Compound* education develops the body and the soul simultaneously. Neither of these conditions is satisfied today. It will be

---

[1] Fourier was greatly concerned with problems of education, and the texts in the present section provide no more than an introduction to the educational theories which he elaborated at great length in the *Traité de l'association domestique-agricole* (*OC*, v, 1–309) and the *Nouveau monde industriel* (*OC*, vi, 166–236). However, a number of the texts which we have included under other rubrics also deal with educational problems. See especially the selections below on "Vocational Training" (pp. 307–310) and "Education and Sexuality" (pp. 364–367). A systematic exposition of Fourier's educational theories may be found in David Zeldin, *The Educational Ideas of Charles Fourier* (London, 1969).

proved in the course of this work that the civilized methods neglect the body and pervert the soul.

*Integral* education is comprehensive; it aims at the perfection of everything related to the body and the soul. It will be proved that our civilized systems serve only to pervert the development of the body and the soul in a piece-meal fashion and to corrupt both with egoism and duplicity. . . .

The educational methods of Harmony tend first of all to promote the discovery of the INSTINCTUAL VOCATIONS of the very young and to adapt the individual to the diverse functions for which nature has destined him. Civilization, on the other hand, prevents the individual from performing the functions for which he is best suited. . . . No question has been more muddled by our theorists than that of vocational guidance. This problem is going to be completely resolved by the mechanism of harmonious education. It will not limit itself to endowing the child with a single vocation; instead it will develop about thirty vocations which will be graduated and dominant in diverse degrees.

Since the first aim of attraction is the creation of *luxury*, education must inspire people to engage in productive work. This requires the elimination of one of civilization's most shameful blemishes, a blemish which is not to be found in savage societies. I am speaking of the coarseness and crudity of the lower classes, the duplicity of their language and manners. This vice may be indispensable to civilized society in which the common people are so burdened by privations that refinement and cultivation would only serve to increase their awareness of their own wretchedness. But in the societary state the common people will enjoy a minimum level of subsistence higher than that of our comfortable bourgeoisie. It will no longer be necessary to brutalize them into accepting their suffering or to compel them to perform disagreeable work. For the serial mechanism will put an end to their suffering and will make their work attractive.

The very success of industrial attraction will necessitate the refinement of the plebeian class in Harmony. Otherwise the coarseness of the common people would serve to counterbalance the enticements that societary work will offer to the upper classes. The wealthy class would never enjoy working with boorish clods and mingling in all their activities. Thus the refinement of the common people will serve two ends: it will increase their own well-being, and it will also serve to make work in Harmony more appealing to the wealthy. . . .

Common norms of civility, speech and behavior can only be established by means of a collective education which will give the poor child the same good manners as the rich. The education that children receive in our society varies according to their wealth: the rich are taught by academicians, children of the middle classes have their pedagogues, and the poor are left to the village schoolmaster. If Harmony followed the same practice, it would attain the same results. Social classes would be mutually incompatible and each would have its own particular style: the poor would be coarse, the bourgeoisie would be petty, and only the rich would be refined. The result would be a state of general discord which must be avoided in Harmony. It will be avoided thanks to a system of education which is THE SAME for a whole Phalanx and for the whole globe. This new system of education will make good breeding universal.

On this point let us be careful not to confuse *unity* with *equality*. The refinement of the lower classes will not constitute a threat to the status of the wealthy; on the contrary, it will be most advantageous for them. Every rich man prefers polite and intelligent servants, such as those of Paris, to provincial clods who are crude and incompetent in the performance of their services.

In any case, servants are not hired contractually in Harmony. They perform their functions out of personal affection. Thus the rich man in Harmony has the two-fold pleasure of being served by pages who are highly refined individuals and his close friends. People think that monarchs are very fortunate in enjoying just one of these pleasures, that of having well-educated young men as their pages. If a Harmonian could enjoy the additional advantage of having friends in all his servants, does it follow that this system has any connection with equality?

Let us make a comparison. Would anyone claim that, in order to avoid equality, the common people should be shorter and slimmer than the rich? No, of course not. *Physical* unity requires bodily stature to be the same among people of all classes. But this is only a *simple unity*, limited to the physical or material realm.

*Compound unity*, which must be *physical* and *passional* and which can only be established in Harmony, requires that humans be identical in everything which concerns the fulfillment of the soul as well as the development of the body. Compound unity requires that men be homogeneous in language and manners even though unequal in wealth.

As soon as work is made attractive, there will be no drawbacks to having the poor refined and well educated. On the contrary, it would be bad for the rich and for work in general if the poor retained the crude manners of civilization. For the poor will constantly be encountering the rich in the *attractive work* of the passionate series. If these meetings are to have charm and intrigue, there must be a unity of manners and a common level of refinement. The Harmonians will be as fond of each other as the civilized are hostile. The Phalanx will regard itself as a single, unified family. But no prosperous family can allow any of its members to be deprived of the education that the others have received.

The most powerful means of creating a unity of good manners among the children in the Phalanx will be the OPERA. For all the children in Harmony participation in the opera will be a semi-religious exercise, a symbol of the spirit of God, of the unity which God has established in the whole system of the Universe. The opera brings together all the material unities. Thus all the children in Harmony will take part in operatic sessions. Training in material unity will direct them toward passionate unity.

I have already pointed out that an opera house will be as necessary for each Phalanx as its plows and herds. Not only will it provide the least community with performances as excellent as those of Paris, London and Naples; it will also serve to educate children and to shape them in the ways of material Harmony. . . .

Unitary education will perfect both men's bodies and their souls. Armed with their whips, paddles and metaphysical abstractions, our civilized teachers mould men like Nero and Tiberius.

They can have their shameful talent, the fruit of *simple partial* education. Let us study the system of *compound integral* education which will take a Tiberius or a Nero at the cradle, or even at the age of three, and turn him into a more virtuous monarch than Titus or the Antonines.

—*OC*, v, 1–7

### EDUCATION BY PEER GROUP

An immense advantage of Harmony's system of education will be to neutralize the influence of fathers, which can only serve to retard and pervert the child. On this point the fathers and philosophers are sure to take umbrage. "So you wish," they will say, "to take the child away from his natural teacher who is the father?" I do not *wish* anything. I do not follow the practice of the sophists who try to pass off their silly educational whims as laws. With their mania for plunging the child into cold water, for example, they are just trying to imitate a few republicans of antiquity. I confine myself to analysing the designs of attraction. . . .

Do you wish to learn the designs of nature in education or in any other matter? There is a perfect way of doing so. This is to take the opposite position from that held by the philosophers, who are always at variance with nature or attraction. But what are the educational precepts of philosophy? It holds that "the father should be the teacher of his child," and that "the father should not spoil his child." You must adopt the two contrary views: that "the father should not be the teacher of the child," and that "the father should allow himself the pleasure of spoiling his child.". . .

We will show in the course of this section that in Harmony the only paternal function of the father is to yield to his natural impulse, to SPOIL THE CHILD, to cater to all his whims in consistency with the rule of *descending gentility* or deference of the superior to the inferior.

The child will be sufficiently reprimanded and jeered at by his peers. The older Babies will be rebuffed by the younger Tots, and the Tots by the younger Cherubs. These rebuffs will instill in the child a spirit of emulation which could never emerge in the company of fathers and mothers who always admire the awkward mistakes of their children. Children are more critical of each other: they pay no compliments and make no concessions. A child with even a slight amount of experience or skill is merciless with regard to blunderers. Moreover, the infant who is chided by children only slightly older than himself does not dare to cry or lose his temper. For the older children would laugh at his anger and send him back to the playpen. . . .

In short, the true teacher of the child, the sole force that can light the *sacred fire* in him, that can inspire him to industrial emulation, is a group of slightly older children. A Baby or Tot should spend a part of his day in the company of children who are six months or a year older than he is and who possess more decorations and honors. Once he has had to put up with the jibes of half a dozen such groups, he will be thoroughly imbued with a sense of his own insufficiency and eager to listen to the advice of the partriarchs and venerables who are good enough to offer him instruction.

After that, no harm will be done if at the child's bedtime his parents indulge themselves by spoiling him and telling him that the other children have been too hard on him, that he is really very charming and very clever. These pleasant effusions will only skim the surface without convincing the child. For the impression has been made. He has been humiliated by the jeers of the seven or eight groups of Tots with whom he has spent the day. It won't matter if the parents tell him that the children by whom he was rejected are barbarians, enemies of commerce and of tender nature. All these paternal platitudes will have no effect; and the next day when the child returns to the infantile serister-ies he will remember only the affronts of the day before. It is he who, in reality, will cure the father of the habit of SPOILING him, by redoubling his efforts and proving that he is conscious of his inferiority.

—*OC*, v, 31–33

THE ENCOURAGEMENT OF THE ARTS AND THE SCIENCES

Each year every Phalanx draws up a list of scientific discoveries and works of art to which it has awarded prizes. Each of these works is judged by the competent series. A tragedy, for instance, by the literary and poetic series. . . . If a work seems worthy of a prize, each Phalanx will decide by majority vote upon the sum to be awarded to the author. For example, one franc might be awarded to Racine for his tragedy *Phèdre*.

Having drawn up its list of prizes, each Phalanx will send it to the administration of its province. The provincial administration will count the votes of the whole province and draw up a list of its own. This list will be forwarded to the regional administration which will prepare another, more comprehensive list. Thus after a number of preliminary countings, the final tabulation will be made by the Ministry at Constantinople, the seat of the Congress of Spherical Unity. It will publish the names of the authors who have been awarded prizes by a majority of the globe's Phalanxes. Each author will be awarded an average of the sums voted by this majority. If a third of the Phalanxes has voted half a franc, a third one franc, and a third one and a half francs, the award will be one franc.

Supposing that the tabulation gave one franc to Racine for *Phèdre* and three francs to Franklin for the invention of the lightning-rod, the Ministry will send Racine a bill of exchange for 600,000 francs, and Franklin will get 1,800,000 francs. The sum is paid by each of the 600,000 Phalanxes of the globe for any work which obtains an absolute majority of 300,001 votes. Moreover, the title of Magnates of the globe will be conferred upon Franklin and Racine. In any Phalanx that they visit on the face of the earth, they will enjoy the same prerogatives as the Magnates of the region. . . .

*Objection.* "Will not this type of remuneration be rather vexatious for those authors who disdain the caprices of fashion and make no concessions to prevailing tastes? Wouldn't such writers be denied an absolute majority, as was Racine who had great difficulty in triumphing over the coterie of Mme. de Sévigné which was devoted to Pradon? Will not the societary world also have its coteries, sects, schools and bizarre modes? Is not this harmful variety a necessary effect of the eleventh passion, the *Alternating* or *Butterfly*, which must have free play as all the others do? . . ."

This objection is applicable to civilization where good taste is always limited to a very few and never extends to the multitude. But it is not relevant to the societary order. For as we are going to show, the educational system of Harmony will serve to spread good taste even among the lower class. Changes of fashion will never provoke a decline in taste. The masses will be taught to appreciate several nuances in any genre. For instance, they will learn to love both the classic and the romantic. They will also learn to appreciate nuances within a given school, and they will choose to recompense the representatives of diverse nuances. Although the prizes will be enormous for the winning authors, they will be no more than a trifle for each Phalanx; they will never amount to more than a thousand francs per community each year. And what is a sum of a thousand francs for a community whose annual income will amount to some three million francs (in real value)? For its own good and to satisfy its own needs, each community will enjoy making a real effort to encourage the sciences, letters and arts.

—*OC*, III, 353–356.

## [4]

## ADVANCED GASTRONOMY

Questions concerning love and gourmandise are treated facetiously by the civilized who do not understand the importance that God attaches to our pleasures. Sensual pleasure is the only weapon that God can use to master us and lead us to the execution of His designs. He rules the universe *by attraction and not by constraint*. Thus in all his calculations God's primary concern is with our pleasures.

To show how sagaciously he has prepared our pleasures, I am going to speak of the fine eating which will be done in the combined order. The reader might prefer a digression on the amorous affairs of this new order. But a discussion of love would offend existing prejudices, whereas no one will be offended by an account of the intensification of gastronomic pleasure in Harmony.

Good food is only one-half of gastronomic pleasure. Appetites need to be whetted by a judicious choice of dining companions; and it is on this point that civilization displays its impotence. The most affluent and refined civilized gentleman cannot, *even at his country house*, bring together as well-matched and varied a selection of guests as the poorest man of Harmony will find at all his meals.

The poor matching of guests at our banquets is the reason why civilized ladies are so bored by the pleasures of the table. Women attach more importance than men to the choice of guests; men are more exacting about the quality of the food. These two pleasures, *exquisite food* and a *piquant and varied selection of dining companions*, are continually associated in the combined order. Civilization cannot provide the one or the other. . . .

—*OC*, I, 160

. . . The material pleasures that I am describing are not all that matters. It will not suffice for the poorest of you to have better food and drink than the richest of kings. As important as it is, this sort of well-being would provide you with only one-half of the pleasures of the dinner table. If good food is vital, there is another and no less essential condition: this is the judicious mixing of dining companions, the art of varying and matching table-mates, the art of making each day's meal more interesting than the last through unforeseen and delightful encounters, the art of providing even the poorest individuals with spiritual pleasures which are not to be found in your sad households.

On this point your civilization is completely ridiculous. Your costly dinners and your most elegant banquets are ordinarily so poorly arranged, and the guests are so ill-matched, that one would die of boredom were it not for the food. But any dirty peasant likes good food when he can get it; and he probably enjoys it more than the gentleman, for at least he is jovial and frisky in his tavern. The pleasures of the tavern appeal to both his soul and his senses, whereas in your salons people yawn at each other for a mortal hour while they wait for dinner. Eh! And the price you pay for the dinner is the boredom of enduring lethargic conversations about the rain and the sunshine, the good health of beloved friends and relatives, the great strides taken by the worthy children of virtuous fathers, the fine character of daughters, the good nature of aunts, and the tender sentiments of tender nature! What a deluge of insipidity and nonsense you get at the most costly and elegant of civilized meals. The occasion is as dull for the guests as it is for the lady of the house who went to the trouble of preparing the meal and inviting the guests. Eh! How do the civilized dare to aspire to gastronomic distinction when they are absolutely ignorant of the art of organizing the piquant and varied gatherings which constitute one-half of gastronomic pleasure. It seems that on this point kings are even worse off than their subjects. They are reduced to eating with their families, as isolated as hermits and as solemn as owls throughout the whole meal. The gastronomic pleasures of even the most powerful king are thus greatly inferior to those of the poorest individual in the combined order. Nonetheless, a civilized monarch can consider himself lucky if, in his meal-time isolation and gloom, he is spared the nagging fear of being poisoned. Oh, how vain are the pleasures of civilization!

—OC, I, 170–171

### A PROBLEM IN BI-COMPOUND GASTRONOMY:
### THE TRIUMPH OF TOUGH OLD HENS

In conformity with the precepts *utile dulci, castigat ridendo*,[1] I will resort to a gastronomic farce to open a discussion of highly important matters. I would run the risk of frightening the reader if I used systematic jargon. It will be better to begin in a light-hearted way with no tedious formulas. This will provide students with a pleasant introduction to one of the most difficult problems posed by the theory of social movement.

The study of transitions or ambiguous types is so new that in all the 70 known (and perhaps 700 unknown) botanical systems, no one has dared to venture a systematic judgment concerning the species which belong to the ambiguous gender.

In the equilibrium of the passions transitions are what pins and joints are in carpentry. The Creator has obviously deemed them to be useful since he has provided such a plentiful assortment of transitions in the realm of nature. Ambiguous species may be found in every series: take, for instance, the quince, the bat, the flying fish, the amphibious animals, the zoophytes. These and many other species provide a link, and often a redoubled link, between the different series of the animal, vegetable and mineral kingdoms.

There are also transitions in the passional kingdom. One is constantly encountering impure or mixed tastes and unusual personalities, which are destined to serve as a link between the societary series. In today's society these ambiguous impulses are generally scorned and ridiculed. . . . I am going to show that in Association these transitional types, these disdained ambiguous or mixed tastes, will become social bonds eminently favorable to the development of the social virtues.

---

[1] "Proceed from the useful to the agreeable." (Horace, *Ars Poetica*, 344); "Criticize in laughing" (Santeuil).

This can be proved by a discussion of the lowliest tastes. Thus I am going to obtain evidence from witnesses whose reputation in affairs of gastronomy is slight: I am referring to *old hens*. They are going to bear witness, along with their partisans, to a thesis of great import, the thesis that attractions are proportional to destinies. They are going to prove: "that all the impulses of attraction, which are ridiculed because they seem bizarre, are usefully coordinated in the societary mechanism, and will become as precious as they are useless and harmful in the sub-divided or family system."

The reader is going to discover that human reason betrays inexperience and stupidity when it criticizes the allegedly bizarre passions and their worthy Creator who would not have given them to man if he had deemed them incapable of serving the general good. What an honor for a tough old hen to bear the burden of so transcendent a discussion!

In fact certain people cannot stand tender poultry; they complain that it turns their stomach. They prefer pickled three-year-old roosters or old and macerated hens. These tough meats have a good deal of flavor; they can be made tender and tasty with the help of sauces and seasoning.

If at a banquet held by some Sybarite one of the guests wants to eat a skinny old hen, he will be told that the host thought it too common a dish to be served. Nevertheless, out of 50 individuals, there is always at least ONE who has this bizarre taste. In a Phalanx including 1200 members there will thus be 24 such individuals above the age of 15, women included.

These partisans of old pickled hens, served in a braising-pan or in gelatin, form one of the transitional groups in the series of hen-eaters. Here is the complete list:

|  |  |
|---|---|
| Anterior Transition: | excessively young poultry. |
| Citerior Transition: | overly tender poultry. |
| Ulterior Transition: | old poultry. |
| Posterior Transition: | gamey poultry. |

We are dealing here with a taste which belongs to the *ulterior* transition. Let us examine the utility of this allegedly bizarre penchant. Let us watch the theory in action.

Chrysante, a dignitary in the Phalanx of Saint-Cloud, is one of these lovers of old pickled hens. The gastronomers of the region cannot tease him about this mania since he has found about twenty co-partisans, both men and women, in the Phalanx. They all share his taste. They often meet for a group dinner at which the principal dish provided by Chrysante consists of a rooster placed between two old hens.

This group meeting adds to the prestige both of the cooks who prepare and pickle these old birds and of the group which feeds them in the hen-house. It serves to establish a passionate bond between these three groups of *consumers, preparers* and *producers*. We will show later that the old hen creates as many discords in civilization as passionate bonds in Harmony.

At the dinner table, and everywhere else, the Harmonians need stimulants which unite their hearts, minds and senses. This bizarre feast of a rooster and two old hens serves to link Chrysante and his co-partisans by a multitude of ties based on the affinity of their tastes and activities and on their schemes to bring credit to their favorite food. The care they take in the preparation of their poultry adds to its reputation. They gain support by forming coalitions with like-minded members of neighboring Phalanxes. Through their efforts they bring such prestige to their old hen that, finally, it is assigned a place of honor at the dinner table as an exemplary type of ulterior transition. There, properly pickled old hens are much sought after by people who seek diversion from tender poultry.

Thus this meagre feast serves to establish a quadruple bond between the hearts, the minds, the pride and the sensual desires of unequal individuals. This is the brilliant result of a skillfully contrived transition. And all transitions will be skillfully contrived in the societary state.

The collective action of these four bonds (two would suffice) will provide the *composite* passion with bi-compound or redoubled gratification. This means that both the senses and the soul will enjoy two-fold pleasure. What marvelous properties are exhibited by an old hen in serial Harmony!

Let us compare the destiny of this mean bird to the role which it plays in civilization. In civilization it will meet its end on some humble bourgeois table where it will provoke discord.

Purchased by a housewife who is reduced to serving cheap food in order to buy herself dresses, the antiquated fowl will be dished up at noon to her tender spouse who would prefer to eat capons if they were not so costly. No sooner has he tasted the miserable bird than he tells his wife: "A plague on this old hen! It's as tough as the devil himself!" "Really!" answers his wife. "Do you think you're going to get tender chicken with the small change you give me! And I even have to tear that away from you. Give me enough to buy good food, and then you'll get it. You always have money to waste at the café with your drunken friends."

This declaration leaves the tender husband speechless. Like Harpagon, he would prefer to eat well without paying. So he finishes his penitential bird in silence, and the left-overs are served to his darling children who are forbidden to make complaints.

Thus the miserable hen, which would have delighted a group of Harmony's *ambiguous gastronomers* (representatives of the ulterior transition), will be an apple of discord in civilization, a cause of peevishness at the dinner table of a parsimonious little household.

*—OC*, IV, 135–138

# VI

## *Attractive Work*

A new moralist, the Vicomte de Villeneuve-Bargement, has
chosen this epigraph for his treatise on pauperism: "We must
recommend patience, frugality, sobriety, work, religion; all
the rest is a fraud and a lie" (Burke). Yes, everything is a
fraud and a lie beginning with those moral tracts and their
authors who advise us to work. If they knew how to make
work agreeable and productive . . . they wouldn't need to
recommend patience, frugality and *RELIGION!!!*

*AN*, 10AS 21 (6)

A large part of our Introduction was devoted to a description
of attractive work. Here we would like merely to call the
reader's attention to the fundamentally libertarian quality of
life and work in the Phalanx. This, it seems to us, is an aspect
of Fourier's thought that has often been overlooked. In fact
Fourier has sometimes been accused of devising—consciously
or unconsciously—a tyrannical set of institutions that would
have destroyed personal freedom and left no room for privacy.
   This charge is not entirely groundless. Fourier's
descriptions and prescriptions are so fantastically minute that
the Phalanx often appears to be more of a prison than a
paradise. It could be argued, however, that the regimentation
in the Phalanx is more apparent than real, for individual
autonomy and self-realization are protected and fostered by

Harmony's serial mechanism and its system of vocational education. Of course we now know that "vocational aptitude" testing, which matches the personality to the job, can be anything but liberating, especially when it is imposed or "administered" from above. But Fourier's scheme, we would suggest, is largely free of the authoritarian tendencies inherent in much "industrial psychology."

During Fourier's own lifetime, he was in fact accused of proposing to establish anarchy where rational order and discipline should reign. The Saint-Simonians, who were competing with Fourier for a following, advocated patently authoritarian psychological and vocational theories, and they contended that their industrial psychology was superior to Fourier's precisely because it was based on the principles of hierarchy and authority. They did not attempt to hide the fact that the Saint-Simonian "priest" of the new order would wield a large amount of "rational" and "scientific" authority. The Saint-Simonians insisted that true freedom would be protected so long as human resources were allocated scientifically on the basis of psychological testing. Human personalities could be divided into three large groups based on physiological characteristics. Since all men were destined by nature to do scientific, artistic, or manual work, the Saint-Simonians felt that it would be a relatively simple matter to put the right man in the right job, thereby insuring individual happiness and industrial efficiency. By comparison, Fourier's vocational psychology is immensely less constricting. Phalansterian education was specifically designed to detect a host of aptitudes and inclinations. According to Fourier, even the simplest, dullest personality, the "monogyne," could not be adequately analyzed by a crude and repressive psychological typology which imprisoned a man in an exclusive sphere of activity. The whole panoply of Harmonic institutions from groups and series to the anarchic sessions at the labor exchange was necessary, not for order's sake, but to insure individual self-realization. The Phalanx may often seem to be a "giant organization and administration,"[1] which is essentially incompatible with

[1] Herbert Marcuse, *Eros and Civilization* (New York, 1955), p. 199.

instinctual liberation, but we feel that attractive labor can be seen in a different light.

Most of Fourier's nineteenth century readers and critics thought that attractive labor was either impossible or undesirable. Even those who agreed that working conditions could be improved did not believe that work could be turned into festive play or, indeed, into a semi-erotic activity. For many critics, attractive labor was not technologically feasible. Others like Marx rejected it for philosophical reasons, while a large and more hostile group objected on psychological and even moral grounds. These opponents of attractive labor felt that ordinary men would not work unless driven to it by fear and hunger. Since idleness bred immorality, God's curse was both morally salutary and socially useful, at least for the masses. Fourier's specifications were never put to the test during his own era and it is unlikely that our post-industrial technology could subordinate its own requirements of rationality and discipline to the disruptive effects of the Butterfly and Cabalist passions. The texts collected in this chapter, however, should allow the reader to come to his own conclusions about Fourier's solution of the problem of work.

# 1

# GENERAL CONDITIONS AND DESCRIPTIONS

### THE SEVEN CONDITIONS AND THE SOCIAL MINIMUM

Until now politics and morality have failed in their attempts to make men love work. Wage-earners and the entire lower class are becoming more and more indolent. Sunday's idleness is being compounded with Monday's idleness. Men work without enthusiasm, slowly and with loathing.

Aside from slavery, the only means by which society can force men to work is to make them fear starvation and punishment. Yet if God has destined us to work, he should not have to use violent means. How can we believe that he is not able to employ a nobler device, an enticement capable of transforming work into pleasure?

Only God is invested with the power to distribute attraction. He wishes to guide his universe and its creatures by attraction alone. To attach us to agricultural and manufacturing work he has devised a system of *industrial attraction*. Once this system is put into practice, it will endow manufacturing and farming tasks with a host of charms. It may even make work more alluring than are the festivities, balls, and spectacles of today. In other words, the common people will derive so much pleasure and stimulation from work in the societary state that they will refuse to leave their jobs to attend balls and spectacles scheduled during work periods.

If it is to attract the people so forcefully, societary work must have none of the loathsome aspects that make work in the present state so odious. For societary work to become attractive it must fulfill the seven following conditions:

1. Each worker must be an associate who is compensated by dividend and not by wages.

2. Each person—man, woman or child—must be paid in proportion to his contribution in *capital, work* and *talent*.

3. Work sessions must be varied about eight times a day because a man cannot remain enthusiastic about his job for more

than an hour and a half or two when he is performing an agricultural or manufacturing task.

4. These tasks must be performed by groups of friends who have gathered together spontaneously and who are stimulated and intrigued by very active rivalries.

5. Workshops, fields and gardens must offer the worker the enticements of elegance and cleanliness.

6. The division of labor must be carried to the supreme degree in order to allot suitable tasks to people of each sex and of every age.

7. The distribution of tasks must assure each man, woman, or child the right to work or the right to take part at any time in any kind of work for which he or she is qualified.

X. Finally, in this new order the common people must enjoy a guarantee of well-being, a minimum income sufficient for present and future needs. This guarantee must free them from all anxiety either for their own welfare or that of their dependents.

—*OC*, III, 14–16

## WORK AND THE DISTRIBUTIVE PASSIONS

The physical organization of the series will pose no problems. . . . The obstacle to fear will involve the action of certain passions that the moralists would like to repress. For the best formed series would lose all its qualities of industrial attraction, of direct harmony of inequalities, of indirect harmony of antithetical elements, etc., if one neglected to develop the three basic drives which I have called the distributive or mechanizing passions.[1] To thwart any one of the three would be to spoil a series and to deprive it of industrial attraction. . . .

By working in very short sessions of an hour and a half, two hours at most, every member of Harmony can perform seven or eight different kinds of attractive work in a single day. On the next day he can vary his activities by taking part in different groups. This method is dictated by the eleventh passion, the *Butterfly*, which impels men and women to flit from pleasure to pleasure, to avoid the excesses that ceaselessly plague the people

[1] On the distributive passions see above pp. 219–220.

of civilization who prolong a job for six hours, a festival six hours, a ball six hours (and that during the night) at the expense of their sleep and their health.

Civilized pleasures are always associated with unproductive activities, but in the societary state varied work will become a source of varied pleasures. Let me illustrate this point by outlining the daily activities of two Harmonians, one rich and the other poor.

## LUCAS' DAY IN JUNE

*Time*
|       |                                                         |
|-------|---------------------------------------------------------|
| 3:30  | Rising, preparations.                                   |
| 4:00  | Session with a group assigned to the stables.           |
| 5:00  | Session with a group of gardeners.                      |
| 7:00  | Breakfast.                                              |
| 7:30  | Session wth the reapers' group.                         |
| 9:30  | Session with the vegetable-growers' group, under a tent.|
| 11:00 | Session with the barnyard series.                       |
| 1:00  | DINNER.                                                 |
| 2:00  | Session with the forestry series.                       |
| 4:00  | Session with a manufacturing group.                     |
| 6:00  | Session with the irrigation series.                     |
| 8:00  | Session at the Exchange.                                |
| 8:30  | Supper.                                                 |
| 9:00  | Entertainment.                                          |
| 10:00 | Bed.                                                    |

*Nota.* An Exchange is maintained in each Phalanx, not for speculation on interest rates and commodities but for arranging work and pleasure gatherings.[2]

I have described here a day with but three meals, a day in the first phases of Harmony. But when Harmony is in full operation, its active life and the practice of short and varied work sessions will make people prodigiously hungry. Men born and reared in Harmony will be obliged to eat five meals a day, and

[2] For an account of the activities of the Exchange see above pp. 253–255.

even these will scarcely be enough to consume the immense quantity of food produced by this new order, an order in which the rich—with their varied activities—will be stronger and hungrier than the poor. This is just the opposite of the civilized system.

I am now going to describe the five-meal day of a rich man in Harmony. His activities are much more varied than those of Lucas, who was one of the villagers enrolled at the outset.

### MONDOR'S DAY IN THE SUMMER

*Time*

|  | Sleep from 10:30 at night to 3:00 in the morning. |
|---|---|
| 3:30 | Rising, preparations. |
| 4:00 | Morning court, review of the night's adventures. |
| 4:30 | Breakfast, followed by the industrial parade. |
| 5:30 | Session with the group of hunters. |
| 7:00 | Session with the group of fishermen. |
| 8:00 | Lunch, newspapers. |
| 9:00 | Session with a group of horticulturalists, under a tent. |
| 10:00 | Mass. |
| 10:30 | Session with the group of pheasant-breeders. |
| 11:30 | Session at the library. |
| 1:00 | DINNER. |
| 2:30 | Session with the green-house group. |
| 4:00 | Session with the group of exotic plant growers. |
| 5:00 | Session with the fish-tank group. |
| 6:00 | Snack, in the fields. |
| 6:30 | Session with the sheep-raising group. |
| 8:00 | Session at the Exchange. |
| 9:00 | Supper, fifth meal. |
| 9:30 | Art exhibition, concert, dance, theater, receptions. |
| 10:30 | Bed. |

It is obvious from this description that only a few moments are left for sleep. Harmonians sleep very little. Advanced hygiene along with varied work sessions will inure them against work fatigue. They will not wear themselves out during the day and they will need only a very small amount of sleep. They will become accustomed to this from childhood thanks to an abundance of pleasures more numerous than the day is long.

To facilitate the constant movement that life in Harmony requires, all the sections of the Phalanstery (or edifice of the Phalanx) will be provided with communicating passageways on the first and second floors. These passageways will be heated by pipes in the winter and cooled during the summer. Adjacent buildings will be linked by elevated walk-ways and there will be graveled tunnels connecting the Phalanstery with the stables. By these means it will be possible to go through the rooms, workshops and stables while remaining under cover and without even knowing if it is hot or cold outside. In the country light eighteen-passenger carriages will be used to transport agricultural groups.

Some of my civilized critics may object that this arrangement will be quite costly. In fact it will cost infinitely less than the money we now spend on carriages, on the cleaning of dampened and mud-stained clothes, and on the curing of colds, inflammations and fevers caused by over-exertion and exposure. Others may say that Harmonians will waste a great deal of time in traveling from one activity to another. In fact transfers will take no more than fifteen minutes when they are working in the fields, and half as much when they are indoors.

Those who regret these pauses in the day's occupations are like the man who would propose to abolish sleep because it takes time from work. To allow for rest is to make work go faster. The Harmonians will work passionately and with great zeal. In one hour they will accomplish what cannot be done in three by our slow, clumsy, bored and loitering wage-earners who stop and lean on their shovels every time they see a bird fly by. The enthusiasm of the Harmonians for their work would become harmful and excessive were it not held in check by the frequent pauses necessitated by the changing of work sessions. My critics fail to understand this because they always try to judge the societary mechanism according to the customs and practices of the civilized system.

I shall now turn to the other two mechanizing passions.

The Cabalist and the Composite are perfect opposites. The first is a calculating and reflective impulse. The second is blind enthusiasm, a state of inebriation and rapture which is produced by the simultaneous gratification of the soul and the body. The *Cabalist* or party spirit is the mania for intrigue. . . .

The principal function of the Cabalist in the operation of a series is to stir up discords or competitive rivalries between groups that are close enough to one another to vie for praise and prizes. There will be no harmony between groups cultivating three similar varieties of pears such as the early white, the late white, and the green spotted pear. These groups are contiguous in their nuances and are essentially jealous and discordant. The same will hold for the three groups cultivating yellow, grey and green rennet apples. Discord between contiguous groups is a general law of nature: the color scarlet goes very badly with its adjacent shades, cherry, nacarat and capucine; but it goes quite well with its opposites, dark blue, dark green, black, white. . . . Let us repeat that in the societary order there must be discord as well as harmony.

But discords cannot break out between groups with divergent tastes, such as the groups which cultivate the pearly pear and the orange pear. There is enough of a difference between these two little pears to make judges hesitate. They will say that both pears are good, but not sufficiently alike to be compared. Consequently, jealousy and rivalry will not break out between the two groups that cultivate them, and the Cabalist will not be in operation.

The groups which constitute any passionate series, whether it is organized for work or for pleasure, must be divided according to a scale of related tastes and functions. This is called the *compact or serried scale*. The use of this scale is a sure way to give free play to the Cabalist, to improve the quality of the goods produced in each group and series, and to make people enthusiastic about their work and their fellow-workers. All of these advantages would be lost if refined taste were not encouraged among consumers as well as among producers. What good would it do the Harmonians to produce the finest foods if they had to deal with a moralistic public of uniform tastes, a public that eats only to moderate its passions and forbids itself all sensual refinements for the sake of a repressive morality? If that were the case, the quality of the food produced would decline from lack of appreciation. The cabalistic spirit would cease to prevail in groups dedicated to the production and preparation of food. Agriculture would once more fall into the grossness that today makes it difficult to find one man in a hundred capable of judging the excellence of a foodstuff. The coarseness and ignorance of civilized consumers is such that the seller who adulterates his goods has ninety-nine chances of making a sale against one chance of refusal. This is why all food is so bad in civilization.

To obviate this disorder, the societary state will encourage children to develop their cabalistic propensities in association with the activities of consumption, preparation and production. They will be taught at an early age to recognize and develop their tastes for particular dishes, flavors and dressings; they will be encouraged to demand that even the most inconsequential foods be prepared in accordance with their diverse tastes. The cabalistic scale thus formed among young consumers will subsequently be extended to include the work of preparation, conservation and production.

This variety in tastes, which would be ruinous in civilization, will become economical and productive in association. It will yield the double advantage of:

Exciting industrial attraction,

Making people produce and consume by series.

The mechanism of the passionate series would break down if it failed to include consumption. Fortunately it is a simple matter to utilize the serial method in consumption; one need only establish two scales of tastes, one for the quality of food, and one for its cooking and preparation. Such preferential scales appear of their own accord whenever men's natural impulses are allowed free reign. For example, in an inn where each guest pays his own bill, where there are neither fathers nor masters, and where no one is obliged to conceal his whims, a variety of preferences will emerge. There will be requests for ten or twelve varieties of the most banal dishes, like a salad or an omelette. If the number of diners does not exceed seven, each will probably call for a different variety.

Thus the penchant for nuances in the cooking and preparation of food springs up whenever it is not repressed. I know that it would be impossible to satisfy this multiplicity of tastes in civilization. A household would be ruined if it tried to prepare food in half a dozen different ways for the father, mother, children and servants. It is for this reason that fathers call morality to their aid. By proving that tastes should be uniform, morality enables each father to impose his own tastes on his whole family. This is necessary in civilization. But we are going to speak of an order of things in which nuanced varieties will be cheaper and easier to prepare and produce than they are now. There will be no need to summon morality to smother the penchant for variety.

The trial Phalanx should encourage its members to develop a great variety of tastes for all types of food. It should accustom them to graduating their fancies in compact scales, in minutely distinguished nuances of taste. Without compact scales, it would be impossible to establish the group rivalries and discords that enable the Cabalist passion to flourish.

The third of the mechanizing passions is the *Composite* or exalting passion, whose main function is to create accords of enthusiasm within each group and series. The energies of intrigue or party spirit alone will not suffice to electrify the groups in their work. It is also necessary to draw upon the two contrasting passions: the reflective impetuosity of the Cabalist and the blind impetuosity of the Composite, which is the most romantic of the passions, the one most inimical to reason. I have said that the Composite arises from the coupling or simultaneous enjoyment of sensual and spiritual pleasures. (Of course a coupling of several passions of the same type, either all sensual or all spiritual, produces only an illegitimate or bastard Composite.) This passion must find expression in all the work of the association. Together with the Cabalist, it must replace the vile incentives which characterize civilized work—the need to nourish one's children, the fear of starvation and of the poor-house.

The constant use of the three mechanizing passions—above all the Composite—will enable the societary order to do without these abject civilized stimuli and to endow the work of each industrial group with a quadruple charm. Each task will provide two illusions for the senses and two for the soul; four bonds or sympathies will thus be formed between the members of any one group.

The two sympathies of the soul are the accords or emotional ties based on identity and contrast.

The members of any group are necessarily linked by an accord of identity: they have a shared preference for a task which they have chosen passionately and which they are free to quit at any time. The accord of identity exercises a powerful charm or attraction when a man finds that he is aided in his work by a group of zealous, intelligent and good-natured collaborators rather than the coarse, inept mercenaries, the ragged rascals that he would have had to associate with in civilization. The company of polite and friendly associates makes people enthusiastic about the work which they perform during their short sessions; it makes them eager to return to work and to meet at other times for group meals.

The soul's second charm is that of contrast. I have said before and I will say again that to create contrasts among the diverse groups that make up a series, it is necessary to establish a consecutive ranking or scale among their related tastes and penchants. The use of the compact or serried scale will serve to create discords and rivalries between adjacent groups and harmonies between groups with divergent tastes.

In addition to emotional ties based on identity and contrast, an industrial group should be stimulated by two other vehicles of sensual charm. The first of these is the charm of specialized perfection, which lies in the recognition of the group's good workmanship, its competence in its own particular domain. The second is the charm of collective perfection, or the appreciation by the members of the group of the excellence of the work done by the series as a whole.

Some groups may lack one of these four charms or possess it feebly. This does not matter since two charms are enough to create industrial attraction. Moreover, as I will show in subsequent chapters, industrial attraction has many other sources. The point is that societary work offers enticements as numerous as the repulsions of civilized work. . . .

To summarize our discussion of the three mechanizing passions, those three driving forces of an industrial series, let us observe that if all three of them are not developed at the same time, industrial attraction will not be generated. Or if it does appear, it will only be to die away and vanish quickly. Thus if work is to be made attractive, the first condition is to form series of groups adapted to the play of the three mechanizing passions. These groups and series must be:

*Set in rivalry* by the CABALIST, the calculating impulse which creates discords between contiguous groups, so long as the groups are divided into a compact scale of related tastes and activities.

*Exalted* by the COMPOSITE, the blind enthusiasm which derives from the linking of sensual and spiritual pleasures and from the four accords cited above.

*Enmeshed* by the BUTTERFLY which supports the other two passions and sustains their activity by means of short sessions and by the opportunities for new pleasure that it periodically offers before people become sated or indifferent.

—*OC*, VI, 66–74

# HARMONY'S ENTERPRISES

### SELECTING THE SERIES

Let us consider the types of series that we might choose for the trial Phalanx. . . . In making our choice we should keep the following criteria in mind:

1. The care of animals is preferable to work with plants and vegetables because it will keep the series permanently occupied during the winter's idleness.

2. Work with plants and vegetables is preferable to work in manufactures because it has more intrinsic attraction.

3. Kitchen work should be stressed because it is permanent, with no periods of seasonal idleness. It serves to initiate workers in industrial attraction. Since it is linked both to production and to consumption, it is the kind of work best suited to maintain the cabalistic spirit.

4. In factory work attraction is more important than profit-making. The policy of the founders of the Phalanx should be to create a fine balance among the passions and not to speculate on profits poorly related to the societary system. Profits are a hoax when they distract us from our goal, which is the speedy activation of the mechanism of industrial attraction. . . .

During good weather fifty series will devote themselves to the cultivation of plants and vegetables. They will work in the forests and meadows and they will also make use of warm and cool greenhouses. Civilization is familiar only with hothouses. On this point as on so many others, civilized minds tend to SIMPLISM, or the simple mode. This is typical of the genius of civilization. Composite greenhouses, or warm and cool greenhouses used jointly will, like the aviaries, be a very powerful source of attraction for the three sexes and especially for the wealthy class. Great care, consequently, should be taken in organizing this kind of industry.

The management of methodically planted and mixed forests will constitute a large item in the Phalanx's enterprises. Each section of every meadow and forest will be planted with varieties suited to it. The *Rustic Pomp* Series will be formed to care for the altars and borders of flowers and shrubs which will surround the various plots of ground set aside for each kind of vegetable. This sort of luxury is a very precious source of attraction and intrigue. Attractive manufactures will not furnish more than ten to twelve series.

### TOTAL ESTIMATED

Animal Kingdom . . . . . 30 series
Vegetable Kingdom . . . . 50 series
Manufacturing . . . . . . 20 series

To reach a total of 135 series,[1] forty more remain to be formed. Let us review the domestic tasks which can furnish this number of series . . .

1.2.3. The *Storehouse* Series for hay, vegetables and fodder. —4.5.6. The *Wine cellar* and *Under cellar* (for beer, cider, vinegar, liqueurs, etc.); and the *Little cellar* which will be very well stocked for paying tourists. —7.8.9. The *Fruit cellars:* an enormous amount of fruit will be purchased to make preserves. This task will support at least three series. —10. The *Ground cellar* to store vegetables underground, either green or in jars after preparation. —11. The *Oil-store.* —12. The *General Seed-shop.* —13. The *Dairy*, minus the *Cheese factory.* (14. 15.) —16. *Waiters* and *Room-servants* who serve the tables and lodgings. —17. *Furnishers*, maintenance of furnishings from mirrors to pots and pans. —18.19. *Irrigation*, including care of the pumps and pipes. —20. *Nursery maids*, caring for the Seristery of the Brats. —21. The *Nurses*, including the supplementary and substitute nurses. —22. The *Nurses* and *Nurse-men*, working with children who are 2 to 3 years old in order to ascertain and develop their industrial vocations. —23. The *Mentors* and *Mentorines*, working with children 3 to 4½ years old to draw out

---

[1] For all of their importance, Fourier's mathematical calculations were often less than rigorous.

and evaluate their personalities in terms of temperament and character. —24. *Medicine*, in all of its functions, up to hospital workers. —25.26. *Teaching*, much more extensive than in the civilized state. I include here agricultural and manufacturing education. —27.28. The *Little Hordes* and *Little Bands*, the principal educational series. —29.30.31. *Harmony*, both vocal and instrumental, or the various series devoted to songs, hymns, stringed instruments and wind instruments. —32. The *Drama*, furnishing a series of well-graduated kinds of plays. —33. The *Opera*, all types. —34.35. *Choreography* and *Gymnastics*. —36. *Periodic Drudge Duty*. —37.38. Finally, two (or perhaps four) ambiguous series for animal husbandry and farming. . . .

I will repeat here the rule given for work in the animal kingdom: do not go in too much for raising large animals such as horses and steers and avoid growing large plants such as forest trees. That sort of work will cost our inexperienced generation too much time.[2] Nevertheless, these activities should not be neglected as they are today. In general, the goal is the formation of a large number of well-integrated series. Series devoted to little flowers and vegetables will be almost as useful as those caring for oaks and pines, the cultivation of which would require ten times as many hours. . . .

There is one important variety of work that remains to be taken into account—work in the kitchens. This kind of labor will increase the total number of series to two hundred because the kitchens will be able to create about sixty series; these will be extremely precious because most of them will be permanent, working throughout the year.

There is hardly any kind of food, either in the animal or vegetable kingdom, that cannot occupy and intrigue one or sometimes several passionate series. The chicken, the pig, the potato, and the cabbage will each of them occupy several series which could be *dualized* by combining the intrigues of preparation with those of production.

Kotzebue says that the innkeepers of Paris know how to

---

[2] Throughout these texts on Harmony's enterprises, Fourier is providing instructions for a trial Phalanx.

prepare eggs in forty-two different ways. (This is the only thing that he found worthy of note at Paris.) Eggs, therefore, could foster three dualized series in the kitchens. Each of these series would be composed of twelve to fifteen groups.

But we can only establish such a large number of series if we adopt a principle opposed to the teachings of the moralists: we must make sure that people's tastes and passions become extremely refined. Otherwise the various culinary nuances would go unappreciated, and it would be impossible to form series for the production and preparation of food. How could we form intrigues among twenty groups cultivating twenty varieties of a given species if consumers ate each of the twenty without being able to distinguish between different qualities and methods of preparation?

The art of cooking, which is held in such contempt by the philosophers, has the same effect on agricultural emulation that grafting has on fruit: it doubles the value. Intrigues concerning farming and the care of livestock will redouble in intensity when they are combined with the intrigues of culinary preparation. Such combinations create *dualized* series which stimulate each other and increase the intensity of industrial attraction.

In the present state agriculture is beset by two vices which stand in opposition to these splendid characteristics of societary cuisine: one is repugnant work, or work done for money and out of necessity; the other is the limitation of fine food to idle men. The man who grows the food does not have a special attraction for his work, and he is not intrigued by cabales concerning his methods or by debates over the preparation of his food. This is so because the only food he gets to eat is what he cannot sell, and even that is very badly prepared. The Phalanx, however, will produce enough meat and vegetables so that even people who eat in the third class dining room will get to taste every variety. Otherwise an important source of industrial intrigue would be lacking.

Thus our agricultural mechanism is flawed in every sense. For there are no intrigues and cabales associated with production, and the only refined consumers are the idle. But their refinement is completely useless since it only serves to fill them with scorn for the sad condition of the common people who cater to their whims.

—*OC*, VI, 130–131, 135–139

THE SUBORDINATION OF MANUFACTURING

Let us refute . . . a strange sophism of the economists who claim that the unlimited increase of manufactured goods constitutes an increase in wealth. This would mean that if every individual could be made to use four times as much clothing as he does, society would quadruple the wealth it derives from manufacturing work.

Nothing of the kind! The economists are wrong on this point just as they are wrong in desiring an unlimited increase in population or *cannon-fodder*. In Harmony real wealth is based on: 1) The greatest possible consumption of different kinds of food; 2) The smallest possible consumption of different kinds of clothing and furniture. . . .

This principle has escaped the civilized economists who, equating manufacturing with farming, believe that overproduction and consumption of cloth is an index of rising prosperity. Harmony seeks just the opposite: *infinite variety* in clothing and furniture but the *smallest possible consumption*.

When I was still rather inexperienced at calculating attraction, I attempted to weigh the amount of attraction inherent in each kind of work. I was quite astonished to discover that, strictly speaking, there was little attraction for manufacturing work. I found that while the societary order will make agricultural work enormously enticing, it will develop only a limited amount of enticement for manufacturing. This seemed inconsistent, a contradiction of man's needs. Little by little, I began to see that, in accordance with the principle that attractions are proportional to destinies, God must have restricted the appeal of manufacturing because of the excellence of societary industry's products. Societary industry achieves the highest perfection in the manufacture of each of its products: furniture and clothing will last an extremely long time. They will become *eternal*.

—*OC*, IV, 209

The principles that I have been setting forth concerning the selection of the Phalanx's industries and the management of its workshops are very much opposed to the principles of the science called political economy. According to this science all industries are useful as long as they create legions of starving men who sell themselves at bargain prices to conquerors and shop bosses. Excessive competition always reduces the populace to the lowest wages when there is work and to indigence during periods of economic stagnation.

The societary order views manufactures as mere complements to agriculture, as a means of diversion during the long passional doldrums which occur during the winter's idleness and the rainy season. Thus, all of the Phalanxes of the globe will have factories, but they will all strive to make the quality of their manufactured goods as high as possible. The great durability of these objects will greatly reduce the amount of time needed for manufacturing work.

On this score let us lay down a principle which has been disregarded by all the economists and which is linked to our discussion in Chapter VIII concerning types and amounts of attraction.[3]

God has endowed manufacturing work with a limited amount of attraction. It should take up no more than a quarter of the working-time of a man in Harmony. The remaining three-quarters of his time should be spent in caring for animals, raising plants and vegetables, working in the kitchens, and serving in the industrial armies. . . .

The whole mechanism of industrial attraction would be perverted if we were to proceed in a confused manner, as the civ-

---

[3] In Chapter VIII of *Le Nouveau monde industriel* (*OC*, vi, 91–95) Fourier distinguishes between three varieties of attraction: direct, indirect, and divergent. Direct attraction is inspired by work which is enjoyable in itself. Divergent attraction is the detestation inspired by loathsome work. Work which inspires indirect attraction lacks intrinsic appeal but may be made to *seem* enticing under certain conditions (for instance, the presence of convivial fellow-workers, the creation of intense group rivalries, etc.). Fourier's point here is that most manufacturing work lacks intrinsic appeal; even in Harmony it will inspire no more than indirect attraction.

ilized do, without maintaining the proper proportion between the amount of manufacturing and the doses of special attraction bestowed by nature.

The proper proportion, moreover, would be upset in all branches of manufacturing if the goods produced were as poorly made as goods are today. Inferior products are ruinous for society; defective and badly dyed cloth reduces the durability of a garment to a half, a third or a quarter of what it should be. This makes it necessary to increase industrial productivity proportionately and hence to decrease the number of men available for agricultural work.

Sophists will reply that this would be a means of increasing population. It is precisely this vice that we seek to avoid in Harmony. As soon as the population of the globe has reached its full strength of about five billion, we will concern ourselves only with ensuring the happiness of its inhabitants rather than increasing their number. Now happiness would decline if we upset the equilibrium of attraction by taking time from agriculture in order to give more time to factories than nature intends. Nature seeks to reduce the time given to factory work as much as possible by organizing the intrigues of the series in such a manner that all products are brought to perfection.

According to this principle, factories will not be concentrated as they are today in cities choked with swarms of wretched creatures. Rather they will be scattered throughout all of the world's rural areas and Phalanxes. Thus when a man engages in factory work in Harmony he will never deviate from the paths of attraction which tends to use factories in an auxiliary role and as a complement to agriculture. They should not be the principal occupation, either for a community or for any of its individual members.

—*OC*, vi, 151–153

AGRICULTURAL METHODS: WORK AND CONVIVIALITY

In order to invest agricultural work with intrigue, charm and variety—as the three mechanizing passions require—societary crops will be divided into three interlocking categories adapted to various localities: 1. The simple or massive order; 2. the ambiguous or vague order; 3. the compound or linked order.

1. The *simple* or *massive* category is the one which precludes any mixing of crops. It dominates our regions of large-scale agriculture where fields, forests, meadows and vineyards are grouped in large masses. Yet portions of each of these fields and forests might be suitable for crop mixing. This is especially true in forests where an occasional clearing would allow the air to circulate, sunlight to penetrate and tree trunks to mature.

2. The *ambiguous* or *vague* and *mixed* category refers to the confused or so-called "English" gardens which were actually invented by the Chinese. This method gathers together as if by chance all sorts of plants. We use it on a small scale, but it is never applied throughout a district. The societary state will make great use of this method because it beautifies the countryside and generates industrial charm. The present large masses of meadows, woods, or fields will lose their sad aspect when the ambiguous order is used.

3. The *linked* or *compound* order is the opposite of the civilized system of enclosures and fences. In Harmony, where one never encounters the problem of theft, the linked method is eminently practical and produces spectacular results. Each agricultural series will make an effort to cultivate various areas of its Phalanx. It will throw out advanced rows and set up detached plots in all of the posts belonging to series whose center of operations is distant from its own. As a result of this mixing (which will be adapted to the terrain), the district will be dotted with agricultural groups. The scene will be animated, the view varied and picturesque. . . .

The massive order is the only one used by civilized farmers. They grow all their grain in one area, and then in their individual vegetable gardens they abuse the linked method by accumulating twenty kinds of plants where there should hardly be three or four.

When a Phalanx farms its land under the combined system, it begins by determining three or four uses suitable for each section. Crop-mixing is always advisable except in very valuable vineyards. Yet even these can bear fruit and vegetables as accessories to the pivotal crops. The purpose of crop-mixing is to bring various groups together and provide them with encounters which will evoke interest in the crops linked to theirs. In this way the isolation imposed on each group by its work is kept to a minimum.

Each branch of agriculture, consequently, strives to establish itself among the other branches. While our flower beds and vegetable gardens are confined to the areas near our dwellings, in Harmony they will be extended throughout the district. They will, it is true, remain centered near the Phalanstery, but rows of flowers and vegetables will be extended into the countryside. Detached clusters of flowers and vegetables will be established in the fields, meadows and even orchards whose soil is suitable. Although these areas are farther from the Phalanstery, they are close to several rallying posts. These posts consist of a few rows or clumps of shrubs or walls set up in the gardens and flower beds.

The method of linkage is attractive to the eye, but it is also useful because it helps to mesh the passions and foster intrigue. A great deal of care must be taken to arrange the *marriage of groups*, or encounters between groups of men and groups of women brought about by the linking of crops. The idea of marriage of groups is amusing and easily lends itself to the wrong interpretation, but these encounters are industrious, very decent and as useful as our gatherings in cafes and drawing rooms are sterile.

If the Series of Cherry-growers, for example, is having a large meeting in its main orchard a quarter of a league from the Phalanstery, it makes arrangements for the following groups to join it during the afternoon session from four to six o'clock:

1. A cohort from the neighboring Phalanx arrives to help the Cherry-growers.

2. A group of lady florists from the district arrives to plant a two-hundred yard row of hollyhocks and dahlias along a near-by road and around a field of vegetables contiguous to the orchard.

3. A group from the Vegetable-growers Series arrives to cultivate the vegetables in this field.

4. A group from the Thousand-flower Series arrives to care for the sect's altar which is situated between the vegetable field and the cherry orchard.[4]

5. A group of Maiden Strawberry-growers arrives at the end of the session. They have been cultivating a strawberry-ringed glade in the neighboring forest.

At five forty-five, a wagon sent out from the Phalanstery brings a snack for all of these groups. The food is served in the castle of the Cherry-growers from five forty-five until six fifteen. Then the groups disperse after having formed friendly ties and arranged industrial or other kinds of meetings for the following days.

—*OC*, VI, 119–121

### WORK AND AESTHETIC PLEASURE: THE ROLE OF ELEGANCE

Luxury assumes different forms and plays different roles at different stages of social development. In barbarism, the fourth period, finery is corporal. An Algerian bedecks himself with gold; he seems to be a Croesus; but if you enter his hut, you will find that its furnishings cannot compare with those in the home of a civilized artisan. The luxuries of the civilized man are different from those of the barbarian. He takes pride in his buildings, his furniture, his carriage and his banquets; but despite his wealth, he is sometimes less well dressed than his servants. . . .

In Harmony luxury is corporative; everyone wants his favorite groups and series to shine. This penchant is foreshadowed in some of the groups and corporations that exist today. Often a rich colonel will go to great expense to make his regiment outstanding for the quality of its dress and orna-

---

[4] These rustic altars are placed at the summit of a knoll. They are bedecked with flowers or shrubs and the statues and busts of patrons of the sect or of the individuals who have excelled in its work and have enriched it by inventing useful methods. These individuals are the mythological demi-gods of the sect or industrial Series. A corybant opens the session by burning incense before the demi-god. Since work, in the eyes of the Harmonians, is the highest function, they take care to unite it to every source of enthusiasm, such as the mythological honors rendered to the men or women who have served humanity by perfecting industry. (Fourier's note.)

ments or of its orchestra. While such a man would spend fortunes to bedeck a thousand of his social inferiors, he might still be quite sloppy in his personal dress.

Every corporate body has its pride. Our customs have made pride a deadly vice; in the passionate series it will become a major virtue, a civic virtue, a stimulus to industrial rivalry and perfection in work.

If our civilized groups loathe the appearance of poverty, it is obvious that the groups of Harmony will be equally hostile to the appearance of mediocrity. The regency of a Phalanx will provide each group with everything it needs to keep neat and clean; but the rich members will be prompted both by vanity and generosity to endow the group with elegant clothing and equipment.

Lucullus is the captain of the group of red cherry-growers, and Scaurus heads the group of maroon cherry-growers. Competition encourages these two rivals to spend as much on their groups as a prince would spend on his country villa. They provide their groups with wagons and sheds that are more splendid than those we see on stage at the opera. Each of them has a magnificent pavillion constructed in the cherry-orchard at his own expense to replace the modest shed furnished by the regency.

The result is that the ornaments and implements of a passionate series are always sumptuous, whether its members are at work or on parade. Gifts from the wealthy members are accepted not as favors but as acts of liberality which tend to cast distinction on a group and on its branch of industry and in its rivalries with other Phalanxes. . . .

The Harmonians attach little importance to many luxuries on which we uselessly spend immense sums of money. To house Lucullus at Rome it would be necessary to build a huge palace. In Harmony he will be content with three or four rooms, because in the new order the social relations of the series will be too active for anyone to spend much time in his apartment.

Everyone is constantly in the Seristeries or public halls, in the workshops, the fields, or the stables. Only sickness or a special rendezvous can keep the members of a Phalanx in their rooms. Thus a bedroom and living room will be enough for most people, and even the very rich will rarely have more than three rooms. . . .

The polite conventions of Harmony are totally different from our own. People do not waste time on useless visits; they see enough of each other at meals, at the exchange, in their work groups, and at the evening entertainments. When a man visits a Phalanx, he will go see his friends at their work sessions. Do you want to pay Lucullus a visit that he will really appreciate? Go look for him at work in the orchard. You will find him dressed in his captain's uniform and surrounded by the red cherry-growers in his group. At the end of the work session you will dine with him and his fellow-workers in the superb castle built at his expense. Over its doors you will see the inscription engraved by the members of his group: *ex munificentia Luculli, Cerasorum clarissimi sectatoris.* It is there that he displays his elegance and that he loves to show off the fruit grown by the cherished colleagues over whom he presides.

Thus the customs and policies of Harmony tend to endow productive work with all the lustre and the luxurious appurtenances which are today attached only to the unproductive functions. . . . Workshops which are now disgustingly dirty, ugly and run down will become luxurious.

This elegance of working conditions will be an *industrial incentive,* for it will help make children as well as adults passionate about productive work. In Harmony the rich will not spend their excess wealth on the construction of useless private castles; instead they will construct fine workshops and beautiful buildings for their favorite groups and series. Once this practice is widely followed, luxury will itself become a productive force. In Harmony luxury will be associated with useful work, with the sciences, the arts, and especially with cooking. Luxury will serve, along with many other vehicles, to make these functions attractive for both children and adults. The young child will enjoy wandering about all the workshops of the Phalanx and trying his hand at the tasks performed in each of the small-scale workshops. The skill, strength and practical knowledge acquired in this way will enable even the very rich to become producers qualified to perform tasks as well as to direct them.

The civilized distinction between producers and consumers will cease to exist in Harmony: everyone will be a producer. It will be shown further on that the system of natural education, which is THE SAME for all members of the five children's tribes, will provide princes as well as plebeians with training in a variety of tasks. It will assure all children of health, dexterity and useful knowledge, three advantages of which children are generally deprived by civilized education.

When physical aptitude is linked to industrial attraction, all men including princes will become at once producers and consumers. The social distinction between production and consumption will lose its sense. This will mark the end of the most absurd of our social duplicities: the existence of a class which consumes without producing anything.

—*OC*, IV, 536–546

# 3

# WORK AS SOCIAL AND PERSONAL THERAPEUTIC

RICH AND POOR IN HARMONY: THE END OF CLASS ANTAGONISM[1]

Before explaining how a Phalanx reconciles the interests of so many unequal members and succeeds in fully satisfying all of them by dividing profit according to their contributions in *work, capital* and *talent,* we must make some preliminary remarks on the moral bonds which unite these disparate individuals and establish sincere friendship, even blind devotion, between the rich and the poor. These classes are completely antagonistic in the civilized system where the rich conspire to despoil the poor, the poor seek to defraud the rich, and the middle class detests both the upper and lower classes.

One of the most powerful means of reconciling the rich and the poor is *the spirit of societary or compound property.* In Harmony even if a poor man owns but one-twentieth of a share, he is nevertheless a *participating* proprietor of the entire community. He is able to say: "our land, our palace, our castles, our forests, our shops, our factories." Everything is his property. He is a partner who shares in the entire assets of the territory.

When a forest is ravaged today, a hundred peasants look on heedlessly. The forest is simple property because it belongs only

---

[1] A wealth of texts could be included under this heading. For all of the institutions in the Phalanx—from its educational system and social minimum to the detailed provisions concerning inheritance rights and profit-sharing—were designed in such a way as to put an end to class antagonism and create the atmosphere of "unity" and social harmony which Fourier regarded as indispensable if work was to become a pleasure rather than a burden. A substantial portion of Fourier's major work, the *Traité de l'association domestique-agricole* (*OC,* v, 377–476), was also devoted to the elaboration of a complex theory of *ralliements* in which he showed how the proper use of the four affective passions would serve to create bonds between people of differing wealth, age, and intelligence. The texts in this section illustrate a few of the means by which Fourier proposed to reconcile the rich and the poor. Equally relevant to the problem, however, are the texts on "Education, Refinement, and Social Harmony," "The Seven Conditions and the Social Minimum," and "Degrading Work: The Servant Problem Solved." See above pp. 257–261, 274–275, and below pp. 311–314.

to the lord of the manor. In fact, the peasants rejoice over anything that harms the lord's interests and they even make furtive efforts to increase the damage. If a swollen river erodes farm land, three-fourths of the people who don't own any land on the river banks laugh at the damage. Often they rejoice when they see a flood ravage the patrimony of a rich neighbor. For his property is merely simple property: his neighbors have no stake in it and they are quite indifferent to its fate.[2]

In Harmony individual interests are combined and everyone is an associate, if only in the sense that he receives a share in the portion of the Phalanx's income which is allotted to labor. Everyone wants to see the whole community prosper because everyone's interests are harmed when the territory suffers the slightest damage. The mere fact that the members of the Phalanx are partners, and not wage-earners, gives them a personal interest in each other's welfare. They know that any reduction in the total income will prove costly to everyone. A loss of just twelve *oboles* will reduce by five the amount to be divided among the poor members who have no capital invested in the community. As we have already pointed out, the income of the Phalanx is divided into three parts: $5/12$ths goes to labor, $4/12$ths to capital, and $3/12$ths to talent. . . .[3]

The effects of association and ownership on workers are well known. A man might appear lazy when he works for someone else for pay. But as soon as a partnership infects him with a sense of ownership and participation, he becomes a prodigy of diligence. People begin to say of him: "He isn't the same man. I wouldn't have recognized him." Why does this change occur? Because he has become a COMPOSITE owner. He still has competitive instincts. But they serve to benefit the whole group to which he belongs and not merely him alone. In this respect the com-

[2] Although Fourier emphatically denounced the civilized "spirit of simple property" or the "tyranny of individual property over the interests of the mass," he did not plan to abolish all forms of private property in the Phalanx. Rather, he insisted that the rights of individual ownership should never be allowed to take precedence over the interests of the community as a whole. See *OC*, IV, 308–309; VI, 390.

[3] See above p. 250.

posite owner is superior to the egotistical small farmer of whom morality makes so much. Poor morality, it is always so clumsy that it extols the very sources of vice.

—*OC*, IV, 516–519

Inequality of wealth and social rank will cease to be an obstacle to friendship once the cabalistic spirit is brought into play and once the social minimum provides the rich with a guarantee against being solicited or tricked by the poor. In times of revolution the rich and the powerful have often been known to stoop to flattering and wheedling the poorest plebeians. During elections Cato and Scipio were quite willing to shake hands with the most humble rural electors.[4] Thus it is evident that the rich are not afraid of contact with the lower class if the stimulus of intrigue is brought into play and if that class is free from want. This is the situation in Harmony.

Let us add that like all other people the rich have a desire for cabalistic rivalries (an expression of the tenth passion). They have a liking for meetings which satisfy their cabalistic inclinations, and there is nothing that satisfies these inclinations as well as the passional series. Thus every rich man will become completely embroiled in the intrigues of his series; and he will love its members, at least a third of whom will come from the lower class. In participating in the industrial cabales of thirty series the rich man will learn to love the poorer members of his Phalanx.

—*OC*, V, 384–385

Mondor would like to grow peaches.[5] But he doesn't want to take part in the job of exterminating the insects which are devouring the peach trees. He wouldn't have to bother with that

[4] In *OC*, VI, 278, Fourier cites similar cases and adds: "Thus in our society there are many seeds which tend to promote class mixing, but the means employed are abject and the motivation is sordid cupidity."

[5] In this text Fourier shows how the division of labor among the various groups of a series can contribute to the reconciliation of rich and poor. His protagonist, the wealthy Mondor, has already made an appearance in this anthology. See above p. 277 for an account of Mondor's Day.

in the series of peach-growers: the extermination of insect pests
is entrusted to several children who are working as candidate
peach-growers under the supervision of the patriarch or dean of
this series. Mondor enjoys both the advantage of not having to
trouble himself with this important task and the pleasure of seeing it perfectly executed by the pupils of the series. Most of the
pupils are poor, but they arouse Mondor's interest because of the
work they perform. Mondor doesn't care much for grafting.
This task he leaves to the grafting group which is composed of a
few skilled workers whose success he admires. Mondor would
rather not undertake the task of seeking out the best varieties of
peaches for use in grafting. For this job he relies on the secre-
tariat of the series which gathers all the necessary information by
corresponding with other peach-growers.

What does Mondor do then? He likes to train espaliers and
is proud of his ability to prune a tree so that it will bear abundantly. It is a real pleasure for him to arrive each spring, pruning
knife in hand, to lead the group of pruners. He gladly provides
the tools and uniforms for a festive two-hour session in which
he is surrounded by well-dressed, polite, conscientious and
benevolent associates who are all as passionately attracted to this
sort of work as he is.

All of the peach-growers congratulate Mondor on his skill.
In turn he praises the groups which have supported his labors by
performing the necessary tasks of pest control, grafting, record-
keeping, etc. As the leader or colonel of the series, it is Mondor
who accepts the compliments of the Phalanx and its visitors.
Thus a work session with the series is a festive occasion for
Mondor. How could he resist being drawn to peach-growing
when he is able to choose only his favorite occupation, the pruning and trimming of trees?

If Mondor wished to cultivate fruit trees in civilization,
what pleasure would he find in doing so? He would encounter
innumerable vexations: fraud, bother, and finally perhaps the
theft of his fruit. This is what happened to a certain Marshall
Biron who was very fond of peach-growing. One night, on the
eve of the harvest, all of his fruit was stolen. He was an old man
and he died of grief. The fear of theft, which will not exist in

Harmony, would be enough in itself to discourage a rich civilized man from growing fruit. . . . Mondor is happy and receives help in his work because he is a *compound* proprietor whose interests are linked with those of everyone who surrounds him. Biron is only a *simple* proprietor whose interests are not shared by his employees and neighbors. He is betrayed by them: that is the law of nature. . . .

The motives which make the rich fond of work in Harmony are the same as those which make the poor fond of the rich. Phebon is not wealthy but his practical knowledge makes him a valuable member of several series. When group leaders give special dinners or hold cabalistic meetings Phebon is in great demand. Ordinarily the groups and series elect their richest members as parade leaders, but the most knowledgeable members are chosen to be managing directors. It is customary for a parade leader to give an annual party for the poorer members of his group in order to honor those whose knowledge enables the series to excel.

On the other hand, in rivalries between the series the poor become firmly attached to their wealthy leader because he appreciates their work and skill and is willing to join them in cabalistic intrigue. As a result of all this even an old man who is very poor and disdained by everyone in civilization will be much sought after by the rich in Harmony. For such a man is sure to have acquired a great deal of knowledge in all of the series he has joined since his youth. The rich leaders of these series will regard him as a precious associate, a valuable ally in their competitive cabales.

Moreover, if Phebon is of an advanced age, he will not be poor. For he can become a member of the fifteenth choir of *Venerables* who have many special privileges, including the right to eat at the second class dinner tables. Now if the poor man has all he wants, there is no reason for the rich to fear him. In Harmony the fears of the rich will also be allayed by an educational system which will give polish to the manners of the poor. Thus there will be an end to all the sources of antipathy which now oblige the rich man to keep himself constantly on guard against the indigent.

If the elderly poor have a great many opportunities to become intimate with the wealthy, poor young people have even more. . . . Here I have considered only the most difficult problem, that of uniting the upper and lower classes on the basis of self-interest. Today the interests of these two classes are in a state of open conflict. The poor incessantly attempt to rob the rich on an individual basis, and the rich continually plunder the poor as a class.

In the following chapters I will discuss the pomp and magnificence of the series, the elegance of their workshops, and other features which the rich are sure to find alluring. Then it will be even easier to understand why a rich man will want to become a member of about forty agricultural and manufacturing series which, for their part, will strive to entice him by offering him the most attractive jobs.

Attraction, moreover, is bizarrely distributed by nature, and it is quite possible that our rich Mondor will have a natural inclination for some of the most tedious jobs. Locksmithing, for instance, really isn't very fascinating. Yet it was the favorite pastime of King Louis XVI. Among children born and raised in Harmony, the very rich will often become passionately attached to jobs which most of us would find disgusting. But they will no longer be disgusting in the splendid workshops of the new order; for, as the saying goes: "There are no stupid crafts, only stupid people."

Let us provisionally accept my assertion that work in Harmony will be agreeable to people of all classes. It will be supported further on by a hundred demonstrations. But at present let us draw a few conclusions from this hypothesis.

Harmony's common people will constantly encounter wealthy persons who have joined their groups and series. The poor will be well provided with the necessities of life, and they will be assured of remuneration and advancement proportional to their labor. They will be offered numerous opportunities to get rich. . . . For these reasons they will be completely purged of their malevolent feelings toward the rich. They will quickly adapt themselves to the urbane ways of the rich; in a few months they will acquire the manners which a parvenu adopts when he sets himself up in a castle. These parvenus, however, lack the stimulus provided by the friendly and frank criticism prevalent in work groups. On the contrary, parvenus are flattered and deceived by everyone around them. This toadyism greatly retards their acquisition of good manners. But in the societary order, where everyone acquires a taste for gentility, the common people, thanks to amicable irony, will be able to develop courteous manners much more quickly than our parvenus whom no one dares correct.

*—OC*, IV, 521–525

### WORK AND THE DESTRUCTIVE PASSIONS: THE CASE OF NERO

My thesis is that all attractions are useful, as long as they are employed in series of groups which work in short sessions.

"What! Could the passions of a Nero, a Tiberius, actually be useful?" Certainly, they will be most useful in societary work. Let us explain this mystery.

Nero is a creature born with bloodthirsty inclinations. Nature's wish is that at the age of three he should begin to take part in several of the butcher's groups in his Phalanx. If he abhorred the shedding of blood, he could not be passionately attracted to the work of the butcher's shop and he could not become a very skillful butcher at the age of twenty as nature wishes.

But I can hear Agrippina's rejoinder: "What a ridiculous vision! How absurd to say that my son, the heir to the throne of the world, was meant to become a butcher!" Whereupon Agrippina has her son indoctrinated by Seneca and other savants who teach him that nature is corrupt, that bloodthirsty inclinations are odious, that a young prince should love nothing but commerce and the constitution,[6] and that he will be demeaned by hobnobbing with butchers.

So there is one of young Nero's passions thwarted. Twenty more of them will be stifled in like manner by the healthy doctrines of sweet and pure morality. That is just what Seneca

---

[6] *La Charte*, or the constitutional charter of the restored Bourbon monarchy.

would want. But Horace and La Fontaine take a different and a much more healthy view when they say:

"Si furcâ naturam expellas, tamen usque recurret."

"If you chase nature out the door, she comes in by the window."

Let us analyze the disastrous results of this repressed passion and of its countermarch or *recurrence* (an expression of Horace which should be adopted to describe this effect of the passions).

The young Nero will pretend to submit to his teachers; but his bloodthirsty inclinations are only hidden and not rooted out. They will reappear when Nero has thrown off the yoke of his teachers, but they will reappear in a reversed and dangerous form, and Nero will become an odious ruler. Later, and at the expense of his friends and family, he will give vent to the passion that they repressed when he was a child. If he had been able to express it freely at that time, however, he would have become one of the foremost butchers of the Phalanx of Tivoli.

What difference does it make anyway if a young man like Nero begins by working as a butcher, since everything is linked in the system of societary studies? Work in the butcher's shop, like any other kind of work, will open the door to all the sciences. Nero will soon learn how to tell at a glance the difference between the flesh of animals fed on one kind of fodder or another and fattened according to one system or another. (These remarks concern the rivalries existing between the butchers of Tivoli and the Phalanxes near it, and also the rivalries among the Tivolians who favor different systems of fattening livestock.) Thus Nero will study agronomy as it relates to the fodder and vegetables fed to the livestock. This bit of knowledge will set him on the road to more.

Let us add that if young Nero had been brought up in a Phalanx, he would have begun by the age of four to satisfy twenty other penchants which the wise Seneca would have stifled for the sake of morality. If these diverse inclinations were allowed to develop early, they would serve to interest the young Nero in twenty different kinds of useful study. Little by little he would find himself initiated into all the sciences solely as a result of penchants which civilization regards as corrupt and which are repressed in children.

What is the result today of this repression? Nature may be thwarted, but it cannot be destroyed. If it is not allowed to express itself usefully in work, it will reappear later—*usque recurret*—and the bloodthirsty penchants of Nero will express themselves at humanity's expense. Thus, it is not Nero who is corrupt; the source of corruption is civilization, which was unable to utilize Nero's penchants and so forced them to reappear in a state of reversal or recurrence. The results of this recurrence are always disastrous: the passions are travestied and rendered as harmful as they might have been useful. This is the way civilization deals with $\frac{99}{100}$ths of the natural inclinations; it treats the passions like someone who wants to turn butterflies into caterpillars. . . .

The example of Nero's passion applies to each of the twelve radical passions and the 810 passional types in a full Phalanx. Nero occupies an eminent place in the general scale of passionate types; for he belongs to the same high degree as does Henri IV. But even though they represent the same degree, their characters are not similar. Both Nero and Henri IV have four dominant passions, but the passions are not the same. This explains why one of them turned out badly and the other, having found the means to express himself in civilization, turned out well. But anyone who undertakes a systematic study of the reversal or countermarch of the passions will soon recognize that if, instead of being born the heir to a throne, Henri IV had been born among the common people, and if as a child he had suffered the vexations that usually beset the poor, he would have become the leader of a band of highwaymen.

Such, in brief, is the secret of the working of the passions. They are all good as long as they are correctly employed. Those which produce evil are comparable to the bad grain which grows when the soil and weather are poor. The fault does not lie in the generating seed but in the circumstances that thwarted its growth and corrupted its fruit.

Accordingly, the most evil of civilized personalities, like

Nero whom I have chosen as the worst of all, will be highly esteemed in the societary order. In that order people will not criticize Nero but civilization, which has perverted the most precious instincts in the bud and made a travesty of the whole mechanism of the passions and passional types. After the extinction of the present generation, those who have grown up in the societary order will have begun during childhood to express and develop all their penchants. Then every member of a Phalanx will be a fully developed representative of one of the passional types and each will be given the name of some famous civilized individual such as Nero or Henri IV, Plato or Robespierre. Among the 810 passional types in each Phalanx there will be eight couples—known as *tetratones*—who will be endowed with four dominant passions. Among these eight couples two will be known as the Nero and Nerona and the Henri and the Henrietta of the Phalanx. They will have a rank in the scale of passional types similar to that of the battalion leaders in our military regiments.[7]

Any three-year-old child has roughly twenty or thirty penchants. But even the freest education in civilization, that which is given to spoiled children, is not capable of developing half of these penchants. At the age of twenty Louis XVI was quite unaware that he was a locksmith by attraction. Had he been raised in a Phalanx, he would have known of this penchant at the age of two and a half. But the most civilized child in civilization, the son of a king, has no opportunity to discover his industrial aptitudes. In Harmony he would have access to miniature workshops which would be provided with skilled instructors and attractive tools like the ones in adult workshops. Out of the twenty penchants of a civilized child, ten are thwarted if only by the absence of materials and workshops. The child's whole personality is warped; and although this obstacle may be involuntary on the part of the father, it will suffice to plant the seeds of ten vices where ten virtues might have flowered.

As for the ten other inclinations that the civilized child will

[7] On the tetratones and their place in Fourier's "general scale of personality types" see above pp. 220–222.

have been able to satisfy, they too will degenerate into vices because they will not be stimulated by group enthusiasm, nor counterbalanced by serial discords, nor refined by group rivalries. In the absence of these stimuli, the child's penchants will become excessive and they will take a harmful direction. Thus civilization is so antipathetic to the dictates of human nature that it makes evil result from the expression of penchants as well as from their thwarting.

This analysis of Nero's bloodthirsty penchants and of the means of utilizing them in the societary state may be applied to all the other harmful passions. They only become harmful as a result of obstacles which have travestied them in a person's childhood and turned them from their natural course.

*—PM*, ii; *OC*, x, 132–136

### VOCATIONAL TRAINING: THE LITTLE PEAS

I have just described the physical phase of education. At this stage education is concerned only with cultivating and refining the senses. Its aim is to preserve them from the perversion which civilization inflicts upon them at an early age. Nine hundred and ninety-nine out of a thousand French children have no ear for music. The other senses are equally spoiled.

We now turn to the period of the child's initiation into industry and industrial attraction. Without industrial attraction everything in education is spoiled. Since the first of man's three goals is affluence or luxury, it can be said that his education is perverted and that he is setting out on the wrong path if, from the age of about two when he takes his very first steps, he does not spontaneously devote himself to productive work, but instead, like the civilized child, spends his time causing mischief, dirtying, breaking and damaging things, all of which stupid parents find charming.

This perverted behavior of the young child, this instinct which diverges from attraction at so early an age, would cast shame on the Creator if He had not invented another mechanism that causes the passions and attraction to work together at any age. Let us examine how this mechanism operates when children are first capable of working.

As soon as a child can walk and act, he leaves the category of Babies and enters that of the Imps and Impesses. If he has been raised since birth in the Seristery of a Phalanx, he will be strong enough at 21 months to join the Imps. Among children of this age the two sexes are not differentiated. They must be left together at this stage so that their vocations will blossom and so that both sexes will learn to collaborate on particular tasks. We begin to differentiate the sexes only in the tribe of Tots.

I have said that nature gives each child about thirty instincts for work. Some of these are primary or guiding instincts, and they will provoke the development of the secondary ones.

The first problem is to discover the primary instincts. Here is a bait that the child will nibble at as soon as it is offered to him. When he is able to walk, to leave the Seristery of the Babies, the *Nurse-men* and *Nursemaids* who care for him will lose no time in taking him through all of the nearby workshops and work groups. Everywhere he will find little tools and miniature industries being operated by Imps of 2½ to 3 years whom he will want to join in ferreting about and handling tools. By the end of two weeks, it will be possible to tell which shops seduce him and to discover his instincts for work.

The Phalanx will be engaged in a wide variety of undertakings. It will be impossible for a child to wander through them without attempting to satisfy several of his dominant instincts. These will burst out as soon as he sees little tools being handled by children who are a few months older than he.

Civilized fathers and school teachers claim that "children are lazy little creatures." Nothing could be more false. From the time they are two or three years old children are highly industrious. But nature wishes them to work *in passionate series and not in civilization;* and one must understand the stimuli which it employs.

All children have the following dominant tastes:

1. FERRETING, or the penchant for handling things, exploring, running around, and constantly changing activities.

2. *Industrial Din*, the taste for noisy jobs.

3. *Aping*, or the imitative mania.

4. *Working on a reduced scale*, the taste for little workshops.

5. PROGRESSIVE ENTICEMENT of the weak by the strong.

There are quite a few others, but I am limiting myself at first to citing these five which are well known in civilization. Let us examine the method we must use in adapting these tastes to work during early childhood.

The Nurse-men and Nursemaids will first exploit the mania for ferreting that is so dominant in the two year old. He wants to get into everything, to pick up and turn over everything he sees. Thus to keep him from breaking everything, civilized adults must lock him up in an empty room. But this penchant for handling everything is a natural enticement toward work. To attract the child to work in Harmony, he will be brought to the little workshops. There he will see children of 2½ and 3 years of age already at work with little tools and little hammers. He will try to satisfy his imitative mania, or the mania for Aping. He will be loaned some tools, but when he tries to join the children of 26 to 27 months who already know how to work they will reject him. He will persist if the task corresponds to one of his instincts. Then the nurse or the patriarch in charge will teach him some portion of the task and he will quickly succeed in making himself useful enough to gain admission into the group.

Let us watch the imitative mania in action. We will take as an example a little task which can be performed by the youngest children—the shelling and sorting of green peas. In civilized society this task occupies thirty-year-old persons. In Harmony it will be assigned to children of 2, 3, and 4 years. Their workroom contains inclined tables which are fitted with various cavities. The Tots are seated at the upper end of the tables, shelling peas in the pod. The slope of the tables causes the peas to roll down to the lower end where three Imps or Impesses of 25, 30, or 35 months are seated. They are entrusted with sorting the peas and have been provided with special tools.

Their task is to separate the smallest peas for sweet ragout, the medium peas for a ragout made with bacon, and the large peas for soup. The Impess of 35 months first selects the small peas. These are the most difficult to pick up. She sends all of the medium and large peas down to the next cavity where the Impess of 30 months is seated. She pushes those which seem large down to the third depression, sends those which are small back to the first, and allows the medium-sized peas to slip into a basket. The Imp of 25 months, seated at the third cavity, has little to do. He sends a few medium peas back to the second child and collects the large ones in his basket.

The inexperienced Imp will be placed at the third position. He will proudly set about pushing the large peas into the basket. This is an insignificant task, but he will think that he has done as much as his companions. He will become impassioned for his work and the spirit of imitative competition will seize him. By the third session he will be able to replace the Imp of 25 months who sits at the lower end of the table because he will then be able to throw the peas of the second size into the second case and collect only those of the first size which are easy to distinguish. As soon as he is able to take part in this modest task, his cap or his collar will be solemnly decorated with a pompon designating him as a candidate for the group of green pea shellers.

In all societary workshops work of little value will be deliberately set aside for very little children. Tasks such as the one I have cited could easily be done as efficiently without the child. But in that case we would lose the enticement to work that must always be offered to an Imp when he first visits a workshop. This is true even in the case of an Urchin or a Cherub, because the child who has not taken part when he was two years old may join in when he is three or four.

This enticement which is offered to children of various ages in all of the workshops can only give the Imp of 24 months the illusion that he is working. It flatters his self-esteem. It persuades him that he has accomplished something and that he is almost the equal of the lower Imps of 26 and 28 months who are already members of this group, bedecked with plumes and ornaments which inspire profound respect in the beginning Imp. The child of two, then, will find in the workshops of a Phalanx a number of enticements that civilization cannot offer him.

—*OC*, VI, 180–183

# [4]

## WORK PROBLEMS IN HARMONY

### DEGRADING WORK: THE SERVANT PROBLEM SOLVED

We come now to the most important problem of domestic harmony, the problem of creating passionate concord between servants and masters, or the art of making these two classes devoted to one another. Is there any art more foreign to civilization? Or better, is not civilization antipathetic to any concord between people of differing social status, especially between masters and servants? We are now going to show how this branch of domestic unity, so impracticable in the present state, can be established in association, without the aid of political wisdom, simply by allowing the passions to express themselves freely.

Nothing is more opposed to social concord than the present condition of domestic servants and wage-earners. In reducing this poor multitude to a state very close to slavery, civilization has also enchained those who appear to dominate. Thus the very rich never dare to amuse themselves openly during years of great suffering for the common people. This is collective servitude; but the rich man is also subject to individual servitude. Many a wealthy man in our societies is the slave of his own valet. In Harmony the valet will be completely independent, and yet the rich man wil be served with a kind of alacrity and devotion inconceivable in civilization. Let us explain how this harmonious relationship is created.

No member of a community in Compound Harmony (eighth period) will be a hired servant. Yet the poorest man will constantly have fifty pages at his service. The announcement of such a state of affairs, or of any part of the Series mechanism, inspires cries of "Impossible!" However, it can be easily understood.

Domestic tasks, like all of the other kinds of labor on a Phalanx, are managed by series which assign a group to each variety of work. When these series are performing domestic services, they bear the titles of "pages and pagesses." We now give these titles to those who serve Kings, but it would be much more fitting to give the titles to those who serve a Phalanx. For a Phalanx is God in action; it is the spirit of God in that it is composed of the twelve passions harmonized by

> Passionate Attraction
> Applied Truth          and Unity of Action
> Mathematical Justice

To serve a Phalanx *collectively*, then, is to serve God. That is how domestic service is viewed in Harmony. If this primordial branch of labor were held in contempt as it is today, passionate equilibrium would become impossible.

In Harmony, domestic service is not only idealized but also ennobled in a real sense: we will abolish the personal domination that debases a man by putting him at the mercy of another's whims. Let us analyze the mechanism of free collective domestic service as it operates in a job chosen at random, the work done by a chambermaid.

The Pagess Délie serves in the group of chambermaids assigned to the right wing of the Phalanstery. Since she is on bad terms with Leander, she doesn't enter his apartment when she makes her rounds. But Leander is as well served as before because Délie's place is taken by Eglé and Phyllis, two other pagesses in the same group, who are fond of him. They clean Leander's apartment.

The same thing happens at the stables. If one of the pages fails to care for Leander's horse, the animal is groomed by another page, who is a friend of Leander, or it is cared for by one of the pages on rotation. In all of the branches of domestic service, then, everyone will be served eagerly by persons who are fond of him. If no one is particularly fond of him, he will be cared for by the group as a whole.

It may happen that when Leander is working at some other job, he will meet the people who have just finished serving him. And the change in tasks may well have made them his superiors. At seven o'clock Eglé served Leander, but at nine there is a work session at the bee hives. Leander is a member who joined the Beekeepers only six months ago, and the work is still unfamiliar to him. Eglé has been working with bees since childhood, and is very experienced. Leander thus finds himself under Eglé's command at the bee hives in any job they perform together.

Under such a regime no one need worry himself over getting someone to do his housework; all he need do is choose one of the applicants. For if twenty pages work in a stable, at least ten of them will be on very intimate terms with Leander because of their cabalistic relationship in other series such as the garden, orchard, or opera series. Leander will never lack a friend to take care of his horse which, in any event, would be quite well groomed by the pages on rotation. But one of the charms of Harmony is to have a friend eagerly serve you in the most trifling household chores. This friend, moreover, is very capable because domestic services in Harmony are minutely subdivided and only experienced associates are assigned to each task.

Phyllis and Eglé have made Leander's bed, but they aren't the ones who will brush his suit. They take it to the brushing room and give it to Clitie, another of Leander's friends. This particular suit has a spot. Clitie, after brushing the suit, takes it to the cleaning room where it is cleaned by Cloris, who is yet another of Leander's friends. In this way every servant, whether man or woman, will be motivated by friendship, love, or some other form of affection, no matter what kind of domestic work he or she chooses.

Work intrigues in the garden and orchards, at the opera and in the workshops provide each member of a Phalanx with a host of friends. Some of them will surely belong to the groups of pages and pagesses; and they will do his housework out of affection. The poor as well as the rich will enjoy this advantage. A man with no money will find a throng of affectionate servants as eager to serve him as to serve a prince. For it is never *the individual being served who pays those who serve him*. A page would be ignominiously dismissed from the series if it became known that he had secretly received tips from those he served. The Phalanx pays the corps of pages a dividend based on its work and its talent. The series then ordinarily distributes this dividend among its members according to their abilities and attendance.

Individual independence is therefore fully guaranteed because every page serves the Phalanx and not a particular person. This is why all are served affectionately. Affectionate service is a pleasure that the rich themselves can't buy for money in civilization. If a rich man pays a servant handsomely in order to insure his fidelity, ambition will make the servant careless, ungrateful and often treacherous. This danger is unknown in Harmony where everyone is guaranteed the friendship of several pages. These pages enter into no monetary contracts; they serve individuals out of preference and are free to leave their service if their affection should cool.

There is nothing mercenary or servile about domestic service in Harmony. A group of chambermaids is, like all of the other groups, a free and honorable society which shares in the gross product of the Phalanx by virtue of the importance of its work.

—*OC*, IV, 526–530

### DRUDGERY: WORK DEVOID OF ATTRACTION

Drudge duty (40th series) includes all jobs which are isolated and devoid of attraction. These include coach driving, mail delivery, sentry duty at the watchtower, the operation of the telegraph, the guarding of the colors, the playing of the carillon, the night watch at the porter's lodge both at the Phalanstery itself and at the stables, the night patrol, the fire-watch, the tending of the beacon light, etc., etc.

The series of Drudges will receive a substantial dividend in addition to the exemption fees paid by the rich who will be able, as they are today, to purchase exemptions from guard duty. These fees will be allocated to the series as a whole and not to individuals, since individual service for wages would be dishonorable in association.

The Drudges will also be encouraged by various favors such as the right to eat at the second class tables. (Most of them would otherwise eat with the third class.) Our intention is to make the day on which they perform their chores—which recurs about once every two weeks—a day of gaiety for them.

These precautions will seem quite superfluous to the civilized, all of whom are accustomed to regarding oppression as moral wisdom. They tend to forget that every page of this book is concerned with the creation of industrial attraction, the harmonious distribution of wealth, and the fusion of the three classes. It is very important, therefore, to avoid degrading any job or displeasing any class. It is necessary to possess reliable methods capable of infusing repugnant and disdained work with gaiety. (See the section on the Little Hordes.)[1]

—*OC*, VI, 136–137

### THE LITTLE HORDES AND DISGUSTING WORK

We shall now see that morality has failed to understand the principles governing education and that, according to its habit, it has classed as vices all of the impulses which nature would employ to create virtues.

Conflict between the instincts and the sexes yields prodigious results in work and virtue. To create such conflict we will divide children between the ages of four and fifteen and a half (the four tribes of Cherubs, Seraphs, Pupils and Students) into two instinctual corps. These are:

The Little Hordes, who perform tasks which are repugnant either to the senses or to self-esteem.

The Little Bands, who are responsible for the maintenance of collective luxury.[2]

---

[1] Elsewhere (*OC*, IV, 37) Fourier notes that drudge duty "will be assigned to a few individuals whose temperaments are appropriate to such tasks, which they will transform into games. . . ."

[2] The Little Bands, most of whom were girls, were to provide material adornment and moral uplift in Harmony. Although their contribution was less essential than that of the Little Hordes, it should not be neglected. The following account of their functions is drawn from *OC*, VI, 214–216:

"The Little Bands are the guardians of *social charm*. Their job is less spectacular than that of the Little Hordes, who are entrusted with the defense of *social harmony*. However, great importance is attached to finery and to collective luxury in the societary system, and the Little Bands make

These two contrasting corporations will usefully employ the instincts that morality vainly seeks to suppress in both sexes: the taste that little boys have for filth, and the love that little girls have for finery. By setting these two tastes off against each other, societary education will lead both sexes to the same goal by different paths. It will lead the Little Hordes to the beautiful by way of the good, and the Little Bands to the good by way of the beautiful.

---

a valuable contribution in this domain. Their main function is the *physical and spiritual* adornment of the whole community. . . .

"Completely different in style from the Little Hordes, they are devotees of Attic restraint and purity. They are very polite; it is the girls rather than the boys who set the tone among them. . . . Only a third of the members of the Little Bands are boys, and they are the studious ones, the precocious scholars like Pascal, as well as those effeminate young lads who show early tendencies to indolence.

"Less active than the Little Hordes, the Little Bands are slower to rise and they do not get to the workshops until four o'clock in the morning. They wouldn't be needed earlier since they have little to do with the care of the larger animals. But they are devoted to those species which are difficult to raise and tame, such as passenger pigeons and other birds, beavers and zebras.

"The Little Bands have jurisdiction over the vegetable kingdom. Anyone who breaks a tree-branch, picks a forbidden flower or an unripe fruit, or accidentally steps on a plant is brought before the Senate of the Little Bands. This Senate renders judgment by virtue of a special penal code similar to the code of animal care which is enforced by the Divan of the Little Hordes.

"Entrusted with the spiritual and physical adornment of the community, the Little Bands perform academic functions similar to those of the French Academy. They censor bad language and faulty pronunciation. . . . The Senate of the Little Bands even has the right to censor literary works produced by adults. It draws up a list of the mistakes in grammar and pronunciation made by every member of the community and forwards the list to the guilty parties, advising them not to repeat the same mistakes. . . .

"Just as the Little Hordes have their Druids and Druidesses, the Little Bands have their own adult associates, who are known as Corybants. They also have their own allies among the groups of voyagers who travel about Harmony. Whereas the Little Hordes are allied to the big hordes of Adventurers and Adventuresses who belong to the industrial armies, the Little Bands are affiliated with the big bands of Knights and Ladies Errant who are dedicated to the fine arts."

This method gives children a freedom of choice which they do not enjoy in a society such as ours, which forces them to accept a single system of morals. The societary state will permit them to choose between two contrasting paths which favor opposite penchants: the penchants for finery and filth.

Two-thirds of all boys have a penchant for filth. They love to wallow in the mire and play with dirty things. They are unruly, peevish, scurrilous and overbearing, and they will brave any storm or peril simply for the pleasure of wreaking havoc. These children will enroll in the Little Hordes whose task is to perform, dauntlessly and as a point of honor, all those loathsome tasks that ordinary workers would find debasing. This corporation is a kind of half-savage legion whose wild ways contrast with the refined courtesy of Harmony. But this contrast is one of style and not of sentiment; for the Little Hordes are the most ardently patriotic of corporations.

The other third of little boys have a taste for good manners and tranquil occupations. They will enroll in the Little Bands. By contrast, a third of all girls have boyish inclinations and love to horn in on boys' games. They are called tomboys. Such girls will join the Little Hordes. Thus the Little Hordes will include ⅔ boys and ⅓ girls, and the Little Bands will include ⅔ girls and ⅓ boys. Each of these two corps will be subdivided into three sections which must be given names. The Little Hordes will adopt vulgar sobriquets, while the Little Bands will assume romantic names. This will emphasize the contrast between these two groups which are both vital to the working of industrial attraction.

Let us first analyze the duties and civic virtues of the Little Hordes. . . . The Little Hordes have the rank of *God's Militia* in the service of industrial unity. By virtue of this title, they should be the first to enter the breach whenever unity is threatened. To maintain unity the Little Hordes will be asked to perform a number of tasks which are so disgusting that it would otherwise be necessary to call upon the services of wage-laborers. In performing these tasks they will be divided into three corps: the first is assigned to foul functions such as sewer-cleaning, tending the dung heap, working in the slaughter-houses, etc.;

the second is assigned to dangerous functions such as the hunting of reptiles or to jobs requiring dexterity; the third will participate in both these kinds of work. The older members of the Little Hordes will ride on their own dwarf horses.

One of the tasks assigned to the Little Hordes will be the maintenance of roads. They will make it a point of pride to keep the roads of Harmony lined with shrubs and flowers and in more splendid condition than the lanes of our country estates. If a highway is damaged in any way, the alarm will be given at once. The Little Hordes will immediately make temporary repairs and raise a warning flag to make sure that no passer-by might have grounds for accusing the community of having a bad Horde. The same reproach would be made if anyone found a dangerous reptile or a caterpillar's nest or heard the croaking of toads near a highway. The presence of such unclean objects would make people scornful of a Phalanx, and the value of its shares would fall.

Although the Little Hordes perform the most difficult tasks in the Phalanx—tasks which are totally lacking in *direct* attraction—they receive the least retribution. They would accept nothing at all if that were permitted in association. The fact that they receive the smallest share, however, does not prevent any of the members of the Little Hordes from receiving large shares for work performed in other groups and series. But as members of the unitary and philanthropic brotherhood of the Little Hordes, their work is inspired by devotion to the community and not by the hope of remuneration. . . .

Since the Little Hordes are the seedbed of all the civic virtues, they should serve society through the practice of the Christian virtue of *self-abnegation* and the philosophical virtue of *contempt for wealth*. They should exemplify and practice all the virtues that civilization dreams of but only counterfeits. As the guardians of social honor, they should crush evil in all its guises. While ridding the countryside of poisonous reptiles, they will purge society of a poison worse than the viper's, the poison of greed. . . . And in performing their foul tasks, they will eradicate the feelings of pride which make men disdain the laborious class and which tend to promote the spirit of caste, to impair social friendship, and to prevent the fusion of classes. . . .

It might seem that to make children so prodigiously virtuous it would be necessary to resort to supernatural means, as do our monastic orders when they accustom the neophyte to self-abnegation through austere novitiates. We will follow an entirely different course; nothing but the enticement of pleasure will be used with the Little Hordes.

Let us analyze the sources of their virtues. They are four in number, and all of them are condemned by morality. They are the penchant for dirt, and the feelings of pride, impudence and insubordination. It is by abandoning themselves to these so-called vices that the Little Hordes will become virtuous. As we consider this paradox, let us recall that the theory of attraction must restrict itself to utilizing the passions as God made them, without modifying them in any way. In support of this principle I have shown that there are a number of infantile attractions which we are wrong to regard as harmful. *Curiosity* and *flightiness*, for instance, are designed to attract the child to a host of Seristeries where he will discover his industrial vocations. The penchant for *running around with older, tougher children* is also useful; for the example of such children will teach the infant to be enthusiastic about his work in Harmony. *Disobedience toward the father and the teacher* is likewise a perfectly natural impulse. For these are not the persons who should educate the child; his education will be provided by cabalistic rivalries in work groups. Thus all youthful impulses are good in infancy and also in later childhood, provided that they are exercised in passionate series.

The Little Hordes will not be inspired to perform disgusting work from the very outset: they must be gradually introduced to it. First their pride must be aroused by giving them a sense of their own preeminence. All authorities, even monarchs, owe the first salute to the Little Hordes. With their dwarf horses the Little Hordes comprise the globe's foremost regiments of cavalry; no industrial army[3] may begin a campaign without them. They also have the prerogative of initiating all work done in

[3] On the industrial armies see below pp. 322–328.

the name of unity. They report to the army on the day set for the beginning of the project. After the engineers have laid out the work, the Little Hordes parade across the battlefield, and in their first charge they are cheered on by the whole army. They spend several days with the army and distinguish themselves in a number of tasks.

The Little Hordes take precedence over all the other corps and groups in the Phalanx. The morning parade is led by a Little Khan who is drawn from their ranks. If visiting legions are camped for the night in a Phalanx (in the cellular camp), the next morning's meeting to honor their departure will be led by the Little Khan. Like a general, he will have his own staff of officers. Such prerogatives, which delight children, are granted only to the Little Hordes and to a few select members of the Little Bands who are admitted under the patronage of the Hordes.

During religious ceremonies the Little Hordes are seated in the sanctuary, and on all other festive occasions they are given the place of honor. The purpose of all these distinctions is to utilize their penchant for foul tasks. They must be impassioned for such tasks by the trappings of glory, which cost nothing. Filth must become their path to glory, and it is for this reason that we encourage their pride, impudence and insubordination.

The Little Hordes have their own slang or cabalistic language, as well as their own miniature artillery. They also have their Druids and Druidesses, who are acolytes chosen from those elderly persons who have retained their taste for foul tasks. This service brings the elderly numerous advantages.

The method to follow with the Little Hordes is to utilize their enthusiasm for filth, but not to *use it up* by fatiguing them. In order to avoid exhausting their enthusiasm, they must be made to work gaily, honorifically, and in short sessions. If, for example, there is a particularly filthy job to be done, the Hordes from four or five neighboring Phalanxes are assembled. They arrive to take part in the *délité* or matinal meal which is served at four forty-five. Then after the religious hymn at five and the parade of out-going work groups, the charge of the Little

Hordes is sounded in an uproar of bells, chimes, drums and trumpets, a howling of dogs and a bellowing of bulls. Then the Hordes, led by their Khans and Druids, rush forward with a great shout, passing before the priests who sprinkle them with holy water. They run off frenetically to their work, which they perform piously as an act of charity toward the Phalanx, a gesture of devotion to God and to unity.

The job done, they proceed to wash and dress. Then, dispersing into the gardens and workshops until eight, they return triumphantly to breakfast. There each Horde receives a crown of oak leaves which is attached to its banner. After breakfast, they remount their horses and return to their respective Phalanxes.

The Little Hordes should be associated with the priesthood as members of a religious brotherhood. When performing their work they should wear a religious symbol, such as a cross or other emblem, on their clothing. Among their work stimulants we must not forget the religious spirit, which is a very powerful means of inspiring dedication in children.

After the Little Hordes have developed an enthusiasm for collective work at difficult tasks, it will be easy to accustom them to unattractive day-to-day jobs in the apartments, slaughterhouses, kitchens, stables and laundries. They will always be up at three in the morning, taking the initiative at work on the Phalanx as they do in the industrial army.

The Little Hordes have supreme jurisdiction over the animal kingdom. They watch over the slaughterhouses to prevent unnecessary suffering and to insure every animal the most gentle death. Anyone who mistreats a quadruped, bird, fish or insect by abusing it in any way or by making it suffer at the slaughterhouse will have to answer to the Divan of the Little Hordes. Whatever his age, he will be brought before a tribunal of children because his reason is inferior even to that of children. Since animals are productive only when they are well treated, it is a rule in Harmony that a man who mistreats them is himself more of an animal than the defenceless beasts he persecutes. . . .

I have now said enough to make it clear that this corps of

children, who indulge all the inclinations that morality forbids, is a device which will realize all the virtuous fancies with which the moralists feed their imaginations:

1. *Sweet Fraternity.* If a particular task is disdained because it is filthy, the men who perform it will become a class of pariahs, degraded beings with whom the rich will not wish to associate. In Harmony all of the tasks which might lead to such bad consequences are performed by the Little Hordes. The Little Hordes ennoble loathsome work and thereby promote unity and social harmony, the fusion of the rich, middle and poor classes.

2. *Contempt for Wealth.* The Little Hordes do not disdain wealth as such, but rather its egotistical use. They will sacrifice a portion of their own wealth to increase that of the whole Phalanx and to maintain the true source of wealth: industrial attraction. When all three classes—rich, middle and poor—become subject to industrial attraction, they will work together affectionately on all sorts of tasks, even including the dirty work which is reserved for children. For children of rich parents will be as eager as those of the poor to join the ranks of the Little Hordes. It is personality that determines which corporation a child will choose. . . .

If our moralists had studied human nature, they would have recognized that most male children like filth and they would have sought to employ this inclination usefully. This is what the societary order does; it makes use of the taste for filth to form a corporation of industrial Deciuses. It encourages the dirty inclinations which are repressed with heavy-handed whippings by a tender morality that makes no effort to utilize the passions as God gave them to us.

—*OC*, VI, 206–214

WORK, LOVE, AND THE INDUSTRIAL ARMIES

Love, which is a source of disorder, idleness and expense in civilization, will become a source of profit and industrial miracles in the combined order. I am going to demonstrate this through a discussion of one of the most difficult administrative problems of civilization: the recruitment of armies. In the combined order this task will be accomplished by means of amorous strategy.

In each Phalanx there are two major series devoted to love, the *half-type* and the *whole type*. The latter is divided into nine groups beginning with the Vestalate which I shall now discuss.[4]

In each Phalanx the virginal members of the choir of Striplings[5] elect a quadrille of Vestals consisting of two parading couples and two meritorious couples. The former are chosen for their beauty and the latter for their accomplishments in the sciences and the arts or for their dedication to work.

The Vestals hold the rank of Magnates. When the poorest girl is elected a Vestal, she travels in a carriage which is studded with jewels and drawn by six white horses. . . . This youthful elite has the privilege of voyaging with the industrial armies. It is during their magnificent campaigns that the Vestals have their first love affairs.

Every day after their work is done the industrial armies hold magnificent festivities. These festivities are all the more splendid in that they bring together young people who have been chosen for their great beauty and talent. They also offer an excellent occasion for displays of courtliness. For each of the Vestals has numerous suitors and he or she must choose between them during the course of the campaign. Those who wish to form bonds with a single lover join the ranks of the Damsels who are constant lovers representing the second of the nine amorous types. Others who have penchants for inconstancy take their places in the seven remaining categories. The principal result of these diversions is that immense industrial armies are formed without any constraint. The only ruse employed is that of showing off and honoring those virgins whom the philosophers would like to keep hidden and surrounded by chaperons and prejudices.

[4] On the Vestals see below pp. 359–364.
[5] Young men and women between the ages of 15½ and 20.

To muster an army it is only necessary to publish a list of the virginal quadrilles chosen by each Phalanx. The suitors of these young people will be sure to follow them by joining the armies and taking part in the campaign during which the Vestals will make their choices. . . . [Once the campaign has gotten underway] the female Vestal is surrounded by her suitors, and she can watch them displaying their talents in the work sessions and the public games of the army. The number of suitors diminishes gradually as she begins to show a preference. Finally, when she has reached an agreement with one of them, they merely send a sealed declaration to the office of the High Matron or to the Vice Matrons who are in charge of each division. (The High Matron is a minister of amorous relations who directs the amorous affairs of the army which concern the Vestals.) Each evening arrangements are made to receive the couples who wish to form secret unions. The ceremonies are witnessed by a functionary from the office of the Matron, and the union is announced only on the following day when the Vestal has exchanged her crown of lilies for a crown of roses. She then appears in the dress of a Damsel with her favorite. . . .

Every night during the campaign of an industrial army a fairly large number of these unions take place; they are announced the following day at the matinal or first meal. The Bacchants and Bacchantes have the responsibility of venturing forth each morning to recover the wounded, that is to say the rejected suitors.

I will suppose that the Vestal Galatea has wavered in her choice between Pygmalion, Narcisse and Pollux. Finally she has chosen Pygmalion and secretly married him. During the course of the night a hundred other Vestals have formed similar unions with their favorites in the building reserved for this ceremony. The next morning before dawn a thousand Bacchants and Bacchantes gather. A clerk from the Matron's office brings them a list of the night's marriages as well as a list of the wounded parties who must be cared for. The names of Pollux and Narcisse are included on this list. Then the Bacchantes to whom Pollux is most attached hasten to his quarters. Others go to find

Narcisse. Similarly the Bacchants go in search of the attractive wounded females whom they have chosen.[6] Thus Pollux will be awakened by Bacchantes bearing myrtle; they will tell him that he has lost his claim to Galatea's affections. They will endure the first shock, the shrieks of perfidy and ingratitude; and to console Pollux they will employ all their eloquence and their charms.[7]

Each morning there is a rout of suitors to the great satisfaction of the legions of bacchanalians who reap benefits from this amorous martyrdom. For the customary remedy for such amorous misadventures is a few days' consolation with the Bacchantes, the Adventuresses and the other philanthropic groups in the army. When I provide more details concerning these diverse activities and the mechanism of the amorous series in the armies of the combined order, people will find the love affairs of civilization so monotonous and pitiful that they will become unable to tolerate the reading of our novels and plays.

[6] It goes without saying that if the unfortunate lovers are themselves Vestals, they will not be consoled by the Bacchants and Bacchantes. In that case consolation will be provided by other groups, such as the Sentimentalists who are the seventh group in the amorous series. There are many similar exceptions which I shall not bother to indicate but which should be taken for granted. (Fourier's note.)

[7] Some of the civilized may claim that Pollux will not be interested in the consolation of the Bacchantes; that if he is really in love with Galatea, he will disdainfully reject the profligates who come to offer themselves to him. It is true that this would be the case in the civilized order. For several days Pollux would have nothing to do with any other woman, and, what's more, he would challenge Pygmalion to a duel. In the barbarian order Pollux would act differently; he would stab Galatea to death while waiting for the chance to do likewise to Pygmalion. And in the savage or patriarchal order Pollux would act still differently. I am not unaware that according to our customs Pollux should disdain the Bacchantes and their consolations. But if you wish to follow civilized customs and condemn Pollux for distracting himself with the Bacchantes, a barbarian could equally well make sport of the civilized man who failed to murder the sweetheart whom he had lost. I go into these details in order to point out once again that the passions work differently in each social period. There are some ways in which the practices of the combined order may seem bizarre. But before judging them, one should understand the circumstances surrounding the introduction of customs so alien to our own. (Fourier's note.)

It is obvious that admission to the industrial armies will become a privilege in the combined order. There will be twice as many volunteers as needed. In utilizing nothing else beside the stimulus of love, it will become possible to gather one hundred and twenty million legionnaires of both sexes to perform tasks the mere thought of which would freeze our mercenary souls with horror. For instance, the combined order will undertake the conquest of the great Sahara desert. It will be attacked at various points by ten or twenty million workers if necessary. Men will transport earth, cultivate the soil and plant trees everywhere. Finally they will succeed in rendering the land moist and the sand firm; the desert will give way to fertile soil. Navigable canals will be made in areas where we are now unable to dig irrigation ditches, and great ships will sail not only across isthmuses like those of Suez and Panama, but even in the interior of continents, as from the Caspian Sea to the seas of Azov and Aral and the Persian Gulf. Ships will sail from Quebec to the five great lakes, and from the sea to all the great lakes whose length equals a quarter of their distance from the sea.

In every empire the diverse legions of men and women will be divided into several armies, and these armies will join with those of neighboring empires. In the combined order no task will be undertaken by a single army; at least three will work together at the same time in order to create rivalry and emulation. If the sandy wastes of Gascony are to be covered with earth, the job will be done by three armies: one French, one Spanish and one English. In return France will send armies to Spain and England to help with their tasks. Thus all the empires of the globe will be mixed. The same procedure will be followed in the exchange of provincial armies and in the performance of local work.

Let us assume that the Phalanx of Tivoli has a field that could be hayed in two hours by 300 men. If the Phalanx has only 60 men available, it borrows four bands from four neighboring communities. It has its ambassadors arrange for these loans at the Exchanges of the other Phalanxes. On the appointed day the four bands of workers arrive and help the Tivolians in their task.

The haying is followed by a meal attended by the loveliest women of the several communities. Later on the Phalanx of Tivoli will send its men and women to the communities from which it is now receiving help. This exchange of workers is one of the means used in the combined order to turn the dullest tasks into festive occasions. Such tasks become pleasant in Harmony:

Because they never last long thanks to help of a large number of workers;

Because they provide an occasion for the meeting of bands of men and women from different Phalanxes;

And because the large scale on which work is performed makes it possible to organize the work in an elegant fashion.

I wish to emphasize the final point. Our present workshops are so filthy, so disgusting, that they inspire a horror for work and for the men who work, especially in France which seems to be the adopted country of dirt. Is there anything more repulsive than the Paris laundries where the linen of high society is cleaned? In the combined order these cesspools will be replaced by buildings ornamented with marble basins and furnished with faucets for various degrees of heat so that women will not ruin their hands by plunging them into freezing or scalding water. Numerous arrangements will also be made to shorten the work by means of mechanical devices of all sorts. Attempts will also be made to create a fascinating atmosphere at the meal shared by the four or five bands of laundresses after their work.

As trivial as all these details may seem, I stress them in order to show that all obstacles to work have been anticipated. The gathering of bands of workers from different communities is only one of the numerous devices by which the combined order will vanquish all difficulties and provide the means to accomplish the most odious tasks *by attraction and rivalry*.

Love, which is so useless today, will thus become one of the most brilliant mainsprings of the social mechanism. And while it takes so much trouble and constraint for the civilized order to recruit the destructive armies which periodically ravage the earth, the combined order will rely only upon attraction and love to form beneficent armies which will erect innumerable

superb monuments. Instead of having devastated thirty provinces in a campaign, these armies will have built thirty bridges,
leveled thirty mountains, dug thirty canals for irrigation, and
drained thirty marshes. Yet these industrial feats will only be a
few of the miracles wrought by amorous liberty and the collapse
of philosophy.

—*OC*, 1, 172–178

# VII

# *The New Amorous World*

We are not going to speculate about civilization. Instead we shall speculate about an order of things in which the least of men will be rich, polished, sincere, pleasant, virtuous and handsome (excepting the very old); an order of things in which marriage and our other customs will have been forgotten, their very absence having inspired a host of amorous innovations which we cannot yet imagine.

—*OC*, VII, 51

It is tempting to view Fourier as a precursor of Freud. The manuscripts comprising *The New Amorous World* make this approach particularly inviting. But even before the publication of these manuscripts in 1967 some scholars were rehabilitating Fourier as a forerunner of psychoanalysis. Emile Lehouck, for example, asserted that Fourier had "discovered the importance of sexuality" in human behavior and "anticipated the fundamental theses of psychoanalysis."[1] Although Fourier was obviously concerned with the origins of neurosis and other more serious forms of mental disease, we believe that such claims are essentially misleading. Fourier did, it is true, formulate a pioneering theory of the dynamics of repression, and he discussed amorous manias in terms which bear some resemblance to the psychoanalytical explanation of neurotic symptom formation. The mere fact that,

---

[1] *Fourier aujourd'hui* (Paris, 1966), pp. 11, 32–33, 101–102.

at the beginning of the nineteenth century, Fourier attempted to discuss sex in a humane and objective manner also gives some point to his rehabilitation as a precursor of Freud. But Fourier, who had a whole world to construct, never tried to develop his psychopathological theories in any systematic fashion. His analysis of manias, for example, shows extraordinary insight and freedom from moralistic prejudices. But, as the following texts show, he was more interested in speculating on the uses of what he called "natural" manias than uncovering the origins of the "artificial" ones caused by repression or deprivation. Furthermore, despite all the importance that Fourier attached to sexuality, his view of it was quite tradition bound in one major respect. Whereas Freud saw the repressed essence of mankind as expressed in infantile sexual urges, Fourier regarded sexuality as an exclusively adult phenomenon. Although he made many penetrating observations on the behavior of children, he had little interest in or understanding of infantile sexuality. To his mind children constituted a third or neutral sex, and he denied that they could be prompted by sexual impulses before they reached adolescence.

Fourier's significance and originality, in our opinion, lie elsewhere. Few social theorists before or after Fourier have probed as deeply and with as much real detachment into the problem of the relationship between man's instinctual life and human society. This is not to argue that other and more profound —if not more original—thinkers had been unaware of the fact that every society had to solve in some way the problem of integrating instinctual drives and social activity. Most of the major social theorists of the eighteenth century had made some effort to take this problem into account. Montesquieu, for example, had established the fundamental sociological premise: the political, economic, legal, religious, and sexual institutions of any society are structurally related. Diderot, too, was acutely aware of the close connection between sexual mores and economic institutions. Yet both Montesquieu and Diderot were content to analyze the passions in a somewhat conventional way. Montesquieu, moreover, was willing to follow his relativism only so far. He could not or would not look beyond monogamy and rejected the idea that women should be free to enjoy sex outside of marriage. Diderot was less prejudiced but rather fatalistic about the possibility of overthrowing the oppressive sexual regime of Christian Europe.

Fourier's critical analysis of civilization was based on a similar view of the structural relationships between human passions and human institutions, but he was far less inclined to "explain" civilized sexual laws as "natural" developments. Both his utopian anger and his thoroughgoing relativism led him to expose how utterly civilization had failed in its attempt to devise a viable "amorous regime." It was to hide their failure, he maintained, that civilization's philosophers preached doctrines of moderation and sternly insisted that instinctual gratification was incompatible with life in society. This freed them from the obligation to design a society which would liberate and utilize the deepest and most severely repressed human energies. The reader may draw his own conclusions about Fourier's attempt to construct such a society. But it raises a question that cannot be ignored.

# 1

# THE NATURE AND USES OF LOVE IN HARMONY

## LOVE: THE DIVINE PASSION

Lost in the black night, misled by the political and moral systems, let us begin by seeking a more dependable guiding light than the so-called reason that has led us astray. Let us rejoin God, let us seek his tracks in the wilderness. Which of our passions bears some mark of the divine spirit? Can we find any trace of that spirit in our frenzies of ambition, in our perfidious administrative and commercial affairs, in the inconstancy of our friendships, in the discords of our families? No, greed, deceit and envy betray the absence of the divine spirit. But there is one passion which retains its original nobility, which keeps the divine fire burning in mortal men, which gives them a share in the attributes of the Deity. This passion is love. Love is a divine flame, the true spirit of God who is love. Is it not in the rapture of love that man reaches toward the heavens and identifies himself with God? Is there any lover who does not deify his or her loved one and who is not convinced that their shared love is a divine happiness? Even among antipathetic types, love is the most powerful agent of passional unions. It is by means of love that the haughty Diana meets the shepherd Endymion on human terms. The other passions have very little of love's capacity for harmonizing people of different ranks.

What are the other passions compared to love? Can any one of them be compared to it? Without love life would lose its charm. When love has gone man can only vegetate and seek distractions or illusions to hide the emptiness of his soul. Women, who have all too few distractions, have bitter knowledge of this truth. Thus in the decline of life they turn to religion in search of some shadow of the God who seems to have departed with their loved one. They continue to live only by hoping for another life in which they may once again enjoy the happiness of loving.

God shares this conviction; he thinks that man is an incomplete being without love. Thus he has taken countless precautions to make sure that in Harmony the aged of both sexes will have amorous illusions and distractions. In civilization old people manage to forget love, but they cannot replace it. The passions of ambition and paternity are often a source of suffering for old people; but any man of sixty exalts and grieves for the love affairs of his youth. No young person would be willing to exchange his love affairs for the distractions of the elderly.

Thus it is love that stands first among the passions; it is their King, their ideal source. It is in love more than in any other passion that the divine spirit should be sought; it is the best index of the designs of God.

Among all the passions, however, love fares worst in civilization. It is given no other outlet than marriage. Isn't this enough to suggest that civilization is an order contrary to the designs of God? . . . And why should love not have been proscribed by a shameless civilization which, after centuries of study, has reached the point of proscribing God himself, of denying God's existence in its metaphysical quarrels and its atheists' dictionaries? We will take a very different line; and it is primarily to love, and to its possibilities, that the theory of attraction will adapt itself in order to determine the passional mechanism wished by God.

*—OC*, VII, 2–3

### POLYGAMOUS PENCHANTS ARE UNIVERSAL

If polygamy merits the attacks leveled against it by the philosophers, how is it that they have found no means of eliminating the barbarian societies which keep five hundred million men in a state of polygamy? How is it that among the three hundred million people who live in savagery and civilization, the former frequently practice polygamy and regard it as a virtue, while the people of civilization are clandestine polygamists despite the fact that they claim to regard adultery as a vice? Would it not be wise to find some means of tolerating a practice which cannot in any case be prevented? When a vice or purported vice is *legally* practiced by a majority of the human race and secretly practiced by the minority, it would be better to try to make use of it than to indulge one's self in sterile declamations against a weakness inherent in human nature. . . .

If men were really inspired by an aversion for amorous inconstancy and secret polygamy, if women likewise hated inconstancy and adultery, one would have to conclude that human nature inclines to amorous fidelity. The political theorists would have to adapt their speculations to the penchant for fidelity. But the actual conduct of the barbarians and the free members of civilization makes it clear that all men have a penchant for polygamy. The behavior of civilized ladies shows that they have the same penchant. They prefer to have a number of lovers, or at least to change their favorites periodically, while their titulary mate serves to orchestrate the whole and provides a mask for their amorous variations. These truths have been established by centuries of experience. How can they be ignored by the savants who claim to study nature and truth? How can the savants disregard the secret insurrection of the human race against any form of legislation which requires perpetual fidelity in love? . . .

The law shuts its eyes to secret polygamy or conjugal infidelity. This is only prudent, for otherwise it would be necessary to create as many tribunals as there are homes. Yet can one imagine any system of legislation more inept than one whose statutes are secretly violated by every family? Is it not time to say: let us try out some new method since nothing could be more absurd than the one we have? . . .

Instead of making such experiments . . . our regenerating philosophers have attempted to proscribe the passion best suited to the formation of social ties. They have confined the amorous tie within the narrowest limits possible. Their conjugal system only tolerates that form of love which is strictly necessary for the propagation of the species. It would be impossible to conceive of a social order any more drastic in its restriction of love. Our customs and our legislation require a young woman to deprive herself of love until her tender father and her tender mother have found her a buyer. They oblige her to love this buyer all her life, and to love no one if there is no buyer. Good sense would seem to allow for a few exceptions. A woman of forty who has neither been sold nor sought after is quite justified in fearing that she will never be married. She might well be entitled, at the age of forty, to a few amorous liberties. But not in civilization. If after twenty-five years of expectant celibacy she finally decides to take a lover, she becomes, according to religion, a fornicator who will burn eternally in Hell. According to our legislation, she is a shameless enemy of the social order, which does not tolerate love outside the sacred bonds of matrimony as contracted before the municipality. Such are the judgments of a century which prides itself on having elevated reason to the perfection of perfectibility.

And what is the aim of this political system which represses love so violently? Is it to reduce society to poverty, deceit, oppression, carnage, etc.? Of course not. But this has been the result of the civilized system which represses love and grants it only a minimum of legitimacy. Do the legal restraints on love have any real effect? None at all. For even the most oppressed creatures practice polygamy furtively; and those who have any liberty whatsoever practice it more or less openly.

The result of this is a double political absurdity. First, legislation is debased by a system against which the immense majority of citizens is, or has been, in a state of secret insurrection. Second, the results of this system—poverty, oppression, deceit and carnage—are wholly contrary to man's desires and to the goal of nature. Nature conceived of love in order to multiply infinitely man's social bonds. These bonds exist between the two sexes only insofar as they are founded either on physical possession or else on sentimental attachments which are impractical within the cynical and deceitful system of civilized love. Love can neither be expressed nor satisfied in civilization, since the only form in which it is tolerated—marriage—is a coercive bond which extends only to the indispensable measures of reproduction. There are no legal sanctions for any form of love which is consistent with the desire of nature to establish bonds between men and to harmonize society. This state of absolute oppression is a fine refutation of the philosophers who claim to be collaborating with nature and encouraging the formation of affective ties. If just one of the philosophers had ever had this intention, and if he had made any effort to give increased scope to free love, he would have discovered a way out of the morass of civilization.

—*OC*, VII, 228, 234–237

### THE SEXUAL MINIMUM

Physical love, which is called brutish, animal, etc., is degraded by civilized legislation and morality as an obstacle to the conjugal system. When it is not allied with sentimental love, it is regarded as a vile passion which reduces us to the level of the animals. Nothing is more true. Nonetheless when we eat a meal in isolation, we are also behaving like animals.[1] Does it follow that we are degrading ourselves, that it is dishonorable to eat alone when one's family or friends are absent? The law would hardly be just if it condemned a hungry man for eating alone rather than not eating at all. However, the same law dishonors a woman who sleeps with a man in order to satisfy an imperious physical need. There are still many parents who allow their unmarried daughters to suffer and die for want of sexual satisfaction. Certainly some provision should be made for a young woman who is languishing and suffering for want of a pleasure which nature dictates. It would be easy for her to reach some understanding with a conscientious and healthy young man who would promise to be discrete and to take the customary precautions to avoid pregnancy. But on this point fathers start citing the 200,000 volumes of theology and the 400,000 volumes of philosophy. The fact remains that they are assassinating their daughters, and that the laws and prejudices which ignore the natural right to physical love are comparable to the vengeful gods who, according to Calchas, exacted the blood of Iphigenia.[2] Those gods were no more unjust than are our 600,000 volumes on amorous matters. This rebellion of parents, philosophers and

[1] Fourier maintained that to eat a meal in isolation was to deny one's self the emotional or "spiritual" satisfaction provided by good company. See above pp. 265–267 for his discussion of the "two conditions" of gastronomic pleasure.

[2] Calchas was the Greek astrologer who advised Agamemnon, during the siege of Troy, to sacrifice his daughter Iphigenia and to build the wooden horse.

theologians against nature is particularly reprehensible in view of the fact that nature has provided a number of men who would be quite willing to satisfy the needs of languishing women and even those whose charms have withered with age. Here is an example.

In 1816 a young man was prosecuted in the French courts for having raped six women whose ages ranged from sixty to eighty. (No doubt he raped a good many others who were not heard of.) His trial was discussed in all the journals. . . . The man was found guilty and sentenced. Yet it might have been wiser to distribute pieces of his clothing as religious relics to inspire imitation of his fine example. It is evident that this young paragon was acting *out of need,* and it is also evident that *the sexual needs of men and women can become just as urgent as their need for food.*

It follows that society should grant a minimum of satisfaction to the two senses of taste and touch. For the needs of these two senses can become much more urgent than those of the other three. The body may suffer if they are not gratified, whereas a lack of pleasures appealing to the eyes, the ears and the nose will do it no harm. . . .[3]

By means of laws and locks we are able to keep physical love in check, but there is no way of stopping the prejudice against sentimental love which has spread throughout high society. In attempting to proscribe physical love and to elevate the sentimental, our law-makers have sacrificed them both. They have created a situation in which laws are universally disobeyed. It is certain that Cato was wiser when he applauded the young men he saw visiting prostitutes. By doing so, he admitted the

[3] All expositions of Fourier's thought call attention to the "social minimum"—to Fourier's insistence that everyone in Harmony should be assured a guaranteed minimum in food, clothing and subsistence. (See above pp. 274–275.) Although the appeal voiced here for a similar minimum in sexual satisfaction occupies an important place in Fourier's doctrine, it was never articulated in the works published during his lifetime and was first made known only in 1967 with the publication of *Le Nouveau monde amoureux* from which this selection is taken. For commentary on Fourier's rather strange formulation of the sexual minimum see our Introduction pp. 55–56.

legitimacy of the sexual need, at least among men, and accepted the necessity of reaching an accommodation with nature.

It is true that since Cato's time, two new developments have served to justify the system of repression. The first is the fear of mortal sin, which did not exist in antiquity when law and religion took some account of the natural desires of men—if not women. The other reason for repression is associated with a recent development, a danger much worse than that of mortal sin. I am referring to the danger of venereal disease, which dates only from the past three centuries. These two developments have served to retard enlightenment about everything concerned with the practice of physical love.[4] But if the policy of sexual repression appears to make some sense in civilization, this should only serve to encourage us in our search for a different social order. For it is evident that, far from harmonizing the passions, civilization is coming more and more into conflict with the designs of nature. It is also clear that nature, which concedes nothing, is eroding the barriers we set up against it. Thus our efforts at repression are illusory, and I will demonstrate that in attempting to limit the domain of physical love, we have only succeeded in widening its scope. We have permitted physical love to destroy the influence of sentiment and to reign despotically over the whole amorous system of civilization. This has been the inevitable result of our legislation which has unreasonably denied a minimum satisfaction to the two senses of touch and taste.

Let us take note of the supreme injustice of our civilized legislators and the noxious spirit which inspires their secret policies. They are not unaware that the sense of taste, the need for subsistence, is the guiding force in the lives of the common people. They know that when food is lacking, the common people and simple soldiers will rebel and overthrow their government. Yet the law provides no guarantee of a minimum of subsistence. In its justice the law condemns to death a pauper

---

[4] The weakening of such restraints on sexual promiscuity is discussed in Fourier's text on "Amorous Anarchy." See above p. 170.

who is driven by hunger to steal a loaf of dark bread, and it protects and honors the hoarder who inflicts famine on thirty million men. Oblivious of their obligation to provide a minimum of subsistence, the law-makers are even less willing to grant a minimum of sexual gratification. They suppose that the sexual needs are less urgent than the need for food. This is an error. Even though a person can do without sexual intercourse but not without food, it is certain that the need for tactile or sensual pleasures causes as many social disorders as does the need for subsistence.

The two senses react to deprivation in very different ways. While the sense of taste goes into open rebellion, the sense of touch protests silently. But if the ravages it causes are less obvious, they are no less real. The failure to gratify men's tactile needs, their need for physical love, has led to the corruption of the whole system of amorous relations and the consequent erosion of the family system. Thus both minor affective passions —love and familism—have been perverted.

Let us demonstrate this truth by a comparison drawn from the sense of taste. Everyone knows what hunger can do to the common people: it can stifle their feelings of honor and duty and drive them into a state of rage. When the lower classes are hungry, they are always ready to commit crimes and misdeeds. But just try to propose a base action to someone whose subsistence is guaranteed. Promise him a dinner with bread, meat and all the wine he wants in return for performing an ignoble act. He won't even listen to you. But a member of the lower class will cock his ears and forget about his honor. The same thing occurs in love when people lack the necessary minimum. Honor means absolutely nothing to them.

Honor plays a greater role in love than one might think. When I have established the rules of social honor in love, it will be evident that civilization knows nothing about it, that the secret customs of civilization are contrary to honor, that it inspires people to rebel secretly against their own social system and to rail against genuinely liberal and charitable ideas. These civilized customs . . . have no other cause than the banishment of sensual pleasure, the fear of doing without physical love. This fear leads people to ridicule sentimental love and it encourages the spread of lasciviousness and deceit among civilized men and women. The disorders caused by the fear of amorous deprivation are not, in fact, as obvious as those caused by hunger riots. But the mutiny of love is only the more effective for being hidden and concealed behind all sorts of masks. This concealed mutiny is the inevitable result of our ignorant and vexatious legislation . . . which does not wish to recognize the need of guaranteeing a minimum of satisfaction to the two senses of taste and touch, which are the two links between the physical and spiritual realms. When either of these senses is denied gratification, deprived of its necessary minimum, all spiritual relations are falsified. The result is that our social system is completely false in both amorous relations and in relations based on ambition.

I am well aware that these abstractions will be incomprehensible to civilized law-makers. For they have absolutely no means of guaranteeing a minimum of food and comfort to the common people. They would be even less capable of establishing an amorous minimum, of forming groups intended to provide everyone with a minimum of physical satisfaction in love. My purpose is simply to demonstrate the incompatibility of civilization with the designs of nature and the necessity of escaping at once from this disastrous social order. The means of escape has been discovered. . . .

We are going to discuss a new amorous order in which sentiment, which is the noble side of love, will enjoy an unparalleled prestige and will endow all social relations with a unique charm. How will sentimental love maintain this dominion? Through the fact that the physical impulses, far from being fettered, will be fully satisfied. Through the fact that the need for physical gratification will no longer be regarded as any more indecent than the appetites of the other senses, the love of feasts, concerts, perfumes, finery, etc. Only by satisfying the need for physical love, will it become possible to guarantee the development of the noble element in love.

—*OC*, VII, 439–445

## THE DECLINE OF EGOISM AND JEALOUSY

If one compares the jealousy displayed by barbarian and civilized lovers, it is obvious that the barbarians are uncompromising in love and that under many circumstances the civilized are quite willing to make accommodations.[5] Like many other passions jealousy undergoes modifications in different social periods. If it is much weaker in civilization than in barbarism, it will be weaker still in the subsequent periods of guarantism, mixed series and Simple Harmony. The reason is that these periods will be characterized by an extension of social bonds which should serve to decrease jealousy. In any case it is not necessary to do away with jealousy in Harmony where a certain number of jealous couples (roughly a third) will be needed. But since the defenders of jealousy, philosophy and the conjugal system deny that it will be possible to find a large number of couples lacking in jealousy, we must show that our present customs contain the seeds of the tolerance to be exhibited in future societies.

I could cite collective exceptions, whole nations which have renounced jealousy. The Spartans, as is well-known, loaned their wives to all virtuous citizens who desired them. The Lapps and other savage peoples offered their wives to strangers; the Tahitians did likewise. But these people were closer than we are to the state of nature. If there were some jealous lovers among them, that is not surprising; for nature wishes to attain a balance in which one-third of all people are jealous lovers and two-thirds are tolerant lovers. Here I am only criticizing civilization which wishes to make an exclusive system out of jealous love. I would be just as critical of a people who made a system out of communal love. A penchant for exclusive systems is one of the radical vices of civilization, and it will be avoided in Harmony.

Although jealousy is encouraged by the conjugal system, it must have feeble roots among the civilized. For other passions are constantly neutralizing and absorbing the spirit of jealousy in civilization. People frequently forget all about their jealousy

[5] For further comment on the historical relativity of jealousy and sexual mores in general see above pp. 171–172 and 333–335.

when it is in their interest to do so. But in Harmony jealousy will be minimized not only by self-interest but also by other equally powerful and more noble stimuli such as general friendship or unityism, the religious spirit, etc. It is obvious that it will not be difficult to establish the appropriate balance between the number of jealous and non-jealous lovers. This will be particularly easy in view of the fact that no fixed roles will be assigned.

Let us take a closer look at the ease with which jealousy gives way to interests of a higher order in civilization. Let us see how accommodating even the most egotistical of civilized men can be upon occasion. Are there not numerous civilized husbands who manage to establish the most fraternal relations with their wives' lovers?[6] Their relationship adds charm to the household and they attempt to outdo each other in attentiveness to their shared partner. The city of Paris, among others, is cited as having an abundant stock of these tolerant and doting husbands. There are three reasons for the Parisians' superiority in this role: 1) It is costly and time-consuming to escort a woman at Paris. Carriages are necessary and expenses are heavy. Cavaliers and helpers are particularly useful for a busy husband who does not have the time to take care of all of these matters. 2) Parisian lovers are more polite than their provincial counterparts. They do not have the trivial mania of young provincials who think that they have only half seduced a woman when they cannot poke fun at her husband or his style of life. This sort of crudity is rare at Paris. 3) Parisians can learn the healthy doctrine of tolerance from the wits in which that city is so abundant. Furthermore, these doctrines of tolerance are put into practice by the courtiers and social lions of Paris; conjugal intolerance is bad form at the court and in society.

As the human spirit advances, like the Parisians, towards the perfecting of perfectibility, it becomes more accommodating about love. Social progress modifies its jealousy. . . . Thus the

---

[6] In the perspective provided by this text Fourier's "Hierarchy of Cuckoldom" acquires a new dimension. It is clear that Fourier did not merely regard cuckoldry as a quaint civilized foible. It was evidence of a widely shared distaste for monogamous marriage and a "foreshadowing" of the amorous tolerance of Harmony.

passion of jealousy can easily be weakened when circumstances create reasons for an accommodation. In Harmony there will be so many motives for a lessening of jealousy that it would take me pages to list them all. Among other bonds which will produce a decline in jealousy one should mention the childhood friendships established in the industrial series. Any series will create at least twenty active intrigues which will serve to unify people who might otherwise be jealous of each other.

—*OC*, VII, 81–84

### THE REHABILITATION OF SENTIMENTAL LOVE

For the past three thousand years we have been confused by the moral sciences which teach us to do without the pleasures that they are unable to provide. Unavoidably then we have made great mistakes in the allotment of the small number of pleasures which are available to us. I maintain that one of the greatest of these mistakes has been our habit of ridiculing such true pleasures as those afforded by sentimental relationships. The few devotees of sentimental love may vainly protest that it still has numerous partisans in polite society; the fact remains that such people have been crushed by ridicule, by the hypocrisy of the majority which pays lip-service to sentiment while scoffing at it in secret.

If sentimental love were legally recognized in civilization, this would be just one more element in the universal falseness. Every woman would claim that her recognized lover was only a sentimentalist with no desire for physical possession. This sort of fraud is legally sanctioned in Italy where women are permitted lovers who are apparently confined to a sentimental role but who actually go beyond the recognized limits. Thus this sort of relationship is properly outlawed in most civilized countries. It is simply a new form of amorous duplicity. . . .

Sentimental love is even more successfully banished from civilization by ridicule, by the widespread tendency to scoff at those who fail to profit from the chance to possess an attractive woman. Women are even more contemptuous than men of such disinterestedness. On this point the people of civilization may be compared to peasants and those vulgar people who think themselves obliged to gobble up everything served by a caterer simply because it is paid for. They claim that they would be fools to leave anything on the table. But who has the greater pleasure? The guzzler who gorges himself until he is sick, or the judicious gastronomer who eats only as much as his stomach can stand? . . . Surely the latter has more pleasure than the boor who devours everything just because it is paid for.

More than any other people the French are guzzlers in love, and they show no mercy to a lover who fails to bring an amorous relationship to a physical consummation. Nevertheless the conduct of such a lover is similar to that of the satisfied man who leaves some food on the table even though it has been paid for. He increases his enjoyment by depriving himself of something. If a man does not have a carnal passion for a woman but only a sentimental inclination, why should he quit his natural role . . . and give up an attractive illusion in order to satisfy public opinion? . . .

The great mistake of the sophisticated world in this matter is its failure to recognize that genuine sentimental ties can only be formed by a few highly refined individuals. The world is full of hypocrites who aspire to play the sentimental role. But to take them at their word is to condemn sentimentalism to the fate of those fashions which are debased by common usage.

One might claim that sentimental lovers have foreseen the risk of debasement. But, if so, what measures have they taken to get rid of the pretenders? None. They have neither defined the uses of sentiment nor designated the small number of psychological types which are innately disposed to sentimental love. On the contrary, they have generally made the mistake of confusing sentiment with the illusions of compound love or of a love that is seeking physical consummation. . . .

The failure to define the uses of sentiment or to foil those who feign it has led to its discredit. Things have reached such a pass that its true disciples would blush to reveal themselves. The only people who boast of their high sentiments are those who do not practice them. They know that the libertines will not be taken in by their masquerade. Only the naive and the credulous will be fooled.

But let us be fair with the mass of simpletons. In civilization love is fettered in so many ways, falseness is so widespread, and deception is so much to be feared that people are right to ask for amorous guarantees, to demand the physical satisfaction without which any civilized relationship is suspect and precarious. It remains true, however, that this demand for physical gratification has served to stifle the development of sentimental ties. Amorous relations have been reduced to the status of a mortgage in which people refuse to accept anything but effective guarantees and in which the role of trust has been reduced to zero. Such is the sad role of sentimental relationships in civilization.

—*OC*, VII, 101–104

You can often hear poor people complain: "How virtuous I would be if I were rich! How charitable I would be! How much I would do to encourage the sciences and the arts!" etc. On this score people joke with them, saying that "it is very easy for a rich man to be virtuous." No, this is not true. Since so many rich people are not virtuous, there must be something which disgusts them or prevents them from leading a virtuous life. Wealth alone is not enough. As for the poor, their virtues cannot be exercised without wealth, and they are quite right to seek wealth as a means for the activation of virtues which are otherwise as useless as sails without a boat or a boat without sails.

The same thing may be said of sentiment. It is only a partial stimulus in love. It is only half of love and can only emerge in conjunction with physical pleasure. If it is to express itself apart from physical pleasure, guarantees are necessary. When sentiment is denied the support of the physical, it becomes as uninteresting as a meal consisting of nothing but delicate spices. If you serve all the spices of Arabia at a meal where there is no meat or fruit or wine, you will sicken your guests who cannot live off odors. They will tell you that spices provide no more than a conditional pleasure. Your spices will be disdained and ridiculed in this case, but if they were served with an excellent meal they would be a precious complement.

Such is the role assigned to sentiment in Harmony. It com-

plements the physical pleasures of love and is not independent
of them. When all the amorous needs of a woman are provided
for, when she has all the physical lovers, orgies and bacchanalias
(both simple and compound) that she wishes, then there will be
ample room in her soul for sentimental illusions. Then she will
seek out refined sentimental relationships to counterbalance her
physical pleasures.

People may say that there will be nothing meritorious about
her sentimental dispositions, that sentimentality will be easy for
her when she has such a variety of sensual pleasures at her
disposal. But the fact remains that the exercise of sentiment is
subject to many hindrances. The problem is to assure its reign, to
give it as much prominence as possible, and to make its influence
equal to that of physical pleasure. This will be done in Harmony
where sentiment will shine because it will be in a proper state of
balance with sensual love.

—*OC*, vii, 97–98

# 2

# STUDIES IN PSYCHOPATHOLOGY

### THE ANALYSIS OF MANIAS

When we see any one of the twelve passions at work in another person it often seems to be a ridiculous mania. Take familism for example: we reproach fathers for being blind to the faults of their children or for playing favorites among them. We think it an unjust mania when they show a preference—as they often do—for the least worthy of their offspring. But such faults are common to all fathers. When anyone criticizes them he succumbs to the vice denounced by the gospels: he sees the mote in his neighbor's eye but not the beam in his own.

The general tendency of fathers to dote on their children is a necessary passion, common to everyone. If public opinion censures this passion, it has all the more reason to condemn the rare passions and especially those which are useless as well as rare, such as the amorous manias which are limited to one person in 1000 or 10,000 or 100,000. These amorous manias have three things against them: their apparent uselessness, their great rarity and their extreme oddness. I have said enough to indicate what sort of prejudices I will have to combat in order to rehabilitate manias, and especially amorous manias, in the eyes of the public. So let us proceed.

Manias are diminutive passions, the effects of the human mind's need to create stimulants for itself. This need is the source of superstition which is so to speak the root of the spiritual manias. People are particularly prone to develop amorous manias, because lovers tend to seek an ideal happiness in habits that are often quite indifferent in themselves such as . . . heel scratching and hair plucking.

If you discuss amorous manias with women who have had many lovers and men who have had many mistresses, you will learn from their accounts that these manias are infinitely variable. Some amorous manias are physical and others are spiritual; some take an active form and others are passive. There are some mixed personalities, or people whose mania can express itself in either an active or a passive sense; and there are also mixed manias, or manias which stem from both physical and spiritual love.

It is a rule in Harmony that all manias shall be completely equal before the law. (This is one point on which the complete equality recommended by the philosophers will be tolerated.) However all manias must be classified and divided into series. The first problem will be to determine the numerical membership of the various series. Once the Courts of Love have been established throughout the globe, their statistical tables will enable us to ascertain quite quickly the numerical [incidence] of every mania. We will know, for example, that a certain mania appears only once in ten Tourbillons[1] and that another will have only one representative in 100 Tourbillons. Some particularly rare manias will be represented only once in 1000 Tourbillons; and others, rarer still, will appear only once in 10,000 or even 100,000. The mania with only one devotee in 100,000 Tourbillons will be in just about the last rank numerically since it will have only 40 representatives on the whole face of the earth. Nonetheless it will constitute a part of the omnigamous series and we must include it in our calculations. In Harmony great efforts will be made to bring together the devotees of such extremely rare manias. For each of them the meeting will be a pilgrimage as sacred as the journey to Mecca is for Muslims. The smaller their number, the more eager they will be to meet at the appointed time and place.

Before describing the activities of the various amorous series, let us first discuss their composition. We will begin with physical manias because they are more easy to distinguish than are spiritual manias. People who indulge in a mania because they are repressed or seek distraction will not be accorded normal membership in a sect. This is the case with most old men, nine-tenths of whom will wish to join the sects of whippers, flagellants, etc., as either active or passive members. These men seek distraction because they are deprived of love. Their manias are not natural expressions of their characters as are the manias and

[1] Phalanxes.

passions of young men of 25 or 30 who are perfectly capable of satisfying all their amorous needs. I have known a healthy man of 30 who loved to watch his mistress make love with others despite the fact that he was in love with her and was quite capable of satisfying her. This mania was truly an expression of character. For the man was in full possession of his manly faculties and his mania did not stem from deprivation.

Amorous and other types of manias may thus be divided into two categories: the natural and the artificial. Artificial manias are simply [expedients] to which we have recourse in order to make ourselves forget the loss of our faculties in old age or to distract ourselves from repression when we are in our prime. Here I will consider only the natural manias and the means of dividing them into groups, leagues or sects, and then into series of sects.

Manias relating to love and to the other passions will be common among young people in Harmony. Today young people disdain manias because to indulge in them is to invite ridicule. People forget that love is the domain of unreason and that the more unreasonable a thing is, the more closely it is associated with love. Since love tends to manifest itself in manias, and since all manias will be highly useful in Harmony, their development will be systematically encouraged. There will be accurate means for the detection of the manias with which everyone is endowed by nature. The methods will be so precise that it will even be possible to predict and ascertain manias before the onset of puberty. . . .

Any mania common enough to occur in one out of 810 persons should be called an intra-mania because it has a place in the scale of personality types.[2] A mania which appears much more rarely, for instance in one out of 100,000 individuals, should be called an extra-mania (the heel-scratchers fall into this category). I have established this distinction by using examples taken from love. Since I have passed my prime, I may be allowed to cite a personal example. I will choose a mixed extra-mania: sapphianism or the fondness for lesbians. My confession should encourage

---

[2] See above, pp. 220–223.

other more reticent persons to admit to their own weaknesses of this sort.

I have said that it is difficult to discover manias in civilization. I was 35 years old when by chance I found myself in a situation which made me realize that I had a taste or mania for sapphianism. I discovered that I loved lesbians and was eager to do anything to please them. In the whole world there are roughly 26,400 people like me (if one calculates at the rate of 33 per million) because every male omnigyne[3] is necessarily a Sapphianist or a protector of lesbians, just as every female omnigyne is necessarily a pederastite or a protectress of pederasts. If this were not the case, these personalities would lack their pivotal quality in love, which is an impulse of philanthropic dedication to the opposite sex and to everything that might please it in both the ambiguous and direct modes. . . .

I have never met a single one of my fellow Sapphianists even though I have admitted to my inclination in various gatherings. This penchant should not be disguised, for it tends only to benefit women. Yet that is the very reason why it is roundly criticized by the philosophers. For all their courtly pretentions, they are selfish in their dealings with women.

Two things have prevented me from encountering anyone who shares my mania. In the first place, the omnigyne is a rare personality type and the fondness for lesbians is essential only to them, even though it can accidentally emerge in less complex personalities. The other obstacle stems from the fact that in criticized by the philosophers. For all their courtly pretensions, fear of ridicule and lack of suitable occasions.

The fact remains that I have on the globe 26,000 colleagues with whom I would be able to form a cabalistic corporation in Harmony. This corporation would be subdivided into a hundred different nuanced series, and its members would obtain all the advantages that any series offers for heightened pleasure and profit.

It can be estimated that of the 26,000 lesbianists which the

[3] The omnigyne (or omnitone) was the rarest of all personality types in Fourier's system: an individual with seven dominant spiritual passions. He placed himself in this category.

globe must contain, not even ¹⁄₁₀₀th, or 260 of them, are fully aware of their mania. This penchant can emerge only in large cities where lesbianism is in style.

—*OC,* VII, 386–390

Great men are more susceptible than others to manias. The most common spiritual mania among them is the mania for talismans or lucky charms. They ridicule superstition and yet they themselves are blindly superstitious concerning everything related to their work and even their persons. Thus Bonaparte conceived a superstitious predilection for a Mameluke . . . without any real motive that could account for this preference. This choice was truly superstitious.

Savants have such a penchant for manias that they are constantly inventing new ones for themselves. They adopt manias about the most trivial things, even the drinking of coffee. In these shadows of manias it is possible to detect the absence of real manias. The seeds of real manias are present. But they cannot be recognized or developed in a civilization where everyone ridicules manias as soon as they appear. . . .

Rare manias or extra-manias which appear in less than one out of 810 individuals will be used as identifying marks in Harmony just as scars are now used on passport descriptions. In Harmony manias will be particularly bizarre and plentiful among the more complex personality types. In civilization on the contrary the complex personalities are those who try hardest to stifle and hide their manias. They do so out of an excessive respect for civilized standards and public opinion and also out of a desire to avoid criticism, of which they already have quite enough.

A lack of self-understanding makes many men criticize and ridicule manias which are actually their own. I have observed that I remained ignorant of my penchant for lesbians until the age of thirty. Prior to the incident which revealed my penchant to me I often declaimed against lesbians in the civilized fashion. I had no idea that I was actually attracted to them. It seems that the penchant for lesbians is esteemed in China. For there is a piece of Chinese furniture at Lyon with decorations depicting the Emperor seated on a circular couch and surrounded by a group of active lesbians.

In Harmony all the amorous nuances will be classified, first according to their frequency (which is no indication of superiority) and then according to their types, species and varieties, whether physical, spiritual, or mixed. Once this is done, the different amorous sects will be organized in such a way as to create magnificent bonds which will link lovers all over the globe. Military quadrilles will be formed with 32 sects and a center, omnigamous orgies will be organized in serial fashion, and there will be thousands of carefully nuanced groups for the representatives of diverse manias. Finally, manias will be utilized in the same way as the diverse personality types. They may be scorned in civilization, but in Harmony manias will play an invaluable function in creating enthusiasm and in unifying the industrial armies.

I will not provide a description of all these activities; the civilized are not sufficiently free from prejudices to be initiated into these mysteries. But by merely lifting a corner of the veil, I can show the depths of their ignorance concerning the destiny of love. This passion will be the object of the most vast and subtle calculations in Harmony. But imbecilic civilization has not even learned how to decipher the alphabet of love. It cannot even divide love into its two elements and analyze the properties of sentimental and cynical or physical love.

It is obvious that God meant love to be one of the two principal mainsprings of the social mechanism. How can people have supposed that He did not mean it to be the object of vast calculations? How can they have thought He intended love to be no more than the agent of a tyrannical bond called marriage, a bond which is only a germ of egotism and universal human discord? How shameful it would be for God if He had created the most noble of the passions only to yield such a contemptible result. How impertinent of men to impute such ineptness to God! And what is the incense that they burn in their temples but another insult. For they offer it to God in His role as the author of their sufferings and their disgusting civilization, a civilization which has never advanced beyond the least of amorous bonds, the forced bond, that of the couple. In their addiction to this lowly form of amorous relationship, the civilized are on a level with the majority of the animals.

—*OC*, vii, 392–394

### THE REPRESSION OF MANIAS: THE CASE OF MADAME STROGONOFF

Every passion that is suffocated produces its counter passion, which is as malignant as the natural passion would have been salutary. This is also true of manias. Let us give an example of their suffocation. . . .

As a Muscovite princess, Lady Strogonoff saw herself growing old, she became jealous of the beauty of one of her young slaves. She had the slave tortured; she herself pricked her with pins. What was the motive for her cruel behavior? Was it jealousy? No, it was lesbianism. Madame Strogonoff was an unconscious lesbian; she was actually inclined to love the beautiful slave whom she tortured. If someone had made Madame Strogonoff aware of her true feelings and reconciled her and her victim, they might have become passionate lovers. But remaining unaware of her lesbian impulse, the princess was overcome by a counterpassion, a subversive tendency. She persecuted the person who should have been the object of her pleasure. Her wrath was all the greater in that the suffocation was caused by prejudice which blinded her to the true aim of her passion. It was thus unable to attain even mental gratification. Any form of forced deprivation, that is to say suffocation by violence rather than by prejudice, would not provoke such wrath.

There are others who subject groups to the same sort of atrocities that Madame Strogonoff practiced on an individual. Nero loved collective or widespread cruelty. Odin made a religious system and de Sade a moral system out of such cruelty.[4] This taste for atrocities is simply a consequence of the suffocation of certain passions. It was Nero's Composite passion and de Sade's Alternating passion which were suffocated, and for Madame Strogonoff it was a variety of love.

[4] Fourier may not have actually read the Marquis de Sade (1740–1814), but this appreciation of the general character of de Sade's thought was uncommon for the time.

The suffocation of minor manias or extra-manias has the same bad consequences. If a man born to be a hair-plucker or a heel-scratcher in love is not able to satisfy his mania, if he is thwarted and mocked at by those to whom he reveals his penchant, he will succumb to other, harmful manias. Everyone has heard about Julius Caesar's amusing mania: he wished to be the wife of all husbands. Today Caesar could not satisfy such a penchant without being subjected to jeers from all sides. He would be thwarted and he might perhaps succumb to atrocious countermanias for which his whole empire would suffer.

*—OC*, VII, 390–392

### MANIAS AND CHARACTER FORMATION

After wounding the pride of the civilized in so many ways, I am at last going to rehabilitate them in their own eyes and become the champion of the manias that they all have. I am going to teach them to take pride in these secret absurdities which they do not understand and attempt to hide. I am going to teach them to take pride even in their amorous peculiarities which are easy to make fun of but which will be highly useful in the calculation of horoscopes. . . .

In discussing amorous manias (the physical as well as the spiritual variety) we are going to begin with the question of horoscopes. We will approach the question through an examination of very rare manias. This will accustom the reader not to scorn the least expression of a passion, and it will demonstrate that in the study of movement the infinitely small is just as worthy of attention as the infinitely large.

There are innumerable passional manias in the intra- and extra-clavier of personality types. For any one person may have several manias related to each of several passions; he may have several manias in love, friendship, ambition, and even in the passions of the senses.

By the term passional deviation or mania I refer to any whim which is held to be unreasonable and outside the range of the passion, outside its accepted scope. For example, if a man of the lower class is a thief, if he steals whenever he gets the chance, this is a passional need, a natural expression of ambition in a man who lacks the necessities of life and takes his subsistence where he finds it, according to the natural law. But if a million- aire who has everything he needs is seized by an impulse to steal trifles—like a hen, a candle or a glass—this is not a natural ex- pression of ambition but a deviated ambition which provokes ridicule. It is on these ridiculous penchants, which everyone has to some degree, that we are going to base our horoscopes. . . .

Everything is related in God's system of movement; and when a number of people are dominated by the most insignifi- cant caprice, it can serve as a beacon to guide us to immense discoveries in the realm of physical and passional horoscopes. I have already referred to the very rare caprice of amorous heel- scratching, and I have estimated that it occurs but once in a hundred million individuals. Other bizarre caprices (for in- stance, that of the astronomer Lalande who liked to eat living spiders) are just as rare, and will be encountered in Harmony in only forty of the four billion individuals on earth. But the fewer representatives a given mania has, the more precious it will be as a means for establishing horoscopes. Let us compare our method with another.

Our physiologists use their theories concerning the four elementary temperaments as a basis for horoscopes concerning people's personalities and passions. They maintain that particular habits and passions are generally dominant among sanguine types, that others are dominant among the bilious, etc. Such horoscopes are so vague and general as to be almost worthless. For predic- tions concerning each of the four temperaments apply to one- quarter of the human race. Out of eight hundred million men, there are two hundred million sanguine types. But what we want is a horoscope for each of them and not for all of them collec- tively. For instance, if we wish to tell if a child is capable of becoming a Homer or a Demosthenes, methods which vaguely refer to two hundred million men will be of no help to us. For there will never be two hundred million poets equal to Homer.

The only sort of horoscopes that our philosophers can formulate are infinitely vague. Our method focuses on the in- finitely small in order to make predictions which apply to individuals. Harmony bases its calculations on infinitely small manias such as the amorous mania of heel-scratching or the gastronomic mania of insect-eating. Other infinitely rare manias may be employed as long as they are present in at least 24 people composing three compound groups. It makes no difference if these individuals inhabit 24 different empires. It will suffice if each of them is observed in his empire. Predictions can even be made on manias with as few as eight representatives.

Before continuing, let us give a brief definition of horoscopes. Although they are not now accorded scientific status, they will play an influential role in Harmony. By the term methodical horoscope I refer to the determination of the echoes of movement or the effect of recurrent correspondences between the physical and passional realms. For example, amenity or grace is a passional echo of the sanguine temperament since it is often found among the sanguine and is very rare among the bilious. Their passional echo is violence. But it is necessary to probe more deeply to obtain detailed information about a child, to discover whether he will be a poet or an orator, an amorous heel-scratcher or a gastronomic insect-eater. It is necessary to study the infinitely rare manias and to observe their recurrent echoes. Only then can we establish tables of related passions and manias.

A mania which is sufficiently widespread to provide one hundred representatives in an empire of twenty million will have 24,000 representatives on the whole planet. This large number would be very difficult to study with any degree of analytical precision. On the contrary a mania represented by just one individual per empire could be studied in just 240 individuals. It would be one hundred times easier to analyze. It follows that the rarest manias will be the most precious in the calculation of the echoes of movement. This will be the triumph of the infinitely small.

In the calculation of a horoscope three facts should be ascertained: 1) Which of the 810 temperaments is relatively or absolutely dominant among the representatives of a given rare physical mania. 2) What sentimental or mixed manias are dominant among these individuals. 3) Which of the 810 personality types are dominant among them. In addition to these three essential questions, there are related matters to be studied. For instance, one should know the age at which a particular mania, such as amorous heel-scratching, manifests itself actively or passively or in both respects.

When seven consecutive generations have been studied by this method, it will be possible to determine the echoes or correspondences of a given mania in the passional and physical realms. If it is established that a majority of heel-scratchers have a particular type of temperament (for instance, number 360) and a particular personality type (for instance, number 240), one may infer that a child in whom this temperament and personality type are recognized at the age of seven is likely to become a heel-scratcher at the age of thirty.

"And what is the use of these magnificent prophecies?" our wits will ask. "What good will it do us to know that a child will eventually take great delight in scratching the heels of his mistress or plucking her hair?" The advantages of such knowledge will be immense. For if we find a means to predict the emergence of the most trivial peculiarity, it will be no problem at all for us to predict the emergence of widely shared characteristics. When a child is seven we will be able to tell if he is going to become a Homer or a Demosthenes. (People with such talents will be much more numerous than the heel-scratchers in Harmony.) Would not the Romans have been lucky if they could have known in advance, by means of reliable calculations, that Nero was destined to become the most cruel of tyrants. They might then have taken steps to keep him from the throne which did not belong to him.

Thus there is nothing more important than the calculation of horoscopes, and it does not matter if the means which we employ seem trivial. When you are trying to capture a fortress, you don't refuse to enter by the back way or by a tunnel. Any means seems good as long as it gets you inside the gates. You are in the same situation with regard to nature. Let us not disdain any means of uncovering her secrets; let us endeavor simply to get inside the gates. . . .

The calculation of horoscopes is not applicable to the present generation. Its manias are not sufficiently developed and will not be until the beginning of Harmony. The study of methodical horoscopes is arduous and can only be undertaken with generations brought up in the new order. Thus in these chapters I am merely mentioning the subject without discussing the methods in any detail.

—*OC*, VII, 394–399

# [3]

## NEW AMOROUS INSTITUTIONS

### EDUCATION AND SEXUALITY: THE CHASTE VESTALS

We have reached the most delicate phase of education, the period of amorous transition. This is the point at which all of our repressive methods break down. For in dealing with any stage of amorous relations, whether the first or the last, they are incapable of producing anything but universal hypocrisy.[1]

It is tiresome to have to keep on accusing the sciences of incompetence. But one is obliged to double the accusations in any discussion of amorous affairs. For the philosophers have shown less competence in this realm than in any other. At least they have tried out a few remedies for administrative, fiscal and legal abuses. But they have not even sought remedies for amorous abuses. Yet they should be particularly ashamed of their accomplishments in this realm. For they have succeeded in creating a state of general falsehood and secret rebellion against the laws. Since love can only satisfy itself through falsehood, it has become a permanent conspirator working ceaselessly to disorganize society and to inspire scorn for all its precepts. . . .

To make work attractive to children who are near, or just past, the age of puberty is the most important role assigned to young love in the societary state. The tribe of Striplings[2] is divided into two principal corps which are formed, like the Little Hordes and the Little Bands, on the basis of sex and inclination. I give these two corps the names of:

---

[1] As has already been pointed out, Fourier believed that young children had no real sexual life or sexual identity. They remained a third or neuter sex until puberty, when the passion of love began to stir within them. In this text and the one that follows Fourier takes up the final phase of education in Harmony and discusses the institutional means by which the "amorous transition" was to be effected so as to benefit both the individual and the community as a whole.

[2] Young men and women between the ages of 15½ and 20.

VESTALATE including ⅔ women ⅓ men.
DAMSELATE including ⅓ women ⅔ men.

The Vestalate remains chaste until the age of eighteen or nineteen. The Damselate gives way earlier to its amorous inclinations.
Everyone is free to choose; a person may join, or leave, either
corps when he or she wishes. But as long as one is a member, it is
necessary to respect the customs of the corps: virginity for the
Vestals and fidelity for the Damsels. On this point the Harmonians have adequate guarantees—even concerning the fidelity
of men, which is more suspect than that of women.

Since few young men are inclined to imitate the chaste
Joseph, it is normal that they should form a minority within the
ranks of the Vestalate. Indeed, this corps would have to offer
great advantages to make a young man impose chastity on himself until the age of eighteen or nineteen. Let us now consider
the advantages of the Vestalate, bearing in mind that the customs
which I am going to describe cannot be established at the outset
of Harmony. They will be *partially* introduced only after ten
years and fully introduced only after forty or fifty years, following the demise of the generation reared in the civilized order.

In general, it is the strong-minded individuals who will
choose the Vestalate and remain in its ranks to the end. More
malleable personalities will ordinarily prefer to become Damsels
and begin their amorous careers at an early age. For the sake of
decency, a girl who has just left the choir of Students will
usually spend at least a few months as a member of the Vestalate.

The Damsels, the young men and women who have given in
to temptation, are not permitted to attend the children's meetings
held each morning. Since they participate in the court of love
each evening from nine to ten, they would be unable to get up
as early as the children and the Vestals, who go to bed at nine
o'clock in the winter. For this and other reasons the Damsels are
held in low esteem by the children, who revere the Vestals. All
of the young tribes regard the Vestals with the sort of affection
that one feels toward a group which has remained faithful after
a schism. While the Little Hordes look upon the Damsels as

Satan's rebellious angels, they escort the chariots which bear the high Vestals.

The older tribes have other reasons to respect the Vestals and their virginity. The result is that the Vestals are held in great esteem both by children and adults. They provide a precious stimulus to the work of a Phalanx and to the labors of the industrial armies.

The chastity of the Vestals is guaranteed in that they are completely free to quit the corps, and renounce its special advantages, whenever they wish. Moreover, this chastity, which lasts at the longest until the age of nineteen or twenty, may legitimately be terminated at the age of seventeen or eighteen if a Vestal finds a suitable partner during her sojourn with the industrial armies about which I shall have more to say further on.

The lodgings of the Vestals are arranged in such a way as to leave no room for doubt about their private life. (Civilization offers guarantees only concerning public behavior.) The male and female Vestals are lodged separately in different parts of the Phalanstery. The surveillance of this corps is not left to fathers and mothers, who are easily deceived by anyone who knows how to flatter them. During the daytime, however, the Vestals are not kept in isolation; on the contrary, they are in constant contact with the other members of the Phalanx, and their daily work requires them to participate in the activities of twenty or thirty groups including members of both sexes.

The Vestals hold their own court and have their own recognized suitors. The title of *recognized suitor* permits an individual to participate in the activities of the industrial army to which a particular Vestal belongs. This title is issued by the Vestalate in cooperation with the male and female dignitaries from the Court of Love. If the would-be suitor is a man, his past behavior is examined. Inconstancy is not held against him, for it has its uses in Harmony; but an effort is made to determine whether he has displayed deference and honesty in his relations with women. Those who are known in France as charming rakes, those who are proud of deceiving the weaker sex, will be refused. Nor will there be any toleration of those moral shysters whose affected modesty is only a ruse to seduce women and girls. These sentimental sneaks are often worse than the rakes; the rakes are only after pleasure but the sneaks are out for money: their virtues are just an act performed in the hope of snapping up a rich heiress. It is unnecessary to add that a woman will be subjected to a similar examination if she asks to be recognized as the suitor of a male Vestal. She will be refused if she has sold her charms either directly or indirectly according to the civilized custom which allows women who are just as venal as prostitutes to call themselves "decent and proper."

Now I can hear our sophisticated wits begin to grumble: "We'll just forget about your Vestals if they are so prudish. Is there any man who would willingly put up with a committee of women empowered to discuss and criticize his acts, his habits and his character? It would take vaudeville to do justice to their prudish synagogue." These are the objections that the civilized would raise. But in Harmony a man would have much to lose if he lost the esteem of the Vestals; his name would be removed from the wills of dozens of old people from whom he was expecting bequests and inheritances. (See the fifth section on disseminated legacies.) The happiness and the pleasures of old people in Harmony will be based on their alliance with four main groups—the Vestals, the Little Hordes, the Fakiresses and the Fairies—and their desire to avoid the sad lot of old people in civilization will make them particularly solicitous with regard to each of these corps.

The Vestals will owe their eminent position to the impulse to idolatry which has always been a human passion. Although the Romans inflicted atrocious punishments on seduced Vestals, they did act wisely in making these priestesses the object of public idolatry, an intermediate class between man and the divinity. Similarly the Harmonians will make their own Vestals guardians of the *sacred fire*. In Harmony the Vestals will not watch over a material fire, an object of vain superstition, but rather a truly sacred fire, that of honesty, generosity and industrial attraction.

Nothing is more praiseworthy in a young woman of sixteen or eighteen than an unchallenged claim to virginity and an ardent devotion to useful work and to study. In their work the Vestals will cooperate with the Little Hordes on all tasks except the filthy ones. When a state of emergency is proclaimed—when, for instance, a harvest is threatened by an approaching storm— the Vestals and the Little Hordes will be the first at their posts. . . .

Each month four Vestals will be chosen to serve as presidents; they will ride the chariot during ceremonies and on festive occasions they will do the honors of the Phalanx. When a monarch comes to visit he will not be plagued by dull dignitaries with their frigid perorations on the beauties of commerce and the constitution and their fawning pleas for pensions and sinecures. Instead of such an insipid escort, the visiting monarch will be greeted at the outskirts of the Phalanx by its most charming Vestals. If the visitor is a princess, the most handsome male Vestals will be sent to welcome her.

When an industrial army gathers, its standards will be borne by the Vestals, who will also play an important role in its festivities and work sessions. The presence of the most renowned Vestals is one of the enticements which will inspire young men to join these armies whose work, performed under a mobile tent, is not in the least fatiguing. Since magnificent feasts and ceremonies are held each evening, there will be no need to force young men to go to work in these armies as our "free" young men are forcibly conscripted for war. A third of the members of each industrial army will be women who will serve as bacchantes, bayaderes, fakiresses, paladines, heroines, fairies, magicians. Thus there will be a superfluity of applicants of both sexes for positions in the industrial armies. Admission will therefore be a recompense, and one conferred first of all on the Vestals. . . .[3]

With all their claims to the admiration of the young and the elderly, it is not surprising that the Vestals are idolized, that they are the object of a semi-religious cult. The human race loves to create idols for itself. As a result of this universal need, the Vestals will become the idol of the whole Phalanx. It will be re-

[3] On the role played by the Vestals in spurring on the industrial armies see the text above on "Work, Love and the Industrial Armies," pp. 322–328.

garded as a divine corps, as the *shadow of God*. The Little Hordes, who pay allegiance to no other power on earth, will lower their flag before the Vestals, whom they reverently serve as guards of honor.

—OC, VI, 226–230

### EDUCATION AND SEXUALITY: THE FAITHFUL DAMSELS

The Vestals owe their prominence to the fact that half of the Striplings, both Lads and Lasses, opt for a different and less elevated way of life. Not everyone is capable of persisting in the path of virginity. Thus we need to learn how to recognize and make use of the penchants of those individuals who incline towards amorous precocity. It always happens that half of the Lads and Lasses are either stimulated by innate amorous propensities or else are simply poorly endowed with the talent, beauty and strength of character necessary to advance in the Vestalate. They promptly rally to the flag of love and take their places in the corps of the Damsels which includes more boys than girls. The Damsels make up one-half of the sect of faithful love which is the first note in the scale of love.

When they enter the sixth tribe at the age of fifteen and a half, young people do not immediately choose between the Vestalate and the Damselate. They all begin as Vestals. It is only little by little that the weaker personalities give way to love. Some quit the Vestalate at sixteen and others later. Usually it is the least attractive who are the first to lose patience; they have less chance of forming a union with one of the princes of Harmony.

In the civilized state women who give way to love at an early age are generally not very honorable. But their number is large: it includes nine out of ten peasants and city wenches. By the age of sixteen most girls of this sort have known more lovers than years. But in the bourgeoisie and the aristocracy one also encounters a number of adventuresses who, for all their prudish affectations, are more debauched than the wenches. Thus a large majority of civilized women are precocious lovers and secret libertines.

The amorous transition is very decent in Harmony, however, because rivalry obliges the damsels not to provide too shocking a contrast with the honor and modesty of the Vestals. To compete with the Vestals the Damsels compensate for their precocious weakness by displaying great refinement and delicacy in love. . . . The critical period of early puberty would become the rock on which the system of Harmony would founder if it allowed its youth to forget the noble sentiments inculcated in them as children. Love should intervene only to strengthen these honorable impulses; it should play a role entirely different from that which it plays in civilization. For in civilization love serves only to inspire contempt for the precepts of education; it teaches the young to be crafty and to conspire secretly against morals and figures of authority; it gives them a taste for excess and often for vice and debauchery. These are the fruits of civilized education which fails to provide a means for the channeling and utilization of love in its early stages.

In Harmony social relations are organized in such a way that no amorous intrigue can remain unknown, above all in the tribe of the Striplings. Moreover, fidelity and straightforwardness enjoy a prestige in Harmony that would be unthinkable in civilization. Thus any Damsel—whether man or woman—would be disgraced if his or her amorous career did not begin in an honorable fashion. . . .

First love is said to leave a lasting impression. Thus the free play of this passion is particularly important in Harmony. Since the choice is free, there will be relatively few lads who become passionately attached to lasses of their own age. Nature loves contrasts and readily links people of disparate ages. Furthermore, so many friendly relations are established in Harmony between people of widely divergent ages that it will become commonplace for a young lad to begin his amorous career with an elderly woman and for a young girl to begin with a mature man. Of course there is nothing predetermined about the matter since everyone's choice will be free. . . .

How long will a Damsel remain faithful to his or her partner? Can those who form amorous relationships at the age of sixteen or seventeen remain constant until nineteen or twenty? Three or four years of fidelity may be too much to ask of a human being. Nevertheless, every effort will be made in Harmony to prolong the period of fidelity as much as possible. The Damsels will only have limited access to the court of love. They will not be invited into the Seristeries where the high degrees of love are practiced. The Damsels are only a transitional group and there are limits to the amorous liberty which they enjoy. Although every degree of love is tolerated in Harmony (as is indicated on the scale),[4] young people are not allowed to participate in the more exceptional varieties until they have finished their education. . . .

Something should be said about erotic weaknesses and peccadillos. Harmony knows that it would be futile to make too many demands on any individual. The Damsels should be kept within wise limits. But it would be a mistake to demand the impossible, as in civilization where people talk about fidelity while behaving like libertines. . . . Is it not wiser to make some concessions to the torrent instead of trying to repress passion which will break the dikes and overturn the whole scaffolding of repression? It is this idiotic method of repression which has turned civilized women into libertines and convinced them that they have the right to take secret reprisals against men. Harmony more wisely compromises with nature, and to obtain the possible it never demands too much.[5]

—*OC*, v, 258–264

[4] Fourier's theory of the passions includes elaborate calculations concerning the various forms and degrees of intensity in which each of the passions manifests itself. Here Fourier alludes to his "exponential scale of the degrees of love" (*OC*, IV, 356–357). According to this scale there are eight degrees or powers of love, running from unrequited love and monogamy to various forms of "transcendent" and collective amorous activity ("ultragamy," "omnigamy").

[5] In referring to a "wise" Harmony which "compromises" with nature to obtain the "possible," Fourier is adopting the moderate language of his enemies, the moralists. And he is as vague and discrete as possible in his whole discussion of the sexual activities of the Damsels. The calculation and dry irony in his treatment of the problem here become particularly apparent when one compares this text (which he published in 1822) with the following excerpt drawn from the unpublished manuscripts comprising the *Nouveau monde amoureux*.

It is customary for the Damsels to remain faithful until they reach the age of twenty. But since everything is done by gradations in Harmony and since it would be difficult, not to say impossible, for a couple to remain faithful for four or five years, the amorous code allows for exceptions to the rule of fidelity. Thus no one is expelled from the Damselate until he or she has committed three infidelities and one inconstancy, or else seven infidelities without an inconstancy. Only half an infidelity is counted if a Damsel has an affair with one of the priests or priestesses who, in view of their age, are given special advantages. Thus a Damsel can commit fourteen acts of infidelity with priests, and she will only be expelled after the fifteenth, whereas expulsion will occur after the eighth act of infidelity with a layman.

A homosexual affair is only counted as half an infidelity. Likewise only half an infidelity is counted when two partners go to the amorous registry and announce their intention to engage in reciprocal infidelity for a period of three days or less. We should add that when infidelity has not been mutually agreed upon, the victimized partner has the right of reprisal. There are also certain acts of redemption and expiation which would enable an unfaithful Damsel to avoid expulsion. Any Damsel may redeem an infidelity by spending two nights with an elderly priest or priestess. The parties involved must testify before the court of love concerning the fulfillment of these expiations. These customs might seem to be libidinous in a corporation which is reputed to be faithful, but in fidelity as in all things exceptions are the rule.

—*OC*, VII, 434–435

### THE CODE OF AMOROUS NOBILITY

In our civilized and barbarian societies love is not a pathway to glory, advancement and esteem when it is practiced nobly according to the laws of honor and truth. But it can enable the crafty and hypocritical man to acquire the protection he needs to get ahead. Thus an adage says that the only way to move up in the world is through the canal of a woman. (And women themselves, whom men keep trying to remove from politics, have acquired many a kingdom by means of amorous trickery.) Love is also a fine means of advancement for the hypocrite who knows how to sentimentalize to a young lady and moralize to her parents. But open and honorable love is not a means of advancement in civilization which has no rewards for amorous behavior compatible with honor, truth and friendship.

In Harmony the situation is entirely different. There amorous celebrity can entitle a person to a world-wide monarchy and to other lucrative and magnificent offices. Thus it is important to classify Harmonians according to their amorous deeds. A fundamental distinction must be made between nobles and commonors in love, and both these categories should be divided into species and varieties of various degrees.

In Harmony the term amorous nobility refers to the class of hardy and refined individuals who are capable of subordinating love to the dictates of honor, friendship and other elevated sentiments. This class . . . considers as commoners all those egoists who are too weak to be truly generous in love. . . . This nobility does not hold its prerogatives by usurpation; it is open to anyone who can pass the necessary tests and show proof of noble penchants. It is known, thanks to the general clavier of personality types, that no more than an eighth of the members of the Phalanx can attain high nobility and that the number of half virtuosi in the middle nobility cannot exceed a quarter of the Phalanx. Thus the total number of nobles in each Phalanx will be limited to one-third or three-eighths of its members. They will be classified in graduated ranks according to the difficulty of the tests they have passed and the degree of their amorous exploits. . . .

Here we will be discussing only the two noble alliances of love with friendship and honor. . . . Let us give these two alliances the names of amical love and honorific love. I have already called attention to the six major branches of honorific love. This includes the Vestalate in the simple mode and the Fakirate in the compound mode. Honorific love is a sacrifice in which honor is allied with pure love and sometimes completely masters it, as in the case of many Vestals who stubbornly resist their amorous penchants despite the solicitations of their suitors.

As for amical love, I have described a few of its branches in my analysis of the amorous accord[6] and the unions which it establishes, with the help of the vehicles of ambition or religion, between people of divergent ages.

We have seen that there are guaranteed recompenses for such sacrifices and that no one in Harmony loses by his generosity either in love or in any other form of social relation. One must keep these recompenses in mind in order to understand why men and women in the new order will have a strong inclination for the generous impulses which everyone disdains in civilization because they always lead to deception and disappointment. Generous impulses are the prerequisite for admission into the diverse classes of Harmony's amorous nobility. These classes are arranged so as to include all varieties of amorous refinement. Before describing each class, I will present a generic scale of the diverse ranks of amorous nobility. The list and the explanations will be brief. We shall then take up the entrance conditions for admission into the amorous nobility.

The corps of amorous nobility is directly associated with the corps of amorous saintliness. The latter is the transcendent corporation in generous love. The other degrees correspond to those of an ordinary scale. They are arranged as follows:

Pivot. Compound active or compound passive saintliness. Both are allied with heroism.

1. Simple active saintliness.
2. Simple passive saintliness.
3. High active nobility.
4. High passive nobility.
5. Middle active nobility.
6. Middle passive nobility.
7. Low and purely passive nobility.[7]

[6] *ralliement.*

[7] Elsewhere in *Le Nouveau monde amoureux* (*OC*, VII, 120) Fourier indicates that similar hierarchies will be organized for adepts of gastronomy, science and art. In *OC*, VII, 126–144 he outlines in some detail the tests which must be passed by candidates for "gastrosophic saintliness." These

The difference between the active and passive types lies in the ability to organize amorous relationships, sympathies, etc. Those who are only practitioners in the various degrees of amorous nobility belong to the passive type. The active type includes not only amorous practice but also amorous theory or the organization of the activities of the court of love. . . .

Each candidate must pass tests which will vary according to his personality type. For example, a tetragyne or a personality type of the fourth degree will not be required to display as much prowess in generous love as one would expect from an omnigyne or a representative of the eighth degree.[8] It would be premature to go into too many details about these matters. . . .

It does not matter what rank an individual may hold in the social order. Even the emperor or hereditary omniarch of the globe will be classified among the commoners if he is a commoner in his amorous penchants. For the court of love recognizes only legitimate titles and does not grant special favors. Anyone who accepted a favor would, in any case, promptly betray himself by his inability to perform the functions assigned to the nobility. His failure would put him to shame. Thus there will be no question in Harmony about the legitimacy of the amorous nobility. . . .

Let us now turn to the conditions imposed on all candidates for admission into the various ranks of amorous nobility. . . . Love and gastronomy have their own special codes in Harmony. These codes, just like ours, require all candidates to submit to tests and show proof of their worthiness. . . .

1. *Test in pure love* or simple sentimental love. This test is wholly alien to our prejudices, for it requires a person to have a sentimental love affair simultaneously with a compound love affair. If a candidate is a man, he must declare himself to be sentimentally attached to one woman at the same time that he is

---

include tests in eating and rapid digestion; tests in the preparation of food so as to accommodate the desires of the members of a whole Phalanx; and finally highly refined tests on the innovative and judgmental capacities of the candidate.

[8] The tetragyne (or tetratone) and omnigyne (or omnitone) are individuals dominated, respectively, by four and seven spiritual passions.

carrying on a compound, or physical and sentimental, affair with another. This situation would be quite distasteful to our casuists who expect lovers to be entirely devoted to one another. This is fine for the monogynes who are incapable of forming transcendent amorous bonds. But what kind of bonds are formed by two individuals who live only for themselves?[9] Theirs is the most banal sort of amorous relationship, a relationship of which anyone is capable. If, however, two lovers remain sufficiently susceptible to amorous intrigue to maintain sentimental ties apart from their own relationship, they will be making a greater contribution to social harmony than a pair of unsociable republicans who love no one else and are courteous and passionate only towards one another.

The multitude of monogynes will claim that such a sentimental relationship is impossible, that a man who is in love with a woman cannot be seized by a sentimental passion for another, that he could not display as much zeal for her as for his initial partner. In any case, they will add, the first partner is likely to become jealous and to suspect her lover. All of these arguments are perfectly appropriate to the civilized situation where everything is false and where there is no such thing as disinterested love. But in Harmony supplementary sentimental attachments will be honored and they will not become a source of deception. They will be all the more readily accepted in that both men and women will be linked by bonds of friendship with people of their own sex and they will not be inclined to distrust anyone who has given his word of honor. Of course I except the monogynes who will retain their jealous inclinations. But jealousy will be greatly diminished in Harmony where people will have sure guarantees on the disclosure of acts of infidelity. There will be nothing alarming about a multiplicity of love affairs in Harmony; on the contrary it will be highly useful for two lovers to have sentimental partners whom they can trust and rely on in all cases. The proof can be found in our own society where every hus-

[9] According to Fourier, even the most faithful and devoted of "exclusive" lovers would have low moral stature in Harmony. For virtue, as he repeatedly insisted, was nothing else than the "multiplication of social bonds." See, for example, *OC*, VII, 168.

band is quickly convinced of the disinterestedness of the "friends of the family."[10] . . .

2. *Test in amical love.* According to philosophy this is one of the gravest sins. This is a polygamous form of love in which a man or woman has concurrent physical relationships with two partners. Each partner consents to the pleasures of the other, and the friendship among all three is redoubled as a result of this bond. In civilization where the seeds of friendship are non-existent such a [relationship] would be infeasible. But in Harmony the passion of friendship will work wonders. Such relationships will also rely in part on the activation of homosexual love, that ambiguous form of love which our customs do not tolerate even though it was accepted in antiquity. . . . I shall say nothing here about compound amical love which will be explained in the chapter on pivotal, polygamous and omnigamous love.

3. *Test in honorific love.* This is a form of love which is allied with sacrifices made out of a sense of honor. The first degree of honorific love is exemplified by the Vestals of whom we have already spoken. Honorific love also includes the keeping of a promise of fidelity to a person of one's own sex. For example, when a man is infatuated with his friend's mistress, he displays honorific love by neglecting an opportunity to seduce her. This sort of delicacy is almost unknown in civilization.[11]

It takes very little intelligence to see that the sentimental code of Harmony will put an end to the civilized perfidies of cuckoldry and seduction. . . . Outside the coteries of the monogynes, all sexual activity in Harmony will be carried on in the open. There will be nothing hidden or secret about any of the polygamous relationships. Thus it will be impossible for people lacking in amorous delicacy to pass themselves off as apostles of sentimental love. Everyone will be free to behave as

[10] Once again Fourier invokes the civilized toleration of cuckoldry as proof of his assertion that the practice of monogamy is alien to human nature.

[11] A more transcendent form of honorific love is described in the following text on the Angelic Couple.

he wishes, but everyone will be assigned to the exact rank that his behavior merits. . . .

Bigots will complain that I am discussing reprehensible actions, like polygamy and adultery, as if they were praiseworthy. But you, the civilized, do something much worse. You declare these actions to be criminal and then you go on to honor and reward them. You have organized your social system so as to encourage behavior which you claim to regard as perfidious. . . .

If your civilized dogmas are good, the fact remains that you either will not or cannot obey them. Would it not be wiser to adopt a code that you can and will obey, a code that would oblige you to do only those things which you wish to do and which all of you do in secret anyway, a code that would make your so-called vices serve the general good? In legitimizing proscribed customs like amorous polygamy, this code will render them useful; it will require you to do openly what you now do in secrecy and confusion. Rather than destroying your passions, it will put them to good use.

—*OC*, VII, 260–271

### THE TRIUMPH OF SENTIMENT: HARMONY'S ANGELIC COUPLE

Almost every town and village has at least one extraordinarily handsome man and one extraordinarily beautiful woman. These individuals excite everyone's desires and passions. Narcisse and Psyche are the most beautiful people in the town of Cnidos; everyone adores them and one could cite at least twenty Cnidian men who have an avowed passion for Psyche and twenty Cnidian women who are burning with the same desire for Narcisse.

According to civilized law Psyche must belong to just one husband and Narcisse to just one wife. Attraction takes a different view of the situation. Attraction requires that twenty couples of lovers receive the favors of Narcisse and Psyche. Unless God has distributed attraction in vain, He must have prepared some means for the satisfaction of the forty people who desire Psyche and Narcisse. He must have prepared some means for satisfying their desires in an honorable way that will serve to stimulate the enthusiasm and sentimental attraction required by Harmony where spiritual fulfillment and physical satisfaction are always on an equal footing. In brief, there must be a decent means of sharing the favors of the handsome couple with twenty other couples. If there were no such means and if the couple shared its favors in an indecent way, there would be no spiritual or sentimental attraction, and one of the essential elements would be missing from the amorous tie. There would be nothing but pure physical love or sheer animal pleasure in its most ignoble form.

—*OC*, vii, 43–44

The mistake of all the civilized philosophers is that they have always thought of love as something which must be limited to the couple. Necessarily, then, they have been unable to emancipate themselves from egoism which is the inevitable result of amorous relations which are limited to the couple. If love is to be a source of generosity, we must base our speculations on the collective exercise of love. This is the approach which I am going to take.

It would be impossible to convince Psyche and Narcisse to bestow their favors on just two other individuals. This would be a double infidelity, an infamous and degrading passion. But I am going to prove that in surrendering themselves to a mass of suitors . . . they will become angels of virtue in the eyes of the public, their suitors, and in their own eyes. This will result in the establishment of a general bond in which the suitors and even the public will share feelings of rapturous admiration for the philanthropic dedication of the angelic couple.

The reader should not hastily prejudge the question before learning the strange stimuli which will be brought into play. Harmony has the means to ennoble everything which can favor wisdom, or the increase of wealth, and virtue, or the extension of social bonds; it dishonors everything which tends to impoverish men and to weaken social bonds.

If Psyche and Narcisse bestow their favors upon the twenty people who are passionately attached to each of them, they can contribute to the progress of wisdom and virtue. But this union must be sacred in the eyes of society; it must be organized in a noble way and not like the dissolute orgies of civilization.

What motives will induce Psyche and Narcisse to cooperate, and what will ennoble their sacrifice? This is the problem of the angelic union. We will see how a pure, refined and transcendent sentimental relationship will not reach physical consummation until the two lovers have had physical relations with all who ardently desire them. We will see how by this act of amorous philanthropy they will obtain the same glory that civilization gives to a Decius or a Regulus and other such martyrs for religious or political principles.[12]

—*OC*, VII, 47–48

Let us now see if the real pleasures of the angelic couple are not superior to those of the selfish couple. The partners are denied reciprocal physical gratification. Let us consider the pleasures which they receive in compensation.

1. The angelic couple . . . has the happiness of being the object of public idolatry. . . .

2. Its ambitions are gratified by the chance of winning a throne of favoritism. . . .

3. It has the pleasure of a transcendent sentimental relationship, or the highest degree of pure love. This is a sort of mental eroticism which lifts the partners above their physical desires by inspiring in them a sort of enthusiasm which postpones their physical desire to another stage of the passion.

4. The partners derive physical satisfaction from the twenty or thirty chosen individuals with whom they have sexual relations during the course of their session.

5. The partners taste the charms of sentimental love in their relationships with these same individuals, each of whom strives to equal the angel in delicacy and refinement. . . .

---

[12] Fourier proceeds to specify the honors which will be bestowed upon the angelic couple and the tests which they must pass before attaining "angelic" rank. His minutely detailed analysis (which includes illustrative *tableaux*) is far too long to be included in the present anthology. In its place we offer his own summary of the "nine pleasures" of the "angelic relationship."

6. The couple enjoys the sense of noble religious enthusiasm which is associated with the performance of pious works. . . .

7. From their relationships with their respective suitors the partners derive the charm of physical and spiritual variety. . . .

8. They take pleasure in postponing the physical consummation of their relationship. They have all the happiness of two lovers who are sure of each other's affection and certain to establish a physical relationship in due course.

9. They gratify the hyperfoyer passion or unityism in their knowledge that they are transcendent personalities on whom general harmony is established.

*—OC*, VII, 92–93

Just think of the enthusiasm of an angelic couple, a couple convinced that the world is watching it, a couple which knows that the brilliance of its sentimental alliance can entitle it to magnificent kingdoms, immense wealth and celebrity. . . . Eh, can one doubt that this bond of pure sentiment, this abnegation of the sensual spirit will reach the highest degree among the Harmonians? It is sure to do so since they will enjoy complete liberty in this bond. They can bring their sentimental relationship to a sensual, civilized conclusion whenever they wish without losing the fruit of their philanthropic endeavors. The relationship must merely last long enough for them to satisfy their most ardent suitors. Two or three months should suffice. . . .

During the course of their trial will anything be lacking in their happiness? They will have a multitude of physical and spiritual pleasures. In offering themselves to their chosen favorites they will not be limited to sensual pleasure. For they will derive real enthusiasm from the knowledge that they are inspiring feelings of religious veneration in their suitors. Each partner in the angelic couple will respect the other as an image of divinity, and they will enjoy privileged positions in the courts of love. Each of them will minister to the sensual pleasures of the other by seeking out and providing suitors. Each will consider the procurement of pleasures for his or her angelic partner as a service of high friendship.

The exercise of pure sentiment which I am describing makes

the couple sublime in the eyes of others and in its own eyes. The partners are as much adored by those who surround them as they adore each other. What a contrast with civilized lovers who are sublime only to themselves but laughable and insipid egoists in the eyes of others. The world rightly regards a civilized love affair as a caricature, a travesty of the generous spirit which it is supposed to represent. It is a league based on pure interest from which the two lovers take all the profit without sharing the pleasures which they continually vaunt. In this respect civilized lovers are comparable to ignoble gluttons who go bragging about their fine dinners in front of wretched people who are deprived of what they need.

The angelic partners respectively encourage each other in the performance of pious works. If any individual has been accidentally deformed by nature, they will religiously offer him their favors: this will only serve to increase the admiration of the public. (I have already said that in Harmony no children will be born with deformities; deformities can only be the result of accidents and not of birth.)

Like any two lovers, the angelic partners could limit their happiness to themselves. But instead they choose to deprive themselves in order to practice generosity. Are they not the finest models of charity? Thus every suitor who receives their favors approaches them with a holy respect which resembles that of Christians taking communion. . . . The favors bestowed by the angelic couple will be a balm of saintliness, a token of amorous concord, of religious unity and of the absorption of human jealousies in the spirit of God. Thus it will often happen in Harmony that the example of the angelic couple will inspire selfish and jealous lovers to return to the path of virtue, to call a halt to fidelity. These selfish lovers will enter the service of the couple as honorary acolytes; they will participate in its august activities and give themselves to their diverse admirers. The joy of the possessors of the acolytes will add to that of the possessors of the couple and contribute to the general rapture. . . .

What will be the duration of the sentimental ecstasy of the angelic partners? There is no fixed limit. Since everything is done freely in Harmony, the length will vary with the individuals involved and the vehemence of their passion. But it is easy for the couple to prolong their sentimental relationship because they always know that it will terminate with the formation of a physical bond. It is necessary to add that an angelic union can only be established between people whose beauty and virtue are capable of inspiring boundless enthusiasm.

—*OC*, VII, 76–81

### CONFESSORS IN HARMONY: THE ART OF MATCHING PERSONALITIES

We will now take up one of the most interesting branches of the calculus of the passions: the art of enabling anyone anywhere, even in places where he is a total stranger, to make instant contact with people with whom he is in complete sympathy. If the theory of attraction offered no other advantage, would it not still be a boon to all mankind? Would it not be a blessing to the people of civilization who often spend years in a city without encountering sympathetic partners in love, friendship or any of the passions? In Harmony any traveler will make such acquaintances on the very day of his arrival in a city. . . . The art of the *sympathist*, which is unknown in civilization, provides the means for the instant matching of personalities and sympathies, anywhere and under any circumstances.

Let us first consider the enormity of the calculations entailed by sympathetic matching and the speed with which they must be performed. . . . Let us suppose that a horde of one thousand adventurers and adventuresses has arrived in a Phalanx at four o'clock in the afternoon. They are immediately served light refreshments and then, even before they take time to wash, they rush off to confession. The most skillful confessors and confessoresses of the region have been gathered. Their job is to examine these thousand knights errant, each of whom must submit a written declaration concerning his or her most recent adventures. The confessors go over these declarations as well as the reports of previous confessors; they study the immediate inclinations and physical needs of each individual, and attempt to provide him or her with appropriate sympathetic relationships. Putting all the relevant information together, the confessors determine, by means of an equation, the balance of contrasts and identities that will be most attractive to each of the adventurers.

When an individual is still basking in the enthusiasm of a romantic passion, the delicious contrast provided by a sympathy in the composite mode, should the confessor intervene to provide a diversion? Yes, very likely. For someone who has just concluded a sympathetic relationship in the composite would probably be incapable of duplicating the experience immediately. Then should the confessor provide the visitor with a cabalistic liaison by offering him a choice among several candidates of identical character? Or should an appeal be made to the visitor's alternating sympathies, his penchant for variety and contrast in both the moral and physical realms? Such are the first questions considered by the confessor. For there are three basic types of sympathies,[13] and the initial problem is to decide which should be employed. A variation may be in order. Or it may be advisable to continue on the same scale of sympathies. For if an individual's appetite has not been exhausted by his previous adventures, he will be capable of engaging the same sympathies in a higher or lower degree.

That is the heart of the matter; now let us turn to subordinate problems. No matter which of the three sympathies is brought into play, should it be presented directly or should it be preceded by transitions or complements? In the latter case, should the individual be subjected to a direct unitary sympathy or to an inverse unitary sympathy or perhaps even a diffracted sympathy? Should simple movement be relied upon?[14] This is sometimes a wise course of action, though rather inglorious, as simple movement always is; but it may be necessary in exceptional cases which will be determined by the confessors and the fairies. It is not for the individual to choose between these alternatives. He is too much absorbed by his recent memories. It is up to the calm and judicious confessor to determine the type of charm that will arouse his enthusiasm. On the basis of his declarations the confessor will decide what sort of relationship is most certain to engage his sympathies. Then the fairies with the best knowledge

[13] Corresponding to the three distributive passions.

[14] By "simple movement" Fourier refers to the attraction of opposites: for instance, the attraction of a tall man for a short woman.

of the Phalanx will designate the matching individuals from whom he may make his choice.

All of this work, which involves the use of algebraic formulas, should be completed for the thousand adventurers within the short time of two or three hours. For if each visitor was not systematically informed concerning his sympathies, if there was no one to inform him about the individuals with whom he could instantaneously establish sympathetic relationships, he would run the risk of getting involved in purely sensual intrigues, intrigues wholly lacking in illusion. Like the people of civilization, he would fall back upon trivial, simple sex. (Sometimes this is necessary, but only as a respite from composite relationships or, as a transition, in moments of hesitation and of overabundant pleasure.) After a two days' visit, at the moment of his departure, he might accidentally encounter people with whom he was truly sympathetic. Then he would regret having spent his two days without having known their merit and without having formed a liaison which might have charmed him. He would leave the Phalanx with a feeling of resentment, with bad memories instead of delicious illusions.

This goes to show that the functions of the confessor are most important and that a skilled confessor is an invaluable member of any Phalanx. The job is not one that can be confided to the first comer, as it is in civilization; it requires the greatest degree of tact, human understanding, and familiarity with local circumstances. Women will excel more than men in this sort of work, and as a rule in Harmony there will be two confessoresses for every one confessor. They will be magnificently paid for their services and promoted to the highest ranks.

As for the formulas used by the confessors in their work of sympathetic matching, they cannot be explained just yet.[15] It will first be necessary to classify the 810 personality types, any one of which may be represented in an equation of sympathy and may appear in a number of cases.

—*PM*, IV; *OC*, XI, 25–28

[15] Fourier does in fact go on to explain—at length—the process whereby the confessors do their matching (*OC*, XI, 29–144). Unfortunately, his "algebraic" formulas do not lend themselves to translation.

# SCENES AND EPISODES FROM THE
# NEW AMOROUS WORLD

### THE ARRIVAL OF A BAND OF KNIGHTS ERRANT AT CNIDOS

The cynic Diogenes claims that love is an occupation of lazy
people. He is wrong; it is an occupation of the rich. However
busy they may be, the rich always have love affairs, whereas a
lazy man who is poor and old does not. The poor man has very
few love affairs even in his youth. If girls from poor families
have more love affairs than men, this is only because prostitution
is a way of earning money. As for the class of young villagers
and laboring people, they are hardly able to do anything else but
earn their living. They have no more than a bare minimum of
love, whereas the rich have all they want even in old age.

In Harmony where no one is poor and everyone can make
love until extreme old age, a fixed portion of each day is devoted
to love. Love becomes an essential concern of everyone in Harmony; it has its code, its tribunals, its court and its institutions,
etc. I am now going to present a few glimpses of the amorous
life of Harmony. They may seem very bizarre, but the reader is
urged to suspend his judgment until the theory of love has been
fully presented. I have had to disseminate it in the different sections of this treatise.

One thousand adventurers and adventuresses belonging to
the jonquil hordes and bands are gathered in Hindustan. They
have traversed Persia and Armenia after having visited the
Bosphorus and Troad, and they are now making their way
along the Asian coast to Ephesus, Halicarnassus and Cnidos.
From there they will proceed to the social holy places—the
Cyclades, Attica, the Peloponnesus—and finally they will reach
Italy and Western Europe. One of their columns, including
about two hundred knights and ladies, has arrived at Cnidos to
visit Rhodes and Candia. The central edifice of the Phalanx[1] of

---

[1] "Phalanx" has been substituted for "Tourbillon," the term used by
Fourier throughout both texts in this section.

Cnidos is situated near the promontory once occupied by the Greek city famous for its cult of Venus and the statue by Praxiteles.

On the eve of its arrival the jonquil horde has sent the Cnidian leaders and priests an offering consisting of four couples of knights and ladies. The members of this quadrille of odalisks have distinguished themselves in the theaters and academies. In courtliness and good manners they have proven themselves to be the equals of the sovereigns for whose pleasures they were destined. The Cnidians are impatient to entertain a horde whose forerunners have been so promising. The youthful members of the priesthood are burning with desire, and the confessors and confessoresses from the whole area have already arrived to organize the opening session of the court of love and arrange sympathetic relationships. Diverse groups of bayaderes of both sexes have gone out to the neighboring communities to help the priests of Cnidos in preparing for a visit which seems likely to be splendid.

At three o'clock in the afternoon the watch-tower at Cnidos announces the capture by the Cnidian bacchantes of an advance guard of adventurers. About sixty Cnidian men and women hasten to the caravansary to discuss the ransom of these captives. . . . Soon the quadrille of prisoners appears. It consists of five groups whose emblem is the jonquil. They are escorted by four bacchantes and the Paladin Electra to whom they have surrendered. For the next twenty-four hours they will be the exclusive amorous property of Electra and her bacchantes.

Let us note here that in Harmony capture is never the result of actual combat. Captives are taken in the course of positional warfare which is carried on according to rules similar to those of chess. All moves and captures are judged by the paladins who always accompany a band on its expeditions.

The captives enter the caravansary and, after washing, they join the Cnidians gathered in the reception hall. . . . They discuss their misfortune in not having found confessors at their previous stop. For in amorous warfare one cannot capture individuals who have recently confessed and who wear badges indicating that they are ready to establish sympathetic relationships.

The bacchantes, who are eager to return to the charge, have declared by signal that they are willing to sell their amorous privileges with regard to the captives, and the meeting is being held to discuss the terms of sale. A certain amount of physical intimacy is necessary if the negotiations are to reach a successful conclusion. Therefore the discussions are preceded by an initial salvo or simple skirmish during which the new arrivals surrender themselves for a few moments to the familiarities of the Cnidians. (Of course the adventurers and adventuresses are free to compensate themselves in like manner during the skirmish.)

After a short skirmish a fanfare announces the opening of the session. The Vice Pontiff Erytheia mounts her throne surrounded by the corybants who are responsible for the supply of perfumes. The confessors and other local dignitaries are placed near the throne and they are led by Chryses, the High Priest of Cnidos. A number of places below the throne are left vacant; they will be occupied by the captives and their possessors as soon as each captive is redeemed.

As the session opens the captives are seated opposite the throne at enough distance from one another to give free access to the Cnidians who may wish to redeem them. Above the captives on a platform sit Sigistan and Iscora, the chiefs of the captured band. They remain free and they keep possession of their jonquil banner, since neither chiefs nor banners are captured in Harmony.

As soon as the herald Hypsipile has proclaimed the opening of the series the corybants Palemon and Clitia offer Sigistan and Iscora two staffs entwined with jonquils and ribbons representing the colors of Cnidos. While Palemon and Clitia pay court to their charming visitors, the other corybants wrap a chain of flowers around each of their captives.

The price of redemption is set at a one-carat diamond or the equivalent for each of the prisoners. (Precious stones are a noble currency in Harmony and they are used in the redemption of captives to distinguish such transactions from purely commercial affairs.)

Prisoners in Harmony must display great strength of character in their moment of adversity. Their virtuous behavior must shed honor on the bands of adventurers to which they belong. Since the jonquil band enjoys a great reputation, the Cnidians have high hopes for their captives.

As the negotiations get underway, the adventurers are offered a variety of redemption proposals. Such propositions cannot fail to be agreeable to them since the length of captivity is reduced by half each time the prisoner changes his or her master. Since nothing is done by force in Harmony, these changes can only be made with the consent of the prisoner. . . .

One of the rights of the priesthood during the negotiations for the redemption of the captives is to claim an amorous tithe. In this session the tithe is allotted to the Vice Pontiff Erytheia who is seventy years old. She casts her eyes on the young Mirza, prince of Raschnir. But she only takes possession of him in order to display her generosity. She declares that she is infatuated by the odalisk Belissan, one of the forerunners sent by the adventurers the previous day. She has been so happy with Belissan that she wishes to express her gratitude to the adventurers by liberating her captive Mirza. However the young princes refuses to accept unconditional liberation and he begs the Vice Pontiff to exercise her rights if only for a short period. He promises to do his utmost to merit as much love as she gave to Belissan. Erytheia graciously consents, telling her corybants: "I charge you with the responsibility of paying my debt to Mirza this evening." Thus for his civility to Erytheia the prince gains the right to choose among four young women. Applauded by the priests, he takes his place at the foot of Erytheia's throne. All eyes now turn to a female captive who is sought in redemption.

Ganassa, a magnificent fakiress from Malabar, has captivated the reverend confessor Philostratus who is eighty years old. He places an emerald in the hands of the bacchantes and tremblingly approaches the fakiress. He asks if she would consent to being redeemed by him with his promise to keep her in captivity for just one hour during which he will seek only the pleasure of looking at her and talking with her. At the end of that time he promises to hand her over to any possessor she might choose.

"No," replies Ganassa, "I will be your captive only on one condition: only if you allow me to be yours without reserve.

You must allow me to display all of my zeal and to make you admit that in the best days of your youth you never had a more passionate lover." Then she locks the venerable Philostratus in her embrace. At this sight the priests raise cries of admiration, declaring the gesture to be worthy of a saint. "You are not mistaken," says Ganassa. And, throwing off her robe, she displays the medal of saintliness, a radiant triangular diamond. "I am a saint," she adds, "and I wished to prove it before saying so."

At this point the corybants sound the salvo of saintliness and the confessors approach Ganassa, humbly requesting her benediction. She approaches Chryses, their august leader; she bestows a kiss upon him and then offers her alabaster hand to the confessors who cover it with caresses. After blessing them all, she withdraws leading the reverend Philostratus to the seats of redemption. The hall echoes with cries of admiration for this virtuous adventuress.

The third captive is Zemaim, a famous sculptor from Delhi. Amphale, the Queen of Cnidos, has taken a fancy to him. Zemaim, who has become enamoured of her, joyfully places himself in her power. She gives the bacchantes a diamond and takes her place with Zemaim.

Lamea, a bayadere from Benares, is sought after by a number of handsome Cnidians. But apart from the group which is pressing around her, she notices a middle-aged man who is watching her with an anxious gaze. She asks him the reason for his distress. He approaches her and says: "I fell in love with you in the days when I was visiting India with the heliotrope band. You were then a Vestal and I was already too old to be attractive to a Vestal. Today I am still older and, furthermore, I have the misfortune of being the poorest citizen of Cnidos. I have never desired to be wealthy as much as I do now. Like Philostratus, I will ask for the happiness of redeeming you and of meriting your friendship. But I will not request favors which, at my age, it is indiscrete to seek." Then Lamea takes a diamond from her finger and gives it to Phebon, saying: "This will enable you to rival in wealth those whom you surpass in unselfishness; and it will show you that the priestesses of the Ganges never hesitate to perform acts of virtue. Go, pay my ransom, and I will be

yours alone." At these words the priests seem upset. The bacchantes refuse the ransom. The Vice Pontiff rises from her
throne and orders that a diamond twice as large as Lamea's be
taken from the palladium of Cnidos to be given to her. Then
she orders that Lamea's jewel be kept in remembrance of a
divinely inspired adventuress.

The hall resounds with a soft murmur. The high priest
draws near Lamea and places a respectful kiss upon the hand that
bore the memorable diamond. Lamea takes her place in the
seats of redemption along with Phebon who is intoxicated with
happiness.

Isaum, the son of the caliph of Baghdad, is twenty-three
years old. He is the fifth captive. Too young to be a knight errant, he has accompanied the horde as an adventuring seraphim.
He has already distinguished himself for his virtue, however, and
at the Phalanx of Scamander he was promoted to the rank of
angelic candidate for having bestowed his favors upon the whole
choir of venerable ladies of Scamander.

Discussion opens concerning the redemption of Isaum. The
paladin Orythia pays court to him. He is willing to become her
captive; but Leucothea, a young girl with whom Orythia is in
love, also wishes to redeem him. Orythia does not wish to dis-
please the charming girl and concedes Isaum to her, begging her
to remember the sacrifice. Isaum intervenes to conciliate the two
and declares that he will not give himself to either of them unless
they promise to enjoy each other's favors. He pledges to collaborate with them as a lesbianist, or a lover at the service of
two ladies and participating only on their orders and to activate
their pleasures. Leucothea, urged on by Isaum and Orythia,
accepts the proposition. The agreement is sealed with a lesbian
kiss and Isaum receives the unanimous applause of the assembly
for his generosity. . . .

The next captives are a pair of adventurers, Zeliscar and
Zetulba of Golconda. They are young and pious students, nineteen years of age and accompanying the horde as its cherubs.
Zeliscar, who is as handsome as Ganymede, is a devotee of antiquity, a lover of ancient Greece which he has come to visit.

Agesilaus, the king of Cnidos, has been charmed by the precocious intelligence of the young man and has conceived a strong passion for him. He praises to Zeliscar the virtues . . . of the most famous Greek legislators and of the greatest of the Caesars. He passionately recites the poetry in which the delicate Anacreon urged the abandonment of women and the love of men. Several Cnidian savants also seem eager to inculcate in Zeliscar the principles of sacred antiquity. But out of respect for their virtuous king, they do not present themselves as his rivals. The young student displays a desire to confer with these learned individuals and to learn their lessons about the mysteries of ancient philosophy. Agesilaus assures him that the next day he will have the opportunity to dine with all of them. Then he redoubles his solicitations to the young man. Finally Zeliscar, who is full of enthusiasm and easy to convince, gives himself to the tender Agesilaus. The latter presents a diamond to the bacchantes and promises Zeliscar that he will taste the charms of virtue.

—*OC*, VII, 156–164

### A SESSION OF THE COURT OF LOVE

The band of adventurers moves forward through a cloud of perfume and a rain of flowers. The choral groups and musicians of the Phalanx welcome them with hymns of joy. As soon as the visitors have reached the colonnades of the Phalanstery, bowls of flaming punch are brought in and a hundred different nectars spurt from the opened fountains. All the knights and ladies are wearing their most seductive clothing. Two hundred priests and priestesses, who are dressed no less elegantly, greet their guests and perform the introductions. After refreshments have been served, the whole group mounts to the throne room where the pontiff Isis is seated. The welcoming ceremonies are concluded there and, after washing, all the visitors proceed to the confesional.

The high priests begin to examine the adventurers and to read their written declarations. A few adventurers, who have been examined at their last stop, give the priests the commentaries written by their previous confessors. Everyone hands over a written summary of his or her most recent confession together with whatever observations may have been added by the consistory of the last Phalanx visited.

While the visitors are eating a light snack, the work of analyzing and classifying their confessions goes on in the consistory. A list of five or six sympathetic relationships is drawn up for each knight and lady on the basis of the examinations conducted by the young priests and priestesses who wish to become sympathetic with the adventurers. Before the snack is over the fairies and genies have completed their task of match-making. Their recommendations are delivered to the office of the High Matron along with a summary of each confession. Sympathetic matching takes everything into account, and the final choices made are those which seem most likely to complement previous encounters either through contrast or identity.

I am only speaking here about young adventurers. The amorous affairs of the older adventurers are handled by the fakirs who use other methods. . . .

The first moments of the visit are taken up by ceremonial activities which should always include an informal meal. This meal will give everyone a chance to satisfy his curiosity, to move about from one person to another and to form some general impression of the visitors. Of course they too need to see how the land lies. People should get a brief look at one another before amorous affairs get underway. This interlude also allows time for the theoretical determination of sympathies; it enables everyone to have his own list of partners in time for the opening of the court of love. It should be added that up until the opening of the court of love the Vestals and the children are free to mingle with the visitors and to satisfy their curiosity about them. This is a most important precaution since the children might otherwise wish to enter the court of love, which they are not allowed to do. Thus the session does not begin until they have seen all they want of the visitors and are quite ready for bed. Only then do the adventurers go to the office of the High Matron to get back their papers and to look at the portraits of their designated sympathetic partners.

When the preludes are over the adventurers and their hosts

gather in the salon. A salvo is fired to announce the opening of the session. On one side of the salon stands the whole band of adventurers. On the other side the priesthood is gathered along with other people who have been designated as sympathetic partners or who have come to take part in the amorous activities. The priests are placed opposite the adventuresses and the priestesses opposite the adventurers.

When the Head Fairy waves her wand a semi-bacchanalia gets underway. The members of both groups rush into each other's arms, and in the ensuing scramble caresses are liberally given and received. Everyone strokes and investigates whatever comes to hand and surrenders himself or herself to the unfettered impulses of simple nature. Each participant flits from one person to another, bestowing kisses everywhere with as much eagerness as rapidity. Everyone also makes a special point of encountering those individuals who caught his or her eye earlier. This brief bacchanalia allows people to verify the physical attributes of those to whom they are attracted, and it can lay the groundwork for the establishment of sympathetic relationships between people who are more inclined to physical than spiritual pleasure.

It would be wrong, however, to suppose that this first confused skirmish exercises a decisive influence on the match-making that is to follow. Indeed, it would be bad form for anyone to make a binding commitment at the outset before formally encountering his designated sympathetic partners. People who have gotten together in the scramble will be able to renew their acquaintance later, and they will only love each other all the more if it turns out that their calculated sympathies, of which they are as yet unaware, are consistent with the preferences revealed in the bacchanalia.

Some of our civilized materialists might wish to conclude their investigations at this point. They would claim that this opening skirmish is all they need to make their choice. It will, in fact, be enough for monogynes dominated by the passion of touch; and they will not be prevented from forming sensual relationships with like-minded partners encountered during the bacchanalia. But such relationships, which are no more than simple amorous ties, deriving from purely physical affinities, will

satisfy no more than a twentieth of the lovers in Harmony. . . .
For the goal of Harmony is to establish compound amorous relationships based on both physical and spiritual affinities. Thus
while the opening sensual skirmish is indispensable, it is only a
prelude. It is the first phase in a process which moves, according
to the law of progression, from the simple to the compound.
Since nature's first thrust is always towards the physical, it would
be contrary to the natural order of things to begin by occupying
lovers with transcendent and spiritual illusions. The natural impulse should first be reinforced by a little opening bacchanalia,
and then the sentiments should be brought into play with the
help of the fairies. When sentimental inclinations are linked to
the physical ties already established, pleasure will be compounded.

Let us return to our narrative. The opening caresses and
exploratory activities should last no more than a few minutes,
barely a quarter of an hour. To break up the skirmish, use should
be made of a divisive agent. Since everything is done by attraction in Harmony, mixed or homosexual attractions should be
employed. Groups of Sapphists and Spartites[2] should therefore
be thrown into the fray to attack people of their own kind.
Such people are easy to recognize in Harmony since everyone
wears plumes or epaulettes designating his passions. These two
new groups will create a general distraction and disunite a number of couples. At that point the senior confessors will have no
difficulty in calling a halt to the skirmish, and everyone will proceed to the reconnoitering-room.

The reconnoitering-room contains two tiered and elevated
stands. These stands face each other in such a way that anyone
on one stand can get a good look at everyone on the other. All
of the adventurers are placed on one side and all the sympathetic
candidates on the other.

The actual matching is done by the matrons each of whom
takes charge of five or six lovers. . . . The matrons point out
the various partners who have been designated for each individual. The individual has been given a list with precise information

[2] Female and male homosexuals.

concerning the spiritual affinities and temporary inclinations of each of his potential partners. He is also able to determine their physical attraction since they are right before his eyes and since he has perhaps already gotten acquainted with them during the introductory bacchanalia. . . .

When the inspection is over, everyone proceeds to the festival hall where the encounter takes place. The encounter is supervised by the fairies and genies whose tasks are much more delicate than those of the matrons. First of all there will be certain problems to resolve. A number of people may desire the same lover. A given priest may be desired by ten adventuresses and a given priestess by ten adventurers. Such conflicting claims would be very troublesome in civilized gatherings. . . . But anyone who has been in love several times knows that people often develop passionate spiritual sympathies for individuals who did not seem at all attractive to them at first. The whole point of the operations of the court of love is to determine these spiritual sympathies at the very outset in order to minimize competition for the most physically attractive individuals. Such competition leaves some people with throngs of admirers and leaves a great many other people in a state of abandonment.

In Harmony sheer physical attractiveness will not have the colossal influence that it has in civilization where everyone is transfixed by the sight of a beautiful woman. Of course the Harmonians will not fail to appreciate physical beauty; in fact their judgment will be considerably more discerning than ours. But when it comes to the selection of sympathetic partners their choices will not be determined by physical charm. For their desire for sensual gratification will be satisfied in several different ways.

First of all the adventurers will never fail to ask for an exhibition of simple nature, a session in which the amorous notabilities of the area, and of their own band, show off their most remarkable attributes. A woman who has only a beautiful bosom exhibits only the bosom and leaves the rest of her body covered. Another who has only an attractive waist bares it and leaves the rest covered. Another who wishes to exhibit everything she has appears completely naked. Men do the same. No one can say after this session that he has been denied a chance to admire all the physical attractions of the region.

In addition to this exhibition of simple nature, the visitors will be able to organize orgies to be held the following day. At these orgies, which will be appropriately harmonized, everyone will have ample opportunity to derive satisfaction from the beauties displayed at the exhibition.[3]

The physical needs of the adventurers are satisfied in this way at every Phalanx they visit. Given the human need for variety and contrast, the most pressing desire of the adventurers when they arrive at a new Phalanx will therefore be for spiritual sympathy rather than for mere physical gratification.

It should also be pointed out that if, at the end of a visit, an adventuress takes a fancy to a handsome priest with whom she has not made love, it will be possible for her to obtain satisfaction during the farewell session. Such gestures of traditional courtesy should not be refused to any member of a departing band.

As a result of these measures, no one will suffer from a lack of physical gratification. Thus the important problems to be dealt with at the court of love will concern the establishment of spiritual sympathies. . . . The encounters which take place in the festival hall will be run in an alternating pattern. First of all the adventurers and adventuresses will be taken by their fairies to meet the priests and priestesses whom they have chosen as their most desirable sympathetic partners. Then the priests and priestesses will go to meet the adventurers whom they have selected. No final decisions will be made until everyone has had a chance

[3] Elsewhere in *Le Nouveau monde amoureux* (*OC*, VII, 329–332) Fourier discusses a variation on these proceedings: a type of "museum orgy" offering no more than visual gratification and designed to encourage the development of the aesthetic faculties of the Harmonians. His discussion concludes: "In civilization such meetings would be no more than bawdy gatherings because artistic taste and knowledge are not widespread. Our generation lacks the means to ennoble the amorous orgy, and especially the museum orgy. We are even more lacking in the general goodwill which will prevail among the Harmonians. Thus it is not surprising that the expression 'amorous orgy' evokes ideas of secret debauchery" (*OC*, VII, 331).

to converse with all his or her candidates. Everyone must have a chance to present himself to those he desires and to inspect the information recorded on their escutcheons concerning their personalities, their habits, current caprices, most recent passions, and their need of alternating and contrasting pleasures.

Little by little, as alliances are established, the group will grow smaller. The first and most rapid matchings will be dictated by romantic inspiration or by pure sensuality. But these sudden alliances may well be compound sympathies since everyone has already had the opportunity to study his list and to scrutinize his potential partners. . . . All those who are definitively matched up withdraw in order to permit the others to proceed with their encounters. Although it may be necessary for repeated enquiries to be made, this should be done without undue haste. Some alliances take a long time to form: preliminary discussions may go awry and a couple may only come to terms in the ballroom or even at supper. Such delays are commonplace among the more refined individuals.

Those who are the last to make up their minds do not run the risk of being left out or badly matched, for the fakirs may always intervene to satisfy them. But in general the tardy couples . . . get along particularly well because they have spent a long time flirting with each other. Moreover, if the sympathies which bind the tardy couples are somewhat lacking in intensity, their pleasures are always compound and never simple.

In all of these encounters great care is taken to avoid wounding anyone's pride. This is the particular responsibility of the fairies. Even when they are serving as protectors to just two individuals, they can make sure that no one's feelings are hurt. For if after a conversation one person wishes to refuse his or her suitor, the reason for the refusal is told only to the fairy who explains things to the rejected suitor with the utmost delicacy. The fairies abandon their protégés only when they are no longer needed, when two potential partners have established a sufficiently intimate relationship to reach an agreement of their own accord.

I have only described a single phase in the workings of the court of love. But it is already clear that in just two or three hours' time it can cement a host of happy alliances or compound sympathetic relationships of a sort that it takes months to establish in civilization. For it takes an extremely long time to understand the character of any civilized individual, and especially of a civilized woman.

The sympathetic intrigues which take place on the morning after the arrival of a group of visitors will be even more lively than those of the night before. For affairs which miscarried or failed to ripen will be renewed, and there will also be cases of infidelity to lend a touch of variety. The sympathetic relationships which endure will be particularly noteworthy in view of the fact that there will be many temptations to overcome. During a visit of three days almost all the adventurers and adventuresses will waver in their sympathies, finally returning to partners whom they barely got to know in the opening session. All this of course is quite independent of their participation in the orgies, the expositions of simple nature, the bacchanalias, etc. These material distractions are interludes in which both partners in a sympathetic relationship generally participate by mutual consent. They are moments of respite which do not destroy a relationship and which are not even considered to be acts of infidelity when they have been mutually agreed upon. Momentary respites of this sort are widely practiced in Harmony not only by sympathetic partners but also by the most faithful lovers. For on special occasions such as the visit of a band of adventurers . . . there are so many temptations that even the most faithful are likely to succumb. In order to avoid losing the privileges of fidelity they agree to break off their relationship for a stipulated period in accordance with the provisions of the code of love. . . .

It is evident that the task of arranging sympathetic relationships cannot be assumed by young people. . . . Decisions must be made which can only be entrusted to elderly and experienced individuals. Without their cooperation a band of visitors would be reduced to forming brutish relationships like the dirty and dangerous orgies of civilization in which partners are chosen uniquely on the basis of simple love and physical attraction. . . .

Let us consider the benefits that the elderly will derive from their services as amorous intermediaries. The task will not be at all wearisome for them. A skilled and knowledgeable pontiff will take pride in his or her abilities as a match-maker. . . . It will also be common for a traveler to become passionately attached to his confessoress. For apart from the fact that many individuals have an innate penchant for elderly people when they are agreeable, there will also be times when this penchant will be aroused by the methodical progression of sympathies. A skillful confessoress will manage to discern this need in the soul of her client and she will even try to call it forth. No one will be taken by surprise in such cases since, according to the custom of the court of love, the confessoress herself will be wearing medals or epaulettes indicating her own spiritual situation, her character, and her most recent impressions. Whenever the need for a sympathetic union between persons of divergent ages arises, it will be very much to the advantage of the confessors and confessoresses.

They say that no one does anything for nothing in this world; and if it is right for the elderly to assist the young in amorous affairs, it is just as right for them to be repaid for their services. . . . I cannot repeat too often, however, that customs so alien to ours cannot be established during the first years of Harmony. It will first be necessary to purge the globe of syphilis and other skin diseases. Until this is accomplished, Harmony will be more circumspect about love than civilization now is.

—*OC*, VII, 209–220

# VIII

## The Mathematical Poem

The social movement is the prototype of all the others. The
animal, organic and material movements are coordinated with
the social movement which comes first. This is to say that the
properties of an animal, a vegetable, a mineral, and even a
cluster of stars, represent some effect of the human passions
in the social order, and that EVERYTHING, from the atoms to
the stars, constitutes a tableau of the properties of the human
passions.

—*OC*, I, 31–32

In our selection of texts we have thus far focused on Fourier's
social thought, and we have presented the doctrine of passionate
attraction primarily as its rationale—as the conception of human
nature underlying his critique of civilized society, his ideas about
love and work, and his plans for the organization of the Phalanx.
To stop at this point, however, would be to do less than full
justice to Fourier's own ambitions as a thinker. For he regarded
passionate attraction as the central element in a comprehensive
vision of the universe. At the very outset of his career he asserted
that its discovery would enable him not only to lay plans for the
harmonious organization of society but also to uncover the
secrets of the natural world. As he wrote in the "Letter to the
High Judge," passionate attraction was the "key" to a host of

new sciences. It was a universal law which would enable him to explain everything from the origins of the heavenly bodies to "the most minute alterations of matter in the animal, vegetable and mineral kingdoms."

In his first major work, the *Théorie des quatre mouvements*, Fourier devoted much attention to the more esoteric aspects of his doctrine. He discussed the sexual proclivities of the stars, predicted the emergence of wondrous new animal species, and chronicled the entire 80,000 year life-cycle of the earth from the first infection of the seas by stellar fluid to the moment when the planet would cease to rotate on its axis. The derision which greeted these prophecies convinced Fourier to adopt a more circumspect tone in the presentation of his doctrine. In his subsequent published writings he concentrated on his theory of social organization and attempted to pass off his more esoteric speculations as mere "entertainment for the ladies." Fourier's earth-bound disciples went further: in their popularizations they practiced what one of them described as a "useful weeding out" of the doctrine. In simply purging it of its more extravagant elements, the disciples set a precedent which was long honored by scholars interested in Fourier. Only in recent years, and thanks largely to the efforts of André Breton and his Surrealist group, has serious consideration been given to the imaginative qualities of Fourier's stellar reveries and his reflections on analogy.[1]

While the texts in this section are intended for those readers whom Fourier described as "the curious," a few words of explanation are in order. The rationale behind most of Fourier's strangest speculations was provided by what he called the "theory of universal analogy." This theory rested on two premises: the universe was a unified system, a web of hidden correspondences or hieroglyphs, and man was at its center. Everything that transpired in the world of man had some echo or correspondence in the world of nature. Each of the twelve basic human passions was represented by its own color, musical

---

[1] See the works by Simone Debout-Oleskiewicz, Emile Lehouck, and Jean Gaulmier, as cited in the Bibliographical Note.

note, geometrical form and celestial body. Similarly every human personality trait, institution or social relationship was faithfully depicted in some animal, vegetable or mineral species.

Since nature mirrored the conflict or harmony of the human passions, the system was anything but static. According to Fourier's cosmogony there were to be 18 (or 26) separate creations during the course of human history. The first creation had endowed the earth with a multitude of poisonous snakes, insects, sea-monsters, and other dangerous beasts. Each of these harmful creatures was a symbol or hieroglyph of some form of conflict or disharmony in the early stages of human history. The 72 different commercial "vices," for instance, were represented by 72 different types of poisonous snakes. But in Harmony, these snakes, along with a great many other dangerous animals, would disappear. New creations would replace them with a vast number of useful and gracious species whose existence would reflect the new-found harmony of the human passions. Even in civilization one could detect portents of the future. The bee's hive and the beaver's dam were models of Harmony just as the wasp's nest was an image of civilization and the parrot an image of the civilized philosopher. As for the transformation of the ugly caterpillar into the beautiful butterfly, what could it represent but man's future metamorphosis?

The reader may choose to regard all this as a waste of time. But it has a coherence and poetry of its own. As gratuitous and arbitrary as it may seem, the theory of universal analogy was, like much else in Fourier's thought, an affirmation of the underlying order and harmony in a world of apparent disorder and chaos. It was also a way of looking at the world so that everything acquired a human dimension. It was one expression, and not the least interesting, of Fourier's desire to end man's separation from nature.

### THE HARMONY OF THE FOUR MOVEMENTS

The Destinies are the present, past and future results of the mathematical laws of God concerning universal movement. UNIVERSAL MOVEMENT is divided into four principal branches: the *social*, the *animal*, the *organic* and the *material*.

1. The theory of *social movement* should explain the laws according to which God has determined the ordering and the succession of the diverse social mechanisms on all the inhabited globes.

2. The theory of *animal movement* should explain the laws according to which God distributes passions and instincts to all beings which have been or will be created on the diverse globes.

3. The theory of *organic movement* should explain the laws according to which God distributes properties, forms, colors, tastes, etc., to all the substances which have been or will be created on the diverse globes.

4. The theory of *material movement* has already been explained by the modern geometricians who have made known the laws according to which God has determined the gravitation of matter on the diverse globes.

There is no effect of movement which cannot be included in one of these four divisions. As a whole they make up universal movement of which we understand *only the fourth branch, that of material movement.* But even material movement has only been partially explained; for in setting forth the laws concerning the order which exists among the stars, the geometricians cannot say what changes the vortices of stars may have undergone a hundred thousand years ago or may undergo a hundred thousand years from now. Finally, they are unable to determine the changes which have taken place or will take place in the universe. The calculation of these changes, which will be made accessible to everyone, is a part of the theory of material movement, which has not yet been completely worked out. . . .

The four movements are subject to two dependences:

*First.* The laws of the four movements are coordinated with mathematics. Without this dependence there would be no harmony in nature, and God would be unjust. In fact, nature is composed of three eternal, uncreated and indestructible elements:

1. *God or the Spirit*, the active and moving element;

2. *Matter*, the passive and moved element;

3. *Justice or Mathematics*, the element which regulates movement.

In order to place these three principles in harmony, it is necessary for God to be consistent with mathematics as He moves and modifies matter. Otherwise He would be arbitrary in His own eyes and in ours; for He would not be in accord with a justice which is both absolute and independent of Himself. But if God submits to mathematical rules which He cannot change, He serves both His glory and His interest in doing so. He serves *His glory* in that He can demonstrate to men that He rules the universe equitably and not arbitrarily, that He moves matter according to laws which are not subject to change. He serves *His interest* in that his consistency with mathematics enables Him to attain, in any movement, the greatest results for the least effort.

It is already known that the material and organic movements are in accord with geometry, that all animate or inanimate bodies are made, moved and modified according to its laws. It is clear then that two of the four movements are coordinated with a justice which is both natural and independent of God.

It remained to be shown that the two other movements, the animal and the social, which concern the activity of the passions, follow the same rule, and that every one of the passions, even the most odious, acts on men and animals in ways that have been geometrically determined by God. . . .

*Second dependence.* The social movement is the prototype of all the others. The animal, organic and material movements are coordinated with the social movement which comes first. This is to say that the properties of an animal, a vegetable, a mineral, and even a cluster of stars, represent some effect of the human passions in the social order, and that EVERYTHING, from the atoms to the stars, constitutes a tableau of the properties of the human passions. . . .

This means that the passions, which the philosophers have done so much to disparage, perform after God the leading role in the movement of the universe. They are what is most noble after God, since He has ordained the whole universe to be organized in the image of the effects that the passions produce in the social order.

It follows from this that if a globe reaches an understanding of the laws of social movement, it simultaneously discovers the laws of the other movements, since they are hieroglyphs of the first in every respect. If we did not yet know the laws of material movement which have been established by the modern geometricians, we could discover them today by analogy with the laws of social movement which I have discovered and which provide the key to the whole system of the three other movements. It is unfortunate for the human race that the savants have begun their studies where they ought to have concluded them, with the discovery of the laws of material movement. For these laws are the most difficult to establish, and their discovery does not make it any easier to acquire a knowledge of the three other categories of laws.

—*OC*, I, 29–32

### THE EARTH'S CREATIONS

The creation whose results we now see is the first of the eighteen which are due to occur during the life-span of the human race. I am only referring here to the creation of the substances which make up the animal, vegetable and mineral kingdoms, and not to the creation of the globe itself.

The earth took approximately *450 years* to create the animals, vegetables and minerals of the old world. The creations on the American continent took place later and according to a different plan. In both hemispheres these creations were accompanied by great upheavals.

The activity of creating is a delight to God, and it is in His interest to prolong it. If the gestation period of a human being lasts nine months, God must take a proportional amount of time to create the animals, vegetables and minerals. According to the theory this time should be equivalent to $\frac{1}{192}$nd part of the life-span of humanity. This means that the first creation should have lasted approximately 450 years.

All creations take place through the conjunction of a northern fluid, which is male, with a southern fluid, which is female.[2]

___

[2] A star can copulate: 1. with itself like a vegetable, the north pole copulating with the south; 2. with another star by means of outpourings

A planet is a being which has two souls and two sexes and which procreates, like animals and vegetables, through the meeting of two generative substances. The procedure is substantially the same throughout nature; for the planets, like the vegetables, include both sexes in a single individual.

To believe that the earth will not produce new creations, that it will limit itself to what it has already accomplished, would be like believing that a woman who has had one child could not have a second, a third, a tenth. The earth will have a succession of creations; but the sixteen harmonic creations will be as easy for it as the two subversive creations, the first and the eighteenth, were and will be difficult.

On every globe the first and last creations take place according to a system which is contrary to that which governs the intermediate creations. The first and last creations yield a multitude of harmful creatures and substances and a very small number of useful ones. The contrary occurs in all intermediate or harmonic creations; they yield a multitude of magnificent and useful creatures and substances, a very small number—an eighth—of useless things, and nothing that is harmful.

Thus the first creation covered the earth and filled the seas with an immense quantity of harmful beasts. Those who believe in demons might well suppose that Hell has presided over this first creation when they see Moloch and Belial vivified in the form of the tiger and the monkey! Ah! could Hell in all its fury concoct anything worse than the rattlesnake, the cockroach, the legions of insects and reptiles, the sea-monsters, the poisons, the plague, leprosy, venereal diseases, gout, and the multitude of venoms which seem invented expressly to torment man and to turn this planet into an anticipation of Hell?

I have already indicated the causes of the noxious character of the first creation. I have said that *"the features of the animal, organic and material movements must represent the play of the*

---

emanating from contrasting poles; 3. with the help of an intermediary: the tuberose was engendered by three aromas emanating from the south pole of the Earth, the north pole of the planet Herschel and the south pole of the Sun. [Fourier's note.]

*human passions in the social order*." Now the first creation was meant to provide a tableau of the seven periods of mankind's childhood. In this creation God was bound to depict the dreadful results of the passions during the first seven periods by covering the earth with a multitude of horrible creatures. But since a few virtues were destined to prevail during the course of the first and seventh periods, God was bound to depict them by creating a few useful and gracious creatures. (There are in fact very few of the latter in this truly demoniac creation.)

We will talk later about the new varieties of land- and sea-animals to be produced in future creations. As for the present, we do not even know how to make use of the few good creatures with which the first creation has provided us. To prove this let me refer to four quadrupeds: the vicuna, the reindeer, the zebra and the beaver. We are deprived of the services of the first two by our incompetence, our malice and our dishonesty. These obstacles make it impossible for us to raise herds of reindeer and vicuna in all the high mountainous regions for which these animals are suited. Other social vices prevent us from domesticating the beaver, whose pelt is no less precious than that of the vicuna, and the zebra, which is the equal of the horse in speed, strength and beauty. There is a harshness and a lack of understanding about our social customs, and about the way we run our stables, that prevents us from undertaking the enterprises necessary to tame these animals. By the eighth period, and even by the seventh, zebras and quaggas will have been domesticated like the horses and donkeys of today; beavers will be building their dams and establishing their communities in the midst of the most heavily populated areas; herds of vicuna will be as commonplace a sight in the mountains as are sheep today; and a multitude of other animals like the ostrich, the deer, the jerboa, etc., will come and join forces with man as soon as his company becomes attractive to them, which it can never be in the civilized order! Thus the first creation, which is wretched and evil enough in itself, is doubly wretched for man who, through social incompetence, deprives himself of most of the benefits which it could offer him.

The new creations cannot begin until the human race has

organized the eighth social period. Until then, throughout the duration of the seven first societies, there will be no second creation.

Nonetheless the earth is violently agitated by the need to create. This is evident in the frequency of the northern lights, which are a symptom of the stagnation of the planet, a useless effusion of creative fluid. This fluid cannot come into contact with that of the other planets until the human race has accomplished the preparatory tasks, and these tasks can only be executed when the eighth social order has been established. The human race must first attain a minimal size of two billion inhabitants. This will take at least a century. For women are much less fertile in the Combined Order than in civilization, in which the conjugal system makes them procreate abundantly. Poverty consumes a third of their children; another third are killed off by the childhood diseases which beset the incoherent societies. It would be much better to have fewer children but keep them. But since this is impossible in civilization, its inhabitants are unable to bring the planet under full cultivation. In spite of their enormously high rate of multiplication, they are barely able to take care of the land which they already occupy.

When the two billion inhabitants have cultivated the planet as far north as the sixty-fifth parallel, they will witness the formation of the Northern Crown.[3] This crown, of which I will speak later, will heat the arctic glacial regions with reflected light. By bringing new land under cultivation the human race will be able to attain its full size of three billion inhabitants.

---

[3] The *Théorie des quatre mouvements*, from which this excerpt is drawn, contains a chapter on "Northern Crown" (*OC*, 1, 41–52). It was a ring which would form around the north pole as a result of the coagulation of the northern lights. Sufficiently large to remain in perpetual contact with the sun's rays, it would warm northern latitudes with reflected light, melting the polar ice-cap and stabilizing climatic conditions throughout the northern hemisphere. Thanks to the Northern Crown, wrote Fourier, Harmony's Siberians would enjoy a more temperate climate than the inhabitants of civilized Florence. Grapes would grow in the suburbs of Saint Petersburg and oranges at Warsaw. The northern seas would be disinfected and turned into "a sort of lemonade" by a fluid emanating from the Northern Crown.

Once the arctic regions have been placed under cultivation, nothing will stand in the way of the harmonic creations. The first will begin about four centuries after the establishment of the Combined Order.

*—OC*, 1, 38–41

### "EPILOGUE ON THE THEORY OF ANALOGY"

Our wits, in writing bombastically about "the great book of nature," its eloquent voice and its beauties, cannot manage to explain a single line of this GREAT BOOK. It is only a tormenting riddle for us without the calculus of analogy which clears up the most impenetrable mysteries. The calculus of analogy solves the riddles of nature in most amusing fashion, for it reveals all forms of hypocrisy, it tears off all the civilized masks and proves that our so-called virtues are vices in the order of nature. Thus it is with good reason that Bernardin de Saint-Pierre called them the "frivolous and dissembling virtues."[4]

Let us consider the great book. A few authors have attempted to expatiate upon the symbolic language of the flowers and the plants. But how could they interpret representations of a societary harmony which is unknown to them. The little flower called the PANSY depicts the relations of the five children's tribes in Harmony: the Cherubs, the Seraphs, the Students, the Pupils and the Striplings. The three older groups exercise paternal functions and discipline the two younger groups. By analogy the two violet petals of the pansy are placed under three yellow petals; thus yellow, the color of paternity, is linked to violet, the color of friendship, in accordance with the following scale:

| X Black, | 1 Violet, | 2 Blue, | 3 Yellow, | 4 Red, |
|---|---|---|---|---|
| *Egoism,* | *Friendship,* | *Love,* | *Paternity,* | *Ambition,* |
| | 5 Indigo, | 6 Green, | 7 Orange, | P White, |
| | *Cabalist,* | *Butterfly,* | *Composite,* | *Unityism.* |

---

[4] Bernardin de Saint-Pierre (1737–1814) is best known for his sentimental novel *Paul et Virginie.* His *Etudes de la nature* are often cited by Fourier.

If our wits do not wish to accept scales, which must however be adopted in music, what guide will they utilize to understand the language of the colors and the symbol appropriate to
each? As long as people refuse to recognize the existence of elementary scales in colors and in the study of the passions, they
cannot be initiated into the science of analogy. But in relying
upon the scales of colors, of which a ray of sunlight provides
just one example, you have at the outset a sure basis on which to
ascertain the passion represented in an animal, vegetable or
mineral hieroglyph. When you see a bird with yellow feathers
such as a canary, you can be sure that it represents one of the
relations of paternity. In fact the canary is a spoiled little child;
it loves to nibble at titbits and sweet things; its twittering corresponds to the constant chatter of spoiled children; it is imperious and moody just as they are; and it is used to being well
taken care of and to getting its way. Thus nature put a crown
on its head to symbolize the dominance of the spoiled child who
is a king in its household, who dictates to father and mother, to
sisters and nurses, and makes everyone yield to its rule.

Since the color yellow provokes much amusement among
the wags, let us make use of it to study greater mysteries. Let us
observe the bright yellow tuft on the head of the cockatoo parrot. Molière would say that this yellow tuft is the emblem of an
unhappy marriage. That is correct, but let us explain why. The
parrot is the symbol of the sophists of the philosophical world: it
is full of glib talk, but its words are merely verbiage without
sense. Such are the brilliant systems of philosophy as represented
by the contrasting variations in the colors of the parrot's plumage: one's wing is yellow on the top and red at the tip; another
has red on the top and yellow at the tip. Likewise the sophists,
like Epicurus and Zeno, preach contradictory dogmas. On what
foundations are their lofty systems constructed? On the family
system, on the division into small conjugal households; all philosophy swings on this old hinge, which is the exact opposite of
the societary system. Analogy requires the pivotal parrot, which
is the white one, to display a yellow stripe as the symbol of the
group of paternity. This group is central to all the social systems

conceived by philosophy. Thus the knight-errant of the parrots, the cockatoo, has yellow plumage on all the lower part of its body.

The study of the parrot would provide us with a rich mine of analogies. But let us not pursue the subject since it would reveal to us all the faults of the philosophers who advocate tolerance and truthfulness but are no more inclined to practice tolerance than to hear the truth about their own cleverness.

The Sophists are strangely contradictory when they make a principle out of "the unity and analogy of the system of nature" (Schelling)[5] and then go on to claim that the guides provided by nature, like the scale of the seven primary colors, are analogous TO NOTHING! If unity and analogy are actually a part of the nature of things, this basic guide must be a symbol of something! And what does it symbolize if not the passions? Could one claim that this scale of primary colors represents only the material harmonies like the seven double ribs and the collar bone, the seven bones of the skull and forehead, the seven different notes plus the eighth rounding out an octave? These are four charges of ignorance to be brought against philosophy. For according to the principle of unity if nature accumulates analogies in the material realm, they must be reproduced in the passional realm, and it must be possible to determine among the passions a scale of seven elemental drives, not including the secondary scales of the twelve half-tones, of the 24 major and minor keys, of 32 with the transitions, etc., etc.

---

[5] Fourier frequently referred to the German philosopher Friedrich Schelling (1775–1854) as an "expectant" who had anticipated his theory of universal analogy. See for instance *OC*, VI, 14: "The philosophers are all agreed in teaching that there is unity and analogy in the system of the universe. Let us hear what one of our celebrated metaphysicians has to say about the matter: 'The universe is constructed on the model of the human soul, and the analogy of each part of the universe with the whole is such that the same idea is constantly reflected from the whole to each part and from each part to the whole.' SCHELLING." Although this citation appears in varied forms throughout Fourier's writings, he does not seem to have actually read Schelling. Most of what Fourier knew about German idealism in general seems to have come from a hasty perusal of a popularization by Frédéric Ancillon.

Let us cut short this tiresome discussion of principles and return to their application. Let us go back to the analogies of colors and, changing from yellow to red, let us consider a charming symbol, the goldfinch, whose head is capped in red, which is the color of ambition according to the preceding scale. This bird is the opposite of the canary. Its plumage is mud-gray but clean and glossy, which indicates an industrious poverty. The goldfinch represents the child born of poor parents who is well-disciplined and brought up to be ambitious and to get ahead. It is preoccupied with this idea, and by analogy its brain is dipped in red, the color of ambition. Its warbling, the symbol of a cultivated mind, is equal to that of the canary, which portrays the rich and well-educated child. Thus the poor but ambitious child will become just as well-educated as the child of a wealthy family; he will manage to filch the learning that is freely given to the rich. Since he will get this education only with the help of his family, nature has colored his wing-feathers yellow to show that his ascent is due to their encouragement, to the group of paternity represented by yellow. This poor child is not frightened by thorny scientific problems; he surmounts the obstacles of learning and he will become a gifted lawyer or a famous doctor. By analogy the goldfinch enjoys nibbling at the thistle, a spiny plant which has affinities with people of the rustic class who are accustomed to the spines of industry. It is to illustrate these relationships that nature has endowed two contrasting creatures with sympathy for the thistle: the goldfinch, the symbol of the studious child from a peasant family; and the donkey which symbolizes the peasant himself with his dialect or ridiculous braying, his meager diet, his resignation in the face of harsh treatment, and his obstinate persistence in bad methods.

Here the thistle offers a double analogy: a sensual one and a spiritual one. The peasant loves strong drink, spicy food, and violent emotions like those aroused by watching corporal punishment. From this it follows that the donkey, the symbol of the peasant, loves feeding on the thistle's thorns and likes to look out over frightening precipices.

So it is that the most despised creatures, the donkey and the thistle, arouse our interest through the medium of analogy. What Boileau said about mythology is even more applicable to analogy:

"There for our enchantment everything is put to use
Everything acquires a body, a soul, a mind, a face."

Without analogy nature is no more than a vast patch of brambles; the 73 systems of botanical classification are only the 73 shafts of the thistle. Rousseau has rightly described botany as a forbidding science which spits Greek and Latin at the ladies. The ladies would be more interested if they were told how a given effect of the passions is represented in a particular plant. If you showed them the varieties of love represented by the iris, the tuberose, the carnation, the hyacinth, the peach, the apricot, the pigeon and the cock, you would make studying much more attractive to them than by reciting your barbarous legends, your academic thorns: TRAGOPOGON, MESEMBRYANTHEMUM, TETRENDRIA, RHODODENDRUM. That chorus is hardly likely to make studies appealing to the fair sex!

To discover gracious analogies there is no need to have recourse to spectacular plants or to talk of the groves of Cythera. The most bourgeois plants like the cabbage and the onion will do perfectly well. Let's try:

The cabbage is a symbol for clandestine love with its secret intrigues, its masks and its hundred ruses. Like the lover it hides its flower under the veil of a hundred nested leaves. These puffy and undulating leaves represent the crafty efforts of lovers who are obliged to conceal their relationship. They are more blue than green, because blue is the color of love. . . .

The cauliflower, which is the opposite of the cabbage, depicts the opposite situation: love without obstacle or mystery, the pastime of youths who are free to fly from pleasure to pleasure. Thus the cauliflower is an ocean of flowers; they depict the delights of youth. Its leaves are neither blue nor bloated, because the emancipated youths who have orgies are rarely in love and have no need to use guile like the fettered youths symbolized by the cabbage.

Like some vegetables the cauliflower has a bad smell when it is cooking; it contaminates the water and leaves a smell in the room in which it is prepared. The artichoke and asparagus can cause contamination of a somewhat different sort: the artichoke contaminates the hand that picks it, and asparagus causes urinary contamination. In this vice which is common to three plants nature depicts a variety of disorders associated with free love. Let us try out this particular analogy with reference to the cauliflower, which symbolizes the young lover, the great seducer, the man for whom love affairs are an ocean of flowers. Such a man sows discord in any family; everyone talks about the wives and daughters whom he has seduced; this leads to gossip, domestic quarrels, disagreeable incidents; and by symbolic analogy the cauliflower contaminates the element that symbolizes the family. Here is the table of analogies between the four elements and the four affective passions plus their pivots:

| Earth, | Air, | Aroma, | Water, | Fire, |
|---|---|---|---|---|
| Friendship, | Ambition, | Love, | Family, | Unity. |

The two types of contamination caused by asparagus and the artichoke may be explained in a like manner by analogy with the disorders of love. But these matters would be too obscene to discuss here: sometimes tender and simple nature is *too simple*, too close to the august truth. Among nature's tableaux there are many which are unacceptable in good company; and I could scarcely explain in writing the symbolic attributes of asparagus and the artichoke. Both are hieroglyphs of amorous scandals which are precisely depicted in their leaves, their fruit and in all their features. The tableau is so faithful that it can only be explained to a male audience—particularly if one includes a discussion of contraries such as the cardoon which is the opposite of the artichoke. The cardoon represents the honorable woman and the artichoke the libertine.

However, the raw truths of analogy are perfectly acceptable when they concern the lower classes and species. If one draws upon the relations of the he-goat and the nanny-goat to provide a tableau of the corrupt sexual practices of the lower classes, this will not offend people who do not know how to read. As for the filthy miser, there is no harm in showing him that his features are mirrored in the hog and the oak-tree which provide two complementary portraits of avarice. The portraits remain faithful even in their details, for there is also an affinity between the piglet and the fruit of the oak, the acorn.

The science of analogy will dissipate our political prejudices as well as our moral ones. An analysis of the contrasts between the bee-hive and the wasp's-nest will show the worthlessness of our prejudices concerning administrative liberties and guarantees. The hive is a model of unified action and the wasp's-nest of duplicity. These are two magnificent analogies.

One of the vices which have led the civilized wits astray in their study of nature is their failure to refer everything to the needs and propensities of man. According to this principle the bees must be a symbol of the good since it serves us in a compound way by making both honey and wax. Similarly the wasp must be a symbol of evil since its useless nest and the harm that it does are a source of compound poverty. Like the wasp, the spider is a symbol of evil; it is the image of lying commerce and the snare of free competition.

Nature's paint-brush is so faithful that her analogies are beguiling even when they are considered in isolation. Although Molière's portrait of Tartuffe has received much praise, the flower called the amaranth and the reptile named the chameleon are even more perfect portraits of hypocrisy. To demonstrate this a long description of all of the features of these two models would be necessary.

Analogies have a double charm when they are presented in contrasting and graduated form. The eagle and the vulture depict two authorities who know how to rule once they have attained the supreme rank. But there are also malingering monarchs who are incapable of ruling. Their symbols are the ostrich, a light-headed bird with a huge body, and the dodo the image of the vain fool. Its empty skull is covered by a ridiculous crest which is as useless to man as is the rest of its body.

To facilitate the study of analogy one should collect galleries of portraits representing a given subject. In concerning ourselves with the august truth, we should study a number of symbols of truth at the same time. The swan, the giraffe, the stag, the fir-tree, the cedar and the lily are all hieroglyphs of the different uses of the truth, which is so thankless for those who practice it. In witnessing the sad consequences of truthfulness, as represented by these diverse animals and plants, no civilized person will be tempted to be truthful, whatever the philosophers may have to say about the matter. Seeking to deceive us, the philosophers do not wish us to know the unhappy fate reserved for the lovers of truth.

The tableaux of our passions become particularly alluring when they are studied in a comparative manner. One could, for instance, establish a scale of the degrees of stupidity, wit and intelligence as represented by the heads of birds: their tufts, crests, appendages, plumes, collars, excrescences and other head ornaments. Since the bird is the creature who rises above all others, it is on its head that nature has placed the portraits of the varieties of intelligence with which human heads are provided. The heads of the eagle, the vulture, the peacock, the dodo, the parrot, the pheasant, the cock, the pigeon, the swan, the duck, the goose, the turkey, the guinea-hen, the canary, the goldfinch, etc., provide so many portraits of the insides of the human head. The comparative analysis of their head-gear affords us an amusing gallery, a tableau of the diverse sorts of wit and stupidity with which nature has endowed each of the human types represented by these birds. . . .

I have said enough to demonstrate that the obscure language of analogy has at last been deciphered. Further study will permit the complete elaboration of the theory of analogy and of *the causes in creation. Quaerite et invenietis.*[6]

When contemporary naturalists extol the beauties of the great book of nature, they are limited to observing *effects.* In this respect do they not resemble the blind senator who caused great amusement in the court of Domitian? In a discussion concerning the preparation of a flatfish, this senator went into raptures about the beauty of the fish even though he was quite

[6] "Seek and ye shall find."

unable to see it. Such is the spectacle created by our writers who vaunt the beauties of the great book when they cannot read a line of it. They are not able to decipher even the most intelligible hieroglyphs such as the caterpillar, which is the disgusting symbol of the four odious societies which precede the establishment of the societary system. These four societies are represented by the four stages in the sleep of the caterpillar. It enters the chrysalis which is the symbol of the transitional social state of Guaranteeism, and its growth is culminated by the emergence of the butterfly, the symbol of societary harmony.

If our moralists are unable to decipher such striking tableaux, how can they explain the more difficult ones such as the bean and the pea which represent the Little Hordes and the Little Bands! If they wish to understand nature's obscure language, they must forget about their academic pride and begin to study the passions and analogy. Whoever leads the way will have all the followers he wants. What an affront for these savants to be reduced, like Cicero, to preaching obscurantism: *latent ista omnia crassis occultata et circumfusa tenebris,*[7] etc. How disgraceful is their ignorance of the true meaning of the things they study! They are not even aware that the swan and the giraffe, which represent the useless, superficial truth, are two portraits of their own war-horse, of the "august truth" which they claim to value so highly. Nor do they understand the tableau of the hunt: the stag pursued by a man and a dog is nature's representation of the attack on truth by the great men and governments of civilization.

–*OC*, vi, 459–465

---

7 "All these things lie hidden and confused in dark shadows."

# Bibliographical Note

Although Fourier has a place in all the standard histories of European socialism and nineteenth century social thought, the scholarly literature on Fourier in English is still relatively limited. The best brief account is Frank Manuel's brilliant chapter "Charles Fourier: The Burgeoning of Instinct" in *The Prophets of Paris* (Cambridge, Mass., 1962), pp. 195–248. Manuel offers both a penetrating psychological portrait of the man and a discerning analysis of his anatomy of love. Other suggestive interpretative essays are Daniel Bell, "Charles Fourier: Prophet of Eupsychia," *The American Scholar* (Fall, 1968), pp. 41–58; and Edward Mason, "Fourier and Anarchism," *The Quarterly Journal of Economics*, XLII, 2 (February, 1928), pp. 228–262. An English scholar, David Zeldin, has published a specialized monograph on an aspect of Fourier's thought rather slighted in the present anthology: *The Educational Ideas of Charles Fourier* (London, 1969). Nicholas V. Riasanovsky's recent *The Teaching of Charles Fourier* (Berkeley, 1969) is a thorough and sympathetic general study of Fourier's thought, the first in English.

There is a vast body of literature on Fourier in French. Among the popularizations of Fourier's own disciples Victor Considerant, *Destinée sociale*, 3 vols. (Paris, 1834–1844) and Hippolyte Renaud, *Solidarité. Vue synthétique sur la doctrine de Charles Fourier* (Paris, 1842) may still be read with profit; and Charles Pellarin's devout and charming *Vie de Fourier* (5th ed., Paris, 1871) has not yet been superseded. Most of the older works by French scholars focus primarily on Fourier's economic writings and on the question of his place within the socialist tradition. The best of these is Hubert Bourgin's massive and richly documented Sorbonne thesis *Fourier: Contribution à l'étude du socialisme français* (Paris, 1905). Although this is not the "definitive" work it was once thought to be, it remains an immensely valuable systematic exposition of Fourier's thought. Fourier is presented as an early exponent of cooperative socialism in a number of lively and informed studies by Charles Gide, notably *Fourier, précurseur de la coopération* (Paris, 1924). Henri Louvancour, *De Henri Saint-Simon à Charles Fourier: Etude sur le socialisme romantique français de 1830* (Chartres, 1913) is an excellent, detailed monograph on the conflict between Saint-Simonians and Fourierists during the early years of the July Monarchy. One of the best of the shorter studies on Fourier's social and economic thought is the chapter entitled "Charles Fourier ou la mathématique des passions" in Maxime Leroy's stimulating *Histoire des idées sociales en France*, 3 vols. (Paris, 1947–1954), II, 252–299.

In recent years there has been a resurgence of interest in Fourier as a psychologist and as an analyst of love and repression. A new look has also been taken at aspects of Fourier's doctrine, such as the speculations on cosmogony and universal analogy, which were formerly regarded as evidence of his "madness." Much of the impetus for this reorientation was provided by André Breton whose *Ode à Fourier* (Paris, 1947) was only the first of Breton's many efforts to rescue Fourier from the political economists. A second edition of the *Ode* (Paris, 1961) includes an introduction by Jean Gaulmier with suggestive commentary on Fourier's influence on French literature from Baudelaire to the Surrealists. Major scholarly contributions to the recent reassessment of Fourier have been made by Emile Poulat and Simone Debout-Oleskiewicz. It was Poulat's admirable *Les Cahiers manuscrits de Fourier. Etude historique et inventaire raisonné* (Paris, 1957) that called attention to the mass of unpublished Fourier manuscripts at the Archives Nationales. Madame Debout-Oleskiewicz undertook the difficult task of preparing an edition of Fourier's treatise on *Le Nouveau monde amoureux* (Paris, 1967) from some of these manuscripts. In addition to her lengthy introduction to that work she has published a number of important articles, notably "La Terre permise ou l'analyse selon Charles Fourier et la théorie des groupes," *Les Temps modernes*, XXII, 7 (July, 1966), pp. 1–55 and

"L'Analogie ou 'le poème mathématique' de Charles Fourier," *Revue internationale de philosophie*, XVI, 60 (1962), pp. 176–199. This number of the *Revue internationale de philosophie* is entirely devoted to Fourier, and it also includes significant articles on the man and the movement by Henri Desroche, Emile Poulat, Jean Dautry, and I. I. Zilberfarb. The best recent general study of Fourier's thought is Emile Lehouck, *Fourier aujourd'hui* (Paris, 1966) which provides a particularly useful introduction to the more esoteric aspects of the doctrine as well as interesting commentary on the literary qualities of Fourier's work.

The only comprehensive study of the various Fourierist movements is I. I. Zilberfarb's *The Social Philosophy of Charles Fourier and His Place in the History of Socialist Thought in the First Half of the Nineteenth Century* (Moscow, 1964: in Russian). Bourgin's *Fourier* includes a detailed account of the evolution of the French Fourierist movement, which may be supplemented by the more recent publications of Desroche and Poulat. Useful studies of English and Russian Fourierism are R. K. P. Pankhurst, "Fourierism in Britain," *International Review of Social History*, I, 3 (1956), pp. 398–432; and Georges Sourine, *Le Fouriérisme en Russie* (Paris, 1936). There is as yet no general scholarly study of American Fourierism. But Donald Drew Egbert and Stow Persons (eds.), *Socialism and American Life*, 2 vols. (Princeton, 1952), I, 173–189 and II, 49–50 offers a concise summary and useful bibliography. John Humphrey Noyes' venerable *History of American Socialisms* (reprint, New York, 1961) is in fact mainly devoted to the American Fourierist communities and provides an engaging first-hand account of their rise and fall.

Extensive bibliographies of Fourierist literature may be found in Giuseppi Del Bo, *Charles Fourier e la Scuola Societaria (1801–1922), Saggio Bibliographico* (Milan, 1957), and in Zilberfarb's *Social Philosophy of Charles Fourier*, pp. 460–532, where the titles of all works are cited in the original language. E. Silberling, *Dictionnaire de sociologie phalanstérienne* (Paris, 1911) is an index of great value, but more so to initiates than to beginners.

# *Glossary*

Does not a new science have the right to make use of a few new words and to provide itself with a whole system of nomenclature if necessary? Many subalternate occupations have their own unmethodical collections of technical terms. How can the same prerogative be refused to a science? I shall be sober in my use of this privilege, and when I am obliged to have recourse to a neologism, I will be careful to avoid arbitrary NEOLOGIZING. My terminology will be adapted to that which is already accepted in the precise sciences.

—*OC*, III, xi

*Accord*. A bond formed between individuals or groups on the basis of shared or contrasting penchants.

*Butterfly*. One of the three distributive passions. The need for variety and periodic change.

*Cabalist*. One of the three distributive passions. The penchant for intrigue.

*Combined Order*. A synonym for Harmony.

*Composite*. One of the three distributive passions. The desire for pleasures appealing to both the senses and the soul.

*Compound*. An adjective referring to any form of activity or relationship which is both material and spiritual.

*Exchange*. "An Exchange is maintained in each Phalanx, not for speculation on interest rates and commodities but for arranging work and pleasure gatherings." *OC*, VI, 67.

*Familism*. One of the four affective passions. The parental instinct.

*Guaranteeism*. A transitional historical stage linking Civilization and Harmony. It is possible (and eminently desirable) for this stage to be skipped.

*Group*. Fourier generally uses this term in a restricted sense.

A group is not any collection of individuals but rather a gathering of at least three (and ideally seven to nine) individuals with a common passion.

*Happiness.* "Happiness, about which men have reasoned or misreasoned so much, consists in having many passions and many means to satisfy them." *OC*, 1, 92.

*Harmony.* A social order organized so that the gratification of individual desire serves to promote the common good.

*Moderation.* A philosophical dogma, incompatible with human nature.

*Monogyne.* An individual endowed with a single dominant passion. Synonymous with *Solitone.*

*Passionate Attraction.* The tendency of every passion to seek its own gratification. This tendency is felt "prior to any reflection" and it is "persistent despite the opposition of reason, duty, prejudice, etc." *OC*, VI, 47.

*Passions.* The fundamental human drives. They are not simply emotional states but rather impulses actively seeking gratification.

*Phalanstery.* The principal building of a Phalanx.

*Phalanx.* The principal social and economic unit in Fourier's utopia. A community or association consisting of from 1600 to 1800 members.

*Philosophers.* A pejorative expression. "By the term philosophers I refer only to the authors of the uncertain sciences, the politicians, moralists, economists and others, whose theories are not compatible with experience." *OC*, 1, 2.

*Pivot.* The principal part or element in a system or mechanism. Unityism is the pivotal passion, just as the sun is the pivot of the solar system and the family system is the pivot of civilization.

*Polygyne.* An individual endowed with multiple dominant passions.

*Serial.* Adjectival form of series, as in "serial order."

*Series.* A mode of organization characteristic of all nature. Fourier most commonly uses the term to refer to the organization of work and play within the Phalanx. In that context the series is a carefully stratified assemblage of groups of individuals of differing age, wealth, intelligence, etc., all of whom share some nuance of a common passion. See *Group*.

*Seristery*. Rooms or halls in the Phalanstery where the members of a series meet.

*Societary Order*. Synonymous with Harmony.

*Solitone*. Synonymous with *Monogyne*.

*Subversion, Subversive*. Terms referring to any social order in which the passions are in conflict. For example, civilization.

*Transition*. When used in a technical sense, this term refers to any passion, species or substance which links one series to another. The eel, for example, occupies a transitional place between the series of fish and snakes. Although transitions are equivocal by nature, they will be eminently useful in Harmony.

*Universal Analogy*. The theory according to which all of nature depicts the harmony or conflict of the human passions.

# Index